BOBS/10/74

GNOSIS

WERNER FOERSTER

GNOSIS

A SELECTION OF GNOSTIC TEXTS

English translation edited by
R. McL. WILSON

I. Patristic Evidence

OXFORD
AT THE CLARENDON PRESS
1972

Oxford University Press, Ely House, London W.1

GLASGOW   NEW YORK   TORONTO   MELBOURNE   WELLINGTON
CAPE TOWN   IBADAN   NAIROBI   DAR ES SALAAM   LUSAKA   ADDIS ABABA
DELHI   BOMBAY   CALCUTTA   MADRAS   KARACHI   LAHORE   DACCA
KUALA LUMPUR   SINGAPORE   HONG KONG   TOKYO

This translation of *Gnosis*, vol. i, edited by
Werner Foerster, is published by arrangement with
the Artemis Verlag, Zürich

PRINTED IN GREAT BRITAIN
AT THE UNIVERSITY PRESS, OXFORD
BY VIVIAN RIDLER
PRINTER TO THE UNIVERSITY

CONTENTS

Contributors to Volume I

WERNER FOERSTER, Professor Emeritus of New Testament, Evangelisch-Theologisch Fakultät, Münster, Westphalia

ERNST HAENCHEN, Professor Emeritus of Systematic Theology, Evangelisch-Theologisch Fakultät, Münster

MARTIN KRAUSE, Wissenschaftlicher Rat and Professor of Egyptology (esp. Coptology), University of Münster

Translators

R. McL. WILSON, Professor of New Testament, St. Mary's College, University of St. Andrews (Introduction, Chapters 1-4, 7, notes)

S. G. HALL, Lecturer in Theology, University of Nottingham (Chapters 5-6, 21-2)

DAVID HILL, Senior Lecturer in Biblical Studies, The University, Sheffield (Chapters 8-13)

G. C. STEAD, Ely Professor of Divinity, University of Cambridge (Chapters 14-20)

INTRODUCTION

GNOSIS*

1

GNOSIS means 'knowledge'. But knowledge of what? Before we ask *what* Gnosis knows, something must be said about the *how*. This in itself marks off gnostic knowledge from philosophy. Where the latter acquires its knowledge by rational and logical methods, and communicates it in the same way to other men, so that they may either accept or reject it—and again with arguments of the same kind—with Gnosis it is different. Gnostic knowledge is basically *one*, and is acquired in *one* act. Thus the gnostic Simon says: 'It is true that in those sciences which are generally practised anyone who has not learned does not possess knowledge, but in matters of Gnosis a man has learned as soon as he has heard',[1] and in a pagan gnostic document it is said, when the Revealer shows himself in his true form: 'And immediately, at one stroke, everything became clear to me.'[2] In the Christian-gnostic writings this is also shown by the fact that it is often said that *one* sentence from the Old or New Testament, from Homer, or any other poet, is sufficient, rightly understood, for Gnosis.[3] Again, in the gnostic writings we find no laborious working-out of the gnostic insights, no gradual drawing near to the truth. In general the gnostics take no account of philosophy; and when they do so it is with a clear rejection at least of the priority of philosophy.[4]

The reason for this is that Gnosis seeks to impart *religious* knowledge, and therefore renounces any rational foundation. Gnosis is not a philosophy.

[1] Ps. Cl., *Recogn.* III 35, 7.   [2] Poim. 4.
[3] In the Megale Apophasis, Hipp. VI 10, 2; 15, 2; 16, 1; elsewhere Hipp. V 7, 19; 8, 7; 9, 10; 21, 12; 27, 4.
[4] *Sophia Jesu Christi*, pp. 80, 4–81, 17. Cl. Al., *Strom.* VI 6 = § 53, 3–5.

* The German term *die Gnosis* is rather wider and more comprehensive than the English 'Gnosticism', which is often used to translate it. Briefly, Gnosticism refers primarily to the Christian heresy of the second century and later, which is only a part of the phenomenon known to German scholars as *die Gnosis*. The present volume includes Hermetic material, the second Mandean. To avoid confusion, *die Gnosis* has been consistently rendered in this book as 'Gnosis'.

We might indeed set Gnosis alongside mysticism. There the aim is a vision, religious or coloured by religion, which can be set alongside gnostic knowledge. But the difference is not to be denied. The mystic believes that in his vision he has a foretaste of conditions after death. Gnosis, on the other hand, is not particularly interested in experiencing, to some extent even now, the conditions after death; rather is it a question of obtaining a proper comprehension of one's self, the world, and God. In Gnosis it is not a matter of an experience, in which cognitive perception is, for the most part, eliminated, but actually of a cognition. Thus it readily speaks of a 'learning'.[5]

Gnosis thus has something all its own in the manner in which it conceives its aim. The central factor in Gnosis, the 'call', reaches man neither in rational thought nor in an experience which eliminates thought. Man has a special manner of reception in his 'I'. He feels himself 'addressed' and answers the call. He *feels* that he is encountered by something which already lies within him, although admittedly entombed. It is nothing new, but rather the old which only needs to be called to mind. It is like a note sounded at a distance, which strikes an echoing chord in his heart. Here is the reason why the basic acceptance of Gnosis can and should take place in a single act.

If we must thus ascribe to Gnosis something peculiar in the manner of its appropriation, something peculiar must also show itself in its very thinking. This has indeed often been misunderstood as a blend of East and West, Orient and Occident, and the emphasis has been laid now on the one constituent, now on the other. But all these efforts have not led to a satisfactory result. We shall follow another path. Just as the essence of Gnosis can be grasped in a *single* act, so the totality of Gnosis can be comprehended in a single image. This is the image of 'gold in mud'.

What does this mean? It gives expression first of all to the distinction between the gold and what surrounds it. This means that what answers the 'call', the 'I' of man, the 'self' or whatever we choose to call it, belongs to another sphere than the world which surrounds that 'I'.

The mud is that of the world: it is first of all the body, which with its sensual desires drags man down and holds the 'I' in

---

[5] e.g. *Ev. Ver.*, 20, 27 f.; Ir. I 24, 6, etc.

thrall. 'Within you is a noble slave, to whom you owe his freedom.' Thus we frequently hear in Gnosis the admonition to free oneself from the 'passions'. In Mandeism—a gnostic sect which survives to our own day—we often hear of the 'stinking body'[6] and similar expressions, and in Tractate VII of the *Corpus Hermeticum*, a collection which also includes gnostic pieces, it is said: 'First you must rend the garment which you wear, the fabric of ignorance, the foundation of wickedness, the fetter of corruption, the black wall, the living death, the visible corpse, the grave which you carry with you, the robber that is in you.' All this applies to the body. It recalls Plato, who at one point calls Eros a tyrant who bites mankind. But Plato would not speak about the human body as here, and the insistence on celibacy, which is the logical conclusion that Gnosis sometimes draws, would have been impossible for the Athenian philosopher. There is the further fact that from this basic theme of hostility to the body Gnosis derived not only asceticism but also its converse, libertinism, in which man shows his contempt for the body and satisfies its desires because fundamentally they are no concern of his. Indeed, it can even come to the point that a gnostic sect propounds the statement that man must have performed all evil deeds in his lifetime (or in a future life of reincarnation), otherwise he cannot be 'saved'.[7] If we add that there are in Gnosis representatives of a respectable ethic, but that all these groups—ascetics, libertines, and advocates of a high ethical standard—are still 'gnostics', then it can be seen that with this hostility to the body we have still not grasped the central core of Gnosis.

The hostility to the body is only part of a more far-reaching hostility to *the world*. The gnostic has no appreciation for the beauty of this earth, for him 'the whole world lies in wickedness', and this because it is dominated not only by the power of sense but, beyond and including it, by the power of Fate. Fate presented itself in that period above all in the world of the stars, especially in the seven planets which the ancients counted (Sun, Moon, Mercury, Venus, Mars, Jupiter, Saturn), but also in the twelve signs of the Zodiac; the 'seven' and the 'twelve' are therefore marked in a special way as the power of evil which

[6] *Left Ginza I 2*, 14. 433, 34 Lidzb. and often.
[7] Carpocrates, Ir. I 25, 4.

enslaves mankind. According to many gnostics, 'demons' also rule in and over this world, and frequently the figure of the devil appears.

These powers of evil are, however, not individual powers in a world good in itself, but are an expression of the view that the whole world, the entire cosmos in the ancient sense, is what the gnostic describes by 'mud' when he speaks of the gold in the mud. There is indeed the view that the cosmos can *also* be used as an indication of the divine world, but even then it is doomed to extinction, with all that is in it.

There are features which especially express the wickedness of the world. To these belongs first of all the transitory character of all that is in it. 'No longer to come into being' is one of the aims of the gnostic. Reincarnation is then the special cause of terror. But death also, the necessity of dying without prospect of a better life, is characteristic of the world; time which rushes on, the inconstancy of all that is on earth, is cause for alarm; the gnostic seeks after what is immutable. Even the separation of mankind into man and woman belongs to this world, which the gnostic yearns to transcend.

When reference is made to the gold in the mud, the 'I', the 'self' of man, is something other than this whole world. This other is God. God or, as Gnosis also expresses it, the Ultimate Ground of Being lies beyond what we can comprehend with our eyes or with our sense-perception generally. Philosophy also, rational thinking, 'wisdom' cannot attain to that point. It is the sphere of 'light', of what is least readily to be grasped with the senses and the understanding.[8] Indeed, one can really speak only of a 'primal cause', a 'depth', or as often happens describe God only in negative terms. He is 'the unknown Father', or 'the unknown God', and frequently the attempt is made to describe this unknown God with an array of negative expressions such as 'ineffable', 'unspeakable', or the like, or even with 'non-existent': not 'existing', that is, in the usual sense of existence. Occasionally even the predicate 'ineffable' is denied. God is not even 'ineffable', for if he were 'ineffable' that would already be to give a definition, and God in reality is exalted above anything of the sort. Another way of expressing what is

---

[8] Another image is that of a perfume which is diffused without any apparent material basis (Hipp. V 19, 3, the Sethians).

unspeakable is to use the prefix 'fore': God is called 'Fore-father' or 'Fore-beginning': while it is natural to speak of the Father and the Beginning, as sometimes happens, the use of *Fore*-father and *Fore*-beginning indicates something that lies *before*, concerning which all that can be said is simply this, that it lies before all that is visible and conceivable.

So God and the world stand apart and in opposition. That we must also say 'in opposition' is connected with the fact that the world has always originated either out of the antagonism of the two principles 'God' and 'World', or else owes its existence to a 'Fall', an illegitimate action on the part of a being created by God. So even if in the beginning only *one* entity, God, exists, we can yet speak of a dualism of particular severity. Thus Basilides, who does not know any proper 'Fall', yet speaks of a 'supracosmic' realm.

Now the image of the 'gold' implies that the 'self' in man to which it alludes belongs to the sphere of God. The image is chosen because it allows the gold to be gold, even in the mud of the world: the divine element in man is not damaged, even if it stays there. The divine element in man cannot be altered in its quality, it is 'good'. Certainly, according to some gnostics, it may perish if it is not 'formed', but if it is formed then it makes its appearance pure, 'in being, power, greatness, per-fection one and the same as the uncreated and unlimited Power'.[9] But generally what is said is that he who possesses the divine element will of necessity enter with it into the other-worldly sphere of the divine. Perhaps the 'gold' must yet be purified, the divine element has still to be trained, but the end is certain: the sphere of the divine, the 'wholly other'. Man consists of the body and the divine 'self', the 'soul' or 'spirit'. If, as also happens, the 'soul' is taken to be an entity inter-mediate between body and spirit, it has no part in the destiny of the divine element and must obtain for itself by its good deeds a lower salvation which is clearly delimited. But at any rate the 'self', this core in man, the soul or the spirit, cannot be created through any kind of effort on the part of man; it is there, or it is not present at all. The decisive thing is not some-thing man must do, he has it; or better, he *is* it. This is the meaning of the expression that the gnostic man or his self is

9 *Megale Apophasis*, Hipp. VI 12, 3; cf. ibid. 14, 6; 16, 5.

'saved by nature', and correspondingly that men who do not participate in Gnosis are 'by nature lost' or perish. One of the Church Fathers says critically: 'If one [a gnostic] knows God by nature . . . then he calls faith an existence, not a freedom, a nature and substance.'[10]

If the world is thus the evil and the world of the divine the good, the question is: how then did the good 'self' of man come into this evil world? To this question a major part of the gnostic endeavours is devoted. The answer takes different forms, according to whether a primal dualism is assumed or the fall of a divine being. In any case the world is now in a state of disorder, even where this disorder is regarded as necessary for the education of the divine element. The divine must find its way back again into the divine world.

Now it would be false were we to assume that the 'self' of man can of itself alone attain to the divine world. The gold lies in the mud, and of itself cannot escape from it. It is 'stupefied', it has 'forgotten' its homeland, evil has placed it in 'drunkenness', 'taken it captive', or whatever other images are used to describe this condition of the 'I'. 'It seeks to escape from the bitter Chaos, and knows not how it is to win through.'[11] The help cannot come from this world, for indeed it is antagonistic to the divine; neither can it come from the 'I' of man, but only from the 'wholly other world', from the 'Pleroma', the 'fullness' as it is also called, probably in contrast to the 'Kenoma', the 'emptiness' of this world. It comes in a 'call', which breaks through man's forgetfulness of himself, makes an end of his stupefaction, and terminates his imprisonment. 'Stand up, shake off your sleep . . . Remember that you are a king's son'— so run the decisive words of the 'letter' with which the call comes to the knowledge of the sleeping 'king's son' in the Acts of Thomas (§110). The reaction also corresponds: 'But at its voice I rose up . . . from sleep . . . and read. Wholly as it stood written in my heart were the words of my letter written. I thought on this, that I was a king's son. . . .' Thus 'only' a recollection is necessary, but the decisive point is that the 'I' cannot recollect of itself. It is a question of a recollection which, as already said, can be accomplished in *one* act, a remembrance which flares up within him as soon as he becomes

---

[10] Cl. Al., *Strom.* V 1 = § 3, 2.   [11] Hipp. V 10, 2.

aware of the 'call'. It is thus a 'redeeming' function of a peculiar kind which the call has. The gold remains gold even in the mud, it requires only to be 'set free', and then 'nobility craves after its nature', as is further said in the passage just mentioned in the Acts of Thomas. The redeemed man can return to his homeland.

The decisive event is indeed named by the 'call', but this does not yet bring the final redemption. Even if the gnostic through the call has found his self, even if he is thereby exalted above the whole world and it can now be said: 'From the beginning you are immortal and children of eternal life, and you willed to distribute death among you, that you might consume and destroy it . . .',[12] however much he knows that he belongs to the world of light—the call does not yet bring the final redemption, for the gnostic still remains fettered to his body. The 'self', the 'seed', as it is here called, works like leaven, in that it 'unites what appeared to be divided, namely soul and body';[13] only the actual deliverance from the body in death makes the 'self' free for that space which is no space but the sphere of light. Strictly speaking, even death does not bring it about, but only the end of the world, in which matter is destroyed and the gnostic enters into the world of light. An anticipation of this condition in a mystic experience does indeed occasionally occur,[14] but is, however, the exception. Gnosis leads man to knowledge of himself, but does not teach him to experience freedom from the body in a mystic ecstasy; it is knowledge, not experience.

This leads to a final point. The gnostic is not called as an isolated person. It may be that only 'one of a thousand, and two of ten thousand'[15] hear the call, but at any rate these unite together into a community. The gnostics do not exist as individuals, but as a community which in each case gathers round one who has received the 'call' and hands it on, as in most Christian 'sects', which are named after the founder, or in Manicheism. This man has the decisive revelation, as, for

[12] Valentinus in Cl. Al., *Strom.* IV 13 = § 89, 2.
[13] Cl. Al., *Exc.* § 2, 2.
[14] Only apparently Ir. II 31, 2: 'They [the gnostics] . . . affirm that the resurrection from the dead is no other than the recognition of their so-called truth.' The author of *Ev. Ver.*, on the other hand, hints towards the end at a mystical experience.
[15] Basilides in Ir. I 24, 6; cf. Gospel of Thomas, Logion 23.

example, it is reported of Valentinus that he saw a little child, who, to the question who he was, replied that he was the Logos;[16] this fundamental revelation is then developed into a myth, such as is reported of Valentinus in the passage mentioned, and then around this myth, this 'system', there gathers a circle of like-minded people. Since the myths are varied, there are also different gnostic 'schools', which, however, stand in a strained relationship to one another. For each group affirms that it alone exactly knows the redeeming call or the Redeemer. 'Those from above . . . , from whence we are, . . . understand Jesus the Saviour not partially but wholly, and are alone perfect from above, the rest know him only in part.'[17]

The gnostics of course feel themselves in this world as 'people divided',[18] who are, however, destined to unity in the kingdom of light. They are 'sparks of light', which go into the kingdom of light from which they came. This takes place as *one* act: all together go into the Pleroma. Only then can the world meet its end, when it is either annihilated by fire, or remains here below, a burnt-out heap of ashes, powerless and dead, or even continues in a contentment free from aspiration or desire with all its parts in that particular sphere which is appointed for it. It is on the gnostics that the end of the world depends.

With the end of the world all tensions are removed, the expansive stream of time, the limiting character of individuality, the tension of the sexes. But that the entire Pleroma is once again taken up into the unity of the 'primal cause' is *not* gnostic doctrine. Valentinianism indeed makes all 'aeons' become alike, and says of them that they all become what the others also are,[19] but further it does not go. The gnostics at the end of the world do indeed come to entrance into the Pleroma and to marriage with the masculine angels, and thus the unification of male and female is attained,[20] but that is all; only expressions such as in the 'redemption' of the Marcosians, who are baptized to 'unity',[21] apparently go further. Admittedly formulae also occur which are suggestive of declarations of identity, as, for example, in the Megale Apophasis, where the developed 'seventh power' becomes 'one and the same with the

---

[16] Hipp. VI 42, 2.   [17] Hipp. VIII 10, 11, the Docetists.
[18] Cl. Al., *Exc.* § 36, 2.   [19] Ir. I 2, 6.   [20] Ir. I 7, 1.
[21] Ir. I 21, 3.

uncreated and infinite power in being, power, greatness, and operation'.[22] But even here there is no thrust forward to an outright declaration of identity; at the very least the 'primal cause', the supreme power, remains by itself.

The main points of Gnosis are thus the following:

1. Between this world and the God incomprehensible to our thought, the 'primal cause', there is an irreconcilable antagonism.
2. The 'self', the 'I' of the gnostic, his 'spirit' or soul, is unalterably divine.
3. This 'I', however, has fallen into this world, has been imprisoned and anaesthetized by it, and cannot free itself from it.
4. Only a divine 'call' from the world of light looses the bonds of captivity.
5. But only at the end of the world does the divine element in man return again to its home.

2

There is a great host of gnostic systems. They all have the one aim, to explain how the opposition of the divine world and the world in which man now lives came about, how it happens that a divine part lies imprisoned in this world in the gnostic. They all contain in themselves the call which is to awaken the divine element, and depict what the end of the world will be, when all the divine returns to its homeland and this world will be destroyed (or become impotent and inactive). At one point, as a summary of the questions to which Gnosis promises an answer, we find mentioned:[23] 'Who were we? Who have we become? Where were we? Where have we been cast? Whither do we hasten? From what are we freed? What is birth? What rebirth?' If the decisive point for the gnostic lies in the 'call' which leads to comprehension of the self, there is given with it a definite understanding of God and the world. The gnostic systems make explicit what is implicit in giving heed to the call. The gnostic needs a 'system' which shows him whence he came, how the world exists, how redemption comes about, and how it is finally consummated. So we have a profusion of

[22] Hipp. VI 12, 3.   [23] Cl. Al., *Exc.* § 78.

gnostic systems which seek to present this. Corresponding to the fact that the essential in man is not his capacity for rational thought but his responsiveness to the 'call', mythological and mythical entities play a decisive role in the process. Even though we can derive individual systems out of one another, it is yet impossible to trace the systems all back to one source.

Hellenism, to be sure, also makes a distinction between the worlds of sense and spirit, but in Gnosis it is a *fundamental* cleavage between the two realms, which Greek thought does not make in this way. For the Greeks the power which created the world, whether it is called God or Demiurge, universal reason or fire, is the supreme and ultimate, out of which this world is derived. Gnosis, however, makes a fundamental cleavage between the world which contains all this, including the universal reason or the fire, and the fullness of the divine existence, the 'light'.

It is then most natural to start out from two principles which from the primal beginning are opposed to one another, light and darkness, good and evil, God and matter. Here the darkness is the aggressive element, rendered covetous by the beauty and order of the world of light and obliging that world to take counter-measures. It sends a figure from its midst, who descends of his own free will and is either wholly or partially swallowed by the darkness. Or a figure of light, 'man', falls in a tragic error down into the darkness. In this branch of Gnosis it is then quite clear how the captivity of the 'gold' in the mud came about. The divine is either the prototype of an event which is accomplished in every man, and man is summoned to put the tragic error of the prototype into reverse. Or the fallen divine element is in man, divided into many parts, as a great flash of light is divided into many small sparks, and there is need for a fresh mission from the world of light to remind the unconscious divine element of its homeland, gather up the divine sparks, and bring them back to their home. H. Jonas[24] has called this branch of Gnosis the 'Iranian' type, because in Iran, or more precisely in the religion of Zoroaster, we hear of two hostile 'twins', the good God and the evil, who, however, both have their realms in the world in which we live. Among the gnostics, on the other hand, the one principle is identical

[24] H. Jonas, *Gnosis und spätantiker Geist* I[3], 256.

with this world, the other entirely opposed to it and not to be grasped by the senses. This branch of Gnosis is represented by the Poimandres and in Manicheism, in part too in Mandeism, and has also left traces of its influence in the West.

The other branch of Gnosis starts from *one* principle, the divine, from which in the course of the development one part is separated, that is falls. The difficulty of this approach is once expressed thus: 'For the present you must not let this trouble you . . . how from one beginning of all things, which is simple and . . . uncreated, imperishable and good, these natures also have come into being, that of perishableness and that of the Midst, which are of a different substance, where the good has [yet] the nature to beget and bring forth what is like it and of the same substance with it.'[25] In contrast to Hellenism, however long the series of the 'aeons' emanating from God is, we do not hear at the decisive point of a gradual slipping into perishability and evil, but of a 'fall', the motive of which is held to be what the Gnosis concerned regards as the primal sin. This fall with its consequences is what separates this part of Gnosis from Hellenism.

Into the foreground now steps the Lord and Creator of this world, derived from the fallen entity: the 'Demiurge',[26] frequently called Ialdabaoth, who is identified with the Creator God of the Old Testament and who, as ruler of the 'seven', is Lord of destiny. Sometimes he also produces a son, the Devil, who in the true sense of the word brings into this world injustice and evil. Ialdabaoth, the lord of the stars and of this world, has received from the fallen entity something from the world of light, and what is at stake is now this particle of light, which is to return to its homeland. That the Demiurge is identified with the God of the Old Testament is characteristic of western Gnosis, in so far as it mentions the Creation at all. For the Creator of this world is for the gnostic not the highest God; his oft-quoted word from Isaiah 45:5, 'I am God, and beside me there is no other', is conceived as an expression of his overweening pride and his ignorance of the true God who stands above all comprehension. The commandments of the Old Testament also are not such that they can give the gnostic guidance for the

---

[25] Epiph. XXXIII 7, 8.
[26] Demiurge = creator or shaper of the world.

road. For if he practises asceticism, there is nothing of that in the Old Testament, and if he yields himself to libertinism, there is certainly nothing of that; but should he wish to strike a middle course, the New Testament is nearer to hand.

Alongside these there are other systems which work with ideas closer to Hellenism. It is said, for example, that the utterly inconceivable God deposited a 'world-seed' which contained in itself all that this world became. An archon[27] is lord over the 'hebdomad', that is, over the sphere of the planets, and another more exalted over the 'ogdoad', the sphere of the fixed stars. Both are finally converted, and at the end of the world remain content in their respective spheres. In the 'world-seed', however, there is also a 'sonship', which cannot of its own effort mount upward; and with that the theme of this form of Gnosis (Basilides according to Hippolytus) has been stated. Others make not the world but the idea of the world consist of three principles, to which is added as a fourth the corporeal element of this world. Other systems speak only of three principles, whose reciprocal action is the motive of world history. At any rate the middle one of the three principles is to be thought of after the manner of a serpent, which brings ideas from the highest principle down into matter; the latter strives with all its power to retain them beside it. Here there need not be any talk of a 'fall'.

The entity which falls is either male or female. Among the Naassenes it is 'Adam' or 'the inner man', who has fallen from the 'primal man' into the 'earthen products of oblivion'; in him and in his fate the gnostic can find himself again. In Baruch-gnosis it is 'Elohim', who unites in love with 'Eden'. It is indeed only in the course of the report that it becomes clear that Elohim belongs on the side of the good God, and with him the spirit of man, while the soul belongs to Eden.

Elsewhere it is a female principle that falls, be it that no real motive for the fall is present, but the 'fallen' betakes herself to the very lowest realm of matter; or that the reason for the fall is an erotic motive, on account of which she is also called Prunikos, 'lustful'; or that a more spiritual reason for the fall is mentioned, namely the desire to be like the highest God. At any rate with her begins the chain of events in the world. In these

[27] Archon = ruler.

systems the biblical creation story has generally stood as god-parent. Several speculations are offered in order to reach from the entity which falls to the fallen men, who in all the mud of the world still bear the 'gold' within themselves. Prunikos, for example, gave to Ialdabaoth something of the light which, as a being from the higher world, she possessed in herself, and induces Ialdabaoth to breathe this into the man whom he created, but could not bring to stand erect; others make 'Sophia', as the fallen entity is also and frequently called, sow the seed from above without Ialdabaoth's knowledge upon particular men, that it may be brought up here on earth.

The idea that the 'self' in man belongs to the divine world can also be expressed in the form of statements about a 'primal man' in the upper world of light.[28] In some passages it is the highest God who is so called, but generally it is not the 'uncreated' but the 'self-originated' who bears the name 'man'. This renders it possible to make earthly man in the core of his being identical with the divine Primal Man, as, for example, in the Naassene Preaching and especially in Manicheism. Where a female being falls, it is not so easy to express this thought, as can be seen, for example, in Valentinianism. Yet even in this form of Gnosis 'man', 'primal man', 'Adamas', Adam, or the like sporadically appears; he is occasionally identified with the Redeemer, as in the *Sophia Jesu Christi*, where it is said: 'In that hour the light became manifest . . . in a first immortal androgynous man, that through this immortal one men might attain salvation and awaken out of their incapacity for knowledge. . . .'[29] That the first man or primal man is elevated above the sexual division into male and female is often stated, and the same is expected for the pneumatics in the world of light.

The descent of the 'gold', the fallen 'I' of the pneumatics, is contained in the events relating to the fallen entity. As already said, the divine element in man cannot of itself escape from its captivity in this world. It is a call from the invisible world, which reveals the heavenly homeland, that brings redemption. Sometimes this call is concealed under the catchword of

---

[28] Review of the whole material in H.-M. Schenke, *Der Gott 'Mensch' in der Gnosis*, Göttingen, 1962.
[29] p. 94 of W. C. Till's edition.

'learning', as in the Megale Apophasis, where it is said: 'When it [the uncreated] now receives the corresponding word and teaching . . .',[30] or among the Sethians, who proclaim: 'The beam of light hastens, when through instruction and learning it has received its own place, to the Logos.'[31] After all, the entire system of the individual gnostic leaders is a call. This is particularly clear in the Poimandres (§ 15), where the author is granted a vision of the highest God which shows how it comes about that man 'in contrast to all other beings on earth is divided, mortal in respect of his body, immortal in respect of the essential man'; but if he recognizes this, has 'learned' that he is immortal, that he is 'gold', then he goes after death into the higher world.

Many gnostic systems have a 'Redeemer', a figure from the world of light who awakens the divine element in man from its stupor and breaks through the spell of oblivion. This figure is for one thing a clear personification of the call itself, like Manda d'Hai, for example, in Mandeism, which means 'knowledge of life'.

In the Christian domain Jesus Christ naturally has the decisive role. The oldest Christian gnostics of whom we have any reports make Jesus wiser and more righteous than all other men, and say that a power was sent upon him from above, through which he could elude the creator of the world; he who can do the same obtains the same power. A similar view affirms that at the Baptism Christ descended upon Jesus, and thereupon he proclaimed 'the unknown Father'; before the crucifixion, however, Christ returned again to the Father. Whether these systems—Carpocrates and Cerinthus—are presented in their full range by our sources can no longer be determined with certainty, but they are simpler than the more complicated later systems, which also have more to say about the redemptive work of Christ. At any rate Christ does not redeem and deliver by the fact that he really suffered death upon the Cross: 'How, if life had been in him, would the body also be dead? Then death would have gained the upper hand even over the Saviour himself, which is absurd.'[32] Thus the (divine) life must have withdrawn before the death. This is the case at its clearest and sharpest in the Basilidian system according to Irenaeus, where Jesus allows Simon of Cyrene to be crucified instead of himself,

[30] Hipp. VI 16, 5.   [31] Hipp. V 21, 9.   [32] Cl. Al., *Exc.* § 61, 6.

and laughs at the Jews who do not notice it. This is the so-called Docetism of the Christian gnostics, i.e. the view that Jesus suffered only in appearance (Greek: *dokein*), but not in reality. But what then is his redeeming and liberating work? For one thing, that he allows the 'call' to go forth. He proclaims the unknown Father. Thus Jesus receives the charge, 'Proclaim to men this word, and inform them about the Father and "the good".'[33] Another method of carrying through his work is to act as a model. Thus, for example, among the Basilidians of Hippolytus, where Jesus has become the first of the 'separation of kinds', and now can separate the 'elect' for himself: it is a question of the separation of the divine element in man from the other ingredients in him; free from these other ingredients, the 'elect' can now ascend to the highest God. In this system indeed Jesus has not only fulfilled in himself the separation of the kinds, but has also himself contributed through his preaching to the purification of the pneumatic part.

Among the Valentinians the situation is that Jesus Christ 'also delivered what he put on'. From 'Achamoth', as the fallen portion from the world of light is called among them, he assumed the pneumatic element, from the Demiurge the psychic Christ and a psychic part. This psychic part is resuscitated by him, in that he sends a ray of his power which destroys death: Here we can speak of a redemptive act in the proper sense, as also in the other speculation that the blood which flowed from the wound in his side indicates allegorically the 'discharge' of the passions, and thereby the deliverance of the psychics. The pneumatic part, on the other hand, requires 'wisdom', it requires 'formation according to knowledge', it must come to its 'authentic nature'. In relation to the pneumatics the conduct of the Saviour has a prototypical character, in that the pneumatic element is compared with the marrow in the bones of the Saviour, which were not broken. He brings the call, he is the prototype. In any case his action is not something which transforms the 'self'. Sometimes, however, we do hear of a victory over death, as for example, in the Letter to Rheginus.[34] The psychics, so far as there is any mention of this intermediate

---

[33] Baruch-Gnosis, Hipp. V 26, 30.
[34] Rheginus 44, 21–9; 45, 22 f. (see vol. II); cf. the 'great champion, Jesus Christ', Cl. Al., *Exc.* § 58, 1.

class, have a salvation on a lower grade, not in the sphere into which the gnostics enter, but still a salvation which affords them an eternal life.

The word 'deliver' is still more richly filled where the image of the serpent is employed. The serpent, usually identified with the Logos or with 'Jesus', carries the 'awakened' upwards (as it has also brought them down). In so far as the bearing upwards is the decisive thing in the return to the invisible world, it is 'redemptive'. But 'knowledge' is combined with it in a peculiar way: the serpent, Jesus, carries aloft those who have become 'free', which means those who have recognized themselves and freed themselves from the world. To this extent the role of 'knowledge', that is the response to the call, comes into play here also.

There is still one special variation of the Redeemer to be discussed: the 'redeemed Redeemer'. If the 'gold' comes from the world of light and the Redeemer also derives from it, then the Redeemer and those whom he is to redeem are of the same nature. In that the Redeemer enters into this world, he even takes on—so it seems—that from which he is to free those to be redeemed, and thus himself becomes one in need of redemption. But he is at the same time the Redeemer, which means that he is the redeemed Redeemer. We may also look at this from above: God seeks himself, as it is said in the Megale Apophasis: 'That is what they say: "I and you are one, you are before me, I am after you." This . . . is the one power, divided above and below, begetting itself, multiplying itself, seeking itself, finding itself, its own mother, its own father. . . .'[35] What is redeemed is ultimately the Redeemer, for the two are substantially the same.

This would be a philosophy if no more were said than this. For it, the world would be a perpetual alternation, a constant up and down. Some gnostic systems in fact come close to this idea. But then there would be no talk of a redeemer, nor of a redeemed Redeemer; for Redeemer indeed means that he *finally* removes a situation, especially since the yearning of the gnostic, again in the Megale Apophasis, is 'no more to come into being'.[36] But if this is the aim of Gnosis, then there is something from which the Redeemer *redeems*: this

[35] Hipp. VI 17, 2–3.   [36] Hipp. VI 14, 6; 17, 7.

world. And here it is noteworthy that the Redeemer actually is *not* redeemed from the realm from which he delivers those to be redeemed: for he has either assumed nothing material at all, or he casts it aside as one casts aside a garment which one no longer requires, and thus he is not 'redeemed' from it. Nor does he open up for those who belong to him the way upward through the spheres of the stars. At any rate not a word with which the ascending spiritual man encounters the 'powers' relates to this fact, but only to this, that the pneumatic is a higher being, that he belongs to the world of light, and this has taught him the 'call'. Finally, it is only very seldom said of the Redeemer that he is or becomes redeemed. When in the Acts of Thomas the idea is expressed that the Redeemer entered into the outer darkness, this is probably an influence from the Christianity of the Church. In western Gnosis at any rate there is no reference to the redeemed Redeemer, nor can he be recognized even in the Poimandres. Gnosis always distinguishes the 'redeemer' from the supreme God and from those to be redeemed; only in the controversy with Gnosis could it be pointed out that 'properly' the Redeemer redeems himself.

We have now outlined the chief possibilities for the solution of the questions which lie in the decisive symbol of Gnosis, the gold in the mud. A few points remain to be presented. Christianity of the great Church has its sacraments, baptism and the Eucharist. For the gnostics a sacrament was strictly superfluous. 'Others say . . . the perfect redemption is the knowledge of the ineffable greatness . . . through knowledge the inner man is redeemed', it is expressly said of some gnostics.[37] If, however, sacraments frequently still appear in the gnostic systems, and in others are at any rate to be conjectured, this may in the first place be connected with the fact that the gnostics broke away from movements which knew sacraments and ceremonial acts, which they then took over and transformed. Thus Mandean baptism probably goes back to the self-baptism of the Jews. The question then is whether the rite still has the same meaning as originally.

Christian Gnosis frequently has several sacraments, the chief being Baptism, Unction, Sealing, Eucharist, and Bridal Chamber. From the reports of the Church Fathers and even from the

---

[37] Ir. I 21, 4.

fragments we learn little about this side of Gnosis. Only from the reports of Irenaeus about the Marcosians do we obtain a few formulae of the sacrament of the Redemption. About Baptism, Unction, and the Eucharist we learn some things in the strongly gnostic-coloured Acts of Thomas. More recently we have, in the Gospel of Philip and in the Exegesis on the Soul, copious allusions to sacraments, especially that of the Bridal Chamber.

Beside the sacraments we may set formulae which the gnostics after their decease must pronounce in the individual starry spheres through which they pass, to the ruler of the realm in question; Irenaeus[38] and Origen[39] offer us some material. These formulae also, like the sacraments, are originally alien to Gnosis. If the central core of Gnosis is the stupefaction induced by the world, then once the 'call' has broken through this stupefaction the self cannot be held back. Nevertheless, this appearance of magical formulae is an indication that for many Gnosis is not yet enough, that the 'powers' may still be a danger to them, and that they still require a token that those passing through their spheres belong to the world of light; this is consequently the content of these formulae.

The ethics of the gnostics appear to be determined by the fact that they regarded themselves as 'saved by nature'. This leads to an indifference to ethical conduct. The Church Fathers understood it thus: 'Hence the most perfect among them actually do all that is forbidden without fear.'[40] But here we must dig somewhat deeper. The Church Fathers measure the conduct of the gnostics by the standard of what in the Church ranks as ethical or not. The gnostic, however, who most sharply emphasizes the *necessity* of 'unethical' action, Carpocrates, still says that 'Faith and love redeem'.[41] It is not the case that life is simply a matter of indifference; conduct flows from that which comes from the supreme God. The gnostic's reaction is directed against all that is called 'law': 'He says that "Mine and thine" were introduced through the law.'[42] Laws, whether introduced by the world creator or enacted by men, cannot place one under an inner obligation; they are and remain laws introduced from without, and from

[38] Ir. I 13, 6.   [39] *C. Cels.* VI 31.   [40] Ir. I 6, 3.
[41] Ir. I 25, 5.   [42] Cl. Al., *Strom.* III 2 = § 7, 3 (Epiphanes).

these the gnostic wants to be free. Hence the chief opposition of the gnostics is directed against the Law of the Old Testament, which more than other laws was clothed with the authority of the world creator. The rule of conduct for them resulted from what came from the true supreme God. The only thing inwardly binding was faith, that is the response to the call, and love, which sees in one's neighbour the man who perhaps is also 'saved by nature', as it is expressed in the Gospel of Truth,[43] or at the very least cannot be roused against him, because the supreme God himself does not do so. From this we can understand the gnostic indifference with regard to confession before the authorities, and above all their participation in so-called meals of idol-offerings, which to Jews and Christians were forbidden but for Gnostics allowed (or even commanded); for the idols, like Athena, for example, or Jupiter, or even the mystery-god Attis, ranked for them as non-existent, and they felt themselves elevated above the powers of fate. Sexual life also could be regarded as unimportant, if life in the body was a matter of no concern.

The opposite conclusion was also possible. If bodily life becomes extinct, then it is false to strengthen it by yielding to it.[44] In this there was probably no thought at all of direct asceticism, even if it may have been practised, as occasional references in the Church Fathers show. On the whole, however, we ought not to be surprised if the libertine side of Gnosis stands forth more prominently among its opponents: this was particularly scandalous to the Church Fathers, while they had little to say against a way of life that was little different from that of 'orthodox' Christians, and perhaps even inclined towards asceticism.

3

How Gnosis expressed itself in the living intercourse of man and man we can learn on a literary basis only from a few examples, such as the Letter of Ptolemy to Flora. It is addressed to a woman apparently not yet initiated, and discusses things which still stand in the forecourt of Gnosis. Apart from this activity of theirs, which we can recognize only to a limited extent, the gnostics were very prolific in literary production. This can be

[43] 43, 2–5.   [44] Cl. Al., *Exc.* § 52, 1 f.

seen in the first place from the reports of the Church Fathers, which at any rate in the majority go back to writings of their opponents, and even in part quote them verbally. The judgement formerly passed on these reports by the Fathers was more unfavourable than today, when we can in some cases control them; and this not only on the basis of the quotations which they offer verbally, but thanks to the library from Nag Hammadi, found in 1945–6 but so far only partially published. This greater confidence, however, does not mean either that the Church Fathers must have understood the gnostics, or that they provide us with complete information about their opponents; we must reckon with the fact that they set in the foreground things which were abstruse, particularly heretical, or scandalous. With these reservations, however, the reports of the Fathers even today are still indispensable for knowledge of Gnosis. Hence they form the skeleton of the present selection.

In the Mandean literature it becomes clear that poetry played a part. From the non-Mandean literature also we have a few specimens. Origen speaks of psalms by Valentinus and hymns by Basilides. One example is contained in Hippolytus' account of the Naassenes, and in the Acts of Thomas two examples of poetry are to be found.

The bulk of gnostic writings, however, consists of revelations which are supposed to have been handed over by one of the gnostic Saviour-figures to a person generally from biblical history. In this garb it becomes evident that the 'system' intends to bring the 'call from above'. There are gospels, not in the sense of the New Testament gospels but secret revelations of Jesus, mostly after his Resurrection, and also gospels which do not make this claim. As recipients Old Testament figures like Seth are also mentioned. Finally, there are book-titles which go back to figures in the doctrine developed by the sect concerned.

With this the range of gnostic literature has not yet been fully reviewed. There are the gnostic Acts of Apostles. These did not sprout (or did so only in a lower degree) from delight in story-telling, but are likewise intended to bring the 'call'. In particular the figure of Thomas, the 'twin', offered the opportunity in a play upon his name to tell of the twin brother of Christ, and in manifold stories to show how Christ conquers the powers of darkness. Here again and again, under the veil of allegory, there appears the gnostic myth, which has pressed the legend of Thomas Didymus into its own service.[45]

The cherished writings of the Greeks and barbarians, Homer, for example, and what the myths related of the destiny of their gods, were also made to serve the same purpose, in part through violent reinterpretation. There is nothing which outside of Gnosis was transmitted as hallowed tradition, which could not on principle appear as the expression of the gnostic myth. The so-called Naassene Preaching is an example of this. It is therefore indeed worth while to trace out the origin of the individual motifs, but for knowledge of Gnosis itself nothing is thereby gained. Where philosophers have made some statement which also appears in Gnosis, they are charged with professing as their own wisdom, without acknowledging the source, an insight expressed by the ancient prophets of Gnosis.

So Gnosis lays hold of the whole of ancient religion, and also of ancient philosophy, if it harmonizes with its system, or can be made to harmonize. That in the process it claimed for itself the New Testament also, and under certain conditions even the Old, is readily comprehensible.

But not only what is thought in the world of religion is adapted to and taken over by Gnosis, but everything that occurs elsewhere as well: medical matters like the composition of the brain or the child in the womb, and in addition all kinds of remarkable things which were known or which rumour brought from distant peoples, such as the attractive power of the magnet for iron, and similar phenomena. These last could indeed make clear with special emphasis the quite insuperable power of the 'call', from which the 'elect' cannot withhold himself. Even the apparently inexplicable fact that in an empty ointment-jar the fragrance of a sweet-smelling ointment can still be traced is put to use by Gnosis.

All this serves to make clear the peculiarity and the effect of Gnosis. But it was itself kept secret, and this because it can only be imagined. With this we come back to the beginning: it is not a matter of the intellect. For other men the thoughts of Gnosis are only a subject for mockery. Thomas says to the

[45] G. Bornkamm, *Mythos und Legende in den apokryphen Thomas-Akten*, Göttingen, 1933.

Saviour: 'The words which you speak to us are for the world ridiculous and contemptible.'[46] Hence the writings of Gnosis are made accessible only to those who are 'worthy' of them. In addition, use is made of ambiguous words, or there is a play on a word such as 'alien', which has for the gnostics a different sense, opposed to that which it has for non-gnostics. Whole narratives also are based on such a difference in thought and language.

Related to this, but already passing over into mere trifling, is number speculation. There are certain numbers which it is desired to find in as many ways as possible, whether it be three, four, thirty, or 365, the number of the days of a year. The possibility of making play with numbers becomes even greater when we add the fact that at that time, both in the Semitic and in the Greek world, the numbers were designated by letters, so that every number could be taken as a letter and every letter as a number. If then the letters of a word are read as numbers, and the total of these numbers is reckoned and employed, the number of combinations becomes simply enormous; indeed the number 666 in the Revelation of John has not even today been identified as a name with any certainty. These matters have this in common with Gnosis, that what is meant by them must be imagined; and this imagining now becomes a more or less ingenious game.

Finally, two further developments of Gnosis must also be mentioned. One is the quite invincible delight in finding ever more and ever new secrets, in inventing names, and attaching speculations to them. Thus in one version of the Apocryphon of John the names are listed of the angels who are supposed to have created each individual part of the human body, and in the Pistis Sophia reference is made to various mysteries and decrees, and endless revelations are presented concerning them. The external trappings, and even the last tendency if we remove what is tagged on to it, are still gnostic, but it almost sinks into an occult and esoteric mysticism. The second is the declension into barren digressions, mostly of a sexual character, such as Epiphanius reports of the so-called Gnostics: even there we can see the connection with what is proper to Gnosis, but the particles of light which are to find their way upwards are

[46] Book of Thomas 142, 23 f. (see vol. II).

quite tangibly present in beasts and plants and in the sexual organs of mankind. What a distance it is from the 'self' of man which answers the 'call' all the way to these sharp practices!

ON THE CHOICE OF TEXTS AND THE TRANSLATION

The first volume of this selection of gnostic texts in translation contains—with the exception of the Apocryphon of John, which has a very close relation with the Barbelognostics—only Latin and Greek texts which are offered by the Church Fathers. That Valentinianism here occupies a relatively large place is connected with its tradition. The texts are chiefly taken from Irenaeus, Hippolytus, and Epiphanius, to whom must be added Clement of Alexandria with his *Stromata* and Origen with an extract from the sixth book of the *Contra Celsum* and from his commentary on John. The Book of Baruch has been edited by Ernst Haenchen. Martin Krause supplied the (German) translation of the Apocryphon of John.

The second volume will bring gnostic texts from the sensational find of Coptic papyri which was brought to light in 1945 at Nag Hammadi, 60 miles downstream from Luxor on the Nile, in a selection adapted to this collection. It will further present selected texts from the realm of Mandeism, a gnostic Baptist community of the Middle East. To this volume, the manuscript of which is already to hand and therefore admits of speedy publication, there will be added an index of the essential key-words and also of biblical passages, for both volumes. The two volumes are thus envisaged as a unity; it was exclusively technical reasons of publication which determined the division into two.

The translator was confronted by the difficult question whether all technical expressions should be translated or not. After long consideration the compromise was decided on: to leave untranslated expressions which offered too much free play, such as *logos* or *nous*, but also Demiurge, the latter, for example, because the translation 'creator' is inexact but, on the other hand, the rendering 'maker of the world' does not allow it to be clearly recognized who is meant. The terms *pneumatikos*, *psychikos*, and *choikos* and related expressions have remained untranslated; on the other hand, every *phēsin* and *phasin* has been correspondingly translated, irrespective of the frequency of its occurrence, in order to keep in mind the character of our texts as reports from the pen of the Church Fathers. In general, stress has been laid on securing as exact a translation as possible.

Round brackets indicate explanatory additions by the translator (see further p. 105 n. 2, p. 226 n. 2, and p. 356 n. 11).

(*Note to English Edition*: Introductory material has of course been translated direct from the German. The actual texts, however, have been translated with the original at hand, and revised to ensure that they are really *English* translations and not merely at third hand through the German. Where the German version shows a preference for one of two alternatives, it has of course been followed. Numbered footnotes are those of the German edition. Those marked by an asterisk have been added by the translators.)

EXPLANATION OF SOME TECHNICAL EXPRESSIONS

Abyssos	Abyss
Achamoth	Transcription of the Hebrew word for 'Wisdom'
Adamas	Invincible
Aeon	World, eternity. In Gnosis exclusively for the other world or worlds
Archons	Powers located between the other world and this earth, who enslave mankind. The singular 'archon' as a designation of the Demiurge is here reproduced by 'ruler'
Barbelo	Name of a female aeon, usually in a high or even the highest place. Etymology unknown
Chaos	The realm of disorder which lies at the root of the world
Chus	Earth (thrown up); in Gnosis a designation of that of which the earth consists
Choic	Men of earth. This term is not translated
Demiurge	The creator of the world, who is, however, not in the proper sense a 'creator', but only a 'shaper'

Ennoia	Thought
Greatness	Occasionally used instead of Pleroma
Horos	Limit, namely the boundary between the other world and everything else
Hylic	The man who is attached to Hyle, matter, and surrenders himself to it
Ialdabaoth	The name of an archon, usually in the role of the creator of this world. The interpretation of the name is uncertain
Kenoma	Emptiness, void. A designation of the world as that which has no true 'existence'
Logos (pl. logoi)	Word, speech, reason. One of the higher aeons
Nous	Understanding, thought. One of the highest aeons
Parhedroi	Spirits who are with man
Pleroma	Fullness. A designation of the other world as that which has true 'existence'. The totality of the aeons
Pneuma	Spirit, breath. Occasionally there is a play on this double meaning, but predominantly 'spirit'
Pneumatic	Spiritual, man who has or is spirit
Prunikos	Lustful (or 'Lechery'). Name of a fallen aeon
Psyche	Soul, usually in a depreciatory sense, in contrast to the Pneumatic
Psychic	Man of soul, who has no more than soul
Sige	Silence. Name of one of the highest aeons
Topos	Place. As a name of the Demiurge not translated

The following terms, translated in the German edition, are here left untranslated:

Autopator	αὐτοπάτωρ: lit. 'self-father'
Hebdomad	ἑβδομάς: a group of seven, especially of the seven planets or the spheres they control
Monad	μονάς: the primal unity
Ogdoad	ὀγδοάς: a group of eight, or the eighth and highest 'heaven' above the spheres of the planets

THE GREEK BASIS FOR SOME TRANSLATIONS

Consort   σύζυγος; the term συζυγία, used of pairs of aeons, is
               left untranslated
Deficiency   ὑστέρημα
Depth   βάθος
Greatness   μέγεθος
Isolation   μονότης
Knowledge, Gnosis γνῶσις
Limit   ὅρος
Midst   μεσότης
One   ἕν
Passion   πάθος, πάθη
Primal cause* βύθος
Save, salvation σώζω, σωτηρία
Saviour   σωτήρ
Unity   ἑνότης

* This seems to be the nearest equivalent for the German *Urgrund*, but does not
carry quite the same meaning. *Urgrund* here means something of unfathomable
depth, the primal ground of being. Buthos is *also* the primal cause (German
Ursache), but this idea is not expressed in the term itself.

1

SIMON AND MENANDER

SIMON MAGUS

Simon Magus is regarded by the Church Fathers as the originator of the gnostic heresy,[1] but whether he actually was—that is, whether the whole of Gnosis took its origin from him—is open to question. He has at any rate some peculiar features which are lacking in the later Gnosis.

The tradition about him is relatively meagre, and by no means free from influences later introduced. The first mention in the Book of Acts runs: 'A man named Simon was in the city, who practised magic and made a great impression on the people of the Samaritans. He said he was a great (man). All, great and small, followed him and said: "This is the power of God which is called great." They followed him because for some considerable time he had made a great impression on them with his sorceries' (Acts 8: 9-11). The Church Fathers unanimously trace back the title 'the great power' to the fact that he was worshipped as a god. Thus Justin already says:

> After Christ was taken up to heaven, the demons put forward men who said that they were gods, who were not only not persecuted by you but even counted worthy of honours. The Samaritan Simon from the village of Gitta, who under the emperor Claudius accomplished magic works of power through the arts of the demons working in him, was in your royal city of Rome considered as a god and honoured with a statue among you as a god; this statue was erected in the river Tiber between the two bridges, and has this Roman inscription: 'To Simon, the holy god.' Almost all the Samaritans, and a few also among other nations, confess him as the first god and worship him.[2]

That he was regarded as a god in Rome is certainly an error, for the god's name was Semo. But that almost all the Samaritans confessed and worshipped him as God is the peculiar thing, for in Gnosis only he and his disciple Menander themselves appear as God.

---

[1] For example, Ir. I 27, 4. [2] *Apol.* I 26, 1-3.

Now Celsus[3] saw in Syria and Palestine prophets who said:

I am God or the Son of God or a divine Spirit. I am come. For the world is already at the point of being destroyed and you, ye men, shall perish because of your unrighteousness. But I wish to deliver you. You shall see me again coming with heavenly power. Blessed is he who now worships me—upon all the rest I will bring fire from heaven, both upon cities and on countries. The men who do not know their punishment shall repent and groan in vain; but those who follow me I will keep safe for ever.

These prophets betray a self-consciousness similar to that of Simon. In addition, not only is the self-consciousness similar but also the role which they play in the drama of world history: it is by the attitude adopted to them that the eternal destiny of men is decided.

In the Greek world it is nothing remarkable for men to be regarded as gods—the cult of the emperor is only one example. It is thus nothing out of the ordinary, and also not improbable, that Simon gave himself out to be God. In view of the fact that this is reported only of him and his disciple, one must regard the report about Simon as not to be rejected out of hand. We have here Gnosis in the form of Greek self-consciousness, or Greek self-consciousness in the form of Gnosis. Only with Simon and his disciple Menander is the founder of the sect at the same time the redeemer who has come from heaven.

Following on the passage already cited, Justin further says: 'And a certain Helena, who at that time went about with him but had formerly maintained herself in a brothel, is said to have been the first Ennoia (Thought) emanating from him.'

Whether this Ennoia whose name was Helena is an original element of the Simonian system has been the subject of dispute. She has been thought a later addition, since the redemption of mankind and that of Ennoia stand in rivalry with one another, and in addition Ennoia as a descending divine being appears to presuppose a developed gnostic system: how should Simon come to that? But the design of the system is still very simple. According to Tertullian's account[4] Ennoia anticipates the Father's purpose, and thus 'falls' as in Gnosis generally; but in the older accounts this is not the case, rather Ennoia is detained by the angels created by her, a relatively simple version which was later developed by the Christian gnostics in manifold ways. From the late-Jewish 'Wisdom'[5] this Ennoia is distinguished not only through their names but also by the fact that, while heaven and earth are indeed made by means of her, she does

---

[3] In Origen, *C. Cels.* VII 9.   [4] *De anima* 34.   [5] *Sap. Sal.* 6–9.

not have Folly set over against her, nor does she ascend again without further ado. The redemption of Ennoia and that of mankind are not in rivalry when there is as yet no thought at all of the union of Ennoia with the men in whom she is to exist. Simon believes he has in himself such a power as the supreme god possesses, and that he is in a position to redeem Ennoia. It would be too strange that the unanimously attested report of the Helen insulted by Stesichorus, who later retracted the insult—a feature which occurs nowhere else in Gnosis—should have been invented by the Simonians. Whether the further elaboration of the Helena legend as it appears in Hippolytus[6] and later in Epiphanius[7]—centring on the theme of Helen's torch—whether this also derives from Simon is not certain.

From what Irenaeus reports it is worthy of note that Simon, like Celsus' Syrian prophets, promised that the world would be dissolved and those who were his delivered from the dominion of those who had made the world; this means, however, that they are also freed from the Law.

Concerning Simon's end, Hippolytus reports that he had himself buried alive and commanded his disciples to dig him up again after three days, but that he was not raised again to life. This sounds like a legend, but may contain a core of fact. For Clement of Alexandria[8] reports that he was called 'the standing', that is, the one who does not fall prey to destruction. If he regarded himself as God, this idea would be very natural.

A special part is played by Simon's ethics. His disciples, whom Irenaeus calls 'mystery priests', went over to libertinarian practices, and the justification for that occasions no surprise. Simon, however, according to Irenaeus, probably did consider the laws of the Old Testament as ordained by wicked angels, but in regard to his conduct itself nothing is known apart from what the Church Fathers call sorcery.

The important thing is that Simon shows no relationship with Christianity. The reports which place him in such a light are to be received with caution. Among these are: that he appeared in Judaea as Son and so forth, that in outward appearance he suffered, that Helena was affirmed to have been the lost sheep, and the speculation about the one who 'stands, stood and will stand'.

At any rate Simon presents Gnosis still in an immature form, diluted with Greek ideas about man. Gnostic ideas here are (*a*) the anti-cosmic attitude; (*b*) the redemption of Helena = Ennoia; (*c*) the 'deliverance' of the men who believe in him.

6 Hipp. VI 19, 2.   7 Epiph. XXI 3, 2 f.

8 *Strom.* II 11 = § 52, 2; So also Ps. Cl., *Recogn.* II 7, 1 and *Hom.* II 22, 3 f.

Irenaeus, *Adv. Haer.* I 23, 2–4

2. The Samaritan Simon, from whom all the heresies take their origin, has the basic ideas of the following heresy. He led about with him a certain Helena, whom he had redeemed as a harlot in Tyre, a city of Phoenicia, and said that she was his first 'thought', the mother of all, through whom in the beginning he had conceived the idea of making angels and archangels. This Ennoia, leaping forth[9] from him and knowing what her father willed, descended to the lower regions and gave birth to angels and powers, by whom he said this world was made. But after she had given birth to them, she was detained by them out of envy, because they did not wish to be considered the progeny of any other. For he himself had remained entirely unknown to them; but his Ennoia was detained by the powers and angels which had been emitted by her, and suffered every contumely from them, that she might not return again to her father, even to the point that she was shut up in a human body and through the centuries, as from one vessel to another, migrated into ever different female bodies. She was also in that Helen for whose sake the Trojan War was joined; hence Stesichorus, who had defamed her in a poem, was deprived of his eyesight, but then afterwards he repented and wrote the so-called *Palinodes*, in which he glorified her, and saw again. In her wandering from body to body, in which she continually endured ignominy, she finally prostituted herself in a brothel—and this was the lost sheep (Matt. 18:19 par.).

3. Hence he himself came, that he might take her first to himself and free her from the fetters; but to men he accorded redemption through the recognition of him. For since the angels were governing the world badly, because each one of them desired the supremacy, he came to bring things to order. He descended in transfigured form, made like to the powers and authorities and angels, so that he might appear to men as a man, although he was not a man; he was thought to have suffered in Judaea, although he did not suffer.[10] The prophets spoke their prophecies inspired by the angels who created the

---

[9] The same image of 'springing forth' also in Ir. I 2, 2 (Valentinianism) and 29, 4 (Barbelognosis).

[10] This last point is certainly Christian but probably also what Irenaeus says about his descent.

world, hence those who have their hope in him and in his Helena trouble themselves no further with them, and as free men do what they wish. For through his grace are men saved, and not through righteous works. Nor are works just by nature, but by convention, as the angels who made the world ordained, in order to enslave men by such precepts. Hence he promised that the world will be dissolved, and those who are his liberated from the dominion of those who made the world.

4. Therefore their mystery priests live licentiously, and perform sorceries, as each one is able. They practise exorcisms and incantations, love potions and erotic magic; the so-called familiar spirits and dream-inducers, and whatever other occult things exist, are zealously cultivated among them. They have an image also of Simon, made in the form of Zeus, of Helena in the form of Athena, and these they worship. They have their name from Simon, the founder of their impious opinion, being called Simonians, and from them the falsely so-called Gnosis took its beginnings, as one may learn from their own assertions.

Hippolytus, *Ref.* VI 19, 5

These became imitators of error and of Simon Magus and do the same things, saying that one must engage in intercourse without consideration, affirming: 'All earth is earth, and it makes no difference where a man sows, if only he sows.' Indeed, they count themselves blessed because of this union, and say that this is perfect love and the holy of holies.

Hippolytus, *Ref.* VI 20, 2–3

2. Peter resisted him (Simon) at length, since he deceived many by his magic. Finally . . . he sat down under a plane-tree and taught.

3. And when at last he was near to being refuted because of the passing of time, he said that if he were buried alive he would rise again on the third day. Commanding a grave to be dug, he ordered his disciples to heap earth upon him. They did as he commanded, but he remained (in it) until this day. For he was not the Christ.

Clem. Alex., *Strom.* II 11 = §52, 2

The adherents of Simon want to be like in conduct to the 'standing one' whom they worship.

Origen, *Contra Celsum* I 57

The magician Simon also, the Samaritan, wanted to win some through magic, and he deceived them at that time. But now one cannot find thirty all told in the world, and perhaps this number is too high. Even in Palestine they are very few, and nowhere in the rest of the world is his name to be found . . .

DOSITHEUS

On Simon's predecessors and disciples not very many reports, and these not very accurate, have been preserved.

According to the Clementine Recognitions and Homilies both Dositheus and Simon were disciples of John the Baptist. Since on John's death Simon was in Egypt, Dositheus took over the position of leader. On his return Simon did not venture to displace him directly from his station, but through a miracle brought it about that Dositheus worshipped him, Simon, as the 'standing one'; shortly afterwards Dositheus died. Among the Church Fathers only Origen has preserved a report about him, that Dositheus gave himself out to be the Messiah or Christ. It is characteristic, and gives the impression of sound information, that it is reported of his followers that they both possessed writings from him and were of the belief that he did not taste of death.

Origen, *In Joh.* XIII 27 (on John 4:25)

Thus a certain Dositheus of the Samaritans came forward and said that he was the prophesied Christ; from that day until now there are Dositheans, who both produce writings of Dositheus and also relate some tales about him, as that he did not taste of death, but is still alive.[11]

MENANDER

Menander from Kapparetaia in Samaria worked in Antioch. He affirmed that his adherents would not die, and that through the baptism which he gave them. Whether in this there is any influence of Christian or Jewish ideas at work remains uncertain.

The adherents of Simon and Menander evidently did not long continue. This is readily comprehensible, since each linked his activity with his own person and for that reason its effectiveness was subsequently bound to go into decline.

[11] According to Origen (*De Princ.* IV 3, 2), Dositheus affirmed that one ought to remain in the garment and in the position in which he was overtaken on the Sabbath, until the Sabbath is past. Whether this refers to the gnostic Dositheus is questionable.

Justin, *Apol.* I 26, 1, 4

1. Thirdly (I adduce the fact) that even after the taking-up of Christ into heaven the demons put forward some men who said that they were gods . . .

4. Concerning one Menander, likewise a Samaritan from the village of Kapparetaia, a disciple of Simon, who likewise obtained power from the demons, we know that he came to Antioch and deceived many through magic arts, and that he alleged to his disciples that they would not die. And even now there are some of them who affirm this.

Irenaeus, *Adv. Haer.* I 23, 5

His (Simon's) successor was Menander, a Samaritan by race, who himself attained to the highest point of magic. He said that the first Power was unknown to all, but that he himself was the one who was sent by the invisible as a saviour for the salvation of men. The world was made by angels, whom he too—like Simon—said had been brought forth by Ennoia. He added that he brought it about through the magic knowledge that was taught by him that he conquered the angels who created the world. His disciples received resurrection through baptism into him, and they can no longer die, but remain without growing old and immortal.

2

THE FIRST CHRISTIAN GNOSTICS

INTRODUCTION

Cerinthus, Carpocrates, and Saturnilus have this in common, that in these cases we can still scarcely speak of a 'system'; even with Carpocrates, concerning whom Irenaeus presents a relatively detailed report, there can be no question of it, since the Church Father occupies himself principally with ethics.

If we assume that Simon and Menander lived to about A.D. 60 or 70, the first account we have of a Christian gnostic, apart from what can be gathered from the New Testament, concerns Cerinthus, whose activity falls in the period of the Apostle or Presbyter John;[1] we are thus brought to the last decades of the first post-Christian century. He was followed by Carpocrates, who is said to have lived under Hadrian (A.D. 117–38).[2] Saturnilus is roughly contemporary, perhaps somewhat earlier than Basilides (still before 150). The Cainites we append here since they fit into this line of descent.

What is common to them is further that they do not *expressly* name the God of the Old Testament as creator of the world; either they speak of angels who made the world, or they ascribe the creation to a 'power'. The Church Fathers would probably have mentioned it, had they either named or intended the God of the Old Testament. Also, the expression 'Ialdabaoth' does not yet appear.

In Cerinthus it is the man Jesus, on whom Christ descended at the Baptism, who proclaims the 'unknown Father'. This Christ was impassible, and separated from him again before the Passion. Jesus Christ is thus the bearer of the call who proclaims the Father, up to that point unknown.

According to Carpocrates the soul of Jesus retained what it had seen in its pre-existence, and thereby obtained power to escape from the world-creators, to disdain the Jewish precepts, and to ascend again to God. Here Jesus is the pattern and example which his adherents may in certain circumstances surpass. All that matters is faith and love; this is intensified to the point of saying that a man *must* despise and transgress all laws, otherwise he is still subject to the creator powers and is reincarnated, until one day the intuition strikes

---

[1] Eus., *H.E.* IV 14, 6.　　[2] Theodoret, *Haer. Fab.* I 5.

him that it *is* only a matter of faith and love, and that it is therefore
needful to trample all 'laws' underfoot. How this freedom was
justified emerges from a fragment of a document by Carpocrates' son
Epiphanes, who died at the age of seventeen, in which he seeks to
prove rationally that 'mine and thine', even in regard to marriage,
is a law introduced by men and contrary to the will of nature.
Following on this fragment, Clement reports concerning the 'love-
feasts' of this sect, which were the occasion for promiscuous unions:
probably we have here something like a sacrament before us.

Saturnilus likewise held man to be a creation of the angels, but
one which—this feature we shall frequently encounter again—could
only crawl. Hence 'the higher power' sent a 'spark of life', which
raised him up. Saturnilus is said to have been the first to distinguish
two kinds of men, the one good, the other evil; this means, then, that
he was the first to assume the natural and unalterable division of
mankind. That Christ delivers only the men who have the spark of
life in them is of course in conflict with the idea that it is the spark
of life which raises man up—this means *every* man; probably this
difference should be traced back to abbreviation in the report or to misunderstanding by the Church Father. Saturnilus was an ascetic, and
forbade marriage; most of his adherents also abstained from the eating
of meat. It is not clear what was the wider context in which stood the
mention of Satan as an angel who acted against the creator angels.

The Cainites held Cain, Esau, and others to derive from the
higher power, which according to Tertullian's account is to be
distinguished from a 'weaker power'; probably behind these two
powers there are concealed the 'unknown God' and the creator or
creators. Judas brought about the 'betrayal' as a good deed, various
justifications being presented, as the same Church Father reports.
Creation they ascribe to the 'Hystera', the 'womb', but whether this
arose from a misreading of the Hebrew divine predicate 'gracious'[3]
is very uncertain. Their ethic was similar to that of Carpocrates.
Irenaeus mentions a Gospel of Judas and quotes from an anonymous
document, from which Epiphanius also quotes, although a somewhat different passage. In addition Epiphanius mentions a writing
of Paul, which was used by the so-called gnostics as well.

CERINTHUS

Irenaeus, *Adv. Haer.* I 26, 1

A certain Cerinthus in Asia[4] taught that the world was not
made by the first God, but by a power which was widely

---

[3] R. M. Grant in *Vig. Chr.* 11 (1957), 146 f.
[4] Hipp.: instructed in the learning of the Egyptians.

separated and remote from that supreme power which is above the all, and did not know the God who is over all things. Jesus, he suggested, was not born of a virgin, for that seemed to him impossible, but was the son of Joseph and Mary, just like all the rest of men but far beyond them in justice and prudence and wisdom. After his baptism Christ descended upon him in the form of a dove, from the power that is over all things, and then he proclaimed the unknown Father and accomplished miracles. But at the end Christ separated again from Jesus, and Jesus suffered and was raised again, but Christ remained impassible, since he was pneumatic.

CARPOCRAETS AND EPIPHANES

Irenaeus, *Adv. Haer.* I 25, 1–6

1. Carpocrates and his disciples say that the world and what is in it was made by angels, who are much inferior to the unbegotten Father. Jesus was born of Joseph and like the rest of men, but he was distinct from the rest in that, since his soul was strong and pure, it remembered what it had seen in the regions of the unbegotten God: and for this reason power was sent down to him that he might escape the world-creators by it. It passed through them all and was set free in all, and ascended up to him, and likewise the (souls) which embraced the like. They say that the soul of Jesus was lawfully nurtured in the traditions of the Jews, but despised them and thereby obtained powers by which he vanquished the passions which attach to men for punishment. 2. The soul which like the soul of Jesus is able to despise the creator archons likewise receives power to do the same things. Hence they have come to such presumption that some say they are like Jesus, some actually affirm that they are even stronger* than he, and some (declare) that they are superior to his disciples, like Peter and Paul and the other Apostles; they are in no way inferior to Jesus himself. Their souls derive from the same surroundings, and therefore likewise despise the creators of the world and are counted worthy of the same power, and return again to the same place. But if anyone despise the things here more than

* '*secundum aliquid* represents the intensive καὶ ἔτι in Greek, [κατά τι] being an error of similarity' (Harvey, *Sancti Irenaei adversus Haereses*, Cambridge, 1857, vol. i, p. 205 n. 2).

he, he can be greater than he. 3. They practise magic arts and incantations, love potions and love-feasts, familiar spirits and dream-inducers, and the other evil things, saying that they already have the power to prevail over the archons and creators of this world, and not only that, but over all that is created in it. . . . They live a dissipated life and hold an impious doctrine, and use the name as a cloak for their wickedness . . . 4. So abandoned are they in their recklessness that they claim to have in their power and to be able to practise anything whatsoever that is ungodly and impious. They say that conduct is good and evil only in the opinion of men. And after the transmigrations the souls must have been in every kind of life and every kind of deed—if a man does not in *one* life do at one and the same time all that is not merely forbidden for us to speak or hear but may not even enter into the thought of our minds, nor may one believe if men in our cities do anything of the sort —so that, as their scriptures say, their souls have been in every enjoyment of life and when they depart (from the body) they are deficient in nothing; but they must labour lest perchance, because something is lacking to their freedom, they be compelled to be sent again into bodies.

That is why Jesus spoke this parable: 'When you are with your adversary on the way, take pains to get free of him, lest he deliver you to the judge and the judge to his servant, and cast you into prison. Amen, I tell you, you will not come out thence until you have paid the last farthing' (Matt. 5 : 25 f. par.). The adversary, they say, is one of the angels who are in the world, whom they call the devil, saying that he was appointed to bring the souls which have perished from the world to the Prince. He, they say, is the first of the world-creators, and he hands over such souls to another angel who serves him, that he may shut them up in other bodies. For they say that the body is a prison. And the saying 'You will not come out thence until you have paid the last farthing' they interpret to mean that one does not come out from the power of the angels who made the world.

So long must (a man) continue to be reincarnated, until he has been in absolutely every action in the world. When no more is lacking, then his soul, set free, goes to that God who is above the creator angels, and so it is saved. All souls, whether they have gone ahead to engage in every action at one coming (into the flesh), or whether they migrate from body to body or, inserted into every kind of life, fill up and pay their dues, all souls are liberated, so that they may no longer be in the body.

5. Now if these things are done among them which are godless and unrighteous and forbidden, I could not believe. But in their writings it is so written, and they themselves explain thus: Jesus, they say, spoke in a mystery to his disciples and apostles privately, and charged them to hand these things on to the worthy and those who assented. For through faith and love are (men) saved. All other things are indifferent, being accounted now good, now evil, according to the opinion of men, but nothing is evil by nature.

6. Some of them mark their own disciples by branding them on the back of the right ear-lobe. Hence also Marcellina, who came to Rome under Anicetus (*c.* A.D. 154–65), since she was of this doctrine led astray many. They call themselves gnostics. They have also images, some painted, some too made of other material, and say they are the form of Christ made by Pilate in that time when Jesus was with men. These they crown, and they set them forth with the images of the philosophers of the world, Pythagoras, Plato, Aristotle, and the rest; and their other observance concerning them they carry out like the heathen.

Clement of Alexandria, *Strom.* III 2 = § 5, 2–9, 3

5, 2. This Epiphanes, whose writings are at hand, was the son of Carpocrates and a mother named Alexandria, on his father's side an Alexandrian, on his mother's a Cephallenian. He lived in all seventeen years, and was honoured as a god in Same on Cephallenia, where a temple of great stones, altars, a precinct, and a museum have been built and consecrated. The Cephallenians gather at the temple at the new moon, celebrate the day of deification as his birthday, and sacrifice to Epiphanes, offer libations, and hold carousal, and hymns are sung. 3. He was taught by his father in the basic sciences and in Plato, and founded the monadic Gnosis, from which also the sect of the Carpocratians derives.

6, 1. He says in his book *On Righteousness*: The righteousness of God is a communion with equality. For the heaven, equally stretched out on all sides in a circle, embraces the whole earth, and the night shows forth equally all the stars, and the sun, the cause of day and the father of light, God has poured forth from above equally upon the earth for all who can see, but they all see in common, for he makes no distinction of rich or poor, people or ruler, foolish and wise, female and male, free and slave. 2. But not even one of the irrational beasts does he treat otherwise, but pours it (the sun) from above equally on all the beasts together, good and bad, and thus establishes righteousness, since none can have more or take away from his neighbour that he himself may have twice as much light as the other. 3. The sun causes common food to grow up for all creatures, and the common righteousness is given to all equally; and in regard to such things the race of cattle is like the (individual) cattle, that of swine like the (individual) swine, of sheep like the (individual) sheep, and so on. 4. For righteousness among them is shown to be community. Then in community are all things sown alike according to kind; common food grows upon the earth for all the beasts that graze, and for all equally, not governed by any law but harmoniously present for all in righteousness through the generosity of him who gives and commands.

7, 1. But not even the things of generation have any written law—it would have been altered—but they sow and give birth equally, having a communion implanted by righteousness. The creator and father of all, ordaining it by his own righteousness, provided for all in common equally an eye to see, making no distinction of female and male, reasoning and unreasoning, in short none of any kind, imparting sight in equality and community to all alike by one command.

2. But the laws, he says, since they could not restrain men's incapacity to learn, taught them to transgress. For the private property of the laws cut up and nibbled away the fellowship of the divine law . . . 3. He says that 'mine' and 'thine' were introduced through the laws, and that (people) would no longer enjoy in community the fruits either of the earth or of possessions, or even of marriage. In common for all he made the vines, which refuse neither sparrow nor thief, and likewise the corn and the other fruits. Fellowship and what belongs to equality when violated gave birth to a thief of creatures and of

fruits. 8, 1. In that God made all things in common for man, and brought together the female with the male in common and united all the animals likewise, he declared righteousness to be fellowship with equality.

2. But those thus born rejected the fellowship which had brought about their birth, and say: 'Who marries one, let him have her', when they could all share in common, as the rest of the animals show. 3. (Later he says that same thing again, adducing in these very words): Into the males he put desire vigorous and impetuous, for the continuance of the race, desire which neither law nor custom nor anything else that exists can remove, for it is an ordinance of God. . . .

9, 3. Hence the word of the lawgiver 'You shall not covet' (Exod. 20: 17, Deut. 5: 21, cf. Rom. 7: 7) must be understood as laughable, and yet more laughable is it to say 'what is your neighbour's'. For the very one who gave the desire as embracing the things of birth commands that it be taken away, though he takes it away from no animal. But that he said 'your neighbour's wife' is even more laughable, since he compels what was common possession to become private property.

Clem. Alex., *Strom.* III 2 = § 10, 1

These then are the teachings which the excellent Carpocratians set forth. Of them and of some other adherents of the same false doctrine it is related that they assemble for meals—for I would not call their gathering a love-feast—both men and women. And when they have satisfied themselves . . . then they overturn the lamps and so remove the light that would uncover the shame of their dissolute 'righteousness', and unite as they will and with whom they will; and after they have exercised themselves in fellowship in such a love-feast, they demand even by day from the women of whom they wish it obedience toward the Carpocratian law—for it would not be right to say toward the divine law.

SATURNILUS

Irenaeus, *Adv. Haer.* I 24, 1–2

1. From these (Simon and Menander) Saturnilus, who was from Antioch by Daphne, and Basilides took their impulse and taught divergent doctrines, the one in Syria, the other in

Alexandria. Saturnilus, like Menander, taught one Father unknown to all, who made angels, archangels, powers, and authorities. The world and everything in it came into being from seven angels, and man also was a creation of angels. When a shining image appeared from the supreme power above, which they were not able to detain, he says, because it immediately sped back upwards, they exhorted one another, saying: 'Let us make a man after the image and likeness' (Gen. 1: 26). When this was done, he says, and their creation could not stand erect because of the powerlessness of the angels, but crept like a worm, then the power above took pity on him because he had been made in his likeness, and sent a spark of life which raised the man up, equipped him with limbs, and made him live. This spark of life, he says, hastens back after death to its own kind, and the rest is resolved into that from which it came into being.

2. The Saviour he assumed to be unbegotten, incorporeal, and without form, but appeared in semblance as a man. The God of the Jews, he says, was one of the angels; and because all the archons wanted to destroy the Father, Christ came for the destruction of the God of the Jews and the salvation of those who believe in him; these are they who have the spark of life in them. He was the first to say that two kinds of men had been moulded by the angels, the one wicked, the other good. And since the demons helped the wicked, the Saviour came for the destruction of the wicked men and demons, and the salvation of the good. Marriage and procreation, he says, are of Satan. Many of his followers abstain also from animal food, and through this feigned continence they lead many astray. Of the prophecies, some were spoken by the angels who created the world and some by Satan, of whom he teaches that he was himself an angel who acted against the world-creators, and especially the God of the Jews.

THE CAINITES

Irenaeus, *Adv. Haer.* I 31, 1–2

1. Others again say that Cain was from the superior power, and confess Esau and (the tribe of) Korah and the Sodomites and all such as their kinsmen. They were attacked by the creator, but none of them suffered any ill. For Sophia snatched

away from them to herself what belonged to her. This Judas the traitor knew very well, and he alone of all the apostles recognized the truth and accomplished the mystery of the betrayal, by which everything earthly and heavenly is dissolved, as they say. And they produce a fabrication, which they call the Gospel of Judas.

2. I have also collected writings of theirs, in which they urge the destruction of the works of Hystera (the womb); Hystera is the name they give to the fabricator of heaven and earth. And they say they cannot be saved in any other way, except they pass through all things, just as Carpocrates also said. And at every sinful and base action an angel is present and instils in him who ventures the deed audacity and impurity; what it is in act they say in the angel's name: 'O thou angel, I make use of thy work; O thou power, I accomplish thy deed.' And this is the perfect 'knowledge', to enter without fear into such operations, which it is not lawful even to name.

Tertullian, *Adv. Omn. Haer.* 2

There also broke out another heresy, called that of the Cainites. For they glorify Cain, as if conceived by some potent power which operated in him. Abel was conceived and brought forth by an inferior power, and was therefore found to be inferior. Those who assert this also defend Judas the traitor, saying that he was admirable and great because of the benefits which he is claimed to have brought to the human race. For some of them think that thanksgiving should be rendered to Judas for this reason. 'For Judas', they say, 'observing that Christ wanted to subvert the truth, betrayed him that the truth might not be overthrown.' Others dispute this, saying: 'Since the powers of this world did not wish Christ to suffer, that salvation might not be provided for the human race through his death, he betrayed Christ out of concern for the salvation of mankind, in order that the salvation which was being hindered by the powers opposed to the suffering of Christ might not be prevented altogether, and therefore through the passion of Christ the salvation of the human race might not be delayed.'

Epiphanius, *Panarion* XXXVIII 2, 4 f.

4. There came also into our hands a book in which they formulated certain things full of lawlessness, including the

following: 'This,' he says, 'is the angel who blinded Moses, and these are the angels who hid those about Korah and Dathan and Abiram (Num. 16) and brought them to another place.'

5. Again they fabricate another little book in the name of Paul the Apostle, full of things unspeakable, which the so-called Gnostics use, which they call the Ascent of Paul; the pretext (for so calling it) they find in the fact that the Apostle says he ascended into the third heaven and heard ineffable words, which it is not permissible for a man to speak (2 Cor. 12: 4). And these, they say, are the ineffable words.

3

ASSOCIATES OF MARCION

INTRODUCTION

Whether Marcion is to be described as a gnostic is questionable. There do appear in him a number of ideas which are also found elsewhere in Gnosis, but, on the other hand, the fundamental concept of the 'call' which strikes home to man's 'self' is not to be found here. He is therefore not included in this collection. His predecessor Cerdo, however, and his unfaithful follower Apelles, who separated from his master, and also Severus, ought not to be omitted.

CERDO

Irenaeus, *Adv. Haer.* I 27, 1

Cerdo, who took his start from the Simonians and came to Rome in the time of Hyginus, the ninth successor in the episcopate since the Apostles (*c.* A.D. 138–42), taught that the God proclaimed by the Law and the prophets was not the Father of our Lord Jesus Christ; for he was known, but the other unknown, and he was righteous, but the other good.

APELLES

According to Hippolytus Apelles, who started out from Marcion's teaching, assumed four Gods, distinguishing from the supreme God first the creator, then the law-giver, and finally the one who was the cause of evil, i.e. the devil. He taught that Christ came down from the good God, that he took on real flesh and died in it and rose again, but that he then gave back his flesh to matter and ascended to his father, the good God. Apelles is said to have associated himself with a virgin Philumene and proclaimed her thoughts. He taught, like Marcion, an ascetic way of life.

Hippolytus, *Ref.* VII 38, 1–5

1. Apelles, who came from these, teaches thus: there is one good God, as Marcion also assumed, but the creator of all things is righteous, he who made what has come into being;

a third is he who spoke to Moses—this one is fiery—and there is another, the fourth, the cause of evil. These he calls angels.

2. He speaks ill of the law and the prophets, saying that what is written is the work of men and false. Of the Gospels or the Apostle he chooses what pleases him. He pays heed to the words of a certain Philumene as to the revelations of a prophetess. Christ, he says, came down from the power above, that is, from the good, and is his son.

3. This one who appeared, he says, was not born of a virgin nor was he without flesh, but he took portions from the substance of the all, that is, hot and cold and wet and dry, and made a body; and in this body, concealed from the cosmic powers, he lived for the time which he lived in the world.

4. Again, when he was crucified by the Jews he died, and raised up after three days he appeared to his disciples and showed them the print of the nails and his side, persuading them that it was he and not a phantom, but that he was in the flesh (John 20: 20, 27; Luke 24: 39).

5. The flesh, he says, he showed and then restored to the earth, from whose substance it was, since he did not claim anything that was another's, but after using it for a season restored to each (part of matter) what belonged to it, loosing again the bond of the body, hot to hot, cold to cold, wet to wet, dry to dry; and thus went to the good Father, leaving behind the seed of life in the world, through the disciples, for those who believe.

Tertullian, *De anima* 23

Apelles says that the souls were enticed down from their seats above the heavens with earthly foods by the fiery angel, the God of Israel and ours, who then bound sinful flesh fast about them.

From Epiphanius, *Panarion* XLIV 2, 6

(Apelles) . . . shows us in what scripture and what kind of things were spoken naturally by him (Christ), and what are those from the Demiurge. 'For thus', he says, 'he said in the Gospel: be you tried money-changers.[1] Make use',* he says, 'of every scripture, selecting what is useful.'

---

[1] Apocryphal saying of Jesus.

---

* Taking χρῶ as the Attic imper. of χράομαι. German 'For I make use'.

SEVERUS

According to Severus there is one good God in an unknown and lofty heaven. The Demiurge (with his principalities and powers) is called Ialdabaoth or Sabaoth. His son is the Devil, the serpent. The latter was cast down upon the earth by the power above (the highest God?) and then brought into being the vine, which produces all manner of sins. Marriage is of Satan. One half of mankind is from God, the other from the evil one. On soteriology Epiphanius has nothing; he reports so briefly on the sect in general because in his time there were at most only a few adherents still surviving.

Epiphanius, *Panarion* XLV 1, 1–2, 3; 4, 1 and 9

1, 1. After these (Lucian and Apelles) followed Severus, either a contemporary or about that time. . . . 2. The fables put out by him are what I am about to tell.

3. He too wants to ascribe the creation of our world to authorities and powers. There is in an unnamed highest heaven and aeon a good God. 4. The Devil, he says, is the son of the great ruler over the host of the powers, whom he now names Ialdabaoth, now Sabaoth. This one who was born from him is a serpent. 5. He was cast down by the power above to the earth and, having come down, being serpentine in form, he was driven into an insane passion and united with the earth as with a woman; and from him, when he shed the seed of generation, the vine sprang forth. 6. Hence in proof of their idle nonsense he interprets the snakelike twisting of the vine mythically, saying that it is because of the lack of symmetry in the plant that it (the twisting) is like a snake. And the white (vine) is like a snake, but the black like a dragon. 7. And the grapes of the vine are like gouts or drops of poison, because the coils of each shoot are sinuous, only short and round.* 8. Wine on this presupposition confuses the mind of man. Now it leads to the enchantment of sexual pleasure, now it rouses to frenzy. Or again it instils wrath, because the body is easily deluded by the power from the vine and the poison of the afore-mentioned dragon. Hence such people abstain completely from wine.

2, 1. They say that woman also is a work of Satan. . . . Hence those who consort in marriage, they say, fulfil the work of Satan. 2. Even in regard to man, half is of God and half of the Devil. From the navel upwards, he says, he is the creation of

---

* Or: because of the globular or ovoid form of each grape's rounded shape.

the power of God; from the navel down he is the creature of the evil power. 3. Hence he says that everything relating to pleasure and passion and desire originates from the navel and below.

4, 1. These people make use of some apocrypha, as we have heard, but also in part of the publicly read books, hunting out only those things which, distorting them to their own taste, they handle in a completely different manner. . . . 9. I have dealt briefly with this heresy . . . since I believe that there are no longer any belonging to it, except a few in the upper regions (of Egypt).

4

THE BOOK *BARUCH*

INTRODUCTION

Hippolytus in his work *The Refutation of all Heresies* gives an account of a book with the title *Baruch*. Ostensibly it derives from a gnostic by the name of Justin. Hippolytus indicates again and again, by the words 'he says', that he is quoting the actual text. Despite this we are not certain that he reproduces the whole of Justin's document. We do not even know whether he had it before him in its original text—such writings were often altered in the copying—and there is much to suggest that here interpolations are present. Be that as it may, what we learn from *Baruch* shows that it occupies an exceptional position in the whole of gnostic literature.

It does indeed share with the rest of Gnosis the conviction that we live in a world created and dominated by evil powers. It is therefore vital to escape from it and attain to the kingdom of light of the 'Good' beyond. This has nothing in the least to do with our world. To this point *Baruch* is not different from any of the other gnostic systems. They all faced the task of making it comprehensible to the reader that once a part of the divine fell, and came into the power of matter, which is hostile to God, and there it now lives as 'spirit', as if imprisoned, in some (or all) men. *Baruch*, however, avoids in a very original fashion the necessity of having to speak of such a fall of the divine. It starts out from *three* primal entities, which are all assumed not to have come into being, but exist eternally. They are, however, of very different kinds, and this difference allows Justin to conceal the doctrine of a fall of the divine. This takes place as follows:

The highest of these three primal powers is called 'the Good'. He lives in a kingdom of light above the creation. Since he is good, he cannot aggressively invade the evil world. He must therefore remain in his kingdom of light, which in this way takes on certain features of a prison. This will become still clearer.

The two other primal powers are of a completely different kind. While 'the Good'—ostensibly at least—foresees everything, the other two do not suspect what consequences their action will have. This makes itself immediately apparent. For Elohim and Eden—with such Old Testament names has Justin endowed the pair—fall passionately in love with one another. Here Elohim in *Baruch* is really something like a heaven-god. Eden, on the other hand, is the earth-goddess. That from the marriage union of these two all life took its origin is related in an old legend, and it still glimmers through here as well. Eden admittedly, according to Justin's description, is anything but attractive, for her virgin body passes down into that of a serpent. Here the ancient lore of the signs of the zodiac plays its part. It called not only the 'fish' and the 'twins' double-bodied, but also Sagittarius and Virgo. For people imagined the archer as a centaur, half man, half horse, and Virgo as she is here described.

At first the marriage seems to be truly happy, for twenty-four angelic beings are the fruit of this union. Twelve are ranged after the father, twelve after the mother. In some peculiar way the third of these angels on each side possesses special power. The third of the 'paternal' angels is called Baruch (properly = the blessed; but it is open to question whether Justin knew that), and the third of the 'maternal' angels is Naas. Naas is a Graecized reproduction of the Hebrew word *nahash*, which in the Old Testament creation story (Gen. 3: 1 ff.) denotes the serpent, but in Hebrew is a masculine noun. We have thus discovered one of Justin's chief sources, which, however, yielded rich produce only through allegorical inter-pretation on the grand scale. In the creation story (Gen. 2: 8) it is said—and Justin quotes these words: 'And God planted a garden in Eden.' What is meant by this is just what we have already heard: Elohim (in the Old Testament = God) produced with Eden (in the Old Testament this is a region) twenty-four angels. They are the 'garden', the 'paradise', of which Genesis speaks. The twenty-four angels are twenty-four trees, and while Baruch is the tree of life, Naas can only be the fateful tree of the knowledge of good and evil. This exegesis strikes us as very arbitrary and fanciful. But at that time people were prepared to engage in something of the sort, if only mysteries were revealed thereby. And of these Justin found no lack.

First of all the angels create man, out of the higher and anthropo-morphous part of Eden, the earth, while from her lower part the animals and other living creatures come into being. Adam and Eve are really intended to be a token and seal of the happy alliance of Elohim and Eden. Hence the latter give them the best that each possesses. But this is just what paves the way for the future cata-strophe. Elohim and Eden are of different natures: he is therefore able to impart to men of his divine 'spirit', while she can only bestow the vital, yearning 'soul'. Through this man has himself become a dual being, upon whom claim can be laid from two quite different sides.

The difference of nature between Elohim and Eden makes it possible for Justin now to separate them finally. Elohim (we have

E

already said that he is properly something like a heaven-god) betakes himself with his twelve angels to the upper region of his
creation, to see whether there also everything is in the best condition.
Eden, the earth, naturally cannot join in such a heavenly journey,
and remains below.

To his great astonishment Elohim sees above a light which
radiates much more brightly than the one he created. He understands immediately that above him there holds sway one yet higher
and more powerful, and he acknowledges that he has wrongly held
himself to be the highest. This feature, that the Demiurge, the
creator of the material world, acknowledges his inferiority over
against the highest divinity, occurs often in Gnosis. In fact, Elohim
plays in Justin the role of the Demiurge. Only the fact that he
himself is able to impart the divine 'spirit'—properly that ought to
be a prerogative of 'the Good'—indicates that Justin here has
combined together different ideas. How consciously he works is made
apparent by a minor detail which can at first sight easily be over-
looked, or noted as surprising: Elohim did indeed take his angels
above with him. But when he is admitted into the kingdom of light
of 'the Good', his angels must remain outside. For this there is good
reason.

We have already said that 'the Good' may not intervene in earthly
events, since his goodness is not consonant with that. This holds also,
however, for anyone whom he receives into his kingdom of light—
and therefore for Elohim. He would gladly go back down again to
earth and fetch his spirit which he gave to men. But 'the Good'
cannot allow him, and precisely in this way (although Justin of
course does not give it prominence) 'the Good' becomes responsible
for the misfortunes of man, which now set in.

Eden does not suspect that Elohim has entered into the realm of
light of 'the Good'—indeed she knows nothing of 'the Good'. But she
observes that Elohim has abandoned her. With this Justin can now
provide the motive for the fury with which she persecutes the spirit
of Elohim in men.

Before this, however, he had already portrayed how men have to
suffer under the angels of Eden. Here Justin turns back again to the
Paradise story. There it is said in Gen. 2: 10 ff.: 'There sprang up a
river in Eden', which divided into four branches: the first is called
Pheison, the second Gihon (the form 'Geon' in Justin betrays only a
different pronunciation), the third and fourth are the Euphrates and
the Tigris. These four rivers which sprang up in Eden are, according
to Justin, the twelve angels of Eden, who appear grouped in four
groups of three. Each such group is mystically called a 'river'. But
they all flow round the earth like a choir moving in a circle—they

are the twelve signs of the Zodiac, of which Justin here mentions only the evil influences which—according to ancient astrology—they have upon the countries and men severally dominated by them. Now since the name of the 'river' Pheison reminds one of the Greek word 'pheidolos' = niggardly, the Pheison brings with it scarcity, famine, and so on!

But Justin makes the angels of Eden bring destruction upon men in another and more individual fashion also. The wicked angel Babel —Justin knows the Revelation of John—operates as a wrecker of marriages; Justin identifies him out of hand with the Greek goddess of love, Aphrodite. But Naas himself is also balefully active here: he commits the primal sin, in that he seduces both Eve and Adam, and so brings adultery and paederasty into the world.

Elohim may not come to the aid of his tormented spirit in men. Instead, Justin now makes Baruch intervene—of course at Elohim's command. Baruch, like all the twelve good angels, did not enter with Elohim into the kingdom of light of 'the Good'; hence he can now take a hand again and again in earthly affairs! Success, however, is denied him, since Baruch is not able to move the spirit in men so strongly as Naas the vital soul. Hence Baruch's intervention in Paradise itself, in the case of Moses, and finally in the prophets, is a failure.

Justin, however, is now struck by yet another new idea. He makes use in his own fashion of the legend of the twelve labours of Hercules: Hercules in reality combated the twelve angels of Eden. Almost had the hero attained his goal when he came to grief on the seductive arts of Omphale who, needless to say, was no other than Babel-Aphrodite!

Thus Judaism and heathenism were incapable of receiving the message of salvation and spreading it further afield. Only with the twelve-year-old Jesus, whom he met keeping the sheep, did Baruch at last find success: here the seductive arts of Naas had no effect. Jesus rather proclaimed the message of Baruch, with which Elohim had charged him: One ought not to allow oneself to be tempted by the world, but ascend to 'the Good'. With this, Justin the Gnostic seems to prove himself a Christian. But he represents a very singular Christianity: brought by Naas to the Cross, Jesus spoke to Eden those words which in the Gospel of John (John 19:26) he speaks to his mother Mary: 'Woman, thou hast thy son'; he leaves the earthly body on the Cross to Eden and gives his spirit into the hands of the Father Elohim, with whom he will now sit together on the throne of 'the Good'. That is a kind of gnostic Trinity which comes into being in this fashion.

We have already mentioned that many parts of *Baruch* have the effect of an alien interpolation. This is true above all of the identification of 'the Good' with Priapus, the god of procreative power. 'The Good' according to the gnostic conception is quite simply beyond the creation, and has absolutely nothing to do with earthly procreation and fruitfulness. He is—if we disregard the message of Baruch—completely unknown. Presumably somebody at this point wanted to enrich the original document, and therefore inserted this section. One can, to be sure, defend him with the argument that Gnosis was concerned to show that its secret doctrines were already everywhere hinted at and cryptically expressed. Hence stories like those of Leda and the swan, Danae and the golden rain, or Ganymede and the eagle could be for it cryptic representations of the cosmic marriage between Elohim and Eden, or of the primal seduction through Naas. But with the identification of 'the Good' with Priapus it is quite a different matter: 'the Good' is located in his other-worldly kingdom of light, and the assertion that his statue with the phallus stands before every temple is from the basic gnostic point of view nothing short of blasphemy.

That the Church Father Hippolytus described *Baruch* as the most monstrous book he had ever set eyes on can be readily understood. But he completely failed to perceive the weakness which Gnosis betrays precisely in this book : it knows no goal for which life is worth living. One's nearest, and therefore love, have not come into sight as such a goal.

Hippolytus, *Ref.* V 26, 1–27, 5

26, 1. This man (Justin) says: There were three unbegotten powers of the All, two male and one female. Of the male, the one is called 'the Good', he alone being so called, knowing all things in advance; the second 'father of all things created', without foreknowledge. . . . The female power is without foreknowledge, irascible, of double mind and double body, in all respects resembling the one in the fable of Herodotus: down to the groin a young woman, but a serpent below, as Justin says. 2. This maiden is called 'Eden' and 'Israel'. These, he says, are the powers, roots, and springs of all things, from which the things that are came into being; and there was nothing else. When the father saw that half-woman Eden, since he was without foreknowledge, he came to a desire for her. Now this father, he says, is called 'Elohim'. Eden was no less desirous for Elohim, and the desire brought them together in heart-felt love. 3. From such a union the father begot for himself from

Eden twelve angels. Now the names of the paternal angels are these: Michael, Amen, Baruch, Gabriel, Esaddaios. . . . 4. And of the maternal angels whom Eden made the names are likewise subjoined. They are these: Babel, Achamoth, Naas, Bel, Belias, Satan, Sael, Adonaios, Kavithan, Pharaoth, Karkamenos, Lathen.

5. Of these twenty-four angels the paternal assist the father and do everything according to his will, and the maternal their mother Eden. The company of all these angels together, he says, is the Paradise of which Moses says: 'God planted a paradise in Eden towards the east' (Gen. 2: 8), that is, in front of Eden, that Eden might for ever see the paradise, that is, the angels. 6. The angels of this paradise are allegorically called 'trees', and the 'tree of life' is the third of the paternal angels, Baruch; but the 'tree of the knowledge of good and evil' (Gen. 2:9) is the third of the maternal angels, Naas. For so he (Justin) wants to interpret the words of Moses, saying: Moses spoke them in veiled language, because not all can comprehend the truth.

7. When the paradise had come into being out of the mutual good pleasure of Elohim and Eden, then the angels of Elohim took of the finest earth—that is, not of the animal part of Eden, but from the human and civilized regions of the earth above the groin—and made man. From the animal parts, he says, the beasts and other living creatures came into being. 8. They made man, then, as a symbol of their unity and love, and set in him their powers, Eden the soul and Elohim the spirit. And he becomes, as it were, a seal and love-token and eternal symbol of the marriage of Eden and Elohim: the man Adam. 9. In the same way also, he says, Eve came into being, as Moses wrote, an image and symbol, a seal of Eden to be preserved for ever. In the same way also there was set in Eve, the image, a soul from Eden and a spirit from Elohim, and commandments were given to them: 'Increase and multiply, and inherit the earth' (Gen. 1: 28), that is, Eden. For thus he will have it to be written. 10. For Eden brought to Elohim all her power, as it were a marriage portion. Hence, he says, women to this day bring dowries to their husbands in imitation of that first marriage, obeying a divine and paternal law which came into being with Elohim and Eden.

11. But when everything had been created, as it is written in Moses, 'heaven and earth and all that is in them' (Gen. 2: 1), the twelve angels of the mother were divided into four powers. And each of these four parts is called a 'river': Pheison and Geon and Tigris and Euphrates, as Moses said according to him (Gen. 2: 10–14). These twelve angels, combined in four groups, travel about and administer the world, having a kind of satrap's authority over the world from Eden. 12. They do not, however, always remain over the same places, but move around as in a circling choir, changing place for place and yielding up at due times and intervals the places appointed to them. But when Pheison dominates places, then arise famine, distress, and affliction in that part of the earth; for niggardly (Greek: *pheidolon*) is what is enacted by these angels. 13. Similarly there arise with each part of the four, according to its power and nature, evil times and origins of diseases, and this stream of wickedness according to the dominance of the fourfold 'rivers' travels for ever unceasingly round the world, according to the will of Eden.

14. This necessity of evil, however, came about on some such ground as this: when Elohim had established and formed the world out of mutual good pleasure, he wished to go up into the lofty parts of heaven and see whether anything was defective in the creation, taking his own angels with him. For he aspired upwards, leaving Eden behind; being earth, she did not wish to follow her consort upwards. 15. So when Elohim came to the limit of heaven above, and beheld a light better than the one he had created, he said: 'Open the gates to me, that I may enter in and make confession to the Lord; for I thought that I was lord!' 16. A voice came to him from the light, saying: 'This is the gate of the Lord, the righteous enter in by it' (Ps. 118 (117): 19 f.). And forthwith the gate was opened and the father went in—without his angels—to 'the Good' and saw 'what eye has not seen and ear has not heard and has not entered into the heart of man' (1 Cor. 2:9). 17. Then 'the Good' said to him: 'Sit at my right hand!' (Ps. 110 (109): 1). But the father said to 'the Good': 'Lord, let me destroy the world which I have made; for my spirit is bound in men, and I want to take it back!' 18. 'The Good' said to him: 'You can do nothing evil when you are with me; for it was out of a

mutual good pleasure that you and Eden made the world. So let Eden have the creation so long as she will. But you stay with me.'

19. Then Eden, knowing that she had been abandoned by Elohim, in her grief set her own angels beside her and adorned herself becomingly, in the hope that Elohim might fall into desire and come to her. 20. But as Elohim, held fast by 'the Good', came down no more to Eden, Eden commanded Babel (who is Aphrodite) to effect adulteries and divorces among men, in order that, just as she herself had been separated from Elohim, so also the spirit of Elohim might be pained and tormented by such separations, and suffer the same as the abandoned Eden. 21. And Eden gives great power to her third angel Naas, that he may punish with every chastisement the spirit of Elohim in men, that through the spirit Elohim may be punished, who contrary to the compacts made by him forsook his consort.

When the father Elohim saw this, he sent out Baruch, the third of his own angels, to the assistance of the spirit which is in all men. 22. Baruch came and stood in the midst of the angels of Eden, that is, in the middle of Paradise—for Paradise is the angels, in whose midst he stood—and commanded man 'from every tree in Paradise to eat and enjoy, but from the (tree of the) knowledge of good and evil not to eat' (Gen. 2: 16 f.), which is Naas; that is, to obey the other eleven angels of Eden. For the eleven do indeed have passions, but they do not have transgression. But Naas had transgression. 23. For going to Eve he deceived her and committed adultery with her, which is contrary to the law; and he went also to Adam and used him as a boy, which also is against the law. Hence arose adultery and paederasty. From that time both evil *and* good held sway over men, springing from one origin, that of the father. For by ascending to 'the Good' the father showed a way for those who are willing to ascend, 24. but by departing from Eden he made a beginning of evils for the spirit of the father that is in men.

Now Baruch was sent to Moses, and through him he spoke to the children of Israel, that they might turn to 'the Good'. 25. But the third angel of Eden, Naas, obscured the commands of Baruch through the soul from Eden which dwelt in Moses, as in all men, and caused his own to be heard. Because of this the soul is ranged against the spirit and the spirit against the soul. For the soul is Eden, but the spirit Elohim, both being in all mankind, female and male alike. 26. Again after that Baruch was sent to the prophets, that through the prophets the spirit which dwells in men might hear, and flee from Eden and the evil creation as the father Elohim fled. In the same way and with the same intent Naas seduced the prophets through the soul which dwells in man along with the spirit of the father, and they were all led astray and did not follow the words of Baruch which Elohim commanded. 27. Finally, Elohim chose Hercules as a prophet from the heathen world, and sent him, that he might prevail against the twelve angels of Eden and liberate the father from the twelve wicked angels of the creation. These are the twelve labours of Hercules which Hercules accomplished in order from the first to the last, the lion, the hydra, the wild boar, and the rest. 28. For these are the heathen names which, he says, have been altered by the working of the maternal angels. But when he seemed to have prevailed, Omphale fastened upon him, who is Babel or Aphrodite, and she seduced Hercules and stripped him of his power—the commands of Baruch which Elohim commanded—and put upon him her own garment, that is, the power of Eden, the power below, and thus the prophecy of Hercules and his works were of no avail.

29. Last of all, 'in the days of Herod the king' (Luke 1: 5), Baruch was sent, dispatched again by Elohim, and coming to Nazareth he found Jesus the son of Joseph and Mary tending sheep, a boy of twelve years old, and he proclaimed to him from the beginning all that had happened, from Eden and Elohim, and what was to be thereafter, and he said: 30. 'All the prophets before you were led astray. Endeavour then, Jesus Son of man, not to be led astray, but preach this word to men and proclaim to them the things concerning the father and "the Good", and go up to "the Good" and sit there with Elohim the father of us all.' 31. And Jesus obeyed the angel, saying: 'Lord, I will do everything', and he preached. Naas, then, wanted to seduce him also, but he could not; for he remained faithful to Baruch. So Naas, enraged because he could not lead him astray, caused him to be crucified. But he left the body of Eden on the Cross and went up to 'the Good'. 32. Saying to Eden: 'Woman, you have your son!' (John 19: 26),

that is, the psychic man and the earthly, but himself yielding the spirit into the hands of the father (Luke 23: 46), he went up to 'the Good'.

But 'the Good' is Priapus, who created before (Greek: *prin*) anything existed. That is why he is called Priapus, because he came before all things. 33. That is why, he says, he is set up in every temple, honoured by the whole creation, and in the streets, bearing the autumn fruits above him, that is, the fruits of the creation of which he was the cause, in that he first made the creation which formerly did not exist.[1] 34. So then, he says, when you hear men saying that the swan came upon Leda and begot children of her, the swan is Elohim and Leda is Eden. And when men say that an eagle came upon Ganymede, the eagle is Naas and Ganymede Adam. 35. And when they say that the gold came upon Danae, and begot children of her, the gold is Elohim and Danae is Eden. And likewise they teach all such stories in the same fashion, adding myths resembling them. 36. So when prophets say: 'Hear, O heaven, and give ear, O earth, for the Lord has spoken' (Isa. 1: 2), 'heaven', he says, means the spirit of Elohim in man, 'earth' the soul which is in man with the spirit, 'the Lord' is Baruch and 'Israel' Eden. For Eden, the consort of Elohim, is also called Israel. 37. 'Israel', he says, 'did not know me' (Isa. 1: 3). For if she had known that I am with 'the Good', she would not have punished the spirit in men because of the paternal departure from thence.

27, 1. There is written also in the first book entitled Baruch an oath which they make those swear who are about to hear these mysteries and be perfected with 'the Good'. This oath, he says, our father Elohim swore, and did not repent of having sworn it; of whom it is written, he says, 'The Lord has sworn, and will not repent' (Ps. 110 (109): 4). 2. And the oath is this: 'I swear by him who is above all things, "the Good", to preserve these mysteries and to declare them to no one, neither to turn back from "the Good" to the creation.' When he swears this oath, he goes into 'the Good' and sees 'what eye has not seen and ear has not heard and has not entered into the heart of man' (1 Cor. 2: 9), and drinks from the living water, which is for them a (baptismal) bath, as they think, a well of living water springing up. 3. For there is a distinction, he says, between water

[1] Cf. the Naassenes, Hipp. V 7, 27 f.

and water, and the water below the firmament is of the evil creation, in which choic (material) and psychic men wash themselves, and there is above the firmament the living water of 'the Good', in which the pneumatic, living men bathe, in which Elohim bathed and did not repent of such a baptism. 4. And, he says, when the prophet is said 'to take to himself a wife of harlotry, because the land will go a-whoring from the following of the Lord' (Hos. 1: 2), in these words, he says, the prophet clearly speaks the whole mystery, and is not heard because of the wickedness of Naas.

5. In that same manner they interpret also the other prophetic writings in several books; but above all they have a book called Baruch, in which he who finds it will learn the whole arrangement of their myth.

5

BASILIDES

Basilides was active from the time of Hadrian to the time of Antoninus Pius.[1] We are faced with two quite distinct accounts of him. One is given by Irenaeus in his work *Adv. Haer.* I 24. Grouped with him, or dependent upon him, are Epiphanius, Ps.-Tertullian, Philaster, and others. According to Irenaeus there arose from the unoriginate Father in descending order six forces, and from these emanated powers and angels who made the first heaven. From these were formed other angels, who made a second heaven, and so on until there were 365 heavens. The last angels created the world and apportioned the nations to themselves. Their chief, the Jewish God, wanted his nation to subjugate the other nations; hence strife arose in the world. The most high God then sent his Nous, that is Christ, in order to liberate the men who believe in him from the power of the creator-angels. He could not suffer, but he made Simon of Cyrene take on his appearance, and laughed at the Jews. One should not therefore believe in the Crucified. That is the distinctive doctrine of the Irenaean Basilides. In addition, Irenaeus ascribes to Basilides and his followers a fondness for idolatry, libertinism, and magic of every sort.

Irenaeus, *Adv. Haer.* I 24, 3–7

3. Basilides, so that he may appear to have discovered something higher and more like the truth, vastly extends the content of his teaching. He presents Nous[2] originating first from the unoriginate Father, and Logos[3] originating from him, then from Logos Phronesis (prudence), from Phronesis Sophia (wisdom) and Dynamis (force), from Dynamis and Sophia the powers, principalities, and angels, who are also called the first,

---

[1] Cl. Al., *Strom.* VII 17 = § 106, 4; Jerome, *De Viris Ill.* III 21.

[2] Nous is thought. But since Nous almost always occupies the place next to the highest God, we must here exclude rational thought and translate by some such word as 'insight'. Nous has been left untranslated here.

[3] Logos means the word and reason. Because of its varying connotation it has been left untranslated.

and by them the first heaven was made. From their emanation other angels were made, and they made another heaven
like the first; and in the same way when other (angels)
were made by emanation from them, copies of those who
were above them, they fashioned a further, third, heaven.
From the third, a fourth group of downward descending ones,
and successively in the same way more and more principalities
and angels were made, and 365 heavens. That is why the
year has that number of days, in accordance with the number
of heavens. 4. But those angels who possess the last heaven, which
is the one seen by us, set up everything in the world, and divided
between them the earth and the nations upon it. Their chief
is the one known as the God of the Jews; because he wished to
subject the other nations to his own men, that is, to the Jews,
all the other principalities opposed him and worked against
him.[4] For this reason the other nations were alienated from his
nation.

The unoriginate and ineffable Father, seeing their disastrous
plight, sent his first-born Nous—he is the one who is called
the Christ—to liberate those who believe in him from the power
of those who made the world. To their (the angels') nations he
appeared on earth as a man and performed miracles. For the
same reason also he did not suffer, but a certain Simon of
Cyrene was compelled to carry his cross for him; and this
(Simon) was transformed by him (Jesus) so that he was thought
to be Jesus himself, and was crucified through ignorance and
error. Jesus, however, took on the form of Simon, and stood
by laughing at them. For since he was an incorporeal power and
the Nous of the unborn Father, he was transformed in whatever way he pleased, and in this way he ascended to him who
had sent him, laughing at them, since he could not be held and
was invisible to all. Therefore those who know these things have
been set free from the rulers who made the world. It is not right
to confess him who was crucified, but him who came in the
form of a man and was supposed to have been crucified and
was called Jesus and was sent by the Father in order by this
dispensation to undo the works of the creators of the world.
Thus (he says) if anyone confesses the crucified, he is still a
slave, and under the power of those who made the bodies; he

---

[4] Similarly, Saturnilus (Ir. I 24, 2) and the Ophites (Ir. I 30, 5).

who denies (him) has been set free from them, and knows the (saving) dispensation made by the unoriginate Father.

5. Salvation is for their soul alone; the body is by nature corruptible. He says that even the prophecies themselves came from the rulers who made the world, and that the law in particular came from their chief, him who led the people out of the land of Egypt (cf. Exod. 20: 1). They despise things sacrificed to idols and think nothing of them, but enjoy them without any anxiety at all. They also enjoy the other (pagan) festivals and all (that) appetite (prompts). They also engage in magic, conjuring of the dead, spells, calling up of spirits, and all the other occult practices. They even invent certain angelic names, and declare that some belong to the first heaven, others to the second; and one by one they attempt to expound the names, the rulers, the angels, and the powers of the 365 false heavens. In this way the name of the world, in which they say the Saviour came down and went up again, is Caulacau (Isa. 28: 10).[5]

6. Accordingly, the person who has learnt these things, and knows all the angels and their origins, becomes invisible and incomprehensible to all the angels and powers, just as it happened also to Caulacau. And just as the son was unknown to all, so they also should be recognized by none; but whereas they know them all and pass through them all, they are themselves invisible and unknown to all. 'For know thou them all', they say, 'but let none know thee.' Thus those who are such are always ready to deny it—or rather, suffering for the name is even quite impossible for them, since they are like everybody (else). Not many, either, can know these (doctrines), but one in a thousand and two in (ten thousand).[6] They say they are no longer Jews, but not yet Christians; and their secrets must not be uttered at all, but they must keep them concealed by silence.

7. They arrange the positions of the 365 heavens in the same way as the astrologers. They accept their principles, and have transferred them to their own brand of doctrine. But the chief of those (365 heavens) is Abraxas, and for this reason (they allege) he has 365 numbers in him (i.e. his name has the numerical value 365).

---

[5] Another speculation on Caulacau among the Naassenes, Hipp. V 8, 4; cf. also Epiph. XXV 3, 6.　　　　[6] See also the Gospel of Thomas, Logion 23.

Epiphanius, *Panarion* XXIV 5, 2 and 4 f.; 7, 6

5, 2. This is what the Juggler (Basilides) says: 'We', he says, 'are the men; the rest are all pigs and dogs. That is why he (Jesus) said: "Do not throw your pearls before the swine, and do not give the holy thing to the dogs." ' (Matt. 7: 6). . . . 4. But he says that of the Father and his own secret they are to disclose nothing at all but keep it in silence among themselves; but to disclose it to one in a thousand and two in ten thousand. He teaches his disciples and says: 'Thou knowest all things, but let none know thee.' 5. But he and his followers say if they are asked, that they are no longer Jews, but that they are no longer (!) Christians . . .*

7, 6. Then consequently, says he, (from the 365 heavens) man also has 365 bodily parts, so that to each individual power one part is allotted.

BASILIDES ACCORDING TO HIPPOLYTUS

The account of Hippolytus sounds entirely different. It is illustrated by a large number of fragments, supplied principally by Clement of Alexandria and his successor Origen, of Basilides, his son Isidore, and his followers.

Basilides is, according to this, the one who harnessed his Gnosis in the most consistent way to a monistic system. A completely ineffable God deposits—without volition—a world-seed. Basilides hides the difficulty of his beginning by calling to mind the egg of a peacock or of an even more variegated bird, or the fact that teeth, intelligence, etc., begin to develop in a small child only gradually, but still are stored up in him right from the start. So the 'world-seed' has everything in itself, divine, etherial, heavenly (the world of the planets is meant), and what our world contains. These things were however—as a fragment also makes clear—thoroughly mixed up together. The purpose and end is that all parts of the world, including the divine, shall be brought each to its proper place. Basilides has thus no need of any evil matter, or of an evil or even a merely mediating creator. He does indeed know two 'Rulers' who govern the spheres of the fixed stars and the planets, but do not control our world, for which the thought with which God created it is sufficient. That means that whereas both the Rulers believe themselves to be supreme, yet they do penance when they learn that the non-existent God exists and that they have no power over the

---

* Probably a scribal error for 'not yet'.

world; they are not 'Fate'. The guilt in this world, which men are burdened with, will be expiated through reincarnation and through suffering.

Now the world-seed has in it a threefold Sonship, a light Sonship, which immediately speeds up to God, a coarser Sonship, and one which needs purification. The coarser Sonship can attain to the Father's region only with the help of the Holy Spirit; the Holy Spirit himself, however, being of another nature, remains in its neighbourhood, but outside. He is the mediator between the world above and what lies below, down as far as this world in which we live.

Then there arose from the world-seed the two Rulers, the governors of the sphere of the fixed stars and the sphere of the planets, who each have one son beside them, surpassing them in wisdom and beauty. The third Sonship, which needs purification, is still in the lower world. Then comes the Gospel, quite really, but in such a way that it does not leave its place in the highest region. The Son of the First Ruler receives the Gospel just as naphtha catches fire from a great distance, and he declares it to his father, who gets very frightened and repents. In the same way it goes also to the Second Ruler. Then in our world the light enlightens Jesus the Son of Mary; everything took place as is described in the (canonical) gospels. The sufferings befell his bodily part, his psychic part returned to the (psychic) Sphere of the Seven and the remaining parts each to its own sphere.

If the third Sonship is described as left behind down here to give and to receive benefit, then it is prefigured in what is attributed to the second Sonship and the Holy Spirit; the Holy Spirit carries the second Sonship upwards into the non-existent realm, but cannot do so without receiving from it the service of being itself brought to the threshold of the non-existent realm. Thus also the third Sonship does the 'souls' the service of carrying them up, probably as far as the realm of the 'Great Ruler'—they cannot go higher, which would be contrary to their nature—but the souls do the third Sonship the service of 'purifying' it, so that it can rise up to the supersensible realm. What in concrete terms this mutual service consists of is not stated; it must be concerned with a mutual 'education' as in the Valentinus of Irenaeus. Without this education the third Sonship would not arrive above, nor would the souls reach the Sphere of the Archon. Libertinism is hereby excluded.

The third Sonship thus becomes pure and therefore returns to the upper world and the first and second Sonships. So Jesus became the first-fruits of the distinction of 'kinds', and the elect must also be divided into their 'kinds', that is, into their constituent parts, and each part returns to the 'region' appropriate to it. Then the great ignorance comes over the world, so that no part knows any of the things above it, and thus can no longer yearn for anything higher.

Hippolytus, *Ref.* VII 20, 1–27, 13 (selections)

20, 1. Basilides and his legitimate son and disciple Isidore say that Matthias spoke to them secret words, which he heard from the Saviour in secret discourse. . . .

2. There was a time, says he, when there was nothing; not even the nothing was there, but simply, clearly, and without any sophistry there was nothing at all. When I say 'there was', he says, I do not indicate a Being, but in order to signify what I want to express I say, says he, that there was nothing at all.

3. For that, says he, is not simply something ineffable which is named (indicated); we call it ineffable, but it is not even ineffable. For what is not (even) inexpressible is called 'not even inexpressible', but is above every name that is named. For the names do not even suffice, he says, for the world, so multiform is it, but fall short. And I do not have it in me to find correct names for everything; rather it is proper to comprehend ineffably, without using names, the characteristics of the things which are to be named. For (the existence of) the same designation(s for different things) has caused the hearers confusion and error about the things. . . .

21. 1. Since therefore there was nothing, no matter, no substance, nothing insubstantial, nothing simple, nothing composite, nothing non-composite, nothing imperceptible (non-subjective), no man, no angel, no god, nothing at all that can be named or can be apprehended by sense-perception, nothing of the mental things and thus (also nothing of all that which) can be simply described in even more subtle ways, the non-existent God . . . without intelligence, without perception, without will, without resolve, without impulse, without desire, wished to make a world. 2. I say 'he wished', he says, for want of a word, wish, intelligence, and perception being excluded. By 'world' (I mean) not the flat, divisible world which later divided itself, but a world-seed. 3. The world-seed had everything in it, as the mustard-seed contains everything together in a tiny space, the roots, the stem, the branches, the innumerable leaves, the grains of seed which come from the plant, which in

turn again and again spread seed for yet more plants. 4. Thus
the non-existent God made a non-existent world from the non-
existent, inasmuch as he deposited and planted one single seed
which contained in itself the whole seed-mixture of the world.
Or, to make plainer what they say, just as the egg of a variegated
and many-coloured bird, such as a peacock or some other even
more variegated and many-coloured (species), although it is
only single, yet has within it many shapes of multiform, multi-
coloured, and heterogeneous things, so, says he, the non-
existent seed deposited by the non-existent God has (within it)
the multiform and heterogeneous seed-mixture of the world.

22, 1. There was thus stored up in the seed everything that
can be mentioned, or if it is not to be found can be left out,
everything that was going to be suitable for the world that
would arise from the seed, the world which of necessity at its own
season expands by enlargement derived from a God so great
and of such a kind. (It is) just as with a new-born child. We
see how later the teeth and the paternal characteristics and
the intelligence are acquired, and whatever else did not previously exist, but gradually comes to a man as he grows up from
infancy. 2. But since it is difficult to say that the non-existent
is an emanation (Gk. *probole*) of the non-existent God—for
Basilides shuns and abhors the essence of things produced by
emanation—for what emanation was necessary, for what
material was the basis present, such that God should manufac-
ture the world as the spider takes its threads, or a mortal man
when he manufactures (something) takes bronze or wood or
some piece of material? 3. Rather, he says: 'He spoke and it
was', and that is what Moses said, so these men say: 'Let there
be light, and there was light' (Gen. 1: 3). Whence, says he,
came the light? From nothing. For, says he, it is not written
where (it came) from, but only (that it came) from the voice
of him that spoke. But the speaker, says he, did not exist, so
neither did what came into being exist. 4. The seed of the world,
says he, came from the non-existent, the word which was
spoken, 'Let there be light'; and that, says he, is what is said
in the Gospels, 'There was the true light, which enlightens
every man who comes into the world' (John 1: 9). 5. It takes
its origins from that seed and is enlightened. That is the seed
which contains within it the whole seed-mixture, which Aristotle

says is the 'genus' which is divided into innumerable species, just as cow, horse, and man are subdivisions of 'animal', which does not exist (which is a non-existent).

6. Given therefore the existence of the cosmic seed, they say this: Whatever I say came into existence after this, do not ask, he says, where (it came from). For it (the world-seed) had all the seeds stored and laid up within itself, since it had been previously determined by the non-existent God that the non-existent should come into being. 7. Let us therefore see what according to them was the first, what the second, and what the third thing that came into being from the cosmic seed. There was, says he, in the seed a threefold Sonship, in all respects the same in substance as the non-existent God, which came into being from the non-existent. Of this Sonship with its triple division, one part was light, another coarse, and a third in need of purification. 8. The light part, therefore, as soon as the seed was first deposited by the non-existent, was first to bubble up, and ascended and sped upwards from below with the swiftness (which the) poet (describes as) 'like a wing or a thought' (Hom., *Od.* VII 36), and reached, says he, the non-existent. For every natural thing strives after him because of his extreme loveliness and beauty, one in one way, one in another.[7] 9. But the coarser (nature), which still remained in the seed, wanted to imitate it, but could not rise upwards; for it fell very far short of the lightness of the Sonship which rose up by itself. 10. The coarser Sonship provided itself with a wing of that kind with which Plato, Aristotle's teacher, equipped the soul in Phaedrus (Plato, *Phaedr.* 246a), but Basilides calls it not a wing, but Holy Spirit, on which the Sonship bestows benefit by putting it on, and receives benefit. 11. It bestows benefit, because just as a bird's wing by itself and separated from the bird would never become high or airborne, and a bird separated from its wing would never become high or airborne; the Sonship had some such relation to the Holy Spirit and the Spirit to the Sonship. 12. So the Sonship was borne aloft by the Spirit as by a wing, and bore aloft its wing, that is the Spirit; and when it came near to the light Sonship and the non-existent God, who had created out of the non-existent, it (the Sonship) could not keep it (the Spirit) with it, for it was not of the same

[7] Cf. the Naassenes, Hipp. V 7, 9 ff.; 10, 19 f.

substance and had no nature (in common) with the Sonship. 13. Rather, just as pure and dry air is contrary to their nature and destructive for fish, so for the Holy Spirit that place of the non-existent God and the Sonship, (a place) more ineffable than the ineffable and above every name, was contrary to its nature. So the Sonship left it (the Spirit) in the vicinity of that blessed place which cannot be approached by the intellect or 'defined' by any word, (but) not utterly and completely destitute and severed from the Sonship. 14. Rather it is like a vessel that has had particularly fragrant ointment poured into it; though it might be emptied with the utmost care, still the fragrance of the ointment remains and is left behind in the jar, even if it (the ointment) is removed far from the jar; and the jar has not ointment but the fragrance of ointment. In the same way the Holy Spirit remained without any part of the Sonship and separated from it, but has within itself, after the manner of the effect of the ointment, a fragrance of the Sonship. 15. This is the saying: 'Like ointment on the head, which runs down on Aaron's beard' (Ps. 133 (132): 2); the fragrance which is borne by the Holy Spirit down from above to the formlessness and the place where we are, whence the Sonship began to ascend as it were carried on the wings and back of an eagle, so he says. 16. For everything, he says, hastens upwards from below, from the worse to the better. For none of those among the better things is so foolish that it may not come down.[8] But the third Sonship, says he, which needed purification, stayed in the great heap of the world-seed, giving and receiving benefit. How it receives and gives benefit we shall describe later when we reach the proper place for it.

23, 1. When therefore the first and second ascent of the Sonship had taken place and the Holy Spirit had remained there in the manner described, set as a firmament (Gen. 1: 7) between the supermundane and the world—2. for the things that exist are divided by Basilides into two adjacent and principal divisions; the one is called according to him Cosmos (World), and the other the Supermundane, and the limit between the world and the Supermundane is that Spirit which both is holy and has remaining within it the fragrance of the Sonship—3. when therefore the firmament, which is above the

---

[8] Obscure. Perhaps the 'not' should be deleted.

heaven, was there, there bubbled up[9] and was born out of the cosmic seed and the heap of the world-seed the Great Ruler, the head of the world, a beauty and greatness and power which cannot be spoken of. For he is, says he, more ineffable than the ineffable and more powerful than the powerful and wiser than the wise, and superior to any beautiful things whatever that you might mention. 4. When he had been born, he lifted himself up and soared and was wholly carried right up to the firmament; he thought that the firmament was the end of ascent and height, and supposed that nothing whatever existed beyond, and he became wiser than all that lay below, whatever in fact was cosmic, (he became) more powerful, more excellent, more luminous, surpassing everything you might call good, excepting only the Sonship which was still left behind in the world-seed. For he did not know that it was wiser and more powerful and better than he. 5. So deeming himself to be lord and master and wise architect he turned to the detailed construction of the world. And first he thought it proper not to be alone, and he made for himself and begot from what lay below a Son much better and wiser than himself. 6. For the non-existent God had purposed all these things in advance, when he deposited the world-seed. When he (the Great Ruler) saw his Son, he was filled with astonishment, admiration, and consternation. Such did the beauty of the Son appear to the Great Ruler; and the Ruler made him sit on the right (Ps. 110 (109): 1). 7. That is what is known among them as the Ogdoad, where the Great Ruler sits. The whole celestial, that is, the etherial, creation was the achievement of the great and wise Demiurge himself. But the Son born from him was effective in this and proposed it to him, being much wiser than the Demiurge himself.

24, 1. This is Aristotle's entelechy of the physical, organic body,[10] the soul which is effective in it, without which the body can achieve nothing, greater, more splendid, more powerful, and wiser than the body. The thought, therefore, which Aristotle expressed previously in connection with the soul and body, Basilides stated in connection with the Great Ruler and the Son associated with him.

---

[9] The same image also among the Naassenes, Hipp. V 9, 1.
[10] Cf. Aristotle, *De Anima* II 1 = 412 a 19 ff.

2. For according to Basilides the Ruler has begotten the Son, and Aristotle says that the soul is work and accomplishment, the entelechy of the physical, organic body. Thus as the entelechy manages the body, so, according to Basilides, the Son manages the God who is more ineffable than the ineffable. 3. Thus all the etherial things, which extend as far as the moon,[11] are purposed and directed by the entelechy of the Great Ruler. For from there on the air is distinguished from the ether. So when all the etherial things had been set in order, another Ruler in turn arose from the world-seed, greater than all that lay below him, apart from the Sonship that had been left behind, but much inferior to the first Ruler. He also is called ineffable by them. 4. This locality is called the Hebdomad and is the controller and creator of all that lies beneath. He too made himself a Son from the world-seed, more prudent and wise than himself, in just the way described in the case of the first (Ruler). 5. What is in this region is the heap itself, and the seed-mixture; and what happens (there) happens naturally as something anticipated by him who contrived the future, when it should be, of what kind it should be, and in what way it should be. Controller, provider or shaper of these things there was none; for sufficient for these things was that contrivance which the non-existent contrived when he created.

25, 1. When therefore the whole world and the supermundane things were, in their account, finished, and nothing was lacking, there remained (still) in the world-seed the third Sonship, which had been left in the seed to give and receive benefit, and it was necessary for the Sonship that was left behind to be revealed and restored to that place above the exalted Spirit, to the light Sonship and the one that imitates it and to the non-existent, as it is written—so he says: 'And the creation itself groans together and is in labour together, waiting for the revelation of the sons of God' (Rom. 8: 19, 22). 2. 'Sons', he says, means us spiritual ones, who are left behind here to order, train, correct, and perfect our souls, whose nature is to stay in this region. 'Up to Moses, from Adam, sin reigned', as it is written (Rom. 5: 13). 3. For there reigned the Great Ruler, whose limit extends to the firmament, in the belief that he

---

[11] This is an error by Hippolytus. The sphere of the Ogdoad is that of the fixed stars, the sphere of the Hebdomad, that of the planets.

alone was God and that there was nothing beyond him. For everything was guarded in a deep silence. That, he says, is 'the mystery which was not made known to the earlier generations' (Eph. 3: 3–5), but in those times, so it appears, the king and lord of the universe was the Great Ruler, the Ogdoad. 4. But there was also a king and lord over this region, the Hebdomad; the Ogdoad is ineffable, but the Hebdomad is effable. This is, he says, the Ruler of the Hebdomad who spoke to Moses and said: 'I am the God of Abraham, Isaac, and Jacob, and the name of God I have not shown them' (Exod. 6: 2 f.)—so they suppose it is written—that is, (the name) of the ineffable God, the Ruler of the Ogdoad. 5. That, therefore, is the source, he says, of what was spoken by all the prophets before the Saviour.

Since then, says he, we, the children of God, had to be revealed, (we) over whom the creation, says he, groaned and was in labour, waiting for (their) revelation, the Gospel came into the world, and passed through every rule and authority and lordship and every name that is named. 6. It really came, although nothing descended from above,[12] nor did the blessed Sonship leave that inconceivable, blessed, non-existent God. Rather, just as Indian naphtha, if it is merely seen from a very great distance, catches fire, so from below the powers penetrate from the formlessness of the heap up to the Sonship above. 7. For the Son of the Great Ruler of the Ogdoad seized and received the thoughts like Indian naphtha, as if he were naphtha,[13] from the blessed Sonship beyond the boundary. For the power of the Sonship in the middle of the Holy Spirit at the boundary shares the thoughts of the Sonship, which flow and drift, with the Son of the Great Ruler. 26, 1. So the Gospel came first he says, from the Sonship, through the Son who sits enthroned beside the Great Ruler, to the Ruler (himself), and the Ruler learned that he was not the God of the universe, but was begotten, and had above him, stored up, the treasure of the ineffable and unnameable non-existent and the Sonship, and he was converted and became afraid, for he perceived what ignorance he was in. 2. This is, he says, the saying: 'The fear of the Lord is the beginning of wisdom' (Ps. 111 (110): 10; Prov. 1: 7; etc.). For he (the Great Ruler) began to grow wise under the instruction of the Christ who sits beside him, as he

---

[12] Cf. Hipp. VIII 13, 4.   [13] Text uncertain.

was taught who is the non-existent, what the Sonship, what the Holy Spirit is, how the universe is arranged, and how (or where) it will be fully restored. 3. That is the wisdom spoken in a mystery, of which, says he, the Scripture says: 'Not in taught words of human wisdom, but in taught (words) of the Spirit' (1 Cor. 2: 13). Instructed, then, and taught, and made afraid, says he, the Ruler acknowledged his sin, which he had committed in magnifying himself. 4. That, says he, is the saying: 'I have recognized my sin, and I know my lawlessness, I will confess this for ever' (Ps. 32 (31): 5). When therefore the Great Ruler had been instructed, the whole creation of the Ogdoad was instructed and taught, and the mystery was made known to the heavenly spheres.

Then the Gospel had to come to the Sphere of the Seven, so that the Ruler of the Hebdomad might also be taught and have the Gospel brought to him. 5. So the Son of the Great Ruler shed upon the Son of the Ruler of the Sphere of the Seven the light which he had himself caught from above from the Sonship; and the Son of the Ruler of the Hebdomad was illuminated, and brought the Gospel to the Ruler of the Hebdomad, and exactly as in the previous account he also became afraid and made (his) confession. 6. When therefore everything in the Sphere of the Seven had been illuminated and the Gospel had been proclaimed to them—according to them there are in the regions interminable creations and governments, powers and authorities, about which they have a very large book with many words, where they also say there are 365 heavens, and that their great Ruler is Abrasax, because his name comprises the number 365, so that the numerical value of his name comprises everything, and for that reason the year consists of that number of days[14]—7. but when, says he, these things had happened thus, the formlessness affecting us had also lastly to be illuminated, and the mystery which had not been made known to previous generations (had) to be revealed to the Sonship which had been left in the formlessness like an abortion, as it is written, says he: 'According to a revelation the mystery was made known to me' (Eph. 3: 3) and 'I heard ineffable words which a man is unable to utter' (2 Cor. 12: 4).

[14] The clauses in 26, 6 between the dashes do not fit here but agree with the account in Irenaeus.

8. So from the Sphere of the Seven the light, which had descended from above from the Sphere of the Eight upon the Son of the Hebdomad, descended upon Jesus the Son of Mary, and he was illuminated and kindled by the light that shone upon him. 9. That is, he says, the saying: 'Holy Spirit will come upon you', (the Spirit) which passed from the Sonship through the boundary Spirit to the Spheres of the Eight and the Seven and reached Mary, 'and power of the Highest will overshadow you' (Luke 1: 35), the power of separation from above, from the apex down through the demiurge as far as the creation, which is the Son's. 10. Up to this point the world has had its (present) constitution, until all the Sonship that was left behind to bestow benefit on the souls in the formlessness and to receive benefit, when it has wholly been transformed (achieved form), follows Jesus, rises upward, and arrives purified; and it becomes extremely light, so as to be able to rise up of itself like the first (Sonship). For it possesses the whole power naturally fixed by the light which shone downwards from above.

27, 1. When the whole Sonship thus arrives (above), he says, and is beyond the boundary, the Spirit, then the creation will receive pity. For up to the present it groans and is tormented and waits for the revelation of the sons of God (Rom. 8: 19, 22), so that all the men of the Sonship may go up from here. When that has happened, God, he says, will bring on the whole world the great ignorance, so that everything may remain in accordance with (its) nature, and nothing desire anything contrary to its nature. 2. Rather, all the souls whose nature it is to remain immortal in this region alone will stay here below, knowing nothing other than or better than this region; in the (regions) below there will be no news and no knowledge of the (regions) above, so that the souls found below may not be tormented by striving for the impossible, like a fish striving to graze on the hills with the sheep—such a desire would, he says, be for them destruction. 3. Thus everything, says he, which stays in (its) place is imperishable, but perishable if it wants to overleap and transgress the limits of (its) nature. So the Ruler of the Sphere of the Seven will know nothing of the things above. For the great ignorance will grip even him, in order that 'sorrow, pain, and sighing' (Isa. 35: 10; 51: 11) may leave him, for he will desire nothing impossible and not feel sorrow. 4. Similarly, this ignorance will grip even the Great Ruler of the Ogdoad and all the created things subject to him in the same way, so that they may in no way strive for what is contrary to (their) nature and feel pain. And thus will come about the restoration of all things, which were founded in the beginning according to nature in the seed of the universe, and will be restored in their proper seasons. 5. That each thing has its proper times is indicated by the Saviour when he says, 'My hour has not yet come' (John 2 : 4), and by the Magi who saw the star; for even this was planned beforehand in the great 'heap' with the birth of the stars and the times of the restoration. 6. This is what they take to be the inner, spiritual man in the psychic man (animal- or soul-man)—that is, the Sonship which leaves the soul behind here, not as being mortal, but as staying here by its nature, just as the second[15] Sonship has left the Holy Spirit on the boundary at the proper place—the spiritual man, who at that time was wearing his own soul.

7. But so that we do not leave out any of their (thoughts), I will set out what they also say about the Gospel. The Gospel is, according to them, the knowledge of the supermundane things, as we have made plain, which the Great Ruler did not apprehend. Then when it was shown to him that the Holy Spirit exists, that is the boundary, and the Sonship and God the non-existent who is the cause of all these things, he rejoiced at (these) reports and was jubilant. That is, according to them, the Gospel. 8. Jesus was born, according to them, in the manner described. When the birth previously described had taken place, all that concerns the Saviour happened in a similar way to what is written in the gospels. These things happened, says he, so that Jesus might become the first-fruits of the 'distinction of kinds' among what was confused. 9. For since the world is divided into the Sphere of the Eight, which is the head of the whole world—but the head of the whole world is the Great Ruler—and the Sphere of the Seven, which is the head of that which lies beneath—but the head is the Demiurge—and this region round us, where the formlessness is, it was therefore necessary that what was confused should be 'distinguished into kinds' through the separation which happened to Jesus. 10. There suffered, therefore, that bodily part of him which derived

---

[15] The text in error has 'first'.

from the formlessness, and it returned to the formlessness. There rose up that psychic part of him (which derived from the Sphere of the Seven), and returned to the Sphere of the Seven. He roused (!) what belonged to the pinnacle of the Great Ruler, and it stayed with the Great Ruler. He bore aloft what was from the boundary Spirit, and it stayed in the boundary Spirit. 11. But the third Sonship was quite purified through him, (the Sonship) which had been left behind to give and receive benefit, and it went up to the blessed Sonship, when it had passed through all these. Their whole system is as it were a confusion of the world-seed, a distinction of kinds and the restoration (return) of the confused things to what is proper to them. 12. Jesus became the first-fruit of the distinction of kinds, and the suffering of Jesus took place with no other object than the distinction into kinds of what had been confused. For he says the whole Sonship which was left behind in the formlessness to give and receive benefit must be distinguished into kinds in the very way in which Jesus also was distinguished into kinds.

13. This then is what Basilides made up while he tarried in Egypt, and from them (the Egyptians?) he learned this mighty wisdom and bore such fruits.

NOTES AND FRAGMENTS IN THE CHURCH FATHERS

From notes in the Church Fathers we learn above all that Basilides was a copious writer. He seems to have written a psalm book;[16] a gospel originated with him;[17] according to a later account he apparently also composed twenty-four books about the gospel.[18] As his prophets, Barcabbas and Barcoph are mentioned, along with others whose names are not given.[19] We have a fragment of Basilides from the thirteenth book, in which he probably does not set out his own point of view, but that of others whom he wishes to oppose.

Fragm. 1. Hegemonius, *Acta Archelai* 67, 4–12

4. Basilides was a fairly ancient preacher among the Persians, not long after the time of our Apostles. Since he was clever and saw that at that time everything had already been anticipated, he wanted to sustain that dualism which was also (accepted)

---

[16] Canon Muratori 83 f.   [17] Orig., *Hom. in Luc.* 1.

[18] See below, *Act. Arch.* 67, 5.

[19] Eus., *H.E.* IV 7, 7. Also, perhaps identical with Barcoph: Parchor, Cl. Al., *Strom.* VI 6 = § 53, 2.

by Scythianus. Finally, since he had nothing of his own to assert, he put it forward in other, contrary terms. 5. And all his books contain many hard and abstruse things. There exists, however, the thirteenth book of his Treatises, which begins like this: 'As we begin the thirteenth book of our Treatises, the salutary saying will provide a necessary and fruitful saying. It shows, in the parable of the poor man (Lazarus) and the rich man (Luke 16: 19 ff.), whence sprouted the nature without root and place, which has come upon the things.' 6. Does the book contain only this one chapter? Does it not contain also another statement? But, as many think, will you not all be offended at the book whose beginning is like that? But to return to the subject, after some five hundred lines Basilides says:

7. 'We will cease from the empty and curious diversity (of quoted opinions) and will ask rather what investigations the barbarians have made about good things and bad, and what conclusions they have reached on all these things. For some of them have said that there are two origins of all things, and with them they have associated good and evil; they say that the origins themselves are without origin and unoriginate, that is, that in the beginning there were light and darkness, which existed of themselves, and not such as were understood to be generated. 8. While these were by themselves, each of them pursued a life of its own, which it chose and which was of an appropriate kind. For everything finds that friendly which belongs to it and seems in no way evil to it. But when each came to recognize the other and the darkness contemplated the light, it conceived a desire as for the better thing, strove after it, and longed to mingle with it and participate in it. 9. The darkness did so, but the light did not in the slightest degree receive anything from the darkness into itself, and did not get into a state of longing for it, except that it felt a desire to gaze. It gazed on it (the darkness), but as it were through a mirror. Thus a reflection, that is, merely an exhalation (*color*) of the light, reached the darkness, but the light itself gazed so far and then drew back, without having acquired anything from the darkness. 10. But the darkness received a glance from the light, and a reflection or exhalation of its substance, so that it was repulsive in appearance to itself. Since the worse had acquired from the better not actual light, but a lustre, a

reflection of the light, with rapid change it put on the reflection of the light. Hence there is no perfect good in this world, and what (good) there is is very weak, because what was received in the beginning was too little. 11. But still, through this little light, or rather, through a certain lustre from light, what was created was able to produce something similar; this goes back to the mixture which it had received from the light. And that is the creation which we see.' 12. His other (views) of the same kind as these are explained in what follows. But I think that it is enough to indicate his view in this part. For in this he has written on the nature of the world according to what Scythianus thought.

Fragm. 2. Clem. Alex., *Strom.* VII 17 = § 106, 4

The teaching of the Lord during his presence (on earth) took place under Augustus and Tiberius, and that of the Apostles, including Paul's ministry, was completed under Nero. But after that, about the time of the emperor Hadrian, there arose those who devised the heresies, and they continued until the time of the earlier Antoninus—such as Basilides, even though he claims Glaucias as teacher, who as they boast was Peter's interpreter.

Fragm. 3. Clem. Alex., *Strom.* I 21 = § 146, 1–4

The (disciples) of Basilides observe also the day of his (Jesus') baptism, in that they spend the preceding night in (scripture-) readings. They say that it happened in the 15th year of the emperor Tiberius, on the 15th of the month Tybi; others, on the 11th day of the same month. Some in their desire for accurate knowledge date his passion in the 16th year of the emperor Tiberius, on the 25th of the month Phamenoth, but others on the 25th of Pharmuthi. Yet others say that the Saviour suffered on the 19th of Pharmuthi, and some even say that it happened on the 24th or 25th of Pharmuthi.

A detailed fragment traces back all the suffering which a man endures to his sins, even if it is only that he must suffer like a little child who, though he has not sinned, yet still has sinfulness in him. Forced into a corner, Basilides concedes that even Jesus sinned, and he refers to Job 14: 4. In this discussion he also cites reincarnation in support of his view that martyrdom must be traced back to the providence of God, which Clement of Alexandria calls a 'deification of the Devil', because the Church Father traces martyrdoms back to the Devil. This attitude to martyrdom contrasts with the rejection of martyrdom which Irenaeus ascribes to Basilides and his disciples.

Fragm. 4. Clem. Alex., *Strom*. IV 12 §81, 1–83, 2

81, 1. Basilides, in the twenty-third book of his *Exegetica*, on the subject of those tortured in the course of martyrdom, says this in so many words: 2. 'For I say of all those who meet the sufferings referred to, they are certainly led to this privilege (by God) because they have sinned undetected in some other misdemeanours, but by the kindness of him who leads them (guides their life) they are actually accused of quite different things, so that they may not suffer as those condemned for admitted crimes, nor pilloried as an adulterer or murderer, but because they are Christians. That encourages them not even to seem to be suffering. 3. Even if an individual who has not sinned at all is faced with suffering, which rarely happens, yet even he will not suffer because a power plots against him,[20] but he will suffer as the child suffers who has apparently not sinned.'

82, 1. Further on he continues: 'Therefore, just as a little child who has not previously sinned or has committed no actual sin, but still has sinfulness in himself, receives benefit when he is subjected to suffering and reaps plenty of unpleasant things, exactly so, though a full-grown man may not in fact have done any sin but has to suffer, he suffers what he suffers like the little child; for he has sinfulness in him, but has (simply) not sinned because he has had no opportunity for it, so that it is not to be reckoned (as creditable) to him that he has not sinned. 2. For just as the one who wants to commit adultery is an adulterer, even though he does not get as far as adultery, and the one who wants to commit murder is a murderer, even though he is not able to murder, so also the sinless man of whom I am speaking, when I see him suffer, even if he has done nothing bad, I will call him bad because he wanted to sin. For I will say anything rather than call Providence bad.'

83, 1. Somewhat later he also speaks about the Lord exactly as if about a man: 'If, however, you leave aside all these considerations and try to daunt me with certain persons, saying

---

[20] Naturally, this must be a supernatural power, but Basilides rejected the dominance of such a power (Hipp. VII 24, 5).

something like this, "So-and-so therefore sinned, for he suffered", then I will say if you allow me, "He did not sin, but he was like the little child that has to suffer." But if you press the argument more rigorously, I will say that whatever man you name is man, but God is just. For as someone says, "Nobody is free from dirt"' (Job 14: 4). But for Basilides his position is that the soul has sinned previously in another life, and endures the punishment here—the chosen in an honourable manner through martyrdom, the other as one being purified by the punishment appropriate to it.

Basilides here ascribes sinfulness to Jesus. We might link that with Hippolytus' account: Jesus became the first-fruits of the 'distinction of kinds'. He is 'archetype'. He thus has no need to be sinless.

In a fragment preserved for us by Origen reincarnation similarly appears as a doctrine of Basilides:

Fragm. 5. Origen, *In Rom.* V 1 (336 f. Lommatzsch, MSG 14, 1015A–B)

'I died' (Rom. 7: 10), he (Paul) says, meaning, since sin was imputed to me. But Basilides does not notice that this has to be understood of the natural Law, and he relates the apostolic word to preposterous and impious fables, and tries to base on this apostolic word the doctrine of reincarnation, that is, the doctrine that the soul keeps passing from body to body. He says: 'The Apostle explicitly said, "I lived once without the Law" (Rom. 7: 9), that is, before I came into this body, I lived in the sort of body that is not under the Law, such as a beast or a bird.'

Another note is here in place, drawing attention to the 'depositing of the seed-mixture' as an original confusion and mixture. Whether that is Basilides' own view or that of his disciples is not apparent from the fragment. Thus reincarnation goes back to an original guilt; it is possible to speak of guilt, because every man has a share in it. Its character as guilt, however, is at the same time removed, inasmuch as the 'passions' are merely 'attachments'.

Fragm. 6. Clem. Alex. *Strom.* II 20 = § 112, 1

Those around Basilides habitually call the passions 'attachments'; these are essentially spirits attached to the rational soul in accordance with an original confusion and mixture.

(In what follows 'Basilides' expands this.)

Fragm. 7. Clem. Alex., *Strom.* II 20 = § 113, 3–114, 1

Basilides' son Isidore himself says in *On the Grown Soul*, being conscious how far he threatens his own doctrinal position, in so many words: 'If you do offer anyone a proof that the soul is not unitary, but that by the strength of its attachments the cravings for evil things arise, wicked men will have an excellent excuse for saying, "I was compelled, I was carried away, I did it against my will, I did it without intending to", whereas he has himself set the example, as it were, of desire for evil things and has not resisted the compulsions of the attachments. We must become stronger through the reason and demonstrate that we control the lower creation within us.'

We learn details of the ethics of the Basilideans from a longer fragment which begins from Matt. 19: 10–12.

Fragm. 8. Clem. Alex., *Strom.* III 1 = § 1, 1–3, 3

The Basilideans say: When the apostles asked whether it is not better not to marry, the Lord answered, 'Not all grasp this saying (Matt. 19: 10 f.). There are (various) eunuchs, some from birth, others from necessity.' They explain the saying like this: 'Some have from birth a natural aversion from woman; these do well to follow this natural bent of theirs by not marrying. These are', they say, 'the eunuchs from birth. Those who are such by necessity are those theatrical ascetics who weigh on the other side the good repute that they want to have, and master themselves. These become eunuchs by necessity and not by rational reflection. But those who have made themselves eunuchs for the sake of the eternal kingdom arrive at this determination—so they say—because of the things that arise from marriage; they dread the bother that goes with providing the necessities of life.'

2. And by 'It is better to marry than to be burnt up with desire' (1 Cor. 7: 9) the Apostle is saying: 'Do not cast your soul into the fire, resisting night and day and dreading that you will lose your self-control; for the soul that is concerned with resistance separates itself from hope. So endure', says Isidore word for word in his *Ethics*, 'a quarrelsome wife, so that you may not be dragged away from God's grace, and when you have slaked the fire of passion through satisfaction you may pray with good conscience. But when your prayer of thanksgiving

turns into petition and you ask for the future not (perfect) virtue, but (only) that you may not fall, then marry. But suppose a man is young or poor or fallible and is unwilling to marry in accordance with reason, he should not be separated from his brother. He should say, "I have entered into holiness, nothing can happen to me." If he does not trust himself, let him say, "Brother, lay your hand on me, so that I may not sin." And he will get help both outward and inward. Only let him be willing to perfect what is good, and he will achieve it.

3. 'Sometimes we say with the mouth, "We do not wish to sin", but our thoughts are set on sinning. Such a man does not do what he wants to out of fear, so that it may not be reckoned to him for punishment. Some things belong to humanity that are necessary and natural, others that are natural only. To wear clothes is necessary and natural; sexual intercourse is natural, but not necessary.' I (Clement) have quoted these words to refute these Basilideans who do not live rightly, whether on the grounds that they have the right even to sin because of their perfection, or that they will in any case be saved by nature even if they sin now, because of their inborn state of election. For the progenitors of (their) doctrine do not even permit the very things they do.

The last comment is directed against followers of Basilides who drew libertinist conclusions from the master's teaching. Here we see how the original system of Basilides with its elevated ethic turned into a form like that found in Irenaeus. An elevated ethic is indicated by the following note about Basilides himself:

Fragm. 9. Clem. Alex., *Strom.* IV 24 = §153, 3

Basilides says that not all sins are forgiven, but only those committed involuntarily or in ignorance; (the other sins are atoned for through suffering).

Further fragments deal with faith. What they say applies also to other gnostics. Only it would be wrong to stick rigidly to the term 'faith', which others reserve for the psychics, while speaking of the 'gnosis' of the pneumatics.

Fragm. 10. Clem. Alex., *Strom.* II 6 = §27, 2

Thus the Basilideans define faith as an assent of the soul to something which does not affect the senses because it is not

present (to them). Hope is the expectation of possessing something good.

This definition could also have come from a follower of Plato,
though he would hardly have approved the addition about hope.
But what Basilides appears to have said besides this makes the
difference from the great philosopher quite clear. The 'exceptional
faith', that is, the faith of the elect, of the pneumatics, is—as the
gnostics in general say—a nature and a substance, and not the
rational assent of a free soul:

Fragm. 11. Clem. Alex., *Strom.* V 1 = §3, 2–3
2. For if anyone knows God by nature, as Basilides thinks
when he understands the exceptional faith as an intuition[21] and
as a kingdom, as a creation of good things, as an essence worthy
to be near the Creator, then he calls faith an essence and not
a freedom, a nature and substance, an infinite beauty of an
arbitrary creation, but not the rational assent of a free soul.
3. Therefore the commandments of the Old and New Testa-
ments are superfluous, if anyone is saved, as Valentinus says, by
nature, or if anyone is faithful and elect by nature, as Basilides
supposes.

'Election' and 'be elect' are used by Basilides where Valentinus
says 'saved by nature'.

Fragm. 12. Clem. Alex., *Strom.* IV 26 = § 165, 3
From this (Heb. 11: 13) Basilides took it upon him to assert
that the election is alien to the world, because it is supermundane by nature . . .

If the 'exceptional faith' is spoken of, it refers to the faith of the
gnostics. For each man has his own faith, which is appointed for
him in accordance with his place in the cosmic whole; but the faith
of the gnostic is 'exceptional'.

Fragm. 13. Clem. Alex., *Strom.* II 3 = § 10, 1 and 3
1. Then those around Basilides think of faith as something
natural and attribute it to the elect; it discovers doctrines by
intuitive apprehension without proof. . . . 3. Those who come
from Basilides say, moreover, that there is a proper faith and

---

[21] *Noesis* is derived from Nous and has the sense of 'intuition', that is, of a sudden
'comprehension'.

similarly a (proper) election for each (interstitial) space.
Corresponding to the supercosmic election there follows the
cosmic faith (that is the faith which each one has in the world)
of each nature, and corresponding to the hope of each one is
also the gift of faith.

That Gnosis does not understand itself as philosophy but as
prophetic knowledge was said explicitly by Basilides' son Isidore:

Fragm. 14. Clem. Alex., *Strom.*, VI 6 = § 53, 2–5

2. Isidore, simultaneously son and disciple of Basilides,
writes in the first book of the (= his) *Expositions of the prophet
Parchor* in so many words: 3. 'The Athenians say that secrets
were revealed to Socrates because of a spirit attendant on him,
and Aristotle says that all men have spirits bound up with them
for the time of their embodiment. He took this prophetic teaching and put it down in his books, without acknowledging the
source of his statement.' 4. Again, in the second book of the
same work he writes thus: 'And let no one think that this, which
we say is the (knowledge) peculiar to the elect (and thus of the
pneumatics), exists already, having been previously said before
by certain philosophers. For it was not their discovery; they
appropriated it from the prophets and attributed it to the wise
one who was not present with them.' 5. Again he says in the
same book: 'Those who pretend to be philosophers seem to me
to be such in order to find out what the feathered oak is and the
many-hued robe spread on it, all the things that Pherecydes
hinted at in what he said of divine things, taking his basis from
the prophecy of Ham.'

Another note illuminates an individual point in the account of
Hippolytus:

Fragm. 15. Clem. Alex., *Strom.* II 8 = § 36, 1

Then those around Basilides say in explanation of this verse
(Prov. 1: 7) that the Archon himself, when he heard the utterance of the ministering Spirit, was shocked through what was
heard and said,* since he received the glad news beyond (his)
hopes, and his shock was called fear, which became the beginning of the wisdom (Prov. 1: 7) of the distinction of kinds and
separation and fulfilment and restoration. For he who is above

---

* So German; Greek says 'was shocked by what was heard and seen'.

all sends out (the Spirit? or the Gospel?), distinguishing not only the world, but also the elect.[22]

[22] Generally Cl. Al., *Strom.* IV 12 = § 86, 1, is also regarded as a fragment of Basilides. It runs 'But if we, as Basilides himself says, have received as one part of the so-called will of God to love everything—for they relate this word to the All—as a second part to desire nothing and as a third to hate nothing, then the punishments also are from the will of God, which it is impious to think.' The 'we', however, refers to the orthodox Christians, the 'they', to the Basilidians who fathered the idea of the will of God here mentioned upon the Orthodox. What is falsely attributed to them is the neuter 'everything', 'nothing'. According to Clement, one ought not to love the Devil. See W. Foerster, 'Das System des Basilides', in *NTSt* 9 (1962/3), 249 f.

6

OPHITES AND OPHIANS

Almost the last account that Irenaeus gives us is that of the Ophites. In particular features it calls to mind biblical accounts. It looks as though this system is still the first stage of a speculation, for the origin of the world is ultimately traced back not to a *fall* of a heavenly figure, but to the fact that she simply cannot contain and hold the abundance of 'light' set in her. In the beginning there were three divine beings, the First Light = First Man, the Son of Man = Second Man, and below him the Holy Spirit. Spirit is in Hebrew feminine, so it is not surprising that it is the female principle. The Second Man is called Ennoia (Thought) and is nevertheless masculine, which is remarkable, since Ennoia is feminine in Greek and a masculine equivalent is hard to find in Hebrew also. At all events there existed below the Holy Spirit the elements of Water, Darkness, Abyss, and Chaos. There is thus a trinity of divine beings and a quaternity of material substances existing from the beginning. It is when the trinity of divine beings turns itself into a quaternity that the world begins to exist: both (!) male principles unite themselves with the female principle and beget a son, the Third Man, Christ. Both mother and son are immediately taken into the Imperishable Aeon, that is, the holy and true Church. At this point for the first time right and left are used as indications of worth; Christ, as being 'on the right', is immediately taken up into the Aeon.

But the mother, who was unable to carry the great quantity of the light, overflowed 'on the left', and what overflowed on the left is surmised to be lower, but still had a suspicion of the light; it is a female figure, Prunicos (the Lewd), Sophia (Wisdom), and Man-woman. She entered the water, and indeed reached its bottom, and obtained a body because everything crowded to the light. Then she tried to escape from the waters, but could not because of the body. Water is at this point a general term for (evil) matter. However, she got strength from the light, lifted herself up and made the heaven. Further strengthened by the light, she also laid aside the body. Then, we are not told how, she got a son, who has a breath of imperishability from his mother and bears the name 'Ialdabaoth'. Thus a name is mentioned which frequently occurs in gnostic systems, though not always in the same place. It cannot be explained with certainty; it is usually derived from *jalda bahuth* = Son of Chaos, which, however, suits neither our account nor most others, especially as the events concerning Ialdabaoth take place not in this world, but in an invisible world for which the Valentinians have the name 'the psychic world'. At all events, he begot a son without a mother, he another, and so on until altogether, including Ialdabaoth, a group of seven was reached. These seven made heavens, powers, authorities, and angels. When these powers then began quarrelling with Ialdabaoth—a theme that we have met quite often[1]—Ialdabaoth embodied his feeling of sorrow and despair in the matter; thence a son was born to him, twisted like a snake, who corrupted his father even more. Ialdabaoth therefore even vaunted himself as the highest God, whereat his mother accused him of lying. In order to distract the attention of his powers, he then proposed to make a man; the powers, however, could not make him stand up—we have already met the theme in Saturnilus. On the advice of his mother Sophia, Ialdabaoth breathed into him the breath of life; but that means some of the power which he had received from his mother, and ultimately the superterrestrial and supercelestial power of light. Thus this system apparently remains fairly close to the biblical account. For the God of the Old Testament likewise puts the strength into the human form—except that in that case the power was his own power (Gen. 2: 7). Once in possession of the power of light the man immediately gave thanks to the 'First Man'. Adam and Eve transgressed Ialdabaoth's command not to eat of the tree in Paradise, and thus they knew the Power which is above all. Ialdabaoth is the Lord of the Law; his men are therefore the men of the Law, who are subject to him. His mother convicted him of lying and said that the First Man was above him; so Ialdabaoth created man in order to rule over him and thus prove his mother wrong. But in the man he created there is still a part of the light from above; hence Adam and Eve transgressed the commandment of the law and immediately confessed the First Man. If they should be cast out of Paradise, that means that already the portion of light is 'imprisoned' in them. Ialdabaoth then drives them out of the Paradise, and likewise the Snake, who from then onwards, together with the demons created by him, opposes the man. The Snake is the Devil, an echo of the biblical account, rabbinic lore, and the New Testament.

The expulsion from Paradise meant for the human beings that they now acquired an opaque, sluggish body. Before the expulsion

---

[1] In Simon, Ir. I 23, 3, Saturnilus, Ir. I 24, 2, and Basilides, ibid. 4.

from Paradise Sophia had taken from them the breath of light, but had later given it back to them. Still the demons were devising all kinds of evil. Because the men did not serve him, Ialdabaoth wanted to destroy them through the flood; but his mother arranged that those who went into the ark with Noah should be saved. Ialdabaoth chose Abraham, and through Moses led the Jews out of Egypt. The prophets are distributed between the seven 'powers', but they also said some things derived from the Mother and from the Imperishable Aeon.

The men could not, however, let the power of light which they had in them from Ialdabaoth be effective, because they wore the sluggish body and in it the demons perpetrated all sorts of evil. So Sophia found no rest, and finally she turned to her mother, who asked the 'First Man' that Christ should be sent as helper. He descended through the seven heavens, and there he took to himself the trace of the light which was in the seven heavens—thus these powers also had some of the light. He then united himself with Sophia and descended at his baptism upon Jesus, who had been born from the virgin Mary and was wiser and purer than the rest of men. He performed miracles, proclaimed the unknown Father, and professed to be the Son of the First Man. Before his death Christ and Sophia were removed again from Jesus into the Imperishable Aeon. Yet Jesus was not forgotten, but arose 'in the body'. The body is not the earthly body, but a more spiritual substance—what the Valentinians later call the 'psychic body'. Now Christ sits at the right hand of Ialdabaoth, and takes to himself the souls which have a breath of the light, until Ialdabaoth can send down nothing more than his own substance. Then the whole trace of light will be gathered up into the Imperishable Aeon. What the fate of Ialdabaoth and the world is, we are not told. We are here presented with a threefold division of the world, as in the case of the Valentinians: the region of light, the region of the stars (Ialdabaoth and his sons), and our world.

Is Jesus Christ not here superfluous? The man created by Ialdabaoth already has a spark of light. Adam and Eve, as soon as they had eaten from the tree of the knowledge of good and evil, knew 'the Power which is above all, and they separated themselves from those who had made them'. But that is *not* the condition of men now. The exclusion from Paradise has the consequence that through the breath of the sweetness of light man came to a recollection of himself, but also knew himself as naked and as one who had death within him. Hence Sophia is unable for the time being to get back the trace of light, and that is why Christ is sent. He first proclaims to men the unknown Father, and takes to himself the portion of light at the man's death, so that at the consummation he may lead it upwards. Thus what we find again and again in Gnosis is also present here: the eschatological hope, which is not anticipated by any ecstasy; the fact that no philosophical efforts, but only a secret revelation, the bearer of which is in this case Christ, is able to lead to what lies above; and the content of this revelation, the unknown God.

Irenaeus, *Adv. Haer.* I 30, 1–15

1. Others[2] yet again speak of monstrous things (saying) that there is a first light in the power of the 'deep', blessed and incorruptible and boundless, which is the Father of all and is called the First Man. His Ennoia which proceeds (from him) they call the Son of the one who emits him, and he is the Son of Man, the Second Man. Below these is the Holy Spirit, and below the Spirit on high the elements are separated, water, darkness, Abyssus, Chaos, over which they say the Spirit hovers (Gen. 1:2); and they call it the First Woman. Thereafter, they say, as the First Man rejoiced with his son at the beauty of the Spirit, that is the Woman, and illuminated her, he begot from her an incorruptible light, a third male, whom they call Christ the Son of the First and Second Man and of the Holy Spirit the first Woman, since both the Father and the Son lay with the woman, whom they call the Mother of the Living (Gen. 3:20). 2. Since, however, she was unable to carry or contain the greatness of the light, they say she was overfull and bubbling over on the left side; and thus only their son Christ, as being on the right and lifted up into the higher parts, was at once caught up with his mother to the Imperishable Aeon. And this is the true and holy Church, which is the designation and gathering together and unification of the Father of all, the First Man, and of his Son the Second Man, and of Christ their Son, and of the aforementioned Woman.

3. The power which bubbled over from the Woman, having a trace of the light, fell downwards, they teach, from the Fathers, but by their will retained a trace of light, and they call it the Left and Prunicos (the Lewd) and Sophia (Wisdom) and Manwoman. She went down straight into the waters when they were still and set them in motion, wantonly stirring them to the

---

[2] According to Theodoret (*Haer. Fab.* I 14) the following derives from the 'Sethians whom some call Ophians or Ophites'.

very depths, and she took on a body from them. For to her trace of light everything rushed, they say, and clung, and encircled her; if she had not had this she would perhaps have been completely swallowed up and submerged by the matter. So being tied and severely weighed down by the body, because it was of matter, at last she again got a savour (of the light), and tried to flee from the waters and rise up to her mother; but she could not because of the weight of the body surrounding (her). Being in a very bad way she devised means of hiding that light which was from above, for fear that it would also be harmed by the inferior elements just as she was herself. When she received power from the trace of the light within her, she leapt up and was carried up to the height, and there she spread out and became a covering, and made this visible heaven from her body; and she remained under the heaven which she made, which still has the appearance of a watery body. Since she had a craving for the light above, and had acquired power through all things, she laid aside her body and was set free from it. This body, which they say she discarded, they call the woman from the Woman. And her son also, they say, himself had a breath of incorruptibility left in him by his mother, and through this he acts. Becoming strong, he too, so they say, produced a son from the waters without a mother, for they will not have it that he knew his own mother. And his son in imitation of his father produced another son. This third also begot a fourth, and the fourth too begot a son; from the fifth a sixth son was, they say, begotten, and the sixth begot a seventh. Thus also the number seven was completed among them, their mother occupying the eighth place. And as in birth so they have precedence over each other in dignity and power.

5. They also give them such names as these in their mendacity: the first one, who came from the mother, is called Ialdabaoth, his (son) Iao, and his Sabaoth; the fourth (is called) Adoneus, the fifth Eloeus, the sixth Oreus, the seventh and youngest of all, Astaphaeus. On their hypothesis these heavens and virtues and powers and angels and creators sit invisible in heaven ranked in the order of their generation, and rule things heavenly and earthly. The first of them is Ialdabaoth, who despises his mother inasmuch as he made sons and grandsons without anyone's permission, and also angels, archangels, powers, forces, and

authorities. When these were made, his sons turned to contention and strife with him about the primacy. Filled with grief and despair at these things, Ialdabaoth fixed his gaze on the dregs of matter lying below, and his desire for it took physical shape, and thus they say a son was born. This (son) was himself a Nous (or a Nun[3]) twisted in the shape of a snake, and thence came spirit and soul and all worldly things; hence arose all forgetfulness, malice, jealousy, envy, and death. They say that this snakelike and twisted Nous (or Nun) of theirs has even more perverted the father by his tortuousness, since he was with their father in heaven and in paradise.

6. Hence Ialdabaoth in exultation boasted about all the things beneath him and said: 'I am Father and God, and above me there is none' (Isa. 45: 5). When his mother heard she called out against him: 'Do not lie, Ialdabaoth, for there is above you the Father of all, the First Man, and the Man the Son of Man.' When all were thrown into confusion at the new voice and the unexpected proclamation, and were asking where the cry (came) from, to divert them and keep them with him, they say that Ialdabaoth said: 'Come, let us make a man in our image' (Gen. 1: 26). When the six powers heard—their mother gave them the thought of the man, so that through him she might empty them of their original power—they came together and fashioned a man, of enormous breadth and length. But while he was only wriggling, they carried him to their father. Sophia contrived this also, so as to empty him (the father) also of his trace of light, so that he would not be able to rise up against those above by the power he had. As he breathed into the man the breath of life, they say that he was unwittingly emptied of power. But the man thus got Nous and Enthymesis (thought), and that is what is saved, they say; and he at once gave thanks to the First Man, forsaking his creators.

7. Full of jealousy, Ialdabaoth wanted to devise means of making man empty through a woman, and from his Enthymesis (thought) he brought forth a woman, whom that Prunicos took up and invisibly emptied of power. But the others, who came and admired her beauty, called her Eve, and lusting for her begot from her sons, who they say are also angels. But their mother tried through the snake to lead aside Eve and Adam

---

[3] Hebrew letter.

into transgressing the command of Ialdabaoth; and Eve, hearing this as if from the son of God, was easily persuaded, and urged Adam to eat from the tree from which God had said they should not eat (Gen. 3: 1–7). When they ate, they say, they knew the Power which is above all, and they separated themselves from those who had made them. When Prunicos saw that they (the creators) were defeated through their own creation, she was very glad, and again called out that since there was an incorruptible Father he lied when once he called himself Father; and since there had long been a Man and a First Woman, she also committed adultery and sinned (?).

8. But Ialdabaoth, who because of the forgetfulness surrounding him paid no attention even to these things, expelled Adam and Eve from the paradise (Gen. 3:23) because they had broken his commandment. For he wanted sons to be born to him by Eve, and did not succeed, since his mother opposed him in everything. She secretly emptied Adam and Eve of their trace of light, so that the spirit which came from the Source should not suffer either abuse or reproach. They teach that, being thus emptied of the divine substance, they were cursed by him and cast down from heaven into this world. But the Snake also, because he worked against his father, was cast down into the world below; and he got the angels who are here into his control, and begot six sons, with himself as the seventh, to imitate the hebdomad surrounding his father. These, they say, are the seven demons of the world, always opposing and resisting the human race because on their account their father was thrown down.

9. Adam and Eve previously had light, clear and as it were spiritual bodies, just as they had been created. But when they came here (to this world) they turned into something more opaque and thick and sluggish. The soul, too, became lax and limp, since they had from the creator only a breath of the world; so much so that Prunicos pitied them and restored to them a whiff of the sweetness of the trace of light. Through this they came to recollect who they themselves were, and they knew that they were naked and had material bodies; and they knew that they were burdened with death. They became patient, knowing that the body is their garment only for a time. They also discovered foods under the guidance of Sophia, and when they

were full came together in intercourse with each other, conceiving Cain. The objectionable Snake and his sons immediately took and corrupted him, filling him with the world's forgetfulness, plunging him in folly and insolence so that, when he killed his brother Abel, he was the first to exhibit envy and death (Gen. 4: 1–8). After them (Cain and Abel) by the providence of Prunicos they say that Seth was conceived (Gen. 4 : 25), and then Norea; from them they say the rest of the human multitude is descended. They were plunged by the lower hebdomad into every kind of evil and rebellion against the higher, holy hebdomad, and into idolatry and the rest of the universal contempt, while the mother was always invisibly opposed to them, and saved what belonged to her, that is the trace of light. They want the holy hebdomad to be the seven stars which are called planets, and the objectionable Snake has, they say, two names, Michael and Samael.

10. Ialdabaoth was angry with men because they did not worship him or honour him as God and Father, and he sent the flood on them to destroy all of them at the same time. But in this also Sophia opposed (him), and those who were with Noah in the ark were saved, because of the trace of light which came from her. By means of it (the trace) the world was once again filled with men (Gen. 9: 1). From these Ialdabaoth himself chose a certain Abraham, and made a covenant with him, that if his seed continued serving him, he would give him the earth as his inheritance (Gen. 15). Afterwards through Moses he led out from Egypt those who were from Abraham, and gave them the law, and made them Jews. He selected seven days,[4] which they also call the holy hebdomad. And each one of them took himself a herald to extol him and to proclaim him God, so that the others also should hear the glories (extolled), and should themselves serve those gods who are proclaimed by the prophets. 11. They distribute the prophets thus: to Ialdabaoth belonged Moses, Joshua son of Nun, Amos, and Habakkuk; to Iao, Samuel, Nathan, Jonah, and Micah; to Sabaoth, Elijah, Joel, and Zechariah; to Adonai, Isaiah, Ezekiel, Jeremiah, and Daniel; to Eloi, Tobias and Haggai; to Oreus, Micah and Nahum; to Astapheus, Ezra and Zephaniah. Each one of these extolled his father and god. But Sophia herself also uttered

---

[4] Text uncertain: perhaps 'Gods' instead of 'days'.

many things through them concerning the First Man, the Imperishable Aeon, and about that Christ, who according to them is above, and she forewarned and reminded men of the imperishable light, and the First Man, and the descent of Christ. At this the rulers were terrified, and amazed at the novelty of the things which were being proclaimed by the prophets. Then Prunicos arranged through Ialdabaoth, who did not know what he was doing, the emanation of two men, one from the barren Elizabeth, the other from Mary the virgin (Luke 1).

12. Since she had herself no respite either in heaven or in earth, in her grief she summoned her mother to her aid. And her mother, the First Woman, took pity at the repentance of her daughter, and asked the First Man that Christ should be sent to her aid. He was sent out and descended to his sister and to the trace of light. When the Sophia who is below knew that her brother was coming down to her, she both announced his coming through John, and prepared a baptism of repentance (Matt. 3: 1–12 par.), and prepared in advance Jesus, so that when he came down Christ would find a clean vessel, and so that through her son Ialdabaoth a woman might receive annunciation from Christ. They say that he descended through the seven heavens, became like their sons, and gradually emptied them of power; for to him, they say, the whole trace of light flowed together. As Christ descended into this world, he first put on his sister Sophia, and they both rejoiced as they refreshed each other. That is what they designate as bridegroom and bride. And Jesus, being born from a virgin by the activity of a god, was wiser and purer and more just than all men. Bound up with Sophia, Christ descended, and so Jesus Christ came to be.

13. Many of his disciples, they say, did not know the descent of Christ upon him, but when Christ descended on him, then he began to perform acts of power, to heal, and to proclaim the unknown Father, and to confess himself openly as son of the First Man. At this the rulers and the father became angry with Jesus and arranged for him to be killed. While he was being led to it, Christ himself and Sophia went off, they say, to the Imperishable Aeon, but Jesus was crucified. Christ did not forget him, but sent a certain power down into him, which

raised him in the body. This body was of soul and spirit; for what was worldly he left in the world. When the disciples saw that he had risen, they did not know him; they did not even know Christ[5] himself, through whom he rose from the dead. They say that the greatest error which arose among his disciples was that they thought he had risen in a worldly body, and did not know that 'flesh and blood do not possess the kingdom of God' (1 Cor. 15: 50).

14. They base their statements about the descent and ascent of Christ on the fact that the disciples report no great deed done by Jesus either before the baptism or after the resurrection. They did not know that Jesus was united to Christ, and the Imperishable Aeon to the hebdomad; and the worldly body they call psychic.[6] He (Jesus) remained eighteen months after his resurrection, and when perception descended into him he taught[7] what is crystal-clear. But to a few of his disciples whom he knew to be capable of such great mysteries he taught these things, and thus was taken up into heaven, where Christ sits on the right of the father Ialdabaoth, so that, after they have put off the worldly flesh, he may take to himself the souls of those who knew them (Christ and Jesus), thus enriching himself. His father does not know—he does not even see him—so that the more Jesus enriches himself with holy souls, the more his father suffers hurt and is reduced, being emptied of power through the souls. For now he will have no holy souls to send down again into the world, but only those which are of his substance, that is, those derived from the giving of breath. The consummation will come when the whole trace of the spirit of light is gathered together, and taken up into the Aeon of Imperishability.

15. Such then are their teachings; from which like the Lernaean Hydra a many-headed monster has been bred from the school of Valentinus. For some say that Sophia herself became the Snake, that she therefore was hostile to the creator of Adam, and put knowledge in men, and for this reason the serpent was said to be wisest of all (Gen. 3: 1). But also because of the position of our intestines through which nutriment flows, and because they have such a shape, they point to the hidden parent with the shape of a snake which is within us.

---

[5] The text has 'Jesus', [6] Text obscure.
[7] Perception: i.e. he became perceptible. The text has in the sequel: he learned.

THE OPHIANS

The Church Father Origen in his book against Celsus mentions a drawing, which Celsus had been able to use in his attack on the Christians, since he made no distinction between members of the Great Church and gnostic 'sects'. Origen acquired a drawing containing closer details, and agreeing in its main features with Celsus' copy. According to Origen, it was known by the name of 'Diagram of the Ophians'.

The details of the drawing are now very difficult to explain from Origen's description, and it is probably impossible to get a 'system' directly from it.

In the drawing were seven circles[8] held together by one large circle, which is called Leviathan or the Soul of the Universe, the soul which permeates all things.

Mention must also be made of Behemoth, who comes 'after' the lowest circle; it probably represents hell and thus the kingdom of evil. Then the highest sphere is mentioned, that of the Father and the Son; the latter is marked with white dye from the tree of life. After death the pneumatics stride past seven aeons and their corresponding rulers; the names of the rulers of the aeons are with one exception given: Ialdabaoth, Iao, Sabaoth, Astaphaios, Ailoaios, Horaios, with Adonaios apparently omitted from the list. These are angelic titles and planetary spheres. The symbol of life, which permits the pneumatics to pass through these spheres, is probably to be identified with the seal which was conferred by the Father on his Son.[9] The names of the rulers of the aeons are related to those of the Apocryphon of John and the Ophites. It is very difficult to discern details. Only this is clear, that those few who get past the starry spheres have a seal, and further, that neither does the Redeemer himself lead them past nor do they refer to him, but they invoke the fact that the power of the archons has become impotent. The language of these formulae is consciously kept enigmatic, although the riddle is soluble to the initiates.

Origen, *Contra Celsum* VI 24–38

24. After the account derived from the disciples of Mithras Celsus declares that anyone who likes can compare a Christian initiation with the initiation of the Persians previously related. . . . Where he was able to give the names of sects, he did not

---

[8] The manuscripts give the number ten but in the sequel only seven circles are mentioned.

[9] Cf. the Naassene psalm: 'with seals', p. 282.

hesitate to set out those he seemed to know. But where it was particularly necessary, if he knew it, to do this, and to explain which sect it is that uses the diagram described, he has not done so. For these reasons, he seems to me to have given a description of the diagram (which is at least) in part based on misunderstood information about the insignificant Ophian sect. . . . We also, although we have travelled through many parts of the earth, and everywhere inquired for those who claimed to know anything, have found no one able to explain the diagram.

25. In this there was a drawing of seven circles, separate from each other, but linked together by one circle which was said to be the soul of the universe and was named Leviathan. . . . The ungodly diagram said that . . . Leviathan was the soul which permeates the universe. . . . We find in it also the so-called Behemoth[10] as one set in position after the bottom circle. The author of that disgusting diagram wrote this 'Leviathan' on the circle and on its centre, thus putting the name twice. Celsus adds that the diagram is divided by a thick black line, and he alleged that he had been told that this was hell (Gk. *Gehenna*), which is also the underworld (Gk. *Tartaros*). . . . 26. . . . Thus neither the diagram nor Celsus knows what should be said about hell. . . .

27. . . . He sets out some odd things, including responses, like this: The one who confers the seal is called Father; and the one who received the seal (is called) Young One and Son, and he answers: 'I am smeared with white dye from the tree of life.' . . . He then defines also a number—seven—which is mentioned by the angels who transmit the seal, who stand on either side of the soul of the person (literally, body) who is about to depart, some (angels) of light, others (angels) of the so-called Archon-powers; and he says that the Ruler of the so-called Archon-powers is called 'accursed God'. . . . (We agree with those who criticize it) if there are any who say that the accursed God is the (God) of the Jews who rains and thunders, the creator of this world, the God of Moses and of his cosmology. . . . 28. . . . He says that such (a God) deserves cursing, according to those who hold this opinion about him, because he cursed the snake when he was teaching men the

[10] Manuscripts: Behemon.

knowledge of good and evil.[11] But he (Celsus) should have
known that . . . the Ophians admit nobody to their assembly
unless he (first) utters curses against Jesus. . . . But these
impious men boast the name of Ophians, after the snake,
hostile and terrible to men, not like human beings, to whom the
snake is an enemy, but like snakes themselves they are proud
to be called Ophians; and they boast a certain Euphrates as the
one who introduced these words. . . . 30. . . . And we find in
the diagram which we ourselves obtained from them, that the
arrangement is exactly as Celsus described it. Celsus said that
the first (circle) is shaped in the form of a lion, but does not
state what those true villains call it; but we have found that
the one who in holy scripture is the ineffable angel of the Demiurge is called by that filthy diagram Michael the lion-shaped.
Again, Celsus called the next one, the second, a bull. The
diagram in our possession called the bull-shaped one Suriel.
Then Celsus said the next was an amphibian hissing horribly.
The diagram said that the dragon-shaped one is Raphael.
Again, Celsus said that the fourth has the shape of an eagle;
the diagram said that the eagle-shaped one is Gabriel. Next,
Celsus said that the fifth has the head of a bear; the diagram
said that the bear-shaped one is Thauthabaoth. Next, Celsus
said that according to their account the sixth has the head of
a dog; the diagram said that it is Erathaoth. Finally, Celsus
said that the seventh had the head of an ass, and he names it
Thaphabaoth or Onoel; but in the diagram we found that this
one with the ass's shape is called Onoel or Thartharaoth. . . .

31. But if anyone wants to learn the inventions of those
tricksters, . . . he should hear what they are taught to say after
they pass through what they call the fence of wickedness,
the gates of the archons, which were shut for ever: 'I greet the
solitary King, the bond of blindness, the reckless forgetting, the
first power, guarded by the spirit of providence and by wisdom.
Thence am I sent forth pure, already a part of the light of the
Son and the Father. Grace be with me; yes, Father, be it with
me.' And they say that the rulers (or: the beginnings) of the
Ogdoad are from there. Furthermore, they are taught to say,
as they pass over the one they call Ialdabaoth; 'But you, archon

---

[11] Celsus means that the cursing of the serpent is logical since the Christians
considered the knowledge of good and evil to be something bad.

Ialdabaoth, to whom power belongs as first and seventh, I go with confidence as a ruling Logos of pure Nous, as a perfect work for the Son and the Father, by the imprint of the blow bearing the symbol of life, having opened for the world the gate which you had by your aeon closed; as a free man I go past your power. Grace be with me; yes, Father, be it with me.' They say that the star Saturn is bound by sympathy to the lion-headed archon. Then they think that the one who has gone past Ialdabaoth and has reached Iao must say: 'You night-shining archon, while the mysteries of the Son and Father are concealed, second Iao, first master of death; a part of the innocent one, wearing already as a symbol my own moustache (?), ready to go past your authority, I have[12] overpowered by living word the one born from you. Grace be with me; yes, Father, be it with me.' Next, Sabaoth, to whom they think they will say: ˸Ruler (Gk. *archon*) of the fifth power, commander Sabaoth, advocate of the law of your creation, which by grace is released, by a mightier pentad let me pass, since you see the symbol which your art cannot attain and is protected by an image of the imprint, the body released by the pentad. Grace be with me; yes, Father, be it with me.' Next to him Astaphaios, to whom they believe they will say this: 'Astaphaios, archon of the third door, overseer of the first source of water, let me pass, since you see one initiate, who has been cleansed by the spirit of the maiden, since you see the essence of the world. Grace be with me; yes, Father, be it with me.' After him Ailoaios, to whom they think they say this: 'Ailoaios, ruler (Gk. *archon*) of the second gate, let me pass, for I wear for you the symbol of your mother, the grace that is hidden from the powers of the authorities. Grace be with me; yes, Father, be it with me.' The last one they name is Horaios, and they think to say to him: 'Horaios, you who fearlessly overcame the barrier of fire, and obtained authority over the first gate, let me pass, since you see that the symbol of your power is made weak by the mark of the tree of life, taken (away) similarly by the image of the Innocent. Grace be with me; yes, Father, be it with me.'

33. Celsus goes on to relate other fables, such as that some have attained to the archontic shapes, so that some become lions, others bulls, yet others snakes, eagles, bears, or dogs. We

---

[12] Correction mine.

find in the diagram which we possess and which Celsus mentioned, a square, and what those wretches call the (sword)
which is over the gates of Paradise. But the flaming sword was
drawn as the diameter of a fiery circle, since it guards the tree of
knowledge and life (Gen. 3: 24). But Celsus would not or could
not describe the speeches which, according to the fables of the
impious, those who enter will recite at each gate. But we have
also done that. . . .

34. Then . . . Celsus says this: 'They add one thing on top of
another, words of prophets, and circles upon circles, emanations
of an earthly Church and of circumcision, the flowing power
of a certain virgin Prunicos, and a living soul, and heaven slain
so that it may live, and earth slain with the sword, and many
people slain so that they may live, and death ceasing in the
world when the sin of the world dies, a narrow descent and
gates which open of their own accord. And everywhere there,
the tree of life and the resurrection of flesh from the tree. . . .' In
this Celsus seems to me to be getting the things he has picked up
muddled. . . .

35. . . . To speak of circles upon circles is perhaps a question
of the aforementioned sect enclosing the seven circles of the
archontic powers with one circle, which they say is the soul of
the universe and Leviathan; perhaps it is a misunderstanding
of something in Ecclesiastes. . . . Emanations from the earthly
Church and circumcision are perhaps derived from the fact that
according to some people the Church on earth is an emanation
of a heavenly Church and of a higher aeon, and the circumcision
written in the law is a symbol of a circumcision which happens
there as a purification. Prunicos is the name which the Valentinians give to Wisdom.[13] . . . A living soul is perhaps an
expression which is secretly used by some of the Valentinians
for their so-called 'psychic demiurge'. . . . I do not know about
the slaying of heaven. . . .

36. . . . A narrow descent would perhaps be spoken of by
those who introduce reincarnation. A gate which opens of its own
accord might very well have been said by some who in riddles
explain the passage: 'Open to me the gates of righteousness,
so that I may go in by them and praise the Lord' (Ps. 118
(117): 19). . . .

[13] According to what we know, the Valentinians did not use this name.

38. But the noble fellow was not satisfied with what he got from the diagram; he intended, in order to increase his accusations against us, who never had anything to do with it, to speak of certain other things in between, and took up their (views) as if they were ours. For he says: 'Not the least marvel among them is this: They declare that between the supercelestial circles above some things are drawn, in particular two (circles), a greater and a lesser, of the Son and the Father.' We find in this diagram the greater circle and the lesser, and on their diameter 'Father' and 'Son' are inscribed; and between the greater, in which is the lesser, and another which consists of two circles, the outer yellow and the inner blue, there is a partition drawn in the shape of an axe; and above it is a small circle attached to the larger of the former, with the inscription 'Love', and below, attached to the circle, one with the inscription 'Life'. On the second circle, which embraces and encloses two other circles and another rhomboid figure, is inscribed 'Providence of Sophia (Wisdom)'; and inside the section common to them, 'Nature of Sophia (Wisdom)'; and above their common section is a circle in which is written 'Knowledge'; and below it another, in which is written 'Insight'.

Origen *Contra Celsum* III 13

Celsus seems to me to have in mind certain sects which do not even have the name of Jesus in common with us. Knowledge had perhaps circulated of the so-called Ophians and Cainites and whatever other similar doctrine has sprung up which has completely abandoned Jesus.

7

BARBELOGNOSIS

The work entitled 'Apocryphon of John' is up to the present the best-attested original gnostic document. It is extant in four copies, of which two present a longer and two a shorter text. The long version is probably a revision and expansion of the short. The two forms of the shorter version also diverge from one another at various points, mostly only trivial. The greater part of the deviations goes back to different methods of working on the part of the translators who rendered the two texts from Greek into Coptic. We present below the translation of the short version now in Berlin (= BG), since its text is better preserved than the one in Cairo.

The Apocryphon of John is a secret document. According to the frame-story, Jesus after his resurrection imparted these teachings on a mountain, probably the Mount of Olives, to John the son of Zebedee, and commanded him to write down the doctrines propounded by him and to pass them on only to gnostics and in secret.

According to its structure, the Apocryphon is a classic gnostic Gospel. It consists of two parts: a report of a vision, and a dialogue.

1. The report of the vision can be subdivided into the frame-story, the description of the supreme deity, who can only be described in negative terms, the cosmogony, and the account of the fall of Sophia.

2. The dialogue consists of ten questions from John, which Christ answers, and a concluding frame-story. Only the questions and answers 4 to 9 fit very well together, and the answers are briefly formulated. In them the destiny of the soul is dealt with. The other answers are very long, and only in a small part of the answer is the question posed replied to. The arguments attaching directly to the answers proper continue the ideas expressed before the questions. If we omit the first three questions and answers, this does no damage to our understanding of the connection of the text. In terms of content also the first three questions and answers stand apart from the six following. With one part of the tenth question they contain a paraphrase of the first seven chapters of Genesis, similar to that

which we find in the Hypostasis of the Archons and in Irenaeus (*Adv. Haer.* I 30). Often different conclusions are drawn from the biblical text, and hence we frequently find the formula: 'Not as Moses said.'

One therefore forms the impression that in the second part of the Apocryphon of John two distinct conceptions have been woven together: a paraphrase of Gen. 1–7 in questions 1–3 and part of 10, and teaching about the soul and its destiny after man's death in questions 4–9 and part of 10. The teaching about the soul seems originally to have been formulated as a dialogue. On the other hand, the paraphrase on Gen. 1–7 arouses the impression that it was only transformed into a dialogue through newly formulated questions.

The literary seam between the two parts occurs in BG 44. 19.

To BG 26. 6–44. 19, that is, to the second part of the description of the supreme being, the cosmogony and the fall of Sophia, we have a parallel in the report of Irenaeus on Barbelognosis (*Adv. Haer.* I 29, 1–4). Between the two accounts there are, however, a number of differences: Irenaeus, for example, describes the supreme being very briefly, while the account in the Apocryphon is much more detailed (BG 26. 6 ff.). The same holds for the emergence of the first five aeons in BG 27. 1–29. 18. We learn in the Apocryphon further details about their origin, which are in part self-contradictory: the first aeon to come into being is Ennoia (BG 27. 2–8), who has various names, for example 'the perfect Pronoia of the All' (BG 27. 10–11), Barbelo (BG 27. 14), 'the first Ennoia' (BG 27. 18). According to this, Ennoia and Pronoia are two names of the same aeon, but later (BG 28. 9–10, 18; 29. 12) Barbelo and Ennoia are different beings, and here (BG 29. 12) Ennoia came into being after Barbelo. Thus the account of the origin of this Ennoia must have been omitted in all four versions of the Apocryphon of John. The aeons who come into being after Barbelo owe their origin to a prayer from Barbelo and the assent of the supreme being. Hence they stand forward and praise the supreme being and Barbelo.

Again, the origin of the light which through anointing became Christ is described in BG 29. 18–31. 5 in greater detail and to some extent differently. We learn, for example, that the spark of light was not of equal birth to Barbelo, while Irenaeus describes the light as equal to Barbelo. He also passes over in silence the exultation of the invisible Spirit over the birth of the light and the praises sung by the light.

The origin of the will in BG 31. 13 f. after that of Nous is missing in Irenaeus. In BG 31. 18–20 it is not clear that the beings which have come into existence form pairs, as plainly emerges from the account in Irenaeus.

Differing from the Apocryphon of John (BG 32. 3 ff.), Irenaeus then portrays the emergence of Autogenes from Ennoia and Logos. According to the Apocryphon Autogenes originated from the first Ennoia (BG 32. 9–12), and likewise the truth that is in him is subjected to him (BG 32. 16–17), whereas according to Irenaeus the truth is produced along with him and from the two a union comes into being.

From the will and eternal life four beings take their origin in Irenaeus, while in the Apocryphon (BG 33. 4–5) it is not clear that these spring from a union of the two. The name of one of the four beings is in Irenaeus Thelesis (willing, volition), but in the Apocryphon (BG 33. 6–7) perception.

The first light is called in the Apocryphon of John (BG 33. 8–9) Harmozel, in the three other versions Armozel, but in Irenaeus Armoges. While the other three beings according to Irenaeus are assigned to the three lights, this statement is lacking in the Apocryphon. The second light is called in the Apocryphon of John Oroiael (BG 33. 13), in Irenaeus Raguel. The Apocryphon in addition also reports that all four lights have three aeons with them as well, and they are mentioned by name (BG 33. 10–12 *et al.*). Further material peculiar to the Apocryphon is contained in BG 34. 7–15. They are then in agreement on the generation of the perfect man Adamas (BG 35. 5: Adam), but in Irenaeus he is produced only through the Self-originate, in the Apocryphon through the Self-originate and other beings (BG 34. 19–35. 3). Instead, Irenaeus offers an etymology of the name Adamas. A further difference to be mentioned is that while in the Apocryphon Adam is set in the first aeon of Harmozel (BG 35. 6–9), according to the account in Irenaeus he is 'removed with the first light by (or: from) Armoges'. And 'with the man there was produced by Armoges "perfect knowledge", and she was united with him, and therefore he too knew him who is above all things'. Both texts agree in reporting that Adam after receiving an invincible power sang a hymn of praise. In Irenaeus the praise is only mentioned, but in the Apocryphon we are given to know the exact text (BG 35. 13–20). From this it also appears that the hymn is directed not only—as in Irenaeus—to the Great Aeon, but to the Father, the Mother, and the Son, which Irenaeus or his source perhaps misunderstood, for there we read: 'hence, they say, there was manifested the Mother, the Father, the Son.' While in Irenaeus it is then reported that from the man and Gnosis the tree was born which is itself called Gnosis, the Apocryphon of John offers a completely different text (BG 35. 20–36. 15).

In the report of the origin and fall of Sophia, Irenaeus and the Apocryphon again diverge from one another. According to the

Apocryphon, Sophia is the last aeon with the fourth light Eleleth (BG 34. 7), but according to Irenaeus Sophia was produced by the first angel, who stands beside the 'Only-begotten'. She is also called Holy Spirit and Prunikos, whereas in the Apocryphon the Holy Spirit is her consort (BG 37. 4–6).

The motive for her fall is also differently portrayed: in Irenaeus, Sophia seeks a partner since 'all the rest have consorts'. When she found no one with whom she could unite, she extended herself downwards and made a leap. In the Apocryphon of John she wants to cause a being to come into existence out of herself, but gains the consent neither of the supreme being nor of her consort (BG 36. 17–37. 13). She therefore brings forth a work 'in which was ignorance and presumption', as Irenaeus reports. The Apocryphon describes the appearance of this creature and his concealment more exactly (BG 37. 13–38. 13). His name Ialdabaoth is also mentioned (BG 38. 14). According to the Apocryphon (BG 39. 5–6) he united with Unreason, according to Irenaeus he associated with Presumption and begot wickedness, envy, jealousy, revenge, and passion. In the Apocryphon there are 360 angelic beings (BG 39. 6–15), of whom some are mentioned by name (BG 40. 5 ff.). When he saw the creation and the host of angels created by him, Ialdabaoth in the Apocryphon (BG 44. 9–15) says: 'I am a jealous God, beside me there is no other' (Exod. 20: 5 and Isa. 45: 6; 46: 9), but according to Irenaeus he so speaks because his mother Sophia, full of grief, had withdrawn to the heights and he therefore believed that he was the only one. The Apocryphon concludes the vision-report with a comment cast in the form of a question (BG 44. 15–19).

The enumeration of the deviations between the two accounts has made it clear what differences there are between the Apocryphon and the account in Irenaeus. The numerous agreements have not been mentioned. We may assume that Irenaeus for his description of the Barbelognostics had at his disposal a source which was indeed not identical with the cosmogony and the fall of Sophia in the Apocryphon (BG 26. 6–44. 19), but yet was similar to it.

The ensuing dialogue section in the Apocryphon, which Irenaeus does not mention, was probably not contained in his source either.

Since the report of Irenaeus was composed before 180, we may set in the same period at least those parts of the Apocryphon which are related to it. The Apocryphon of John in the short version now before us will certainly have come into being not much later. We present first the text of Irenaeus, then that of the Apocryphon.

THE BARBELOGNOSTICS ACCORDING TO IRENAEUS
Irenaeus, *Adv. Haer.* I 29, 1–4

1. Apart from those who come from the above-mentioned Simonians, there has arisen a multitude of Barbelognostics, appearing like mushrooms out of the ground. The principal doctrines held among them we now relate.

Some of them postulate an aeon that never grows old in virginal spirit, which they call Barbelo. There, they say, is an unnameable Father, and he wished to manifest himself to Barbelo. This Ennoia (Thought), however, when she had come forth, stood in his presence and asked for Prognosis (Foreknowledge). When Prognosis also (!) had come forth, Incorruptibility emerged, again at their request, and after that Eternal Life. As Barbelo exulted in these, and looked on the Greatness, and rejoiced over the conception, he generated in her a light like her. This was the beginning of the enlightenment and the generation of all things. And when the Father saw this light, he anointed it with his goodness, that it might become perfect. This, they say, is Christ. He again requested, as they say, that Nous be given him as a helper, and Nous came forth. And in addition to these the Father emitted Logos. Unions were now formed of Ennoia and Logos, and of Incorruptibility and Christ; and Eternal Life was united with Thelema (Will), and Nous with Prognosis. These praised the great light and Barbelo.

2. Thereafter, they say, the Self-originate was emitted from Ennoia and Logos, as a representation of the great light, and was greatly honoured, and all things were subjected to him. With him was emitted Truth, and there was a union of the Self-originate and Truth. From the light which is Christ and from Incorruptibility four luminaries were brought forth to stand around the Self-originate, and from Thelema again and Eternal Life four (beings) were produced to minister to the four luminaries, which they call Charis (Grace), Thelesis (Willing), Synesis (Understanding), Phronesis (Prudence). Charis was attached to the first great light, whom they want to be the Saviour and call Armoges; Thelesis to the second, whom they name Raguel; Synesis to the third luminary, whom they call David; and Phronesis to the fourth, whom they call Eleleth.

3. When these had all thus been established, the Self-originate produces the perfect, true man, whom they also call Adamas

(Indomitable), because he is neither dominated himself nor were those from whom he came into being. And he was removed with the first light by Armoges. With the Man, however, Perfect Knowledge was put forth by the Self-originate and united with him; hence he too knew him who is above all things; also an invincible power was given him by the virginal spirit; and at this they all rejoiced and praised the great aeon. Hence, they say, was manifested mother, father, and son. From the Man and Knowledge was born the tree, which itself they call Knowledge. 4. Thereupon, they say, from the first angel who stands beside the Only-begotten, there was put forth Holy Spirit, whom they also call Sophia (Wisdom) and Prunikos (lewd). When she saw that all the rest had a consort, but she herself was without a partner, she sought for one with whom she might unite; and when she did not find one she took it sorely, extended herself, and looked down into the lower regions, thinking to find a consort there. And when she found none she leapt forth,[1] disgusted also because she had made the leap without the goodwill of the Father. Then, moved by simplicity and goodness, she generated a work in which was ignorance and audacity. This work of hers, they say, was the Proarchon, the creator of this present condition. They relate that he stole from his mother a great power and departed from her into the lower regions, and made the firmament of heaven, in which also they say he dwells. And since he is Ignorance, he made the powers which are under him, angels and firmaments and all terrestrial things. Then, they say, he united with Presumption and begot Wickedness, Envy, Jealousy, Revenge, and Passion. When these had been born, the mother Sophia, full of grief, fled back and withdrew to the higher regions, and became for those counting from below the Ogdoad. After she had withdrawn, he thought that he was alone and therefore said: 'I am a jealous God (Exod. 20: 5), and beside me there is no one' (Isa. 45: 5; 46: 9). Of such a kind are their lies.

THE APOCRYPHON OF JOHN[2]

(BG 19. 6) It happened on one of these days, when John the brother of James came up—these are the sons of Zebedee—

---

[1] The image of the leap also among the Valentinians, Ir. I 2, 2.

[2] The parallels to the Apocryphon of John in other Coptic gnostic writings are

when (10) he came up to the Temple, there met him a Pharisee named A[ri]manias and said to him: 'Where is your master, whom you followed?' He said (15) to him: 'He is gone again to the place from which he came' (John 16: 5, 28).[3] The Pharisee said to him: 'This Nazarene has led you astray through a deception [and he has . . .] (20. 1) and he has closed [your hearts and] turned you away from the traditions of your fathers.' When I heard this, I turned away (5) from the Temple to the mountain (Mark 13: 3; Acts 1: 12), to a deserted place, and was greatly grieved in my heart and said: 'How was the Saviour appointed? And why was he (10) sent into the world by his Father who sent him? And who is his Father? And of what nature is that aeon to which we shall go? He said to us: (15) "This aeon has taken on the form of that imperishable aeon", and he did not teach us concerning that one, of what nature it is.' Immediately, as I thought this, (20) the heavens opened and the whole creation gleamed in a light which (21. 1) [came down from] heaven, and the [whole] world [trembled]. I was afraid, and [threw myself down]. And behold, a child [appeared] to me. (5) But [I saw] the form as an old man, in whom is light. [I looked] upon him, (but) did not [understand] this wonder, how it is possible for it to be a [unity] although its external forms (10) [in the] light are many. Its external forms [revealed themselves] reciprocally. If it is one, how (then) has it three forms of appearance? He said to me: 'John, (15) why do you doubt?', then: 'Prove yourself, for [this phenomenon] is [indeed not] strange [to you]. Be not faint-hearted, [for] I am with you at all times (Matt. 28: 20). I am (20) [the Father], I am the Mother, I [am the] Son. I am the (22. 1) eternally existing, the unmixable, [since there is none who] mixes with him. [Now I am come] to make known to you [what] exists, and what has come into being, (5) and what is to be (Rev. 1: 19), that you may know the invisible and the visible things, and to [teach you] concerning the perfect man. (10) But now lift up your face [and] come and hear and [know what I] will say to you

presented in our second volume. Round brackets ( ) indicate text inserted for clarification or to complete the sense. Restoration of lacunas in the manuscript has been put in square brackets [ ]; angled brackets ⟨ ⟩ contain text wrongly omitted by the scribe who wrote the manuscript, as can be seen from the parallels.

[3] Cf. Apocryphon of James 2. 19 (Hennecke, *New Testament Apocrypha* I, 336).

today, [that] you may make it known also to your fellow spirits who are of the (15) race, which does not waver, of the perfect man.' And [I said: 'Speak, that I may] know it.' He said to me: 'Over the unity, since it is a monarchy, no one rules. The [true] God, (20) the Father of the All, the Holy Spirit, the invisible, who is over the All, who exists in his imperishability, since he is [in] (23. 1) the pure light into which no eye may look. Concerning him, the Spirit, it is not fitting to think of him as God, or that he (5) is of this sort; for he is more excellent than the gods: he is a kingdom over which none rules. For there is none before him, nor does he need them; he does not even need life, (10) for he is eternal. He needs nothing, for he is not capable of being perfected, since he did not require anything to make him perfect, but is at all times entirely perfection. He is light. (15) He is illimitable, since there is none before him to limit him; not subject to judgement, since there is none before him to judge him; the immeasurable, for (20) no other has measured him as one who was before him; the invisible, because (24. 1) no one has seen him; the eternal, who exists for ever; the indescribable, because none has comprehended him in order to describe him. (He is) the one whose name cannot be named, because (5) there is none who was before him, to give him a name. This is the immeasurable light, the pure holy purity, the indescribable, perfect, imperishable. He is not (10) perfection, nor blessedness, nor divinity, but he is something far more excellent than these. He is neither infinite nor was he ever limited, (15) but he is something more excellent than these. He is not corporeal, nor is he bodiless; not great, nor small, he is not a measurable greatness, nor is he a creature, nor can anyone (20) conceive of him. He is nothing at all that exists, but something more excellent than these. Not as if he were excellent (in himself), but (25. 1) because he is his own, he had no part in an aeon. Time is not a property of his; for he who has part in an aeon, others have (5) prepared him. And time has not been assigned to him, since he has not received from any other who assigns. And he needs nothing. No one at all exists before him. He who (10) craves for himself in the perfection of light knows the unmixed light. The immeasurable greatness, the eternal, the giver of eternity, the light, (15) the bestower of light, the life, the giver of life, the blessed, the giver of blessedness, knowledge, the bestower of knowledge, who is at all times good, who bestows good, who does good; (20) not according to what he has, but according to what he gives; the compassionate compassion, the grace that bestows grace, the immeasurable light. (26. 1) What shall I say to you concerning him, the Inconceivable? He is the image of the Light. According as I shall be able to know him—for who will (5) ever know him?—according as I shall be able to speak with you, ⟨I will say it⟩. His aeon is imperishable, he is in rest, he rests in silence, he who exists before the All (= all things). But he is the head (10) of all the aeons, if there is any other thing with him. For none of us knew how it is with the immeasurable, except him who has dwelt in him. He it is who has told these things to us (John 1: 18). (15) He who perceives himself in his own light which surrounds him—he is the source of the water of life (Rev. 22:1), the light which is full of purity. The fount of the (20) spirit streamed from the living water of life, and he supplied all aeons and (27. 1) worlds in every kind. He knew his own image when he saw it in the pure water of life which surrounds him. And (5) his thought accomplished a work, it revealed itself, stood before him out of the glory of the Light—this is the power which is before the All, which (10) revealed itself, this is the perfect Pronoia of the All, the light, the likeness of the light, the image of the invisible. She is the perfect power, Barbelo, the (15) perfect aeon of glory. She praised him because she was manifested through him, and she knew him. She is the first Ennoia, his image. She became a first Man, which is the virgin spirit, the threefold male, the one (28. 1) with the three powers, the three names, the three begettings, the aeon which does not grow old, the bisexual, which came forth from his Pronoia. And (5) Barbelo asked of him to give her a First Knowledge. He granted it. When he granted it, the First Knowledge was manifested. She took her stand with (10) Ennoia (Thought)—which is Pronoia—praising the Invisible and the perfect power Barbelo, because they had come into being through them. Again this power requested that (15) Incorruptibility be given her. And he granted it. When he granted it, Incorruptibility was manifested. She took her stand with Thought and First Knowledge, praising the Invisible (20) and Barbelo, because she had come into being because of her.

She requested that (29. 1) Eternal Life be given her. He granted it. When he had granted it, Eternal Life was manifested. And they took their stand, (5) praising him and Barbelo, because they had come into being because of her, through the revelation of the invisible spirit. This is the pentad of the aeons of the Father, that is (10) the First Man, the image of the Invisible, which is Barbelo, and Thought and First Knowledge and Incorruptibility and Eternal Life. This (15) is the bisexual pentad, which is the decad of the aeons, which is the Father of the unbegotten Father. (20) Barbelo gazed steadfastly into him, the purity of light. (30. 1) She turned to him, and gave birth to a blessed spark of light, but it was not equal to her in greatness. This is the (5) Only-begotten, who appeared to the Father, the self-originate God, the first-born Son of the All, of the Spirit, of the pure Light. The (10) invisible spirit rejoiced over the light which had come into being, which was first manifested in the first power—which is his Pronoia, Barbelo. And he anointed (15) it with his goodness, so that it became perfect and there was no deficiency in it (and it became) Christ, because he anointed him with his goodness for the invisible spirit. He revealed himself to him and (20) received the anointing through the (31. 1) virginal spirit. He stood before him, praising the invisible spirit and the perfect Pronoia, him in whom he had dwelt. (5) And he requested that one thing be given him, Nous. The invisible spirit granted it. Nous appeared to him (and) took his stand with Christ, praising him and Barbelo. (10) But all these came into being in silence and a thought. The invisible spirit wanted to do a work. His will became embodied (and) was manifested, (and) took his stand with Nous (15) and the light, praising him. The word followed the will, for through the word Christ created all things, the self-originate God, Eternal Life and the will. (20) But Nous and First Knowledge (32. 1) took their stand, praising the invisible spirit and [Barbelo], because through her they had come into being. [He was perfected] through the spirit, the (5) eternal self-originate God, the son of Barbelo, for he came to him, the eternal virgin invisible spirit. It was the self-originate God, Christ, who (10) honoured him with great honour, because he originated from his first thought, he whom the invisible spirit set as God over the All. The (15) true God gave him all power, and caused the truth that is in him to be subject to him, that he might know the All, he whose name will be spoken to those who are worthy of it. (20) But from the light—which is Christ—and Incorruptibility, at the instigation of God (33. 1) [the spirit], his four great lights were manifested out of the self-originate God, that they might stand beside him and (?) the three: Will, (5) Thought, and ⟨Eternal⟩ Life. (5) His four, however, are Grace, Insight, Perception, and Prudence. Grace (is) in the first light Harmozel, which is the angel of the light in (10) the first aeon, in which there are three aeons: Grace, Truth, Form. The second light, Oroiael, which he appointed over the second aeon, (15) has three aeons with it, which are Pronoia, Perception, Recollection. The third light, Davithe, which he appointed over the (20) third aeon, has three aeons with it, which are (34. 1) Insight, Love, [and Idea]. And the light, Eleleth, which he set over the fourth aeon, (5) has three aeons with it, which are Perfection, Peace, and Wisdom. These are the four lights which stand by the self-originate God, the (10) twelve aeons which stand by the child, the great self-originator, Christ, through the resolve of God, the invisible spirit. The twelve aeons belong to the (15) Son, the self-originated. All things became established through the will of the Holy Spirit, through the Self-originate. But from First Knowledge (20) and the perfect Nous, through God (35. 1) and at the resolve of the great invisible spirit and at the resolve of the Self-originate, there (came into being) the perfect true Man, the first (5) manifestation. He called him Adam. He set him over the first aeon with the great God, the Self-originate, Christ, in the first aeon of Harmozel, (10) and his powers are with him. And the invisible spirit gave him an invincible spiritual power. He said: "I honour and praise the invisible spirit, for (15) because of thee did all things come into being, and all things are in thee. But I praise thee and the Self-originate and the aeons, the three, the Father, the Mother, and the Son, (20) the perfect power." And he appointed his son Seth (36. 1) over the second ⟨aeon in the second⟩ light Oroaiel. And in the third aeon were set the seed of Seth, the souls of the (5) holy ones, who are for ever in the third light, Davithe. In the fourth aeon were set the souls which knew their perfection, (10) and did not repent in haste but persisted for a time, yet at last repented. They will remain with the fourth light, Eleleth, which has bound them to itself, (15) while they praise the invisible spirit.

'Now our sister Sophia, who is an aeon, thought a thought of herself. And through the thought of the spirit and of First Knowledge (20) she wanted to reveal (37. 1) the likeness out of herself, although the spirit had not consented or granted it, nor again (5) had her partner consented, the male virgin spirit. So she did not find one in harmony with her, when she was about to concede it without the consent of the spirit and the knowledge of her own (10) partner, when she emitted (?) because of the passion that was in her. Her thought could not be inactive, and her work came forth, incomplete (and) hateful in its (15) appearance, because she had made it without her consort. And it was not like the appearance of the Mother, since it was of another form. But she looked upon it in her considera- tion that it was of the (20) stamp of a different appearance, since it was of the appearance of a serpent and a lion. Its ⟨eyes⟩ (38. 1) shone with fire. She cast it away from herself, out of those places, that none of the immortals (5) might see it, because she had borne it in ignorance. She bound with it a cloud of light. She set a throne in the midst of the cloud, that (10) none might see it except the Holy Spirit—whom they call Zoë (Life), the Mother of all. And she gave it the name Ialdabaoth. This is the first (15) Archon, who drew a great power from the mother. He removed himself from her. He turned away from the place in which he had been born. He (39. 1) took possession of another place. He made for himself an aeon, flaming with shining fire, in which he now dwells. And he (5) united himself with the Unreason which is with him. He brought into being the powers that are under him, twelve angels, each one of them for his aeon after the pattern of the (10) incorruptible aeons. And he created for each one of them seven angels, and for the angels three powers, so that all who are under him (15) produce 360 angelic beings and his third power, according to the appear- ance of the first pattern, which was before him. Now when the powers made their appearance (40. 1) out of the First Begetter, the first archon of darkness, out of the ignorance of him who begot them, their names were these: the (5) first is Jaoth, the second is Hermas—which is the eye of the fire—the third is Galila, the fourth is Jobel, the fifth is Adonaios, (10) the sixth is

Sabaoth, the seventh is Kainan and Kae, who is called Cain—
which is the sun—the eighth is Abiressine, (15) the ninth is
Jobel, the tenth is Harmupiael, the eleventh is Adonin, the
twelfth is Belias. But they all have other names also from desire
(41. 1) and from wrath. All these also have other, double names
which are given to them. These were given to them by the glory
of the heaven, (5) but these correspond to the truth, which
reveals their nature. And Saklas called them by these names
according to appearance and their power. Through the times
(10) they withdraw and grow weak, but through these (again)
they become powerful and increase. And he commanded that
seven kings should rule over the heaven, and five (15) over the
chaos of the underworld. The names of glory of those who are
over the seven heavens are these: the first is Jaoth, the lion-
faced; the second is Eloaios, the ass-faced; (20) the third is
(42. 1) Astaphaios, the hyena-faced; the fourth is Iao, the
serpent-faced with seven heads; the fifth is Adonaios, the dragon-
faced; the sixth is (5) Adoni, the ape-faced; the seventh is
Sabbataios, with the face of flaming fire. This is the hebdomad
of the week. These are they who control the (10) world. But
Ialdabaoth—Saklas—the many-formed, so that he shows himself in every form according to his pleasure, assigned to them
some of his fire which belongs to him, (15) and his power. But
of the pure light of the power which he had drawn from the
Mother he did not give them. Therefore he lorded it over them,
because of the (43. 1) [glory which] was in him from the power
of [the light] of the Mother. Because of this he had himself called
"God", being disobedient (5) to the substance out of which he
had come into being. And he combined with the authorities
seven powers. By the fact that he spoke they came into being.
And he gave them names (and) set up (10) authorities. He
began from above. The first, then, is Pronoia with the first,
Jaoth; the second is Divinity with the second (15), Eloaios; the
third is Goodness with the third, Astaphaios; the fourth is Fire
with the fourth, Iao; the fifth is the (20) Kingdom with the
fifth, Sabaoth; (44. 1) the sixth is [Insight] with the sixth,
A[doni]; the seventh is Wisdom with the seventh, Sabbataios.
(5) These have a firmament in each heaven, and an aeon after
the likeness of the aeons, which exists from the beginning in the
type of the incorruptibles. But he saw (10) the creation which

is under him, and the multitude of angels under him, who originated from him, and he said to them: "I am a jealous God (Exod. 20: 5), (15) apart from me there is none" (Isa. 45: 5; 46: 9), already indicating to the angels under him that there is another God; for if there was no other, of whom should he be jealous?

'The Mother now began (45. 1) to be agitated, knowing her deficiency, since her consort had not concurred with her when (5) she was degraded from her perfection.'

But I said: 'Christ, what does "be agitated" mean?' He smiled and said: 'Do you think that it is as Moses said, (10) "over the waters"? (Gen. 1: 2). No, but she saw the wickedness and the apostasy which would attach to her son. She repented, and as she went to and fro in the darkness (15) of ignorance she began to be ashamed and did not dare to return, but went to and fro. Her going and coming is "to be agitated". (20) Now when the (46. 1) Self-willed had received a power from the Mother, he was ignorant of a multitude which are superior to his mother. For he thought of his (5) mother that she alone existed. He saw the great multitude of angels which he had created, and exalted himself above them. But when the Mother (10) recognized that the abortion of darkness was not perfect, because her consort had not concurred with her, she repented (and) wept bitterly. (15) He heard the prayer of her repentance, and the brethren prayed for her. The holy invisible spirit assented. (20) Now when (47. 1) the invisible spirit assented, he poured upon her a spirit from the perfection. Her consort came down to her (5) in order to put right her deficiency. He resolved to put right her deficiency through a Pronoia, and she was not brought up to her own aeon, but (10) because of the great ignorance which had become manifest in her she is in the nonad until she puts right her deficiency. A voice came to her: (15) "Man exists, and the Son of man." The first archon, Ialdabaoth, heard it (and) thought that the voice [came (20) from his mother]. (48. 1) The holy perfect Father, the first man, [taught] him in the form of a man. The blessed one revealed (5) to them his face. And the whole archon company of the seven powers assented. They saw in the water the likeness of the image. (10) They said to one another: "Let us make a man after the image of God and his likeness" (Gen. 1: 26). They

created out of (15) themselves and all their powers. They
moulded out of themselves a creature, and each one of the
[powers] (49. 1) [created out of its] power [a soul]. They
created it after the image which they had seen, in imitation of
(5) him who exists from the beginning, the perfect Man. They
said: "Let us call him Adam, that his name and his power may
become for us light." And the powers (10) began from below.
The first is Divinity, a bone-soul; the second is Lordship, a
sinew-soul; the third is (15) fire, a flesh-soul; the fourth is
Pronoia, a marrow-soul, and the whole structure of the body;
the fifth is the Kingdom, (50. 1) a [blood-]soul; the sixth is
Insight, a skin-soul; the seventh is Wisdom, a hair-soul. (5)
And they adorned the whole body. And their angels stood by
them. ⟨They created out of the souls⟩, which had first been
prepared by the powers, the (10) soul-substance, the arrangement of the limbs ⟨and⟩ the joints. And they created the whole
body, which was fitted together by the multitude of angels
which I have already mentioned.

'(15) And it lay for a long time without moving, since the
seven powers were not able to raise it up, nor were the 360
angels who fitted together (51. 1) [the joints. The Mother wanted
to recover again] the power which she had given to the archon
in compulsive desire. She came in innocence (5) and prayed
the Father of the All, whose mercy is great, and the God of
light. He sent, by a holy decree, the Self-originate and (10) the
four lights in the form of angels of the first archon. They gave
him advice, so that they might bring out of him the power of
the Mother. They said to him: (15) "Breathe into his face
something of the spirit that is in you (Gen. 2: 7), and the thing
will raise itself up." And he breathed into it of his spirit—
which is the power of the Mother—(20) into the body, and it
moved (52. 1) at [once. And] immediately [the rest of the]
powers became jealous, because it came into being from them
all and they gave (5) to the man the powers which derive from
them; and he bore the souls of the seven powers and their
abilities. His understanding became far stronger than all of
them (10), (stronger) than the first archon. But they recognized
that he was free from wickedness, since he was more clever than
they and (15) had come into the light. They took him and
brought him down to the regions beneath all matter. But the

blessed Father is a merciful benefactor. (20) He took pity on the power (53. 1) [of the Mother] which had been brought out from the [first archon], that it might prevail over the body. He sent out the (5) good spirit and his great mercy as a helper for the first who had come down, who was called Adam, (namely) the Epinoia of light, who (10) was called by him Zoë (Life). But it is she who works at the whole creation, labouring at it, setting it up in her own perfect temple and (15) enlightening it concerning the coming down of its deficiency and showing it its way upwards. And the Epinoia of light was hidden in him, that (20) the archons might not know but (54. 1) our sister, who [is like] us, might put right her deficiency through the Epinoia of light. (5) And the man shone because of the shadow of the light which is in him, and his thought was exalted above those who had created him. And they looked up. They (10) saw the man. He had exalted himself far above them. They made a resolve with the whole angelic company of the archons and the rest of their powers. Then (15) they mingled fire and earth with water and flame. They bound them together with the four winds, breathing in fire, uniting with one another, (55. 1) and causing [a great] confusion. [They brought him] into the shadow of death. They made again another creature; but out of earth (5) and water, fire and wind, that is, out of matter, darkness, desire, and the antagonist spirit—this is the fetter, (10) this is the tomb of the creation of the body, which was put upon the man as a fetter of matter. This is the first who came down, and (15) his first disruption. But the Ennoia of the first light is in him, and revives his thought. The first archon brought him and (20) set him in Paradise, (56. 1) of which he said that it was a delight for him, which means that it would deceive him; for their delight is bitter and their (5) beauty is unseemly. Their delight is deception, and their tree was hostility. Their fruit was a poison against which there is no cure, and their promise was (10) death for him. But their tree which they have appointed is the tree of life (cf. Gen. 2: 8 ff.).

'I will make known to you the secret of their life, which is their counterfeit spirit (15) which derives from them that it may turn him away, in order that he may not recognize his perfection. That tree is of the following nature: its root is bitter, its branches are (20) shadows of death, its (57. 1) leaves are hate and deception, its sap is a balm of wickedness, and its fruit is the desire of (5) death. Its seed drinks of those who taste it, the underworld is their dwelling-place. But the tree which is called by them (10) "to know good and evil" (Gen. 2: 9), this is the Epinoia of light; because of it they gave command not to taste, that is (15) not to listen to it, since the command is directed against him that he may not look upwards to his perfection, and recognize his deprivation of perfection. (20) But I have raised them up, (58. 1) to make them eat.'

I said to him: 'Christ, was it not the serpent who instructed her?' He smiled and said: 'The serpent (5) taught her the sowing of the desire of defilement and corruption, for they are useful to it. And it knew that she would not listen to it, since she (10) is much more clever than it. It wanted to bring out the power which had been given him by him. And he cast an oblivion upon Adam.'

I said to him: (15) 'Christ, what is oblivion?' And he said: 'Not as Moses said: "He caused him to fall asleep" (Gen. 2: 21), but he covered his perception (20) with a veil, he weighed him down with (59. 1) a stupor. For indeed he said through the prophet: "I will make heavy the ears of their heart, that (5) they may not understand and may not see" (Isa. 6: 10). Then the Epinoia of light hid herself in him (Adam). And in his will he (Ialdabaoth) resolved to bring her out from the rib. But she, (10) the Epinoia of light, is unattainable. When the darkness pursued after her, it could not reach her (John 1: 5). He decided to bring the power out of him, to make a creature once again (15) with a female form. And he made her rise up before him. Not as Moses said: "He took a rib, made the woman, ⟨and left her⟩ beside him" (Gen. 2: 21–2). (20) At once he became sober from the intoxication of darkness. She (60. 1), the Epinoia of light, took away the veil that was upon his mind. At once, when he knew his substance, he said: "This is (5) now bone of my bone, and flesh of my flesh (Gen. 2: 23). For this reason man will leave his father and mother and cleave (10) to his wife, and the two will become one flesh" (Gen. 2: 24), for they will send out the consort of the Mother and raise her up. (15) Because of this Adam called her "the mother of all living" (Gen. 3: 20). Through the authority of the height and the revelation the Epinoia taught him about knowledge.

(61. 1) Through the tree in the form of an eagle she instructed him to eat of knowledge, that he might remember (5) his perfection; for the fault of both was ignorance.

'Ialdabaoth recognized that they withdrew from him. He cursed (10) them, but he also added this, that the man should be master of the woman (Gen. 3: 16), since he did not know the secret which had come into being through the (15) decree of the holy height. But they were afraid to curse him and to expose his ignorance. All his angels cast (62. 1) them out of the Paradise (Gen. 3: 23). He wrapped him in murky darkness. Then Ialdabaoth saw the maiden who stood beside Adam. (5) He became full of stupidity, since he wished to raise up seed from her. He defiled her and begot the first son, likewise (10) the second: Jave the bear-faced and Elohim the cat-faced. The one indeed is righteous, but the other unrighteous. Elohim is the righteous, Jave is the (15) unrighteous. The righteous he set over the fire and the wind, the unrighteous he set over the water and the earth. These are they who (20) by all generations of men (63. 1) are called Cain and Abel to the present day. Marital intercourse came into being through the first (5) archon. He planted in Adam a desire of seed, so that it is this which through marital intercourse brings forth a likeness from their counterfeit ⟨spirit⟩. But the two (10) archons he set over kingdoms, that they might rule over the grave. He knew his substance, which is like him. Adam begot Seth. And (15) as with the race which is in heaven among the aeons, so the Mother sent ⟨the spirit⟩ which belongs to her. The spirit came down to her, to rouse up the substance which is like (64. 1) him, after the pattern of the perfection, to rouse them out of the forgetfulness and wickedness of the grave. And so he remained for a time (5) (and) worked for the seed, in order that when the spirit comes from the holy aeons he may raise them up out of the deficiency (10) to the standing of aeons, that he may become a holy perfection, that he may become now without defect.'

But I said: 'Christ, (15) will the souls of all be saved into the pure light?'[4] He said to me: 'You have come to a consideration of great things, such as are difficult to reveal (20) to

---

[4] In the text the wording of the other version in Codex III from Nag Hammadi has been printed. The text of the Berlin papyrus, 'Christ, will the souls of all live more than the purity of light?', diverges and is probably corrupt.

others, except (65. 1) to those who are of that race which does not waver. Those on whom the spirit of life comes down and who have united (5) with the power will be saved, become perfect, and become worthy to go up to the great lights; for they will be worthy to purify themselves with them (10) from all wickedness and the seductions of evil, in that they set their hearts on nothing except the imperishable gathering and concern themselves with it, without (15) anger, envy, fear, desire, and satiety. By all these they are not affected, nor by anything else except (20) the flesh alone, (66. 1) of which they make use while they watch for (the time when) they will be brought out and taken up (5) by the Receivers into the dignity of the eternal incorruptible life and the calling; they endure all things and bear all things, (10) in order that they may finish the fight and inherit eternal life.'

I said: 'Christ, if they have not done this, what will the souls (15) do into which the power and the spirit of life has come, that they too may be saved?' He said to me: (67. 1) 'Those to whom that spirit has come will in any case live, and these come out of wickedness; for the power (5) comes into every man, for without it they could not stand. But after it has been born, then the spirit of life is brought to it. (10) Now if the strong divine spirit has come to the life, it strengthens the power—which is the soul—and it does not go astray to evil. But with those (15) into whom the counterfeit spirit enters, it is seduced by it and goes astray.'

But I said: 'Christ, (68. 1) when the souls of these come out of the flesh, where will they go?' But he smiled and said: 'To a place of the soul (5) which is the power that was far superior to the counterfeit spirit. This is strong; it escapes from the works of wickedness and (10) through the imperishable oversight it is delivered and brought up to the repose of the aeons.'

But I said: 'Christ, those who have known nothing at all— (15) what are their souls, or where will they go?' He said to me: 'Over these a counterfeit spirit gained the mastery as (69. 1) they stumbled. And in this way it weighs down their soul and draws it to the works of wickedness, and thus brings it (5) to oblivion. After it (the soul) has unclothed itself, it (the counterfeit spirit) hands it over to the powers which came into being under the archon. Again, they are flung into (10) chains and dragged about, until they are delivered from the oblivion and it receives knowledge and so becomes perfect and saved.'

But I said: 'Christ, (15) how does the soul shrivel up and go again into the nature of the Mother or the Man?' But he rejoiced when I asked him, and said: (70. 1) 'You are blessed with an understanding. Because of this they are given to the other, in whom the spirit of life is, for (5) obedience to him. And if it hears through him, it is saved. It does not, however, go into another flesh.'

I said to him: 'Christ, but those who knew (10) and turned away—what are their souls?' He said to me: 'These will go to the place to which the angels of poverty will withdraw, to whom (15) no repentance has been accorded. They will be kept until the day on which they are punished. Every one who has spoken against the Holy Spirit (Matt. 12: 31 f. par.) will be (71. 1) tormented in eternal punishment.'

But I said: 'Christ, whence came the counterfeit (5) spirit?' He said to me: 'When the Mother, whose mercy is great, and the Holy Spirit, the compassionate, who exhausted himself with us—he is the Epinoia of light—(10) and the seed which he awakened in the thought of the men of the race of the perfect eternal man of light (*text corrupt*), then the (15) first archon recognized that they surpassed him in the height of their wisdom. He wanted to take possession of their power of thought. Since he is ignorant, he did not know (72. 1) that they are more cunning than he. He formed a resolve with his powers. They brought Heimarmene into being. And (5) with a measure, times, and seasons they bound the gods of heaven, angels, demons, and men, that they might all be in its (i.e. Heimarmene: Fate) (10) fetter and it be lord over them all—a plan wicked and perverse. And he repented (Gen. 6: 6) of all that had come into being through him. He (15) resolved to bring a flood upon the whole pride of mankind. And the greatness of Pronoia—which is the Epinoia of light—(73. 1) communicated it to Noah. He proclaimed it to men, and they did not believe him. Not as Moses (5) said: "He hid himself in an ark" (Gen. 7: 7), but he sheltered in a place. Not Noah only, but (several) men from the race that does not waver (10) went to a place (and) covered themselves with a cloud of light. And he knew his lordship, with those who were with him in (15) the light that

shone for them; for darkness was poured out upon everything
on the earth. He made a resolve with his angels. (74. 1) They
sent their angels to the daughters of men (Gen. 6: 4), that they
might raise up seed from them for their (5) pleasure. And at
first they had no success. And they came, having all resolved to
create the counterfeit spirit, remembering the (10) spirit which
came down. And the angels changed their form to the likeness
of their husbands ⟨and⟩ filled them with the spirit, which tormented them (15) in the darkness. Out of wickedness they
brought them gold, silver, gifts, and the metals: copper and
iron and all kinds. (75. 1) They led them into temptation, that
they might not think of their Pronoia, which does not waver.
And they took them and begot children (5) out of the darkness
from their counterfeit spirit. They closed their hearts. They
became hard through the hardening of the counterfeit spirit
(10) to this day. The blessed one—that is, the Father-Mother—
whose mercy is great, took form in their seed. First I came up
to the (15) perfect aeon. But I tell you this that you may write
it down and give it to your kindred spirits in secret. For this
mystery (20) belongs to the race that does not (76. 1) waver.

'But the Mother came once again before me. These are the
things which she has done in the world: she has raised up her
(5) seed. I will proclaim to you what will happen; for indeed
I have given you this to write it down, and it shall be securely
stored away.'

Then he said to (10) me: 'Cursed is everyone who gives these
for a gift, or for food or drink or clothing, or for anything else
(15) of the sort.'

He gave him (John) the secret, ⟨and⟩ immediately became
invisible to him. And he (John) (77. 1) came to his fellow
disciples. He began to tell them what had been said to him by
(15) the Saviour.

The secret book of John.

8

VALENTINIANISM I
THE SYSTEM OF PTOLEMAEUS

VALENTINUS AND HIS SCHOOL

We have more accounts of Valentinus and his school in the Church Fathers, and more literal quotations as well, than we have of any other gnostic teacher. In addition, we have a Coptic text which comes from Valentinus himself or from disciples closely associated with him, and also other Coptic writings which are to be attributed to his school. As a result of this, we are comparatively well informed about Valentinian Gnosis. Apart from the so-called Gospel of Truth, the origin of which is not definitely attributable to Valentinus, we have only a few fragments from the leader of this strand of Gnosis, Valentinus, and it is only with difficulty that we can form a picture of him. At all events, he was born in Egypt and became familiar \ with Greek culture in Alexandria. His eloquence is frequently stressed by the Fathers. In this connection Jerome says:[1] 'No one can bring a heresy into being unless he is possessed, by nature, of an outstanding intellect and has gifts provided by God. Such a person was Valentinus.' When we are told that he also composed psalms,[2] that is probably true. He is said to have come to Rome later and, because of his intellectual and spiritual gifts, to have had expectations of becoming a bishop. When a martyr was given preference over him, he is said to have separated himself from the church.[3] This would probably be the choice of Pius in A.D. 143.[4] His teacher is reputed to have been Theodas.[5] He is said to have worked under Anicetus (A.D. 154–65). Among his pupils were Ptolemaeus, Heracleon, Secundus, Marcus, Theotimus, and Axionicus; the last-mentioned is reputed to have preserved most faithfully the genuine teaching of his master;[6] another account mentions also (B)Ardesianus.[7]

[1] *In Hos.* 11, 10.
[2] Tert., *De carne Christi* 17 and Orig., *Enarr. in John* 21, 11.
[3] Tert., *Adv. Valent.* 4.   [4] Ir. III 4, 3.
[5] Cl. Al., *Strom.* VII 17 = § 106, 4. The report that he was excluded in the Episcopate of Eleutherus (Tert., *Praescr. Haer.* 30, 2) is not credible.
[6] Tert., *Adv. Valent.* 4.   [7] Hipp. VI 35, 7.

It is common to the teaching of all Valentinians that the heavenly world, the Pleroma, contains (at least) thirty aeons, thirty worlds. One aeon, or one world, is called Silence, another Truth, and yet another Man and Church, worlds which, however, are not employed simply as abstract entities. Two Tetrads are stressed, and these together are called an Ogdoad.[8] Furthermore, from the last of the aeons, Sophia, there proceeds the Fall and, in the long run, the creation of the world. Between the pneumatics and the choics the Valentinians set, additionally, an intermediate class, the psychics, and to them they granted a graded salvation, not of course in the Pleroma, and accordingly they ascribed to the Demiurge a friendly attitude towards the pneumatics, so far as the end-effect is concerned at any rate. Consequently, a triadic note runs through the Valentinian system, and, for example, the letter of Ptolemaeus to Flora and the account of Irenaeus show this clearly. An important feature, deriving perhaps from Valentinus himself, is that the world owes its continued existence to error or ignorance: if error were to be removed, then all that has its existence by reason of it would be destroyed; which in the most distinctive form of Valentinianism is expressed as follows: the fire of ignorance lies at the root of everything in the world and this fire will one day bring the world back to nothingness and will itself also be extinguished. One effect of this conception is that matter becomes only a necessary product of the intellectual reality of ignorance, or error, not the bearer of what is truly evil.

Valentinus is supposed to have created his system, not *ex nihilo*, but in dependence upon another system.[9] It could have been that of the Ophites, which Valentinianism changed in the following ways: it introduces first of all the Pleroma, with its thirty aeons, and thus makes it larger. Wisdom, the last of these aeons, falls, though not completely, for it is restored again, and only its 'abortion' or its 'thought' cannot remain in the Pleroma. The 'abortion' is finally given form by the Saviour and by it the world and its creator are fashioned: the world and its history stand, from the beginning, under the control of Sophia and, in the last analysis, of the Saviour: thus it does not now come to a struggle between Ialdabaoth and the Mother. The paradise story recedes into the background, and over the whole there lies a gentler disposition which reveals itself also in the special place of the psychics. The Devil as the arch villain also recedes. It seems as if the development of these ideas proceeded only gradually: consequently we shall touch on the probable evolution of the Valentinian system only at the end.

---

[8] Summary of the different Ogdoads in Sagnard, *Gnose Valentinienne* 255–7.

[9] Tert., *Adv. Valent.* 4: He found the seed of an older doctrine.

THE ACCOUNT OF IRENAEUS

In accordance with the triadic theme which runs through the Valentinian system, everything takes place on three levels, all three of which are non-material. Irenaeus' account begins with Bythos and Sige, that is, with the Primal Cause and Silence. The two names—beside which stand others which have been chosen from the Prologue to the Gospel of John or for some other consideration—signify that no one and nothing can fathom this Primal Cause or break the Silence. Thus it is during endless ages; and then Bythos brings forth through Silence a couple (*syzygy*) called Nous and Truth. In this connection one should keep in mind the fact that not only the Primal Cause and Silence, but Nous and Truth as well, though they are counted as two and treated as two, in fact form a single male-female substance or entity: this should be borne in mind in all that follows. Nous alone comprehends Bythos. Nous appears many times in a special position. It cannot signify the organ of philosophical inquiry which seeks to grasp the supreme God; rather it indicates the central faculty of the gnostic, and, in fact, 'understanding' (*Verständnis*) rather than 'intellect' (*Verstand*) would be a suitable translation. In point of fact, Nous is not translated. Nous brings forth Logos and Zoë, that is, the Word and Life, and these produce Man and Church. These are the two Tetrads which together make up the Ogdoad. The names of the aeons proceed from cause to effect, and correspond to the names and concepts which emerge in the Prologue to the Gospel of John, where the 'Only-begotten' takes the place of Nous, which does not occur there. These desire to praise the Forefather, Bythos, and bring forth aeons, Logos and Life ten, and Man and Church twelve. The ten aeons bear in the female series names which suggest the union of man and woman, whereas the twelve aeons derived from Man and Church have names which recall the Christian virtues. Their origin from a father and mother gives to them their 'formation according to substance', but, on the express desire of the Father, the 'formation according to knowledge' is not given to them: this is certainly not stated in the same words, but it follows from the system as a whole; for the two formations, that according to substance and that according to knowledge, are uniformly differentiated at the three stages of the system.

The last and youngest of the aeons, Sophia, called Wisdom, wished to know the Father, and that was certainly an impossible undertaking. By means of Horos, Limit, she is drawn away from her senseless project and convinced that the Father is incomprehensible: she lays aside the idea of knowing the Father, and, at the same time, the passionate enthusiasm with which she had pursued it.

Now the purpose of Sophia, together with the passion with which it was pursued, is ultimately the cause of the origin of the world. Let us make clear at this point what this means: ignorance with regard to the supreme God has resulted in *one* aeon desiring to know him: this aeon is called Sophia (Wisdom) probably because in her preposterous effort the desire of Greek philosophy—to know God—is condemned.[10] And this perverse attempt is in fact lack of knowledge concerning God, and from it follows everything else.

After Sophia had been freed from the purpose which clung to her, Nous, the Only-begotten as he is also called, brought forth another pair of aeons, Christ and the Holy Spirit. He brought to the aeons the knowledge of the Primal Cause, to the effect that he is not to be grasped, but known only through Nous. Now the 'formation according to knowledge' is given to them as well, and all become alike in knowledge; and then the aeons all together bring forth for the Father, as the fairest thing they have, the 'fruit', Jesus. That he is without a female associate is only temporary. Along with him the accompanying angels were created. This is what happens at the first stage. Here already it is evident that the 'full existence in the Pleroma' is a matter of (intuitive) knowledge and that what prevents it from being realized is ignorance, error, and passion. These can be simply stripped away.

Thus the purpose of Sophia is separated from her and outside the Pleroma, and since it is born of a female only, without the aid of a male, it is completely without form and shape. Christ and the Holy Spirit extend themselves outwards over the Pleroma and give to it the 'formation according to substance', and the purpose or thought, which is now called Achamoth (*Chokhma* is Hebrew for Wisdom), becomes an independent substance. Christ and the Holy Spirit immediately draw back again into the Pleroma, and Achamoth, becoming conscious of that, falls into all sorts of distress: the passion is now dissolved, as it were, into its contributory aspects. These are called sorrow, fear, and distress, but all in ignorance. These still belong, as it were, to her, and only the pining after Christ impels her towards the Pleroma, but she cannot enter it because of the 'Limit'. She remains surrounded by passions, but there comes upon her another disposition too, namely, that of turning (conversion) to him who makes alive. At her request, the Saviour named Jesus is sent to her with his accompanying angels, and he gives to Achamoth the 'formation in accordance with knowledge' and releases her from the passions. The saving activity of the Saviour thus consists in the giving

[10] G. Quispel, *Gnosis als Weltreligion* 87–9; J. Zandee, 'Gnostic Ideas . . .', *Numen* 11 (1964), 23.

of knowledge and in the stripping away of the passions. Achamoth now gives birth to fruits, which are as spiritual as the Saviour and his attendants. The Saviour makes the separated passions into incorporeal matter, with result that, in principle, he has created everything.

Achamoth can now give form. Out of her 'turning towards' (or: 'conversion')—whose separation from Achamoth has not been expressly mentioned by Irenaeus—she forms the Demiurge, who, in due course, gives form to everything further. To be sure, his giving form is not an independent creative act, for he performs everything just as Achamoth desires, only he does not know that. So he creates the Right and the Left, that is, the psychic and the hylic realms, and man as well—but all of them are still in the realm of the not seen; only thereafter does he make bodies out of incorporeal matter and put on man the 'coat of skin', that is, the tangible flesh. But something spiritual was introduced into some men by Achamoth, and it was done invisibly, that is, without the Demiurge noticing it. There are thus three classes of men: all men share in flesh and 'dust'; many have in addition souls from the Demiurge; but not many have a spiritual part as well. Matter and flesh perish by nature, for, in the last analysis, they derive from passion, and it must disappear. That which is spiritual cannot perish, for, as the saying goes, it is 'delivered by nature' and is destined for entry into the Pleroma. Only the psychic has free will, by reason of which it can turn either towards passion—in which case it perishes—or towards the 'better', and then it has its lot cast with the Demiurge. Here on earth, that which is spiritual is 'yoked together' with what is psychic in order to be trained together with it in conduct. A reason for the spiritual requiring this training is not directly obvious: for the companions of the Saviour are in fact created in the Pleroma, and it is in this way that Achamoth, after being separated from her passions by the Saviour, conceives the spiritual seed. But according to the system in its entirety *this* spiritual element also must acquire both the 'formation according to substance'—which takes place with birth—and that 'in accordance with knowledge', and its being yoked together with what is psychic is said to prepare for the latter. Probably it is like this: just as the passions which surround her became a reason for the mother to request the Saviour, so also the struggle with the passions which the psychic yoked with the spiritual engages in is meant to lead to the turning towards the Redeemer. But the fact remains: that which is spiritual is spiritual and enters in any case into the Pleroma. It is not clear when the 'formation in accordance with knowledge' takes place, but it must certainly be associated with the coming of Jesus. The statements relating to this, however, are not quite clear.

The Saviour is composed of four ingredients: he is the 'Saviour', he has put on from the mother the spiritual part, then from the Demiurge he has put on the psychic Christ and a body which was prepared with ineffable art in such a way that it was visible, tangible, and capable of suffering. It is this passible part which died on the cross, and this part will be raised up by a ray of the power of Jesus, the Saviour, after he has destroyed death. On the 'salvation' of what is spiritual there are several speculative views. At one point it is said that Jesus also saved what he assumed, but that idea is not pursued any further. Then it is said that the spiritual is, as it were, marrow in the bones of the psychic and is not broken up; and again it is said that the spiritual needs wisdom and that it thus stands in need of the 'formation according to knowledge'. The saved psychics accompany the pneumatics into the Ogdoad, the Eight, the sphere above the planets where the mother Achamoth is. The pneumatics have the souls as garments. When the end of the world comes, the pneumatics will then throw off these souls and enter with Achamoth into the Pleroma. The mother then receives as her bridegroom Jesus, and the pneumatics become the brides of the angels who accompany the Saviour. The visible world is consumed by the fire of ignorance, and simultaneously with the fire. The system in Irenaeus is thus based on and controlled by ignorance and knowledge. In the last resort, it is lack of knowledge of the Father which sets in motion the creation of the world.

A word has yet to be said about the Demiurge. The fact that he (and his angels?) is the creator of the world is common gnostic teaching. But that he takes up an intermediate position is striking, as also is the way in which this intermediate position is worked out. For, at least according to the wording of Irenaeus, no ruler of *this* world is appointed beside him, and it is he himself who creates 'the Left and the Right'. That, according to the system, it is Achamoth who does it secretly is another feature which arouses astonishment. That the Demiurge then knows nothing is only consistent, for otherwise the world would not in fact be evil and condemned to destruction. However, his fate and that of the psychics is worthy of note: they obtain a 'salvation', but it is outside the Pleroma. What then still exists after the fire has consumed the world, matter in its entirety? They reach a position for which probably a Jewish periphrasis for God—'the place'—is used. It is the Ogdoad, and ought thus to be the sphere of the fixed stars, but more probably it is thought of as the region beyond the stars. The system in Irenaeus calls it 'the Middle'. But in the end there is no Middle any more! The anti-cosmic attitude of the gnostics also is moderated here. The Demiurge controls everything in the world in accordance with his care for the community or church (of the gnostics), and this is an attitude which is remarkably exceptional in the whole of Gnosis. In addition there is the fact that, as the letter of Ptolemaeus to Flora shows, no strongly emphasized libertinism and no strongly emphasized asceticism is represented.

All of this points to the conclusion that with ideas like these the aim was accommodation to mainstream Christianity.

Irenaeus, *Adv. Haer.* I 1, 1–8, 6 (Selection) = Epiphanius, *Panarion* XXXI 9, 1–27, 16

1, 1. They say that there exists in the invisible and ineffable heights a pre-existent, perfect aeon, whom they also call Pre-beginning, Forefather, and Primal Cause (Bythos). . . . He is incomprehensible and invisible, eternal and ungenerated, and he has existed in profound stillness and serenity for infinite aeons. Along with him there existed also Ennoia (Thought), whom they also name Grace and Silence (Sige). Once upon a time Bythos determined to produce from himself the beginning of all things and, like a seed, he deposited this production which he had resolved to bring forth, as in a womb, in that Sige who was with him. She then, on receiving this seed, became pregnant and gave birth to Nous, who was both like and equal to him who produced him, and who alone comprehended the greatness of his father. This Nous they also call Only-begotten, and Father, and Beginning of all. Along with him there was produced Truth, and this makes up the first and original Pythagorean Tetrad, which they also call the root of all things: Primal Cause and Silence, then Nous and Truth.

When the Only-begotten perceived for what purpose he had been produced he himself brought forth Logos and Life, since he was the father of all things that come into being after him, as well as the beginning and forming of the whole Pleroma. From the union of Logos and Life there was produced another pair, Man and Church. This constitutes the primordial Ogdoad, the root and substance of all things, which they call by four names: Bythos, Nous, Logos, and Man. Each of these is male-female, in the following way: first, the Forefather was united with his Ennoia, then the Only-begotten, that is Nous, with Truth, then Logos with Life, and finally Man with the Church.

2. These aeons, brought forth for the glory of the Father, themselves desired to praise the Father by their own efforts,

and they produced emanations by means of uniting. Logos and Life, after having brought forth Man and Church, produced ten other aeons whose names are as follows: Deep and Mingling, Unageing and Union, Self-existent and Pleasure, Immovable and Blending, Only-begotten and Blessed. These are the ten aeons which, according to them, were produced from Logos and Life. Man with the Church also produced twelve aeons, on which they bestow the following names: Paraclete and Faith, Paternal and Hope, Maternal and Love, Everlasting Nous and Intelligence, Ecclesiastical and Blessedness, Desired and Sophia (Wisdom).

3. These are the thirty aeons of their erroneous system, concerning whom silence prevails and consequently they are not known. This is the invisible and spiritual Pleroma which is divided into three, namely, an Ogdoad, a Decad, and a Duodecad. It was for this reason, they say, that the Saviour—for they do not wish to call him Lord—did nothing in public for thirty years, thus setting forth the mystery of these aeons. In the parable of the labourers in the vineyard (Matt. 20: 1–16) these thirty aeons are clearly indicated (according to them) for some are sent (to the vineyard) about the first hour, others about the third, and others about the sixth, ninth, and eleventh hours, and when the hours named are totalled up they make the number of thirty—for $1+3+6+9+11$ equals 30. By means of the hours they wish to see the aeons indicated. These are the great, wonderful, and unspeakable mysteries which they themselves invent wherever in the Scriptures something is indicated by numbers and can be accommodated or adapted to their speculative fiction.

2, 1. This Forefather of theirs, they maintain, was known only to the Only-begotten who came into existence from him, that is, to Nous, while to all others he was invisible and incomprehensible. And Nous alone took pleasure in beholding the Father and rejoiced in perceiving his immeasurable greatness. He proposed to communicate to the rest of the aeons the greatness of the Father—how mighty and vast he was, and how he was without beginning, beyond comprehension, and incapable of being seen. But, by the will of the Father, Sige (Silence) restrained him, because he desired to lead them all to the comprehension of and an ardent longing for the aforementioned

Forefather. Likewise, the rest of the aeons quietly wished to see the one who had produced their seed and to acquire knowledge of the root which had no beginning.

2. The very last and youngest aeon of the Duodecad, which had been produced from Man and Church, that is Sophia, rushed forth in advance and experienced a passion apart from the embrace of her consort 'Desired'. This (passion) in fact began among those associated with Nous and Truth, but burst forth in this erring aeon, on the pretext of love, but (in reality) out of temerity, because she had no communion with the perfect Father such as Nous shared. The passion is said to be the search after the Father, for she wished, according to them, to comprehend his greatness. Since she was unable to do this, because she had undertaken an impossible task, she was in very deep distress, because of the greatness of the depth and the inscrutability of the Father, and because of her love for him. Consequently she was ever extending herself further and further forwards and would have been finally absorbed by his sweetness and dissolved in his total essence, if she had not encountered the power which supports all things and keeps them outside the unutterable greatness. This power they name Horos (Limit). By it she was halted, supported, and, with difficulty, brought back to herself and convinced that the Father is incomprehensible. So she laid aside her original purpose, together with the passion which had arisen from that stupefied wonder. 3. Some of them recount the passion of Sophia and her restoration as follows. . . . 4. . . . By this Horos (Limit)—so they claim—Sophia was purified, established, and restored to her partner. For when the desire had been separated from her, along with the supervening passion, she herself remained within the Pleroma, but her desire, with the passion, was separated from her by Horos, fenced off, and left outside it (the Pleroma). It was indeed a spiritual substance, since it was the natural instinct of an aeon, but it was without shape and form, because it understood nothing. Therefore they call it a frail and female fruit. 5. After the substance had been separated from the Pleroma of the aeons and its mother restored to her own partner, the Only-begotten again brought forth another pair, in accordance with the Father's prudent design, that none of the aeons should experience passion in the way this one (Sophia) did. This pair was

Christ and the Holy Spirit, brought forth for the consolidation and strengthening of the Pleroma, and by them the aeons were brought into order. For Christ taught them the nature of their partnerships, that they, being begotten, were not capable of the comprehension of the unbegotten one, and he proclaimed among them the knowledge of the Father—that he cannot be understood or comprehended, that he cannot be seen or heard, but is known only through the Only-begotten, and that the reason for the eternal permanence of the others (the aeons) is the fact that the Father is incomprehensible, and that the reason for their origin and formation is that which is comprehensible in him, that is, the Son. Christ who had just been brought forth effected these things among them.

6. The Holy Spirit made them all alike and taught them to give thanks to the Father, and ushered in the true rest. Thus, according to them, the aeons were made equal in form and in perception, and they all became Noes (pl. of Nous), all Logoi, all Men, and all Christs; similarly, the females became all Truths, all Lives, Spirits, and Churches. When everything was thus established and had attained perfect rest, with great joy, he says, they praised the Forefather, for they had become very glad. And because of this beneficence the entire Pleroma of the aeons, with *one* desire and *one* purpose, and with the consent of Christ and the Holy Spirit, and with the approval of the Father—each of the aeons having brought together and contributed whatever he had in himself of greatest beauty and sweetness—harmoniously wove together and skilfully united these and brought forth, to the praise and glory of Bythos, the most perfect beauty and star of the Pleroma, its perfect fruit, Jesus, whom they also call Saviour and Christ, and Logos, after his father, and All, because he is derived from all. In his honour angels of the same kind were brought forth simultaneously to act as his bodyguard.

3, 1. This then is what took place within the Pleroma, as they narrate it, and the misfortune of the aeon which desired passionately and which nearly got lost in deep sorrow,* because of her search after the Father: and the formation of him who is known as Horos (Limit), Cross, Redeemer, Emancipator, Limit-setter, and Bringer-back-after-struggle; and the generation of the first

---

* Greek: 'in deep matter' (corr. Holl).

Christ, with the Holy Spirit, after the repentance (of Sophia), a generation which took place through the Father, subsequent to that of the aeons; and the formation—deriving from the combined contributions of the aeons—of the second Christ, whom they also call Saviour. This is not openly spoken of, they say, because not all are capable of the knowledge of these things, but it is revealed, as in a mystery, by the Saviour through parables to those who are able to understand. So, for example, the thirty aeons are indicated by the thirty years during which they say the Saviour performed no public work (Luke 3: 23), and by the parable of the labourers in the vineyard (Matt. 20: 1–16). Paul also frequently named these aeons quite openly, they affirm, and even preserved their order, when he said 'To all the generations of the aeons of the aeon' (Eph. 3: 21); and we too (Christians belonging to the Church), when we say at the Eucharist 'to the aeons of the aeons' (that is, 'for ever'), are said to be referring to these aeons. Indeed, wherever an aeon or aeons are mentioned they want to relate the reference to these (beings).

2. The production of the twelve aeons is indicated by the fact that the Lord conversed with the scribes at the age of twelve years (Luke 2: 42), and by the selection of the apostles, of whom there were twelve. The other eighteen aeons are signified by the fact that he spent eighteen months with the disciples after his resurrection from the dead. The eighteen aeons are also clearly indicated by the first two letters of his name (in Greek), Iota and Eta.[11] And, in the same way, the ten aeons are indicated by the letter Iota, with which his name begins. Therefore the Saviour said, 'One iota or one tittle shall not pass away until everything takes place' (Matt. 5: 18).

3. The catastrophe which befell the twelfth aeon is signified, they say, by the apostasy of Judas, who was the twelfth apostle, and by the fact that he (Jesus) suffered in the twelfth month. For they maintain that he preached for only one year after his baptism. Furthermore, this is quite clearly shown in the case of the woman with an issue of blood. . . . For the one who suffered for twelve years, they say, is that power which extended itself and would have flowed into the immensity of substance. If she had not touched the garment of the Son, that is, the Truth

---

[11] The numerical value of Iota and Eta is 10 and 8.

of the first Tetrad—which is signified by the hem—she would have been dissolved into the general essence. But she stood still and ceased from her passion. For the power which went forth from the Son—and that they maintain is Horos—healed her and separated the passion from her (Matt. 9: 20–2 par.).

4. That the Saviour who is from All is himself Everything they would find indicated in the expression 'Every male (neuter gender in Greek) that opens the womb' (Luke 2: 23): he was everything and opened the womb of the desire that belonged to the aeon who fell into passion and which was banished from the Pleroma. They also call this the second Ogdoad, concerning which we shall have occasion to speak a little later. And for this reason, they affirm, Paul said plainly, 'He is the All' (Col. 3: 11), and again, 'All things are unto him and from him are all things' (Rom. 11: 36), and again, 'In him dwells the entire fullness of the godhead' (Col. 2: 9), and 'All is summed up by God in Christ' (Eph. 1: 10). Thus do they interpret (these passages) and others in the same way.

5. Then, with regard to that Horos of theirs, whom they call by several names, they claim that he has two methods of operation, namely, consolidating and dividing. In so far as he consolidates and supports, he is Cross: in so far as he divides and separates he is Horos (Limit). The Saviour, they say, indicated his two methods of operating as follows: first, the consolidating, by his saying, 'Whoever does not bear his cross and follow me cannot be my disciple', and, 'Take up your cross and follow me' (Luke 14: 27). His separating power is signified in the saying 'I come not to bring peace, but a sword' (Matt. 10: 34). John (the Baptist) is regarded as having said the same thing in the words, 'The winnowing-fan is in his hand. He will purify the threshing-floor and gather the wheat into his barn, but will burn the chaff with unquenchable fire' (Matt. 3: 12 par.). In these words the activity of Horos is indicated: they interpret the fan as referring to the Cross which consumes all material objects, as the fire does chaff, but purifies those who are saved, as the fan does wheat. The apostle Paul himself is also supposed to have mentioned this Cross in the following words: 'The word of the Cross is folly to those who are perishing, but to those who are being saved it is the power of God' (1 Cor. 1: 18), and again, 'In nothing whatsoever will I glory save in the

Cross of Christ, by which the world is crucified to me and I to the world' (Gal. 6: 14).

6. Such is the account they give concerning their Pleroma and the formation of all things, by violently adapting the fair message to what has been wickedly invented by themselves. And it is not only from the writings of the evangelists and the apostles that they attempt to derive proofs by falsifying the interpretation and dealing unscrupulously with the exposition, but from the law and the prophets as well, because many parables and allegories are set forth there which can be pressed into the service of various views by reason of the ambiguity of their meaning: by adapting the interpretation, forcibly and cunningly, to suit their own system, they draw away from the truth those who do not maintain a firm faith in one God, the Father Almighty, and in one Lord Jesus Christ, the Son of God.

4, 1. The account they give of the things outside the Pleroma is as follows. The desire of that Sophia who is above, whom they also call Achamoth and who was removed from the Pleroma above along with her passion, was—according to them—of necessity 'violently excited' amid the shadows and the places of vacuity. She was outside the light and the Pleroma and was without shape and form, like an abortion, since she comprehended nothing. But Christ on high took pity on her, extended himself forward beyond the 'Cross' and, by his power, imparted to her form, but only in respect of substance, not of knowledge. After this he hastened back above and withdrew his influence. He left her in order that she might become aware of the passion which belonged to her by reason of her severance from the Pleroma and might strive after better things, since she possessed a certain fragrance (lit. aroma) of immortality,[12] which had been left in her by Christ and the Holy Spirit. For this reason she is called by two names—Sophia, after her father, for her father is named Sophia, and Holy Spirit after the Spirit which is related to Christ. Since she had now received form and become intelligent, but, at the same time, had been deserted by the Logos who had been invisibly present to her, that is, by Christ, she strained herself to search after the light which had departed from her, but she was not able to comprehend it, because she was prevented by Limit (Horos). And as he

[12] The image of the perfume or fragrance also in Basilides (Hipp. VII 22, 14).

prevented her striving any further, Limit said 'Iao', and thus the name Iao is said to have originated.

Since she could not pass through Limit (Horos) because she was entangled with the passion and had been abandoned alone outside, she fell into all sorts of suffering which has many forms and varieties: she experienced sorrow, because she had not comprehended; fear, lest life might abandon her, as light had done; and, in addition, perplexity: but all these (she suffered) in ignorance. The sufferings were not for her something alien, as they were for her mother, the first Sophia, who was an aeon, but rather antagonistic. Moreover, there came upon her another disposition, namely, that of turning to him who gave her life. 2. This, they say, was the formation and substance of the matter from which this universe came into being. From that returning of hers (or: conversion) every soul in the world and that of the Demiurge had its origin: from her fear and sorrow, all the rest took its beginning. . . .

5. When their mother had passed through all her suffering and had, with difficulty, emerged from it, she is said to have turned her attention to supplicating the light which had left her, that is, Christ. He had gone up into the Pleroma, and was naturally reluctant to descend a second time, and so he sent to her the Paraclete, that is, the Saviour, to whom in fact the Father gave all power and put all things under his authority, and the aeons too, that 'in him all things might be created, visible and invisible, thrones, deities, dominions' (Col. 1: 16). But he was sent to her along with the angels, who were his coevals. Achamoth, they say, put a veil over her countenance out of reverence for him, but then, when she had seen him with all his fructifying power, she ran to him and received strength from his appearing. And he gave to her the formation that is in accordance with knowledge and healed her of her passions and separated them from her, but he still was concerned about them, because it was not possible for them to disappear, like those of the former (Sophia), for they had already become fixed by habit and powerful. Therefore he separated them and made them solid and transformed them from an incorporeal passion into (an) incorporeal matter. Then he implanted into them an aptitude and nature such that they could come together into compounds and bodies, so that two substances might come

into being, the one evil, resulting from the passions, the other passible, resulting from the conversion. In this way, they maintain, the Saviour in effect created (all). But Achamoth, freed from her passions, received with joy her vision of the lights coming with him (that is, the angels with him), became pregnant, and—so they teach—gave birth to progeny after their image, a spiritual offspring which was formed after the likeness of the Saviour's bodyguards.

5, 1. These three substances underlie all else, in their opinion: one from the passion, and this was matter; a second from the conversion, and that was (the) psychic; and, thirdly, what she herself brought forth, and that was (the) spiritual. Next she turned her attention to giving them form. But she was not able to give form to the spiritual because it was of the same nature as herself. So she turned to the forming of the psychic substance, which was derived from her conversion, and she projected what she had learned from the Saviour. And first of all, they say, from the psychic substance she formed the Father and king of all those things which are of the same nature as he is, that is, the psychics, which they call the Right, and of those things which sprang from the passion and the sorrow,* which they call the Left. For they declare that he formed all that came after him(self), being secretly moved by his mother: hence he is called by them Mother-Father, Fatherless, Demiurge, and Father, and indeed they name him Father of those on the right (that is, the psychics), but Demiurge of those on the left (that is, the material ones), but (he is) king of all. For the desire (*enthumesis*) wished to make all things to the glory of the aeons and, they say, made images of them, or rather the Saviour did so through her. And she retained the image of the invisible Father which was not known by the Demiurge; he (the Demiurge himself) kept the image of the only-begotten Son, while the archangels and angels created by him retained the image of the rest of the aeons. 2. They maintain therefore that he became Father and God of all things outside the Pleroma, because he was the creator of all that is psychic and material.

He then separated the two mixed natures and made corporeal substances from the incorporeal, fashioned things heavenly and earthly, and became the shaper (Demiurge) of the material

* Greek 'matter'.

and psychic beings, the Right and the Left, the light and the heavy, as well as of those which tended upwards and of those which tended downwards. He also prepared seven heavens above which the Demiurge was to dwell. And, for this reason, they name him Hebdomad, and the mother, Achamoth, Ogdoad: she thereby preserves the number of the original and primary Ogdoad of the Pleroma. The seven heavens are (not) intelligent. They regard them as angels, and the Demiurge himself as an angel, and indeed as one like to God: likewise Paradise, which is above the third heaven, is said to be the fourth archangel in power, and from him Adam received something while he sojourned in him.

3. They say that the Demiurge believed that he had created all this of himself, but in fact he had made them because Achamoth prompted him. He made the heaven without knowing the heaven; he formed man without knowing him; he brought the earth to light without knowing it. And, in every case, they say, he was ignorant of the ideas of the things he made, and even of his own mother, and imagined that he alone was all things. But the reason for this creative activity was, in his case, the mother, who desired that he should so proceed, (he who was) head and beginning of his own nature and lord of the entire undertaking. This mother they also name Ogdoad, and Sophia, Earth, Jerusalem, Holy Spirit, and, with a masculine reference, Lord. She has the place of the Middle and is above the Demiurge, but below or outside the Pleroma until the consummation.

4. Since then the material substance is said to be derived from three passions, fear, sorrow, and perplexity, the psychic substance is said to be composed of the fear and the conversion. From the conversion the Demiurge is said to have derived his being, but from the fear comes all the rest of the psychic substance, such as the souls of the irrational animals and beasts and men. For this reason, he (the Demiurge), too weak to know anything spiritual, imagined that he was himself the only God and said through the prophets, 'I am God, and apart from me there is none else' (Isa. 45:5). From the sorrow the 'spiritual powers of wickedness' are supposed to be derived, whence the devil (whom they call 'world-ruler') also took his origin, and the demons, angels, and all the spiritual substance of wickedness.

The Demiurge they represent as a psychic son of their mother, but the world-ruler as a creation of the Demiurge. The world-ruler knows what is above him, since he is a spirit of wickedness, but the Demiurge does not, for he is psychic. Their mother (Achamoth) dwells in the supra-heavenly place, that is, in the 'Middle', and the Demiurge dwells in the heavenly place, that is, in the Hebdomad, but the world-ruler dwells in this world of ours. The corporeal elements of the universe (*stoicheia tou kosmou*) sprang, as has been said before, from the terror and perplexity, as from a more permanent* source: earth, as a result of the state of terror; water, as a result of the agitation of fear; air, as a result of the congealing of sorrow. Fire is inherent in all of these elements as death and decay, just as they also teach that ignorance is hidden in the three passions.[13]

5. When he (the Demiurge) had formed the world, he made the choic man, not out of this present dry land, but out of the invisible substance, the liquid and flowing part of matter, and into him he breathed the psychic (man), and this is he who came into being 'after the image and likeness' (Gen. 1: 26): 'after the image' refers to the material which is similar to God but not of the same substance: and 'after the likeness' is the psychic man, and therefore his substance is also called the 'spirit of life' (Gen. 2: 7), for it derives from a spiritual emanation. Finally, they say, there was put on him the coat of skin, by which is meant, according to them, the flesh that is subject to sense-perception.

6. But the offspring of their mother, Achamoth—which she brought forth as a result of the vision of the angels around the Saviour and which is said to be spiritual like the mother herself—was according to them unknown to the Demiurge, and was inserted secretly into him (the Demiurge) without his knowing it, in order that through him it might be sown in the soul which derives from him and in the material body, and, having been born and increased there, might be prepared to receive the perfect Logos. For the Demiurge was not aware of the spiritual

---

[13] Here two accounts—or even more—have been combined. For either the 'remaining psychic substance' or the water is from the fear, and the Devil as ruler of the world, who knows what is above him, is not again mentioned in the report of Irenaeus.

---

* Greek: 'more ignoble' (corr. Holl).

man which had been sown simultaneously with his inbreathing by Sophia, with ineffable power and providence. For, as he did not know the mother, so he did not know her seed. This (seed) is known by them as the Church, the image of the church above; and they believe that this is the man who is in them. Thus, they have their soul from the Demiurge, the body from the dust (*chus*), flesh from matter, and the spiritual man from the mother, Achamoth.

6, 1. There are then three substances: the material, which they also call 'left', must of necessity, they say, perish, because it cannot receive any afflatus of imperishability; the psychic, which they also term 'right', stands midway between the spiritual and the material, and consequently passes to whichever side it is inclined; the spiritual was sent forth in order that, after being linked with the psychic, it might be shaped and trained with it in conduct: and this is the salt and the light of the world (Matt. 5: 13–15). It needed psychic and perceptible means of instruction, and, for this reason, they maintain, the world was created. The Saviour is said to have come to the psychic, since it possessed free will, in order to save it. For they maintain that he received the first-fruits of those whom he intended to save; from Achamoth he acquired the spiritual, from the Demiurge he put on the psychic Christ, from the Oikonomia (the dispensation) he was endowed with a body which had a psychic substance, but was so constructed by ineffable art that it was visible, tangible, and capable of suffering. He received nothing whatever material, they say, for matter is not capable of being saved. The end will come when all that is spiritual is shaped and perfected through knowledge, and that means spiritual men who possess the perfect knowledge of God and are initiated into the mysteries of Achamoth: they claim that they themselves are these persons.

2. The psychic men have been instructed in psychic matters; they are strengthened by works and mere faith, and do not have perfect knowledge; and these, they teach, are we of the Church. Therefore they affirm that for us good conduct is necessary—for otherwise it would not be possible to be saved—but they themselves, in their opinion, will be for ever and entirely saved, not by means of conduct, but because they are spiritual by nature. For just as it is impossible that the choic should

participate in salvation—since, they say, it is incapable of receiving it—so again it is impossible that the spiritual—and by that they mean themselves—should succumb to decay, regardless of what kind of actions it performs. Just as gold, when placed in mud, does not lose its beauty but retains its own nature, since the mud is unable to harm the gold, so they say that they themselves cannot suffer any injury or lose their spiritual substance, whatever material actions they may engage in. 3. . . . (see pp. 313–14).

4. . . . Therefore continence and good works are necessary for us, whom they call psychics and describe as being of the world, in order that by means of them we may come to the place of the 'Middle', but for them, who are called spiritual and perfect, they are not at all required. For it is not conduct that leads to the Pleroma, but the seed, sent forth from there in an immature state, but brought to perfection here.

7, 1. When the whole seed is perfected, then, they say, will the mother, Achamoth, leave the place of the Middle, enter into the Pleroma, and receive her bridegroom, the Saviour, who came into being from all (the aeons), with result that the Saviour and Sophia, who is Achamoth, form a pair (syzygy). These then are said to be bridegroom and bride, but the bridal chamber is the entire Pleroma. The spiritual beings will divest themselves of their souls and become intelligent spirits, and, without being hindered or seen, they will enter into the Pleroma, and will be bestowed as brides on the angels around the Saviour. The Demiurge passes into the place of his mother Sophia, that is, into the Middle. The souls of the righteous will also repose in the place of the Middle, for nothing psychic enters the Pleroma. When this has taken place, then (they assert) the fire that is hidden in the world will blaze forth and burn: when it has consumed all matter it will be consumed with it and pass into non-existence. According to them the Demiurge knew none of these things before the advent of the Saviour.

2. There are also some who say that he also brought forth Christ, his own son, as a psychic being like himself, and spoke concerning him through the prophets. This is he who passed through Mary as water passes through a pipe; and there descended upon him at baptism, in the form of a dove, the Saviour from the Pleroma, formed by all (the aeons). In him

there existed also the spiritual seed which proceeded from the mother. They hold, therefore, that our Lord was compounded from these four (parts) and thus retained the image of the original and primal Tetrad: from the spiritual, that which came from Achamoth; from the psychic, what came from the Demiurge; from the Oikonomia (the dispensation), what was prepared with ineffable art; and from the Saviour, what the dove was which came upon him. And he is said to have remained free of suffering—for it was impossible that he should suffer, since he was unconquerable and invisible—and accordingly, when he was brought before Pilate, the spirit of Christ placed in him was taken away. Moreover, in their opinion, the seed which was from his mother did not experience suffering, for it too was impassible, being spiritual and invisible even to the Demiurge himself. What suffered, in their teaching, was the psychic Christ, and he who was formed mysteriously from the Oikonomia, in order that thereby the mother might show forth the type of the Christ above, who extended himself through the Cross and imparted form to Achamoth, as far as substance is concerned. All these things are said to be counterparts of those things (above).

3. The souls which have the seed of Achamoth are said to be better than the rest and are therefore loved by the Demiurge more than the others, although he does not know the reason for it, but imagines they are as they are because they come from him. For this reason he is said to have destined them to be prophets, priests, and kings, and they explain that many things were said by this seed through the prophets because it is of a higher nature. They affirm that the mother also spoke many things concerning the things above, but she did so through him (the Demiurge) and through the souls originating from him. Then, in other respects, they divide the prophecies, maintaining that one part was spoken by the mother, another by the seed, and the third finally by the Demiurge. In like manner also, they hold that Jesus spoke partly under the influence of the Saviour, partly of the mother, and partly of the Demiurge, as we shall show in the course of our exposition.

4. Since the Demiurge was ignorant of the things above him, he was indeed moved by the things said, but treated them lightly, attributing them to all kinds of causes—to the spirit

of prophecy which has a certain movement of its own, or to man, or to the involvement with inferior things. And so he remained in ignorance until the coming of the Saviour. But when the Saviour came, he is said to have learned everything from him and to have gladly agreed with him, with all his power.[14] He is supposed to be the centurion in the gospel who said to the Saviour, 'I have soldiers and slaves under my authority, and whatever I command they do' (Matt. 8: 9 par.). He will continue the administration (Oikonomia) in the world until the appointed time, especially out of concern for the Church, but also because he knows the reward that is prepared for him, namely, that he will go to the place of his mother.

5. They assume three types of men; the spiritual, the choic, and the psychic, corresponding to Cain, Abel, and Seth, in order that they may represent by these the three natures, not with reference to an individual, but with reference to kinds of men. The choic ends in corruption; the psychic, if it chooses what is better, reposes in the place of the Middle, but if it chooses what is worse, it goes to what corresponds thereto. The spiritual beings which Achamoth sowed in righteous souls up till now will, since they were sent forth immature, be trained and brought up here, and later, when they are accounted worthy of perfection, they will be given (according to their teaching) as brides to the angels of the Saviour, whilst their souls rest, of necessity, with the Demiurge for ever in the Middle. And again they make a division among the souls, teaching that some are by nature good, and the others evil. The good are those who are capable of receiving the seed; those by nature evil would never receive that seed. . . .

8, 2. . . . They attempt to make passages of Scripture relevant for the things outside of their Pleroma. They say that in the last times of the world (cf. Heb. 1: 2; 1 Pet. 1: 5, 20) the Lord came to endure suffering that he might show forth the suffering of the last of the aeons, and by his own end make known the end of the affair concerning the aeons. The twelve-year-old girl, the daughter of the ruler of the synagogue, whom the Lord raised from the dead by his presence (Matt. 9: 25 par.) is said to be a type of Achamoth to whom their (the false teachers') Christ, by extending himself, gave form and led to perception of the

[14] Similarly in Basilides (Hipp. VII 27, 7).

light which had left her. But the fact that the Saviour manifested himself to her when she was outside the Pleroma, as an abortion, they say Paul affirmed in the first letter to the Corinthians: 'Last of all he appeared also to me, as to one untimely born (an abortion)' (1 Cor. 15: 8). The coming of the Saviour with his peers to Achamoth he indicated in like manner in the same letter by the words, 'The woman ought to have a veil on her head because of the angels' (1 Cor. 11: 10). The fact that, when the Saviour came to her, Achamoth placed a veil over her face out of shame, was also made manifest by Moses in that he put a veil over his face (Exod. 34: 33). They assert that the sufferings which she endured were signified by the Lord through the cross. In the words, 'My God, why hast thou forsaken me' (Matt. 27: 46 par.) he is said to have shown that Sophia was forsaken by the light and restrained by Limit from making any movement forward; her sorrow was indicated in the words, 'My soul is exceedingly sorrowful' (Matt. 26: 38 par.); her fear in the saying, 'Father, if it be possible, let this cup pass from me' (Matt. 26: 39 par.); and her perplexity too in the saying, 'And what I should say I do not know' (John 12: 27).

3. They teach that he pointed out the three kinds of men as follows: the material, in that to him who said 'I will follow thee' he answered, 'The Son of Man has nowhere to lay his head' (Matt. 8: 19 par.); the psychic, in that to him who said to him, 'I will follow thee, but first let me say farewell to those at my house', he replied, 'No one who puts his hand to the plough and looks back is fit for the kingdom of heaven' (Luke 9: 61)—this person is said to be one of the intermediate class. And that man who claimed to have performed most aspects of righteousness and then refused to follow, being overcome by riches so that he did not become perfect (Matt. 19: 16 ff.), him also they want to place in the psychic class; the spiritual ones (are indicated) by his saying, 'Leave the dead to bury their own dead; go thou and preach the kingdom of God' (Matt. 8: 22), and by his declaring to Zacchaeus, the publican, 'Make haste and come down, for I must abide at your house today' (Luke 19: 5). These, they assert, were of the spiritual descent. The parable of the leaven which the woman is said to have hidden in three measures of meal also reveals, in their view, the three kinds of men. They teach as follows: the woman represents

Sophia, the three kinds of men, spiritual, psychic, and choic, are the three measures of meal, and the leaven is the Saviour himself (Matt. 13: 33 par.). Paul too explicitly mentioned the choic, the psychic, and the spiritual when he said, 'As is the choic, so also are the choic' (1 Cor. 15: 48), and, 'A psychic man does not accept the things of the Spirit' (1 Cor. 2: 14), and, 'A spiritual man (pneumatic) judges everything' (1 Cor. 2: 15). The saying 'A psychic man does not accept the things of the Spirit' is supposed to have been spoken of the Demiurge, who, because he was psychic, knew neither his mother who was spiritual, nor her seed, nor the aeons in the Pleroma. That the Saviour received the first-fruits from those whom he was to save Paul declared, saying, 'And if the first-fruits are holy, so also is the lump of dough' (Rom. 11: 16). On the basis of this they teach that 'first-fruits' denotes the spiritual, and 'lump' denotes us, that is, the psychic church, the lump of which he assumed and raised up with himself, since he himself was the leaven.

4. Moreover, the fact that Achamoth wandered outside the Pleroma, was formed by Christ, and sought after by the Saviour, he himself revealed when he said that he had come for the lost sheep (combining Matt. 15: 24 and 18: 12 f. par.). They explain that the lost sheep must represent the mother from whom the Church here is said to have been sown. The wandering is her stay in the midst of all kinds of suffering outside the Pleroma, from which matter in their opinion derived its origin. The woman who cleaned her house and found the coin (Luke 15: 8) is explained as referring to Sophia above, who lost her desire but later found it again when all things had been cleansed by the advent of the Saviour. Wherefore, they say, she was restored again within the Pleroma. Simeon, who took Christ in his arms and praised God in the words, 'Lord, now lettest thou thy servant depart in peace according to thy word' (Luke 2: 25 ff.) is said to be a type of the Demiurge who, when the Saviour came, learned of his translation (to the Middle) and gave praise to Bythos. And through Anna, who in the gospel is called a prophetess and who had lived seven years with her husband, but had remained a widow all the rest of her life until she saw the Saviour and recognized him and spoke of him to all (Luke 2: 36–8)—through her, they maintain, Achamoth is quite clearly indicated, for she saw the Saviour with his peers

for a little while, but remained all the rest of the time in the Middle waiting for him until he should come again and restore her to her proper partnership. Her name was made known by the Saviour when he said, 'And Wisdom (Sophia) is justified by her children' (Luke 7: 35), and by Paul, as follows, 'Wisdom (Sophia) we speak among the perfect' (1 Cor. 2: 6). Paul is said by them to have made mention of the couplings within the Pleroma when he indicated them by means of one. For in writing of the conjugal union in life (that is, of marriage) he said, 'This is a great mystery: I refer to Christ and the Church' (Eph. 5: 32).

5. Moreover, they teach that John, the disciple of the Lord, made mention of the first Ogdoad, and they express it in these words:[15] 'John, the disciple of the Lord, desiring to declare the origin of all things in accordance with which the Father produced everything, posits as a beginning that which was first brought forth by God, and was called Son, Only-begotten, and God, in whom the Father brought forth all things, after the manner of a seed. By him (he says) the Logos was generated and in him the entire substance of the aeons to which the Logos later imparted form. Since then he speaks of the first origin of things, he rightly proceeds in his teaching from the beginning, that is, from the Son and the Logos; for he says: "In the beginning was the Logos, and the Logos was with God, and the Logos was God. He was in the beginning with God" (John 1: 1 f.). First of all, he distinguishes the three: God, Beginning, and Logos. Then he combines them again in order to show how each of them, the Son and the Logos, was brought forth, and how they were combined with one another and with the Father. For in the Father and from the Father is the Beginning (*archē*: that is, Nous), but in the Beginning and from the Beginning is the Logos. Rightly, then, did he say, "In the beginning was the Logos", for he was in the Son. "And the Logos was with God", for the Beginning (was with the Father), and "the Logos was God", and that is logical, for what is generated from God is God. "He was in the beginning with God" discloses the order of production. "All things were made through him, and without him was nothing made" (John 1:3), for to all the aeons after him the Logos was the cause of formation and origin. But "what

was made in him" he says, "is life" (John 1: 3 f.),[16] and here
he has also indicated the union (syzygy). For he said that all
things were made through him, but that the life is in him. Life
that is in him stands closer to him than all that came into being
through him. For it exists along with him and brings forth fruit
through him. When he adds "And the life was the light of men"
(John 1: 4), he has, by mentioning "man", signified also the
Church (which has the same meaning as "man"), in order that
by means of the one name he might indicate the fellowship of
the pair, for from Logos and Life spring Man and Church.
He styled life as the light of men because they are all illumined
by it (the light), that is, formed and made manifest. This Paul
also declares in the words, "For whatever becomes visible is
light" (Eph. 5: 13). 6. Since then life manifested and generated
Man and Church, she is called their light.

'By these words, then, John clearly discloses, among other
things, the second Tetrad, Logos and Life, Man and Church.
But he also indicated the first Tetrad. For when he treats of the
subject of the Saviour and says that all things outside the
Pleroma were formed through him, he says that he is the fruit
of the entire Pleroma. For he has called him a light which shines
in the darkness and is not comprehended by it, since, when he
had shaped everything which had its origin from the passion,
he was not known by it (John 1: 5). He (John) also calls him
Son, Truth, and Life, and the Logos made flesh "whose glory
we beheld" he says, "and his glory was as that of the only-
begotten, which was given to him by the Father, full of
grace and truth" (John 1: 14). But in fact John says, "And
the Logos became flesh and dwelt among us, and we beheld his
glory, glory as of the only-begotten of the Father, full of grace
and truth" (John 1: 14). Thus indeed has he distinctly referred
to the first Tetrad, in speaking of the Father, Charis (Grace),
the Only-begotten, and Truth. So then John spoke of the first
Ogdoad, the mother of all the aeons, for he made mention
of the Father, Grace, the Only-begotten, and Truth, Logos and
Life, Man and Church.'

Epiphanius, who quotes Irenaeus' account, ends with the words,
'And thus (is the account of) Ptolemaeus', from which one concludes
that it is derived from Ptolemaeus.

16 'What was made' is attached to the following verse.

CLEMENT OF ALEXANDRIA, *Excerpta ex Theodoto*
43, 2–65, 2 (Selection)

This section of the *Excerpta* is parallel to the long account by Irenaeus and is, as a whole, so closely related to it that it must be assumed that the same source underlies both accounts. Specially characteristic of the version given here are the Old and New Testament reminiscences, whereas Irenaeus generally provides the New Testament references and, in particular, parables with a brief explanation, and almost entirely omits the Old Testament reminiscences: moreover, he placed the quotations together in blocks at the end of chapter 3 and in 8, 2–4, whereas the *Excerpta ex Theodoto* provides them scattered throughout its text.

One may in certain respects compare the relationship between the two accounts with that between Matthew and Luke, who both used the same sources but often diverge widely from one another or have omitted something which the other includes (although there the situation is really more complicated).

The section begins with the sending of the 'Saviour' to Achamoth = Sophia and has no reference backwards.

43, 2. And when the Father had given to him all authority, 'the angel of the counsel' (Isa. 9: 6) was also sent forth, with the consent of the Pleroma. And he became head of all things after the Father. 3. For 'in him all things were created, the visible and the invisible, thrones, dominions, kingdoms, divinities, jurisdictions' (Col. 1: 16). 4. 'Wherefore God has exalted him and given him the name above every name, that every knee should bow and every tongue confess that the "Lord of glory is Jesus Christ"' (Phil. 2: 9–11), the Saviour, the same one who ascended and descended (cf. Eph. 4: 10). 5. What does 'ascended' mean but that he also 'descended'? The one who descended into the lowest parts of the earth is the same who also ascended above the heaven.

44, 1. When Sophia saw him, she recognized him as similar to (resembling) the light which had left her, and she ran to him, rejoiced, and worshipped. But when she beheld the angels who had been sent forth with him she was filled with shame and put a veil over her face. 2. Because of this mystery Paul commands that women 'must wear an authority (*exousia*) on their heads because of the angels' (1 Cor. 11: 10).

45, 1. Immediately therefore the Saviour bestows on her the

form according to knowledge and healing from her passions, showing to her the things in the Pleroma from the unbegotten Father as far as herself. 2. He removed the passions from her who had suffered them and made her impassible, but, having separated the passions from her, he kept them. And they were not dispersed, as in the case of the inner (Sophia), but he made both them and those of the second disposition into substances. So, by the appearance of the Saviour, Sophia becomes passionless and what is outside (the Pleroma) is created. For 'all things were made by him and without him was not anything made' (John 1: 3).

46, 1. So, from incorporeal and contingent passion he first moulded them (the passions) into a still incorporeal matter and then, in the same way, changed them into compounds and bodies—2. for it was not possible to turn the passions into substances all at once—and he created in the bodies a capability according to (their) nature.

47, 1. The first and universal Demiurge is the Saviour, but Sophia, as the second, 'built herself a house and supported it with seven pillars' (Prov. 9: 1). 2. And first of all things she put forth, as an image of the Father, the god through whom she made 'the heaven and the earth' (Gen. 1: 1), that is, the heavenly and the earthly, the Right and the Left. 3. He, being an image of the Father, becomes a father and brings forth first the psychic Christ, an image of the Son, then the archangels, as images of the aeons, then angels, as images of the archangels, (all) from the psychic, luminous substance, of which the prophetic word says, 'And the spirit of God hovered over the waters' (Gen. 1: 2). Because the two substances made by him were combined he declares concerning the pure that it 'hovered over', and concerning what was heavy, material, muddy, and dense, that it 'lay underneath'. 4. That this also, in the beginning, was incorporeal he indicates by calling it 'invisible' (Gen. 1: 2 LXX), though it was invisible neither to man, who did not then exist, nor to God, for he in fact formed it; rather, he has somehow expressed in this way the fact that it was unformed, unshaped, and undesigned.

48, 1. The Demiurge separated the pure from the heavy, since he perceived the nature of both, and made light, that is, he let it appear and brought it to light and form, for the light of the sun and of the heaven was made much later. 2. And of the material he made the one out of the sorrow, creating substantially 'the spiritual powers of wickedness' (Eph. 6: 12), with whom we have to struggle—therefore the apostle says, 'And grieve not the Holy Spirit of God with which you were sealed' (Eph. 4: 30)—3. another (he made) from the fear, namely, the wild beasts, and another from the terror and perplexity, namely, the elements of the universe. 4. In these three elements fire floats about and is implanted and hidden in them, and is kindled by them, and perishes with them, for it has no place appointed for it, like the other elements as well from which the compound substances are formed.

49, 1. He did not know her who was acting through him and believed that, being industrious by nature, he was creating by his own power. Therefore the apostle said, 'He was subjected to the vanity of the world, not of his own will, but by reason of him who subjected him, in hope that he would be made free' (Rom. 8: 20 f.), when the seeds of God will be assembled. 2. A proof of the compulsoriness (of the subjection) is that he blessed the Sabbath and specially welcomed the rest from labour (Gen. 2: 3).

50, 1. 'He took dust (*chus*) from the ground' (Gen. 2: 7)— not a piece of dry stuff, but of the diverse and heterogeneous matter—and fashioned the earthly, material, irrational soul, which is of the same substance as that of the wild beasts. This is man 'after the image'. 2. The one 'after the likeness' (Gen. 1: 27), that is, of the Demiurge himself, is the man whom he breathed and inseminated into him, putting into him through angels something consubstantial with himself. 3. Since he is invisible and incorporeal, he called his substance 'the breath of life' (Gen. 2: 7). After being given form, it became a 'living soul'. That this is so, he himself confesses in the prophetic writings.

51, 1. (A) man is therefore in man, the psychic in the choic, not as a part in a part, but the whole in the whole, by the ineffable power of God. Therefore he was formed in paradise, the fourth heaven. 2. For no choic flesh ascends there, but to the divine soul the material was as flesh. This is what the saying 'This is now bone of my bones' signifies—it mysteriously indicates the divine soul, hidden in the flesh, which is solid, susceptible to passion, and moderately strong—'and flesh of my flesh' (Gen. 2: 23) (signifies) the material soul which is the body of the divine soul. 3. Concerning these two (souls) the Saviour also speaks, 'One must fear him who can destroy this soul and this body, the psychic one, in hell' (Matt. 10: 28 par.).

52, 1. This flesh the Saviour called an 'adversary' (Matt. 5: 25 f. par.) and Paul 'the law which wars against the law of my mind' (Rom. 7: 23), and the Saviour warns (us) to 'bind' it and to 'plunder the goods of the strong one' (Matt. 12: 29), that is, of him who wages war against the heavenly soul, and he exhorts 'to be quit of him on the way so that we do not come to prison and to punishment' (Luke 12: 58 f.). 2. Likewise (we should) 'be well disposed' to it, not nourishing and strengthening it by the power to commit sin, but putting it to death here and now and thereby showing it as transient by our refraining from evil in order that at its dissolution it may be secretly broken up and scattered and not retain for itself any actuality and thereby keep an enduring power in its passage through fire.

53, 1. This (flesh) is called 'a tare' (Matt. 13: 25) which grows up together with the soul, the good seed. It is also called a 'seed of the devil' (Matt. 13: 28, 38) because it is of the same substance as he is, a 'serpent' (Gen. 3: 1), 'the bruiser of the heel' (Gen. 3: 15), and a 'robber' attacking the head of the king. 2. But Adam also possessed the spiritual seed that was sown, unknown to him, in the soul by Sophia, 'ordained' he says, 'through angels by the hand of a mediator. The mediator is not representative of one, but God is one' (Gal. 3: 19). 3. The seeds which were brought into being by Sophia are ministered to, so far as it is possible, by the male 'angels'. 4. For just as the Demiurge, secretly moved by Sophia, believes that he acts as a free agent, so also with men. 5. So Sophia first brought forth a spiritual seed in Adam in order that the bone, the rational and heavenly soul, might not be empty, but be filled with spiritual marrow.

54, 1. From Adam three natures are derived: first, the irrational, from which Cain comes; secondly, the rational and just, from which Abel springs; and thirdly, the spiritual, from which Seth comes. 2. The choic is 'after the image'; the psychic 'after the likeness' of God (Gen. 1: 27); the spiritual is after its own nature. Of these three, without the other children of Adam, it

is said, 'This is the book of the generations of men' (Gen. 5: 1).
3. And because Seth is spiritual, he neither keeps the flocks nor
cultivates the soil, but brings forth children, as spiritual beings
do. And him who 'hoped to call on the name of the Lord'
(Gen. 4: 26), who looked 'upwards', whose 'citizenship is in
heaven' (Phil. 3: 20)—him the world does not comprehend
(contain).

This is similar to Irenaeus I 7, 5. The Sethians and the Apocryphon
of John also affirm that Seth is the spiritual one.

55, 1. In addition to these three incorporeal (parts) Adam is
clothed, as a fourth, with the choic (man), the coats of skin
(Gen. 3: 21). And therefore it is neither from the Spirit nor
from that which was breathed into him that Adam sows. For
both are divine and both are put forth through him, but not
by him. 3. His material (nature) has the power to beget and
give birth, for it is mingled with the seed and cannot disengage
itself from this bond in this life. 56, 1. To this extent therefore
is Adam our father 'the first man of the earth, earthy' (1 Cor.
15: 47). 2. But if he had sown from the psychic and spiritual in
the same way as from the material substance, then they would
all have become equal and righteous, and the teaching would
have been in all. Consequently, the material (beings) are many,
the psychic are not many, and the spiritual are few.

3. The spiritual is saved by nature; the psychic, being possessed
of free will, has an inclination towards faith and towards
incorruptibility, but also towards unbelief and destruction,
according to its own choice; but the material perishes by nature.
4. When the psychic 'is grafted on to the good olive-tree', into
faith and incorruptibility, and has a share 'in the fatness of the
olive-tree', and when 'the Gentiles enter', then 'will all Israel
be saved in this way' (Rom. 11: 16–26). 5. Israel is interpreted
allegorically as the spiritual man who will see God, the genuine
son of faithful Abraham by 'the free woman', not the one
'according to the flesh' born from the Egyptian slave (Gal.
4: 22–5). 57. From the three species there takes place both the
shaping of the spiritual and the changing of the psychic from
slavery to freedom.

58, 1. After the kingdom of death, which had made a great
and specious promise, but was none the less a ministry of death,

the great combatant Jesus Christ[17] performed a saving work in that, whilst all authorities and divinities refused, he took upon himself the Church, that is, the chosen and the called—the spiritual from her who had borne it, but the psychic from the Oikonomia (dispensation)—and bore aloft what he had assumed and thereby what was consubstantial with them. 2. 'For if indeed the first-fruits are holy, so also is the lump of dough; and if the root is holy, then so are the branches' (Rom. 11: 16).

59, 1. First of all he put on the seed from her who had given it (the seed) birth, not in such a way that he was contained in it, but he contained it forcibly, and it is being given form gradually through knowledge. 2. But when he came to the 'place', Jesus found, ready to be put on, the Christ who had been foretold, whom the prophets and the law had proclaimed, who was the image of the Saviour. 3. But this psychic Christ whom he put on was invisible. Therefore it was necessary that he who was to come into the world, that he might be seen and touched, and be active in affairs there, should also wear a body perceptible to the senses. 4. A body was therefore woven for him out of invisible, psychic substance, and, by the power of a divine preparation, it came into the world of sense.

60. The saying 'Holy Spirit will come upon thee' indicates the coming into being of the Lord's body; 'the power of the Highest will overshadow thee' (Luke 1: 35) refers to the formation on God's part which he gave to the body in the virgin.

Paragraph 60 differentiates the body prepared with ineffable art (to use Irenaeus' terms) from the 'formation of this body', that is, from the psychic Christ whom the Demiurge, here called 'God', formed.

61, 1. That he himself was other than that which he assumed is made clear from what he confesses: 'I am the life', 'I am the truth' (John 14: 6), 'I and the Father are one' (John 10: 30). 2. The spiritual (nature) which he assumed and the psychic are indicated by him thus: 'The child grew up and increased in wisdom' (Luke 2: 52): the spiritual needs wisdom, the psychic size. 3. By means of that which flowed from his side (John 19: 34) he makes it clear that by the outflowing of the passions from the one who experienced passion, the substances, becoming

---

[17] The designation of Jesus as the 'great champion' is new compared with the account of Irenaeus, but cf. the Acts of Thomas, ch. 50.

passionless, will be saved. 4. And when he says, 'The Son of Man must be rejected, insulted, crucified' (combining different Passion predictions), he appears to be speaking of another person, namely, of him who experiences passion. 5. And he says, 'I will go before you on the third day into Galilee' (Matt. 26: 32): for he goes before all things and indicates that he will raise up the soul that is being invisibly saved and will restore it again to the place to which he is now leading the way.

6. He died, when the Spirit which had come upon him in Jordan departed from him; not that it might exist separately, but rather it withdrew in order that death might operate. For how would the body have died, if life had been present in him? Death would then in fact have had dominion over the Saviour, which is absurd. But death was outwitted by craftiness. 7. For when the body died and when death had taken hold of it, the Saviour sent forth the ray of power which had come upon him and destroyed death, and he raised the mortal body after he had scattered the passions. 8. The psychic element is raised again in this way and is saved. The spiritual who have believed obtain a higher salvation, receiving the souls as wedding garments.

62, 1. The psychic Christ therefore sits on the right hand of the Demiurge, as David says: 'Sit thou on my right hand', etc. (Ps. 110 (109): 1). 2. He sits there until the consummation 'in order that they may see him whom they pierced' (Rev. 1: 7). They pierced the visible, which was the flesh of the psychic one, for 'A bone of him will not be broken' (John 19: 36), he says, just as in the case of Adam prophecy (allegorically) calls the soul bone. 3. When the body suffered, the soul of Christ deposited itself in the hand of the Father. The spirit (situated) in the bone he does not yet hand over, but himself saves it.

63, 1. Now the pneumatics rest 'on the Lord's day' (Rev. 1: 10), in the Ogdoad, which is called the Lord's day, with the mother, having the souls as wedding garments, until the end; the other faithful souls (rest) beside the Demiurge, but at the end they too go into the Ogdoad. 2. Then (comes) the wedding-feast, common to all the saved, until all become equal and mutually recognize one another.

64, 1. The pneumatics then lay aside the souls and, at the same time as the mother receives her bridegroom, each of them too receives his bridegroom, the angels; then they enter the bridal chamber within Horos (Limit) and attain to the vision of the Father, and become intellectual aeons, (entering) into the intelligible and eternal marriage of the union (syzygy).

65, 1. The 'ruler of the feast' (John 2: 8 f.), the best man of the wedding, the 'friend of the bridegroom', stands outside before the bride-chamber and greatly rejoices on hearing the voice of the bridegroom. 2. This is the fullness (pleroma) of joy and of repose.

The section of the *Excerpta* which begins at 43, 2 commences with the sending of the Saviour, here called the 'angel of the counsel', the 'fruit' of all the aeons (Irenaeus I 4, 5), but Irenaeus does not have the citation given in 43, 4. 5. The encounter with the Saviour—of which Clement relates that Achamoth, here known as Sophia, recognized him from the likeness to the light which she had lost —is narrated in a slightly different way from the account in Irenaeus. That 'the second disposition', namely, the 'turning to him who gave her life', is made into 'substances' by the Saviour is not specially mentioned by Irenaeus, although he presupposes it.

Clement does not expressly relate the creation of the Devil, and as Irenaeus also becomes obscure at this point, there is a suspicion that he is mixing up different systems. In any case, according to Irenaeus I 5, 4 and *Excerpta ex Theodoto* 48, 2, the spiritual powers of wickedness are formed from the sorrow, the beasts from the fear, and the elements of the universe from the perplexity. Heracleon accepts the Devil without hesitation, whereas Ptolemaeus in his Letter to Flora does so only with hesitation. One may understand the hesitation to name him, for the Demiurge in fact created all things, and in the end is converted, with the result that there is no place for an original evil being. Perhaps the Devil is only representative of the passions, which are not a matter of intention but purely instinctive.[18]

In paragraph 49 a notable feature is the way in which the creation by the Demiurge, 49, 2, is depreciated.

The separation of man 'after the image' from man 'after the likeness' is here more fully explained and worked out. The material soul is, as it were, flesh of the divine soul; here we must not forget that divine means: from the Demiurge. That Adam was formed in the fourth heaven is indicated also by Irenaeus I 5, 2 (end).

What Clement tells us in 52 is very significant, but relates to conduct. The 'adversary',[19] the law which in our members makes war on the law of the mind, the strong man who has to be bound and robbed

---

[18] See Fragm. 46 f. of Heracleon.
[19] The same expression also in the letter of Ptolemy to Flora (Epiph. XXXIII 3, 2).

of his goods, is the 'flesh' of the divine soul. One should be 'well disposed' to this 'adversary', because by abstinence from evil things one may put it to death. This certainly does not apply to the spiritual part of man, to which Clement first refers in 53, 2, but we may here adduce the idea which Irenaeus reports about their being yoked together in conduct: accordingly, the psychic has a significance even for the spiritual.

In 53, 5 the bone is the divine, that is, the psychic soul, and the marrow therein is the spiritual seed, as is clear in 62, 3.

LETTER OF PTOLEMAEUS TO FLORA

The letter of Ptolemaeus to Flora is very clearly constructed and requires no commentary. It is a document through which a lady, not yet initiated into Valentinianism, obtains instruction on a certain point, from which it will be possible to develop the system proper. *For us*, however, the letter has this significance, that it shows that Ptolemaeus was certainly no libertine and no ascetic, but adhered to the Sermon on the Mount. Alongside it stands the metaphorical significance of Old Testament commandments, like fasting, etc., but Ptolemaeus says that even physical fasting was retained by the Valentinians: we are here miles removed from libertinism and asceticism.

The law, which is contained in the five books of Moses, is divided, first of all, into three parts: the law of God, the additions of Moses, and the 'precepts of the elders'. The law of God is again divided into three: the law = the ten commandments which Jesus fulfilled through the 'but I say unto you'; the law which is to be understood typically or symbolically, although the Jews understood it literally, namely, the laws on fasting, circumcision, sanctification of the Sabbath, bringing of offerings, etc.; and, thirdly, the law which is bound up with evil, the law of 'an eye for an eye, a tooth for a tooth'.

The God who speaks in the Old Testament stands between him whose nature is 'corruption and darkness', on the one hand, and him whose nature is 'incorruptibility and light', on the other: he is appropriately called just: he has indeed a twofold nature, but is himself an image of the better. How he, with this double nature, and the adversary, whose nature is corruption, came into being, when there is still only *one* beginning which is incorruptible and good —these matters Ptolemaeus promises at the end to reveal to Flora in a further course of instruction.

Although we cannot get a *direct* insight here into the ethics of the Valentinians, nevertheless some conclusions may be drawn from the

fact that they highly esteemed the Decalogue as intensified by the
Sermon on the Mount. The special position of Valentinianism is also
clear from the fact that the world is the work not of the devil, but
of a 'righteous God, who hates evil'.

Epiphanius, *Panarion* XXXIII 3, 1–7, 10

3, 1. The law ordained through Moses has not been understood by many before us, my dear sister Flora, for they had accurate knowledge neither of him who ordained it nor of its instructions: this, I think, you will easily realize when you have learned the different opinions about it.

2. Some say that it was decreed by God the Father; others, on the other hand, adopting the opposite course, obstinately and firmly maintain that it was ordained by the adversary, the Devil who brings about destruction, just as they ascribe to him also the creation of this world, because they declare that he is father and maker of this entire universe. 3. They are completely in error, for they do not agree with one another, and each side has missed the very truth of the matter with which it is concerned. 4. For it is evident that this (law) was not ordained by the perfect God and Father—for it is secondary—because it is not only imperfect and in need of completion by another, but also contains commands which are not consonant with the nature and disposition of such a God. 5. Nor (can they) ascribe to the injustice of the adversary a law which forbids the doing of injustice; that is the conclusion of people who do not understand the words of the Saviour, that 'a city or a house which is divided against itself cannot stand' (Matt. 12: 25), as our Saviour declared. 6. Moreover, the apostle says that the creation of the world is due to him—for all things came into being through him and without him nothing was made (John 1: 3)—and removes the supports from under the baseless wisdom of the false accusers: (it is due to him) and not to a God who brings corruption, but rather to a God who is just and hates evil. This is the view of unintelligent men who do not recognize the reason for the creator's providence and have blinded not only the eyes of the soul, but the eyes of the body as well. 7. It is clear to you from what has been said that these people completely miss the truth. Each of the groups has experienced this in its own way: the one, because they do not know the God of righteousness, and the other, because they do not know the Father of all

whom alone the one who knew him revealed by his coming. 8. It remains for us who have been counted worthy of the knowledge of both of these to provide you with an accurate and clear account of the nature of the law and of the law-giver by whom it was ordained. We shall draw the proofs of what we say from the words of our Saviour, for through these alone are we led without stumbling to the comprehension of that which is.

4, 1. First of all you must learn that the entire law which is contained in the Pentateuch of Moses was not decreed by one (person), I mean, not by God alone, but that there are some commandments in it which were even decreed by men. And the words of the Saviour teach us that it is divided into three parts. 2. There is that section which is attributed to God himself and his legislating activity; the second division is that belonging to Moses—not in the sense that God gives laws through him, but in the sense that Moses, starting from his own ideas, gave some laws; and the third part (is attributed) to the elders of the people, who are responsible for having introduced some commandments of their own.

3. You will now learn how it can be shown from the words of the Saviour that this is in fact the case. 4. Once the Saviour was talking with people who were discussing with him the subject of divorce, where the existing legal prescription permitted divorce. Now the Saviour said to them, 'Because of your hard-heartedness Moses permitted you to divorce your wives. From the beginning it was indeed not so. For God', he went on, 'joined together this union, and what the Lord joined together', said he, 'man shall not dissolve' (Matt. 19: 8; 6, par.). 5. Thus he shows that there is a law of God which forbids the wife being divorced from her husband, but that there is another law, that of Moses, which permits the dissolving of the union because of hard-heartedness. 6. So Moses laid down a law which is contrary to that of God, for dissolving is contrary to not dissolving. If, however, we examine the intention of Moses in giving this (regulation), it will be found that he did not give it on the basis of his own decision, but of necessity, on account of the weakness of those for whom the law was given. 7. Since they were not in a position to observe the intention of God, according to which they were not permitted to divorce their wives, with whom some of them were reluctant to live, and as a

result ran the risk of turning even more to unrighteous behaviour and thence to destruction, Moses, wishing to remove this reluctance through which they were in danger of coming into destruction, of his own accord gave a second commandment, exchanging a lesser evil for a greater one, namely, the law on divorce, so that, if they were not able to keep the first one, they might at least keep this one and not turn to injustice and evil, out of which utter destruction would result for them. 10. This is his intention, in terms of which he is deemed to have laid down a law contrary to that of God. In any case, we have demonstrated that the law of Moses is different from the law of God, and this is indisputable, even though we have demonstrated it now from only one case.

11. The Saviour further makes it clear that there are also some traditions of the elders interwoven with the law. 'For God', he says, 'has said: "Honour thy father and thy mother that it may be well with thee", but you', he says, addressing the elders, 'you have declared that that by which you might have been helped by me (must be) a gift to God; and have annulled the law of God by the tradition of your elders. Isaiah also proclaimed this in the words, "This people honours me with their lips, but their heart is far from me. In vain do they worship me, whilst they teach as precepts the commandments of men"' (Matt. 15: 4–9). 14. From this it is obvious that the law in its entirety is divided into three parts: for we find in it the legislation of Moses, of the elders, and of God himself. This division of the entire law which we have proposed brings to light the truth that is in it.

5, 1. That one part, the law of God himself, is in turn divided into three parts: the pure legislation which is not mixed with evil, which is therefore properly called 'law', which the Saviour came not to destroy but to fulfil—for that which he fulfilled was not alien to him, (but required fulfilment), for it was not perfect; next, the law which is intertwined with baseness and injustice, which the Saviour destroyed because it was not consonant with his nature. 2. The third division is that (law) which is exemplary and symbolic, that which is ordained according to the image of the spiritual and transcendent (things). This the Saviour changed from being perceptible (to the senses) and phenomenal into the spiritual and invisible.

3. Now the law of God which is pure and unmixed with evil is the Decalogue, those ten sayings engraved on the two tablets for the forbidding of those things which one must avoid and for the enjoining of things which we must do. Although these contain pure legislation, nevertheless, since they had not reached perfection, they required fulfilment by the Saviour.

4. The law which is interwoven with injustice is that which is laid down for the recompense of and the requital of those who had previously sinned. It ordains that an eye should be cut out for an eye and a tooth for a tooth, and that a murder should be avenged by a murder (Lev. 24: 20 f.). For the second one to commit an injustice sins no less, for he changes only the order of events, but commits the same action. 5. This commandment was and is just, in that it was laid down, in the event of transgression of the pure law, because of the weakness of those who observe the law, but it is alien to the nature and the goodness of the Father of All. 6. Perhaps it was something appropriate (to the circumstances), but it was even more inevitable. For he who does not wish one murder to take place, saying, 'Thou shalt not kill' (Exod. 20: 13) has, when he commands that the murderer be killed in turn, ordained a second law and differentiated between two kinds of murder. Thus he who forbade the one murder failed to observe that necessity deceived him. 7. Therefore, the Son who came from him destroyed this part of the law, admitting that it too was a commandment of God, since with other passages it is considered to belong to the old way of life, especially that passage where it is said, 'God said, "Whoever curses father or mother shall certainly die"' (Exod. 21: 17).

8. But the part which is exemplary is that which is ordained according to the image of the spiritual and transcendent things, I mean what is laid down about offerings, circumcision, Sabbath, fasting, Passover, unleavened bread, and other such matters. 9. All these are images and symbols and they were changed when the truth appeared. As far as their phenomenal appearance and literal fulfilment are concerned, they were destroyed; but as far as spiritual meaning is concerned, they were restored; the names remained the same, but the content changed. 10. For the Saviour instructed us to make offerings, but not those which are made by means of irrational beasts or with

incense, but (offerings) which (are made) through spiritual praise and glorification and thanksgiving, and through liberality and kindness to our neighbours. 11. And he desires that we should be circumcised, but not in the physical foreskin, but in relation to our spiritual hearts (cf. Rom. 2: 28 f.). 12. He wants us to keep the Sabbath: for he wishes us to be idle with reference to evil actions. 13. As to fasting, he wants us to be engaged not in physical fasting, but in spiritual fasting, which amounts to abstinence from all that is evil. External, physical fasting is observed even among our followers, for it can be of some benefit to the soul, if it is engaged on reasonably, whenever it is done neither by way of imitating others, nor out of habit, nor because of the day, as if it had been specially appointed for that purpose. 14. At the same time (we fast) as a way of remembering the true fast, in order that those who are not yet able to keep that fast may have a reminder of it from the physical fast. 15. So also with the Passover and the unleavened bread: that these were images Paul the apostle makes clear when he says, 'Christ our passover has been sacrificed' and 'in order that you', he says, 'may be unleavened, not containing leaven'—by leaven he means evil—'but may be a new lump of dough' (1 Cor. 5: 7).

6, 1. Thus then that which is universally admitted to be the law of God is divided into three parts. First, that which was fulfilled by the Saviour, for the commands 'Thou shalt not kill; thou shalt not commit adultery; thou shalt not swear falsely' are included in the forbidding of anger, lust, and swearing (Matt. 5: 21 ff.): 2. the second division is what was completely destroyed, for 'an eye for an eye and a tooth for a tooth', being interwoven with injustice and itself comprising an act of injustice, was destroyed by the Saviour through its opposite. 3. For opposites cancel out one another. 'But I say unto you, Do not resist at all the evil man, but if anyone gives you a slap in the face, turn the other cheek to him' (Matt. 5: 39). 4. (Finally) there is the part which is translated and changed from the literal to the spiritual, the symbolic (legislation) which is ordained as an image of transcendent things. 5. For the images and the symbols represent other things and were good so long as the truth had not come. But when the truth comes, one must do what belongs to the truth, not what belongs to images. 6. This his (the Saviour's) disciples, as well as the apostle Paul, have demonstrated, in that for our sakes he (Paul) pointed to the symbolic meaning in referring to the Passover and unleavened bread, to the law interwoven with injustice in the words 'The law of commandments contained in ordinances he destroyed' (Eph. 2: 15), to that part which is not mingled with anything inferior or base, when he says, 'The law is holy and the commandment is holy, just and good' (Rom. 7: 12).

7, 1. As far as one can in brief compass I have shown you sufficiently, I think, both the legislation smuggled in by men and the threefold division of the law of God. 2. There remains (the question) who this God is who ordained the law. But I think that I have shown you this as well in what has been already said, if you have listened carefully. 3. For if this (law) was ordained neither by the perfect God himself, nor by the Devil (which is something that cannot possibly be affirmed), then the one who ordained the law must be other than these two. 4. But in fact he is the Fashioner[20] and Maker of this entire universe and of what is in it. He is different from these two realities and since he stands in the midst between them, he rightly bears the name 'Middle'. 5. And if the perfect God is good by his own nature, as he in fact is—for our Saviour declared that the one and only good God is his Father whom he revealed—and if the one of the opposite nature is evil and wicked, characterized by injustice, then the one who is situated in the midst of the two and who is neither good nor evil and unjust, can be properly called just, the rewarder of the justice which conforms to him. 6. This God is inferior to the perfect God, and lower than his justice, since he is generated and not ungenerated—one only is ungenerated, the Father from whom come all things, since all things in their own special ways depend on him—but he is greater and more powerful than the adversary, and is of a substance and of a nature other than the substance of either of these. 7. The nature of the adversary is corruption and darkness, for he is material and multipartite. The nature of the ungenerated Father of All is incorruption and self-existent, simple, and homogeneous light. But the substance of this (latter) brought forth a twofold power, but he himself is the image of the greater.

[20] Greek *demiurgós*.

8. For the present do not let this trouble you as you desire to learn how from *one* beginning of all things, which is simple and, as we acknowledge and believe, ungenerated, incorruptible, and good, there were constituted these natures, namely that of corruption and that of the Middle, which are of different substance, although it is the nature of the good to generate and produce things which are like itself and of the same substance. 9. If God permit, you will learn in the future about their origin and generation, when you are counted worthy of the apostolic tradition which we also have received by succession, because we can prove all our statements from the teaching of the Saviour.

10. My sister Flora, I have taken great pains to tell you this concisely and I have written with brevity, but at the same time I have treated the subject adequately. In the future this will be of exceptional benefit to you, if you, like good and fair soil which has received fertile seed, allow to spring forth the fruit that grows therefrom (cf. Matt. 13: 23 par.).

9

VALENTINIANISM II
THE FRAGMENTS OF HERACLEON

Heracleon is one of the most important disciples of Valentinus; indeed, according to Clement of Alexandria,[1] the most celebrated. In his Commentary on the Gospel of John, Origen (d. A.D. 254) has transmitted to us a number of verbal citations from the gnostic relating to John's Gospel, and two more are preserved in Clement of Alexandria. We can bring these into relation with Irenaeus' great section on the Valentinian system, and, in so doing, interpret the statements of the one by those of the other.

Fragment 1, on John 1: 3; Origen, *in Joh.* II 14

Violently and without evidence, in my opinion, has Heracleon (who is said to be a disciple of Valentinus), in interpreting the (saying) 'All things came into being through him', expounded 'all things' as meaning the world and what is in it, and excluded from that 'all', to suit his own view, that which is different from the world and the things therein. For he says: 'Neither the aeon nor what was in the aeon came into being through the Logos'—for that, he believes, came into being before the Logos. . . . to the 'And without him nothing came into being' he adds, to the 'nothing', 'of the things in the cosmos and in the creation'. . . . Moreover, he has understood in his own way the words 'Everything came into being through him', saying, 'The one who provided the Demiurge with the cause for creating the world, that is, the Logos, was not the one "from whom", or "by whom", but the one "through whose agency" (lit. "through whom").' . . . 'For the Logos did not create as if he were energized by another, so that "through his agency" might be understood thus, but he gave the energy and another created.'

Irenaeus also says that the Saviour who released Achamoth from her passions in effect created everything (outside the Pleroma).[2]

---

[1] See in following Fragm. 50.   [2] Ir. I 4, 5; *Exc.* § 43, 2.

Heracleon here calls the Saviour 'Logos', because of the passage being commented on: cf. Fragment 5.

Fragment 2, on John 1: 4; Origen, *in Joh.* II 21

In the saying 'What was made in him was life' he (Heracleon) understood 'in him' as meaning 'for spiritual men'. . . . And he says, 'For he provided for them the first formation according to their generation in that what had been sown by another he brought to form, illumination, and to an individual delineation, and set it forth.'

Heracleon too has related 'what was made' to what follows: cf. on Irenaeus I 8, 5. The Logos-Saviour lets the spiritual seeds become men. The 'first formation' is the formation according to substance. The sowing is then the activity of Christ, from whom the one who appears here as Saviour is differentiated: Irenaeus I 2, 6 says this, but certainly not explicitly.

Fragment 3, on John 1: 18; Origen, *in Joh.* VI 3

Heracleon says that the words 'No one has ever seen God, etc.' were said 'not by the Baptist, but by the disciple'.

Fragment 4, on John 1: 21; Origen, *in Joh.* VI 15

The difference between 'the prophet' and '(a) prophet' escapes the majority, including Heracleon, who literally says, 'John acknowledged that he was not the Christ, and neither a prophet nor Elijah.'

Fragment 5, on John 1: 23; Origen, *in Joh.* VI 20 f.

Heracleon . . . says: 'The Logos is the Saviour, the voice in the wilderness is that symbolized by John, and the echo is the entire prophetic order.' . . . I do not know how, without any explanation, he asserts that 'the voice which is akin to Logos becomes Logos, just as woman is transformed into man'. . . . And he says that 'the echo will undergo a change into a voice, giving the place of a disciple to the voice which changes into Logos, but the place of a slave to that (which changes) from echo into voice'. . . . According to Heracleon, the Saviour calls him both prophet and Elijah, but he himself denies that he is either of these. 'When the Saviour calls him "prophet" and "Elijah" as well (Matt. 11: 9, 14) he is not making an assertion about the man himself'—he maintains—'but about his attributes. But when he calls him "greater than a prophet" and "among those born of women" (Matt. 11: 9, 11), then he is characterizing John himself. But when he himself', he goes on, 'is asked about himself, he answers (as) John himself, and not (as) his attributes.' . . . He uses a simile: 'His attributes (lit. the things about him), like clothes, were other than himself, and if asked about his clothes, whether he himself was his clothes, he would not have answered with a "yes".' . . .

In his desire to explain why priests and Levites were sent by the Jews to ask questions (John 1: 19) he says, not inappropriately, 'It was fitting for these men to concern themselves with and investigate these matters, for they were firmly devoted to God.' But without much precision he adds, 'for he himself was of the Levitical tribe'. Again, on the question 'Art thou the prophet?' . . . he says: 'They asked if he was a prophet, for they wanted to learn about the more common subject' (John 1: 21). . . . He (Heracleon) thinks it was so arranged that Isaiah should prophetically call him 'greater', since no one of those who ever prophesied was deemed worthy of this honour by God.

Fragment 6, on John 1: 25; Origen, *in Joh.* VI 23

Heracleon regards the word of the Pharisees relating to the fact that baptizing is the duty of Christ, Elijah, and of every prophet, as having been spoken quite reasonably, and he speaks in these words: 'On them alone is there an obligation to baptize.' . . . But, not unwisely, he goes on to say: 'The Pharisees asked the question out of malice and not out of a desire to learn.'

Fragment 7, on John 1: 26; Origen, *in Joh.* VI 30

Heracleon thinks that 'to those sent by the Pharisees John gave reply, not in relation to what they asked, but as he himself wished'.

For Heracleon, John the Baptist is at one moment a symbol for the psychics, or for the Demiurge; at another, a symbol for the pneumatics. The latter enter into the Pleroma, and that is a transformation like that of a woman into a man.[3] The psychics enter some day with the Demiurge into the Ogdoad, where Achamoth previously abode. With this Irenaeus I 7, 1 agrees. When John the Baptist is called a prophet, that, according to Heracleon, is a statement about his clothing. When he is called 'greater than a prophet', he himself being named, as a symbol of the pneumatics. He is so styled

[3] Cf. *Exc.* § 21, 3; 68; 79.

because those who speak prophetically in the Old Testament are only psychics.

Fragment 8, on John 1 : 26 f.; Origen, *in Joh.* VI 39

Heracleon says that the words 'He stands in your midst' are spoken with the meaning 'He is already here and is in the world and among men, and is already manifest to you all.' . . .

Not improbably is it said by him: 'The statement "he who comes after me" indicates that John is the fore-runner of the Christ.' . . . He has interpreted 'I am not worthy to loose the thong of his sandal' much more simply to mean, 'The Baptist acknowledges in this word that he is not worthy to perform the lowliest service for Christ.' After this interpretation he expressed himself not unpersuasively: 'I am not worthy that on my account he should come down from the "greatness" and assume flesh, as a sandal, of which (that is, of the flesh) I can give no account, nor can I describe it, or unloose (explain) the dispensation concerning it.' With greater force and skill Heracleon also interprets the sandal as being the world, and then changes to impiety, saying that everything must be understood in relation to that person who was indicated through John. He in fact believes that 'the creator (Demiurge) of this world, who is inferior to Christ, acknowledges this through these words', which is the most impious thing of all.

The 'greatness' is here a name for the Pleroma, and John a symbol of the Demiurge: the allegorical interpretation fluctuates.

Fragment 9, on John 1 : 28; Origen, *in Joh.* VI 40

In Heracleon's work we read 'Bethany'.

Fragment 10, on John 1 : 29; Origen, *in Joh.* VI 60

When Heracleon comes to this point, he comments without any explanation or quotation of authorities: 'John said the "Lamb of God" as a prophet, the "which takes away the sin of the world" as more than a prophet.' And he thinks that 'the first was spoken with reference to his (Christ's) body, the second with reference to him who is in the body, because, since the lamb is imperfect in the genus of sheep, so the body is (imperfect) in comparison with him who dwells in it. For if he had wished to attribute perfection to the body', he says, 'he would have referred to a ram which was to be sacrificed.'

Here again John the Baptist plays a double role: as prophet, he says, 'This is the Lamb of God', which is taken to refer to the body of Christ, which is psychic; as more than a prophet he says, 'which takes away the sin of the world', and that must refer to the pneumatic realm. There is, however, no talk of forgiveness of sins among the pneumatics.

Fragment 11, on John 2: 12; Origen, *in Joh.* X 11

In his exposition of 'After this he went down to Capernaum' Heracleon says, 'There is again revealed here the beginning of a new dispensation, for "he went down" is not said idly.' And he goes on, 'Capernaum means the uttermost ends of the world, the realm of the material, into which he descended. And since this place was alien[4] (to him),' he says, 'there is no account of his having done or said anything in it.'

Another 'dispensation': at the moment the Saviour descends into the world.   .

Fragment 12, on John 2: 13; Origen, *in Joh.* X 19

Heracleon says 'This is the great feast. It was a type of the passion of the Saviour, for the sheep was not only slain, but, on being consumed, provided rest as well. When sacrificed, it signified the passion of the Saviour in the world; when consumed, the rest that is in the marriage.'

'Rest in the marriage' = Irenaeus I 7, 1: the blessed final state of the pneumatics.[5]

Fragment 13, on John 2: 13–16; Origen, *in Joh.* X 33

Let us see what Heracleon says when he takes 'the ascent to Jerusalem' to mean 'the ascent of the Lord from the realm of the material to the psychic place which is an image of Jerusalem'. 'The statement "He found (them) in the sanctuary (*hieron*)" and not "in the temple (*naos*)" is made', he thinks, 'so that it may not be thought to be the mere "calling", apart from the Spirit, which elicits help from the Lord.' For he claims that 'the "sanctuary" is the Holy of Holies, into which only the High Priest enters, into which'—I think he says—'the pneumatics go. The temple forecourt, where the Levites also

---

[4] Cf. the 'alien' and 'one's own' in the Acts of Thomas.

[5] Or should we think, after Cl. Al. (*Exc.* § 63, 2), of the wedding feast of the neumatics *and* the psychics?

are, is a symbol of the psychics who attain a salvation outside the Pleroma.' In his interpretation he adds that 'Those who are found in the sanctuary selling oxen and sheep and doves, and the money-changers sitting there, represent those who give nothing away out of charity, but who rather consider the entry of strangers into the sanctuary as an occasion for trade and profit-making, and who, for their own gain and love of money, provide the sacrifices for the worship of God. The whip made from small cords by Jesus, who did not receive it from another person', he explains in his own way, saying, 'The whip is an image of the power and energy of the Holy Spirit which blows away the wicked'; and he adds, 'The whip, the linen cloth, and the winding-sheet, and all such things, form an image of the power and energy of the Holy Spirit.' To assist his interpretation he adds something which was not written—'The whip was tied to a piece of wood.' This piece of wood he takes to be 'a type of the Cross', saying, 'With this wood there were consumed and destroyed the merchants who were intent on gain and all wickedness.' And (then), talking rubbish in some way or other, he says: 'Out of these two substances the whip was made', and he asks how Jesus made it, and says, 'For he did not make it out of dead leather, but in order that he might construct the church as no longer a den of robbers and merchants, but as the house of his Father.'

Fragment 14, on John 2: 17; Origen, *in Joh.* X 34

Heracleon very rashly believes that the word 'Zeal for thy house has consumed me' was spoken 'from the mouth (lit. from the person) of the powers which were cast out and destroyed by the Saviour'.

Heracleon makes the cleansing of the Temple express, and according to Origen's report as its main emphasis, something in favour of the pneumatics. It is significant that 'the calling', that is, the psychics, are saved apart from the Holy Spirit.[6] The whip is here an image of the Holy Spirit, more precisely of the Cross, which 'blows away' the wicked. The choice of this image gives expression to the fact that in the case of the pneumatics it is a matter of an event running its own course, without any action on the part of the one concerned. It is like what is said in Irenaeus I 4, 5 about the passions being 'separated' from Achamoth: it is an event 'of nature'.

[6] See also Fragm. 27.

Fragment 15, on John 2: 19; Origen, *in Joh.* X 37

Heracleon of course says that the words 'in three (days)' are used instead of 'on the third (day)', without posing the question —though he sticks to the expression, 'in three'—how the resurrection is accomplished in three days. He adds, 'The third (day) is the spiritual day' on which they believe 'the resurrection of the church is revealed.' It follows then that the first day is called the choic, the second the psychic, because the resurrection of the church did not take place on them.

The church does not mean the great Church, but the community of the pneumatics.

Fragment 16, on John 2: 20; Origen, *in Joh.* X 38

Without paying attention to the story Heracleon says 'the fact that Solomon completed the temple in forty-six years is an image of the Saviour, and the number "six" refers to matter, that is, to the structure (*plasma*), and the "forty", which is the uncombined Tetrad,' he says, 'refers to the inbreathing and to the seed (contained) in the inbreathing.'

At this point Heracleon is making a forced interpretation, not only because he divides the number 46 into 40+6, but above all because he makes the six, the number of matter,[7] signify the body of the Saviour, whereas it usually (for example, in Fragment 18) signifies the evil which the Saviour did not in any put on. Consequently, Heracleon explains the 'matter' as being the 'structure', by which is meant the psychic body which was prepared 'with ineffable art' so that it might be tangible.[8] The 'forty' is then related to the 'inbreathing' and the seed contained therein: the pneumatics are seeds, and the inbreathing refers probably to the moment of baptism when Jesus (the Saviour) descended on the psychic Christ: those sown by another he brings to the formation according to substance.

Fragment 17, on John 4: 12–15; Origen, *in Joh.* XIII 10

Let us look at Heracleon's (commentary) on these verses: he says—'Insipid, temporary, and unsatisfying was that life and its glory, for it was', he affirms, 'worldly.' And he thinks to draw a proof of its being worldly from the fact that 'the cattle of Jacob drank from it (the well)'. . . . 'But the water which the Saviour gives is from his spirit and his power.' . . . And the

[7] See Fragm. 18.   [8] Ir. I 6, 1 towards the end.

words 'he will never thirst again' (v. 14) he literally renders:
'For his life is eternal and never perishes, as does the first (life
which) the well (provides), but rather is lasting. For the grace
and the gift of our Saviour cannot be taken away, and is not
consumed or destroyed in the one who shares therein. The first
life is perishable.' Not improbably he interprets the 'springing
up' (v. 14) as referring to those 'who receive what is richly
supplied from above and who themselves pour forth for the
eternal life of others that which has been supplied to them'.
And he praises the Samaritan woman 'because she showed the
kind of faith that was inseparable from her nature and corre-
sponded to it, in that she did not hesitate over what he told her'.
. . . But I do not know how Heracleon, in expounding what
does not stand written, says on the phrase 'Give me this water'
(v. 15): 'Having been only just pricked by the word, from then
on she hated even the place of the so-called living water', and
on 'Give me this water that I may not thirst nor come here to
draw' he says: 'The woman says this and thereby reveals
that that water was toilsome, difficult to obtain, and not
wholesome.'

Fragment 18, on John 4: 16–18; Origen, *in Joh*. XIII 11

Again, on the words 'he says to her' Heracleon comments:
'It is clear that he was saying something like this—"If you wish
to receive this water, go, call your husband".' And he thinks
that 'the husband of the Samaritan woman mentioned by Jesus
is her Pleroma, so that, on coming with him to the Saviour, she
may obtain from him power and union and the mingling with
her Pleroma. For', he says, 'he was not speaking to her about
an earthly husband and telling her to call him, for he knew
quite well that she had no lawful husband.' Quite clearly he
does violence (to the text) when he says, 'The Saviour said to
her, "Call thy husband, and come hither", and meant by this
her partner from the Pleroma.' . . . But since, as Heracleon
says, 'in the spiritual (or, allegorical) sense she did not know her
husband, in the simple sense she was ashamed to say that she
had an adulterer and not a husband' . . . he then adds, on 'Thou
hast rightly said that thou hast no husband' (v. 17), 'In the
world the Samaritan woman had no husband, for her husband
was in the aeon.' . . . In Heracleon we find 'Thou hast had six

husbands' (v. 18), and he explains that 'by the six husbands there is indicated all the material evil with which she was intertwined and with which she consorted when she debauched herself, contrary to reason, and when she was insulted, rejected, and abandoned by them (the six husbands)'.

Fragment 19, on John 4: 19 f.; Origen, *in Joh.* XIII 15

On these very words Heracleon comments: 'the Samaritan woman properly acknowledged what was said to her by him. For it is characteristic only of a prophet', he asserts, 'to know all things.' . . . After this he praises her 'because she behaved in a way suited to her nature, for she neither denied nor explicitly acknowledged her shame', and he says that 'she was convinced that he was a prophet and, by her question, she revealed at the same time the reason for which she had committed immorality, (namely) that because of ignorance of God and of the worship agreeable to God, she had also neglected all the things that were essential for her life, whereas what is necessary in life was always otherwise available to her. For she would not have come', he says, 'to the well which was outside the city.' . . . 'Wanting to learn in what way, and pleasing whom and worshipping God, she might be released from her immorality, she said, "Our fathers worshipped on this mountain", etc.'

Fragment 23, on John 4: 23; Origen, *in Joh.* XIII 20

Heracleon says, 'Lost in the deep matter of error is that which is akin to the Father, which is sought after in order that the Father may be worshipped by those who are akin to him.'

Origen has handed down many quotations of Heracleon's interpretation of the story of the Samaritan woman. In the first fragments (with which we take Fragment 23 as well) the Samaritan woman is the pneumatic, who regarded the water of the well from which the cattle of forefather Jacob drank as being difficult to obtain (= the Old Testament) and who, corresponding to her nature, immediately agrees with the Saviour's words. She has had six husbands, not five, and this represents, for Heracleon, the evil character of matter; the one husband whom she is to call and whom she cannot name represents the husband in the Pleroma, that is, probably, one of the angels who had come with the Saviour to Achamoth. Heracleon admittedly assumes that they are in the aeon, whereas, according to Irenaeus (I 4, 5), they came with the Saviour, but he says nothing about where they stay until the consummation. The reason for her fall is ignorance of God, and on account of this she had neglected everything that was essential for her life.

Fragment 20, on John 4: 21; Origen, *in Joh.* XIII 16

... 'The mountain represents the Devil or his world, since the Devil was *one* part of the whole of matter', says Heracleon, 'but the world is the total mountain of evil, a deserted dwelling-place of beasts, to which all (who lived) before the law and all the Gentiles render worship. But Jerusalem (represents) the creation or the creator whom the Jews worship.' But, in the second place, he thinks that 'the mountain is the creation which the Gentiles worship, but Jerusalem is the creator whom the Jews serve. You, then', he adds, 'as the pneumatics will worship neither the creation nor the Demiurge, but the Father of truth. And he (Jesus) accepts her (the Samaritan woman)', he goes on, 'as one already faithful and to be counted with those who worship in truth.'

Fragment 21, on John 4: 22; Origen, *in Joh.* XIII 17

Heracleon interprets the 'you' as standing for 'the Jews and the Gentiles'. ... (Heracleon has quoted from the *Kerygma Petri*), we (Origen) wish only to draw attention to the fact that he asserts as the teaching of Peter, 'We must not worship as the Greeks do, who believe in the things of matter and serve wood and stone, nor worship the divine as the Jews; for they who think they alone know God do not know him, and worship angels, the month, and the moon.'

The tripartite division of mankind is clearly expressed here. For the Jews' 'worship of angels, months, and demons' cf. also Gal. 3: 19 and Col. 2: 16. Probably Irenaeus does not mention the Devil at all or does so only marginally.

Fragment 22, on John 4: 22; Origen, *in Joh.* XIII 19

'We worship', thinks Heracleon, means 'the one who is in the aeon and those who have come with him.[9] For they', he goes on, 'knew whom they worship because they worship in truth.' The words 'salvation is of the Jews' 'are said because he was born in

---

[9] i.e. the Saviour and his companions.

Judea', he asserts, 'but not among them (for he was not pleased with all of them) and because from that race salvation and the word (Logos) came forth into the world.' As far as the allegorical (or, spiritual) sense is concerned, he explains that 'salvation came from the Jews because they are considered by him as images of those who are in the Pleroma'.... By way of comment on the words on 'worshipping God in spirit and in truth' he says: 'For the previous worshippers worshipped in flesh and in error him who is not the Father', ... and Heracleon adds, 'they worshipped the creation and not the true creator (cf. Rom. 1 : 25), who is Christ, since "all things came into being through him, and apart from him nothing came into being"' (John 1 : 3).

Fragment 24, on John 4: 24; Origen, *in Joh.* XIII 25
On 'God is spirit' Heracleon says, 'Undefiled, pure, and invisible is his divine nature.' On the phrase, 'those who worship him must worship him in spirit and in truth' he says, thinking to make it clear: 'Worthily of him who is worshipped, in a spiritual, not a fleshly fashion. For those who have the same nature as the Father are themselves spirit, and they worship in truth and not in error, as the Apostle teaches when he calls this kind of piety "a rational service"' (Rom. 12: 2).

Here Heracleon distinguishes between the literal sense and the spiritual understanding, and in terms of the latter the Jews are 'images of those in the Pleroma', probably because the attendants of the Saviour who are destined for marriage with the pneumatics are in the aeon and come forth from it. For Christ as the true creator, see also Fragment 1. One should observe the role which error plays here, as also in Fragment 23, to which should be added ignorance in Fragment 19.[10]

Fragment 25, on John 4: 25; Origen, *in Joh.* XIII 27
Look what Heracleon says: he asserts that 'The Church received Christ and was persuaded concerning him that he alone understands (knows) all things.'

Fragment 26, on John 4: 26; Origen, *in Joh.* XIII 28
On 'I who speak with thee am he' Heracleon says: 'Since the Samaritan woman was convinced concerning Christ that, when

---

[10] Cf. the introduction to Valentinianism, Ir. I 5, 4 towards the end; 5, 2; 7, 1; and the Gospel of Truth.

he came, he would announce everything to her, he said, "Know that I who speak with thee am he whom you expect." And when he acknowledged that he, the expected one, had come, then, he says, "his disciples came to him", for on their account he had come to Samaria.'

The Church = the community of the pneumatics; the Samaritan woman is a symbol of the pneumatics.

Fragment 27, on John 4: 28; Origen, *in Joh*. XIII 31

Heracleon assumes that 'the water-jug which is capable of receiving life is the disposition and thought of the power which is from the Saviour. She left it', he says, 'with him, that is, she had with the Saviour such a vessel, with (lit. in) which she had come to fetch living water, and she returned to the world to announce the good tidings of Christ's coming to the "calling". For through the Spirit and by the Spirit the soul is drawn to the Saviour.' . . . And he interprets the statement 'They went out of the city': '(This is explained) as meaning out of their former way of life, which was worldly. And they came', he says, 'through faith to the Saviour.'

According to Irenaeus the pneumatics are 'yoked together' with the psychics and 'trained in conduct'. But also the account of Irenaeus allows us to recognize the effect of the pneumatic on the psychic, for it is the salt and the light of the world, Irenaeus I 6, 1. At any rate, the Samaritan woman is here already 'formed according to knowledge', and she no longer needed the psychic method of training. She has now a task in relation to the 'calling', that is, the psychics. These obtain a salvation apart from the Holy Spirit, as Fragment 13 affirms. But here the 'calling' is actually led through the Spirit to the Saviour. This appears to be a contradiction, and in a sense it is. But it should be observed that Heracleon—without support in the text—emphatically stresses the fact that the Samaritan woman leaves with him the 'jug', the 'thought of the power of the Saviour', and betakes herself without it to the psychics. This must be of significance for Heracleon, else he would not have introduced this feature into the text. I conjecture, consequently, that Heracleon wants to say that the spiritual disposition and insight into the power of the Saviour is something pneumatic which cannot pass over to the psychics. The Samaritan woman is pneumatic, but the specific thing which makes her a pneumatic does not pass to the psychic, but remains with the Saviour.

Fragment 28, on John 4: 31; Origen, *in Joh.* XIII 32

But Heracleon says: 'They wished to share with him some of what they had obtained by purchase in Samaria.'

Fragment 29, on John 4: 32; Origen, *in Joh.* XIII 34

(On the words 'I have food to eat that you do not know'): Heracleon said nothing on this text.

Fragment 30, on John 4: 33; Origen, *in Joh.* XIII 35

Even if Heracleon supposes that this was said by the disciples in a fleshly way, as if they 'understood in a rather low way and imitated the Samaritan woman when she said, "You have no bucket to draw with, and the well is deep." . . .'

Fragment 31, on John 4: 34; Origen, *in Joh.* XIII 38

Heracleon says that 'with the words "My meat is to do the will of him who sent me" the Saviour explains to the disciples that this was what he had discussed with the woman, calling the will of the Father his "meat". For this was his food, rest, and power. The will of the Father', he goes on, 'is that men should know the Father and be saved. This was the work of the Saviour, on account of which he was sent to Samaria, that is, into the world.'

Fragment 32, on John 4: 35; Origen, *in Joh.* XIII 41

. . . Heracleon . . . says: 'He speaks of the harvest of crops as having still a fixed period of four months, whereas the harvest of which he was speaking was already fulfilled.' And the 'harvest' he related, I know not how, 'to the souls of believers', saying, 'They are already ripe, ready for harvest, and suitable for being gathered into the barn, that is, through faith into rest, all those who are ready. For they are not all (ready). Some (souls) were already ready,' he says, 'some were on the point of being ready, some are near to being ready, and some are still being sown.'

Fragment 33, on John 4: 36; Origen, *in Joh.* XIII 44

Heracleon says . . . 'What is indicated by the text "The harvest is great, but the labourers are few" is the same as is said by means of the other statement: it refers to being ready for harvest and suitable for being gathered already into the barn, through faith into rest, and suited for salvation and for reception of the Logos.'

It is clear that Heracleon has related the 'harvest' to the souls of the faithful, that is, to the pneumatics—in spite of the expression 'souls'. There comes to expression here what is for Heracleon the final hope: to be gathered into the barn, that is, into rest (into the marriage, as Irenaeus puts it). Salvation may also be indicated by the words 'the Logos rests upon the pneumatics', as in Fragment 34.[11] But this state of 'readiness' is achieved through activity which requires at least a period of time, and the 'getting ready' recalls the idea of 'becoming trained' in Irenaeus. The view that some are still being sown is in opposition to Fragment 2.

Fragment 34, on John 4: 36; Origen, *in Joh.* XIII 46

Heracleon is of the opinion that the words 'The reaper receives a wage' are said 'because' (as he asserts) 'the Saviour calls himself a reaper'. And the wage of our Lord, he assumes, 'is the salvation and restoration of those who are harvested, brought about by his resting upon them'. 'And he gathers fruit for eternal life', he maintains, 'is stated either because what is gathered is the fruit of eternal life or because it is itself eternal life'.

The word 'restoration' (*apokatastasis*) is worthy of note here.

Fragment 35, on John 4: 37; Origen, *in Joh.* XIII 49

The words 'that the sower and the reaper may rejoice together' are interpreted by Heracleon as follows: 'For the sower rejoices', he says, 'because he sows, and because some of his seeds are gathered already, and he has the same hope for the rest of them. The reaper (rejoices) likewise because he harvests. But the former began by sowing, the latter by reaping. They could not both begin at the same time, for sowing must come first and reaping afterwards. When the sower stops sowing, the reaper is still reaping. But, at present, both fulfil their individual tasks and both rejoice because they consider the perfection of the seeds as a common joy.' And on the words 'Herein is the saying true, one sows and another reaps' he says: 'The Son of Man above the "Place" sows; the Saviour, himself also Son of Man, harvests and sends as reapers the angels represented by the disciples, each for his own soul.'

Fragment 36, on John 4: 38; Origen, *in Joh.* XIII 50

Heracleon says, 'Neither through them nor by them were these seeds sown.' He means the apostles. 'Those who toiled

---

[11] Cl. Al., *Exc.* § 67, 4.

are the angels of the dispensation, through whom—as mediators
—it (the seed) was sown and brought up.' 'You have entered
into their labours' he explains as follows: 'Those who sow and
those who reap have not the same work. The former in cold and
rain and with much toil dig up the earth and sow, and through
the entire winter care for it by hoeing and clearing away the
weeds; but the latter enter upon a prepared fruit in summer and
joyfully reap.'

The Son of Man above the 'Place' is the Christ, who is also called
Son of Man, see on Fragment 2; but that he should be regarded as
still 'sowing' is hard to understand. Here is a difficulty which has
probably been caused by different interpretations of the image of
sowing. In Fragment 36 it is only the angels of the dispensation
through whom, as mediators, the seed was sown and brought up.
The fact that they are represented as mediators allows this statement to be reconciled with the preceding Fragment: Christ sows
through them: but who are these angels? Mention is made of a
'training' by them, and the thought is of a hard and difficult task,
as the sequel shows. We might recall the psychic training,[12] and
the fact that the Demiurge, after having been 'instructed' by the
Saviour, assists the pneumatics. But then we should have to regard
the sowing also as something which results through the mediation
of the psychic angels.

Fragment 37, on John 4: 39; Origen, *in Joh*. XIII 51

Heracleon has interpreted the words 'out of the city' as
meaning 'out of the world'; and the phrase 'because of the
woman's report' means 'because of the spiritual church'. And
on the word 'many' he says: 'Because there are many psychics.
But the one, in his view, is the imperishable nature of the election, uniform and unique.'

Many psychics, few pneumatics = Clement of Alexandria,
Excerpta ex Theodoto 56, 2.

Fragment 38, on John 4: 40; Origen, *in Joh*. XIII 52

Heracleon comments on this verse as follows: 'He remained
"with them", not "among them" and "for two days", signifying
either the present aeon and the one to come in marriage, or
the time before the passion and the period after it, during which

---

[12] Ir. I 6, 1; 7, 5.

he remained with them, converted many more to faith through his own words, and then departed from them.'

Fragment 39, on John 4: 42; Origen, *in Joh.* XIII 53

Heracleon interprets the words 'We no longer believe because of your word' quite simply, and says, 'The word "only" is missing.' And on 'We ourselves have heard and know that this is the Saviour of the world' he says, 'At first men believe on the Saviour because they are led to that point by men, but when they encounter his words they no longer believe because of human testimony alone, but because of the truth itself.'

Fragment 40, on John 4: 46–53; Origen, *in Joh.* XIII 60

Heracleon seems to say that the 'royal officer' (v. 46) was the Demiurge, 'for he himself ruled like a king over those under him. Because his domain is small and transitory he was called a royal officer', he says, 'like a petty princeling who is set over a small kingdom by the universal king.' He interprets 'his son in Capernaum' as one who (sojourns) in the lower part of the Middle, which lies near the sea, that is, which is linked with matter: and, he goes on, 'his proper man was sick, that is, his condition was not in accordance with his nature, and he was in ignorance and sins'. Then the words 'from Judaea to Galilee' (v. 47) are said to mean 'from the Judaea above . . .'. But I do not know how, being moved by the expression 'he was about to die', he thinks 'that the teaching of those who claim that the soul is immortal is refuted', assuming that 'in agreement with this is the statement that "the soul and the body are destroyed in Hell"' (Matt. 10: 28, par.). Heracleon affirms that 'the soul is not immortal, but is possessed (only) of a disposition towards salvation', for he points out that 'it is the perishable which puts on imperishability and the mortal which puts on immortality, when "its death is swallowed up in victory"' (1 Cor. 15: 54). On 'If you do not see signs and wonders, you will not believe' (v. 48) he comments: 'It is fittingly said to the kind of person whose nature is determined through works, and who is convinced by means of sense-perception and does not believe the word.' The words 'Come, before my child dies' (v. 49) were spoken, he thinks, 'because death is the goal and end of the law which kills through sins. Before he was utterly put to death through sins', he goes on, 'the father asks the only Saviour to help his son, that is, the nature thus constituted.' The words 'Thy son lives' (v. 50) 'were said by the Saviour modestly', and he interprets thus: 'for he did not say, "Let him live", nor did he make it known that *he* himself had provided the life.' But he says that 'he went down to the sick man and healed him of his illness, that is, of his sins, and, having raised him to life through forgiveness, said, "Thy son lives."' And to the words 'the man believed' (v. 50) he adds: 'For even the Demiurge is very ready to believe that the Saviour, even if not present, is able to heal.' But he explains 'the servants of the royal officer' (v. 51) as the angels of the Demiurge who bring tidings in the words 'Thy son lives' that he is behaving fittingly and rightly, and no longer doing what is unseemly; and for this reason, he thinks, 'the servants bring news to the royal officer about the salvation of his son, since the angels', he imagines, 'are the first to see the actions of men in the world, whether they have conducted themselves well and sincerely since the sojourn of the Saviour'. On the seventh hour (v. 52) he comments: 'By the hour the nature of the man healed is defined.' In addition he claims that 'he and his whole house believed' (v. 53) 'is said with reference to the order of angels and to the men who are akin to him (the Demiurge)'. But he goes on: 'there is a question about some angels, whether or not they will be saved, namely those who descended to the daughters of men' (Gen. 6: 2). And he thinks that 'the destruction of the men of the Demiurge is made clear in the words "The sons of the kingdom will be cast out into outer darkness" (Matt. 8: 12, par.). Concerning them Isaiah prophesied, "Sons did I rear and bring up, but they have rejected me" (Isa. 1: 2), and them he calls alien sons, and a wicked and lawless seed, a vineyard which produces thorns' (Isa. 5: 6).

Origen has collected in one place what he wants to convey about Heracleon's exposition of the story of the royal officer. Heracleon explained Capernaum in Fragment 11 as 'the uttermost ends of the world, the realm of the material'. But here Capernaum is 'the lower part of the Middle, which lies near the sea', that is, adjoining matter. By the officer the Demiurge is meant: his son denotes 'the nature thus constituted', that is, the psychic. The soul can die[13] and dies through the sins which the law condemns. In Fragment 48 it is

---

[13] Ir. I 6, 1 f.; 7, 1.

Moses who judges; Moses is the law-giver: law and law-giver are one. The psychics believe by reason of signs and wonders, not, like the pneumatics, in the word alone. The healing takes place through the separation and through the forgiveness of sins. The Demiurge is very ready to believe, just as, according to Irenaeus I 7, 4, he 'joyfully' agreed with the Saviour. It is Heracleon's opinion that not all psychics and not all the angels like them are saved, and he refers to Gen. 6: 1 ff. and to verses like Matt. 8: 12 and Isa. 1: 2.

Fragment 41, on John 8: 21; Origen, *in Joh.* XIX 14

Heracleon has nothing to say on the pericope about the treasury. But on the words 'Whither I go you cannot come' he says: 'How can they come to a state of imperishability when they are in ignorance, unbelief and sins?'

Fragment 42, on John 8: 22; Origen, *in Joh.* XIX 19

Heracleon speaks as if 'He will not kill himself, will he?' had been more simply expressed, 'The Jews said this because they entertained evil thoughts and considered themselves greater than the Saviour, and supposed that they themselves would go away to God for eternal rest, but the Saviour, making away with himself, to corruption and death, unto which they thought they would not go.' In his own words he says: 'The Jews believed that the Saviour said, "I am about to do away with myself and go to corruption, whither you cannot come."'

Fragment 43, on John 8: 37; Origen, *in Joh.* XX 8

We might ask those who introduce the natures and who interpret 'Because my word has no place in you' with Heracleon as 'It has no place for the reason that they are unsuitable for it either by their substance or by their disposition'—we might ask them how those who are unsuitable by substance could hear (anything) from the Father.

Fragment 44, on John 8: 43; Origen, *in Joh.* XX 20

Heracleon supposes that 'the reason why they were unable to hear Jesus' words and understand what he said is provided in the words, "You are of your father the devil."' He says, 'Why are you unable to hear my word? Because "you are of your father the Devil" (is said) to mean "of the substance of the Devil". Thus he makes clear to them their nature, after convincing them in advance that they are neither the children of

Abraham, else they would not have hated him, nor children of God, because they did not love him.' . . . Now it is clear that he considers some men to be of the same substance as the Devil, men who are of a different substance, as his disciples maintain, from those they call psychics or pneumatics.

Fragment 45, on John 8: 44; Origen, *in Joh.* XX 23

Heracleon comments: 'Those to whom the word came were of the substance of the Devil.'

Fragment 46, on John 8: 44; Origen, *in Joh.* XX 24

So much then on Heracleon's statement when he says that 'This verse, "You are of your father the Devil" is to be understood as meaning "of the substance of the Devil".' Again, on 'and your wish is to perform the desires of your father', he makes a distinction, saying, 'The Devil has not will, but desires.' . . . After this Heracleon says: 'This was said not to those who are by nature children of the Devil, the choics, but to the psychics who have become sons of the Devil by intent; some who are of this nature may also be called sons of God by intent.' And he adds: 'Because they have loved the desires of the Devil and performed them, they become children of the Devil, though they were not such by nature.' He draws a distinction by saying: 'The word "children" must be understood in three ways: first, by nature; secondly, by inclination; and thirdly, by merit. By nature', he goes on, '(the child) is one begotten by someone himself begotten, and is properly called "child": by inclination, when one who does the will of another person by his own inclination is called the child of him whose will he does: by merit, when some are known as children of hell, or of darkness and lawlessness, and offspring of snakes and vipers. For', he claims, 'these (all) do not produce anything by their own nature; they are destructive and consume those who are cast into them; but, since they did their works, they are called their children.' . . . Again, he says: 'He now calls them children of the Devil, not because the Devil produces any of them, but because by doing the works of the Devil they became like him.'

Fragment 47, on John 8: 44; Origen, *in Joh.* XX 28

Heracleon comments: 'His nature is not of the truth, but of the opposite to the truth, error and ignorance. Therefore', he says, 'he can neither stand in truth nor have the truth in himself; from his nature he has falsehood as his own, and by nature he can never speak the truth.' But he adds: 'Not only is he himself a liar, but he is also its (falsehood's) father', since he really understands 'his father' to mean 'his nature, since it is composed of error and falsehood'.

These fragments all revolve around John 8: 43–4, on the children of the Devil. In Fragment 46 Heracleon clarifies his view. He distinguishes the children of the Devil by nature from those by intent: children of the Devil by nature are the choics and they are of his 'substance': children of the Devil by intent are those who, out of love for the works of the Devil, do his deeds; they are not by nature his children, nor are they by nature of his substance, but they perform willingly what he desires. Here at once it becomes clear what is intended by the inclination to good or to evil: there is an act of will, in which a man can decide for the good as well as for the evil, Irenaeus I 6, 1. In Fragment 47 the Devil's nature originates from error and ignorance. This agrees with the view that fire, ignorance, lies at the basis of all matter, Irenaeus I 7, 1. If the Devil has no will, but only desires, then he is like the beasts who also have no will, that is, no responsibility, but simply desires. With this we cannot reconcile what Irenaeus I 5, 4 says of the Devil: that passage derives from a different account from the one which the Church Father otherwise follows in Chapters 1–8.

Fragment 48, on John 8: 50; Origen, *in Joh.* XX 38

Heracleon does not refer the words 'There is one who seeks you and judges' to the Father, saying, 'He who seeks and judges is the one who avenges me, the servant commissioned for that purpose, who does not bear the sword in vain, the avenger of the king; and this is Moses, as he said to them previously in the words, "on whom you set your hope"' (John 5: 45). He goes on: 'He who judges and punishes is Moses, that is, the law-giver himself.' Heracleon then raises an objection against himself, saying, 'How then, does he not say that all judgement has been delivered to him?' (John 5: 22). He thinks that this objection can be refuted, and he says, 'He affirms it rightly: for the judge does this will as a servant when he judges, as happens clearly among men as well.'

It is noteworthy that Moses fulfils the will of the Saviour in his judging.

Fragment 49, on Matt. 3: 11; Clement of Alexandria, *Eclogae Propheticae* 25, 1

John says, 'I baptize you with water, but there comes after me one who baptizes you with spirit and with fire.' He baptized no one with fire. But some—so Heracleon says—have marked with fire the ears of those who are sealed, and have thus understood the apostolic word.

Heracleon says only that some Gnostics, not himself, branded the ears of those sealed with fire; we know this about some Carpocratians, Irenaeus I 25, 6.

Fragment 50, on Luke 12: 8; Clement of Alexandria, *Strom.* IV 9 = § 71, 1–73, 1

In interpreting this verse Heracleon, the most celebrated of Valentinus' school, says: 'The confession is on the one hand that made in faith and in conduct, on the other that made with the mouth. Confession with the mouth takes place also before authorities, and this', he says, 'the multitudes consider to be the only confession, but not correctly, for even the hypocrites can make this confession. But it will be found that this word was not spoken universally. For not all who are saved made the confession by mouth, among whom are Matthew, Philip, Thomas, Levi, and many others. The confession by mouth is not universal, but relates to a part. What is universal is the one he now mentions, the one in works and action which correspond to faith in him. And this confession is followed by the partial one before the authorities, if it is necessary and the situation requires it. That man will make the confession by mouth who has previously confessed rightly in his disposition. 72. And of those who confess he rightly said "in me"; but in the case of those who deny he added a "me". For the latter, even if they confess him with their mouth, deny him, since they do not confess him in action. Only those who live in confession and action which conform to him confess "in him", and in their case he confesses himself, since he has grasped them and is held by them so that they can never deny him. For those who are not in him deny him. For he did not say "Whoever denies in me", but "me": for no one who was ever in him will deny him. "Before men": (the confession takes place) in similar fashion before those who are saved and before the Gentiles, before the former by conduct also, and before the latter by mouth.' 73, 1. So says Heracleon.

This fragment provides us with a glimpse of the conduct of the Valentinians. Literally, Luke 12:8 reads, 'Whoever confesses in me before men, in him also will the Son of Man confess before the angels of God. But whoever denies me before men will also be denied before the angels of God.' Before men: it is not said 'before the Gentiles', but the confessing goes on before companions in the faith *and* before Gentiles, and it takes place in conduct *and* with the mouth— with the mouth before the authorities as well, in which case it may lead to martyrdom. If Heracleon considers the latter an easier confession, in that one can say it lightly, he may perhaps have in mind some instance or other, but at any rate martyrdom stands in the background. Confession in conduct is more difficult, for it is demanded every day. Consequently, Heracleon links this confession in conduct with the act of confessing 'in him', which he explains as 'in whom he lives': and whoever lives in him can never deny him.

Fragment 51, on John 1:17; Photius, *Ep.* 134, *MPG* 101, 984 C

It is not out of maliciousness or for the purpose of denying the law that the words 'Grace and truth came by Jesus Christ' are added to the words of the evangelist. Heracleon and his disciples in fact say that.

This passage is not a direct quotation from Heracleon. The statement about grace coming through Jesus Christ is said by Heracleon and his disciples to show that the law which 'was given through Moses' is inferior, and to set the grace of Jesus Christ in opposition thereto. This, however, is a view not confined to Heracleon alone.

10

VALENTINIANISM III
THE ACCOUNT OF HIPPOLYTUS

INTRODUCTION

We have thus recognized Irenaeus' account through the formulation of Epiphanius as that of Ptolemaeus, and found it confirmed by the *Excerpta ex Theodoto* 43–65, by the Letter of Ptolemaeus to Flora, and by the Fragments of Heracleon, but Hippolytus' account of the Valentinian system provides many divergencies, although its relationship to Valentinianism is clear. Here the main divergencies can be only briefly mentioned.

Hippolytus' system starts out not from a pair, Primal Cause (Bythos) and Silence (Sige), but from *a single* Father. He is not counted in the number of the aeons, but transcends all as Beginning and Depth. Being unbegotten, he alone can bring forth, and he creates the Dyad, Nous and Truth, and these bring forth Logos and Life, and these in turn produce Man and Church. The ten aeons derive from Nous and Truth, the twelve from Logos and Life, and the names individually correspond with those in Irenaeus. The last of the aeons, Sophia, defects here as well, but it is because she desires to achieve a work in the way the Father does, that is, alone; she fails to recognize the difference between the uncreated and the created, in terms of which the female produces the substance, whereas the male gives it form. Here we see how the 'formation according to substance' and that 'in accordance with knowledge' (Irenaeus) and the 'production' and the 'formation' of substance (Hippolytus) are two different ways of setting forth *one* viewpoint.

Sophia brought forth an 'abortion', without form and incomplete: according to Irenaeus it was without shape and form. When, according to Hippolytus, the word 'The earth was invisible and incomplete' (Gen. 1: 2 LXX) is employed in connection with it, and when, furthermore, this abortion is equated with the heavenly Jerusalem, this is so because at this stage of events it is equated with the psychic. By Nous and Truth there are produced Christ and the Holy Spirit, and these separate and give form to the abortion: Sophia is now 'given form like a perfect aeon'. Thereafter the Father brings forth Horos (Limit), in order that the aeons may no longer be disturbed by the abortion, and then there is brought forth for the Father by the thirty aeons, that is, by the twenty-eight aeons plus Christ and the Holy Spirit, the 'Joint Fruit of the Pleroma', Jesus. Through the return of Christ into the Pleroma, the 'Sophia outside', as the abortion is called in what follows, falls into distress, out of which the 'Fruit' helps her. He takes away the passions from her and creates from her fear the psychic, from her sorrow the material, from her distress the demonic, and from her turning back again (or: conversion) the psychic essence which is called 'the right'. The distribution of the three passions is clear and meaningful: the psychic denotes the animal soul; the material the body and, in general, matter; the demonic denotes man's possession by evil spirits. The material man is perishable and is indeed made out of devilish substance, but real evil first enters into the world through the demons.

The Demiurge is twofold: on the one hand, he is from the 'fear' fiery, but on the other hand, he is from the 'conversion' and, as such, accepts the instruction of the Sophia outside, but he certainly says nothing to anyone about this. The Old Testament is derived only from the Demiurge; no prophet said anything concerning what is spiritual. That the soul has a double destiny, according to whom it 'makes itself like', is the same in the accounts of both Irenaeus and Hippolytus. But this presentation of the system says nothing about anyone 'educating'. The Fruit and the mother together produce seventy Logoi, which is probably a taking over of a Jewish speculation on seventy angels of the nations. These Logoi are sown in a soul in which no demons reside, and this is a rejection of libertinism, such as the Valentinianism of Irenaeus also achieves with its idea of 'being yoked with the psychics'.

The Saviour is spiritual, but he has a body from the Demiurge. His soteriological work is the 'setting to rights' of (as Hippolytus says) the passions of the soul, or else of 'this world of ours'. According to the view of Valentinus himself, which we may here refer to, he sets the soul free from demons, in which case the Logoi can dwell in it. Probably the souls in which neither demons nor Logoi reside, which have brought themselves thus far by means of their own efforts and their own works, reach a destiny with the Demiurge in the Ogdoad. But Hippolytus has not pursued this part of the system any further.

Two points unite this system and that of Irenaeus in contrast to Valentinian systems shortly to be discussed: Christ is brought forth within the Pleroma, and the Demiurge has an ultimately friendly disposition towards the pneumatics.

Hippolytus, *Ref.* VI 29, 2–36, 4 (Selection)

2. For these (Valentinus, Heracleon, Ptolemaeus, etc.) the beginning of all things is a Monad, which is unbegotten, imperishable, inconceivable, incomprehensible, productive, and a cause of the generation of all created things. The aforementioned Monad is called by them Father. . . .

5. There was a time when there was nothing whatsoever created, and the unbegotten Father alone existed, without place, without time, without counsellor, without any other entity capable of being thought of in any way. He was alone, solitary, as they say, and reposing in isolation within himself. But since he was productive, he decided once to generate and bring forth the fairest and most perfect that he had in himself, for he was not fond of solitariness. Indeed, he was all love, but love is not love if there is nothing which is beloved. 6. Thus the Father himself, since he was alone, brought forth and produced Nous and Truth, that is, a Dyad, which was mistress, beginning and mother of all the aeons which they number within the Pleroma. 7. Nous and Truth, being brought forth by the Father, productive entities from a productive (sire), also brought forth Logos and Life, in imitation of the Father. Logos and Life produced Man and Church.

Nous and Truth, on seeing that Logos and Life, their own offspring, had become productive, gave thanks to the Father of all and produced for him a perfect number, ten aeons. 8. For, he affirms, Nous and Truth could not offer to the Father a more perfect number than this. It was necessary that the Father, who himself was perfect, should be celebrated by a perfect number. Now ten is a perfect (number) for it is the first perfect (number) of those which are reckoned by quantity. But the Father is more perfect, for he alone, unbegotten, was able, by means of the first and single pair, Nous and Truth, to produce all the roots of the created things.

30, 1. But when Logos and Life saw that Nous and Truth celebrated the Father of all by a perfect number, then Logos along with Life desired to glorify their own father and mother, Nous and Truth. 2. But since Nous and Truth were begotten and did not possess the paternal perfection of being uncreated, Logos and Life could not magnify their father, Nous, by means of a perfect number, but (only) with an imperfect one. Logos and Life produce twelve aeons for Nous and Truth. 3. These are, according to Valentinus, the primary roots of the aeons: Nous and Truth, Logos and Life, Man and Church; ten from Nous and Truth, twelve from Logos and Life, and twenty-eight in all.

4 and 5 proceed with the enumeration of names, as in Irenaeus I 1, 2, with the observation that some make the ten proceed from Logos and Life, and the twelve from Man and Church.

6. Now when the twelfth of the twelve, the youngest of all the twenty-eight aeons, a female, Sophia (Wisdom) by name, observed the quantity and power of the aeons brought into being,* she hastened back into the depth of the Father and perceived that all the other aeons, being begotten, were pro-creating in pairs, but that the Father alone was procreating without a partner. 7. She wished to emulate the Father and to produce offspring of herself alone, without a partner, in order that she might achieve a work which would not be in any way inferior to that of the Father. She did not know that he, being uncreated, the beginning of all things, root, depth, and origin, is capable of procreating alone, but that Sophia, being begotten and born (only) after many others, cannot have the power of the unbegotten one. 8. In the unbegotten, he affirms, all things exist simultaneously, but in the begotten the female brings forth the substance, while the male gives form to the substance brought forth by the female. So Sophia brought forth that of which she was capable, an unformed and incomplete substance. 9. And this, he says, is what Moses declares: 'The earth was invisible and incomplete' (Gen. 1: 2 LXX). This, he says, is the good, 'the heavenly Jerusalem' (Heb. 12: 22) into which God has promised to lead the children of Israel, saying, 'I will bring you into a good land, flowing with milk and honey' (Exod. 3: 8).

31, 1. Since then there was within the Pleroma ignorance by reason of Sophia and formlessness by reason of Sophia's off-spring, uproar broke out in the Pleroma. For the aeons were terrified by the thought that the progenies of the aeons would be similarly unformed and incomplete and that, in the not far distant future, destruction would one day lay hold upon the aeons. 2. So all the aeons had recourse to pleading with the

---

* Greek: 'the begetting aeons'.

Father to give rest to the grieving Sophia. For she wept and bewailed greatly over the abortion which had been produced by her; for thus they term it. The Father then had compassion on the tears of Sophia, accepted the supplication of the aeons, and ordered (something) additional to be brought forth. For he did not himself produce (he asserts) but Nous and Truth did, and (they brought forth) Christ and the Holy Spirit for the sake of the formation and the separation of the abortion, and for the consolation of Sophia and her release from her groaning. 3. They became thirty aeons with the addition of Christ and the Holy Spirit. . . . 4. When Christ and the Holy Spirit were produced in addition by Nous and Truth, he immediately separated the abortion of Sophia—which was without form, had been born of one (only) and without a marriage-partner—from the entirety of the aeons in order that the perfect aeons might not be embarrassed, on seeing it, because of its shapelessness.

5. In order that the formlessness of the abortion may not at all be manifest to the perfect aeons, the Father produces again a further aeon, the Cross: being created great, as from a mighty and perfect Father, and brought forth for the guarding and defence of the aeons, he (the Cross) becomes a limit of the Pleroma, having within himself at one and the same time all thirty aeons; for that number had been produced. 6. He is called Horos (Limit) because he separates from the Pleroma the deficiency outside, and Participant, because he shares in the deficiency, but Cross because he is fixed unwaveringly and immovably, with the result that nothing of the deficiency can come near the aeons within the Pleroma.

7. Outside the Limit, the Cross, the Participant, is the Ogdoad, as they call it, which is the Sophia outside the Pleroma whom Christ, after he had been additionally produced by Nous and Truth, formed and made into a perfect aeon, which would be in no way inferior to those (aeons) within the Pleroma. 8. Since the Sophia outside had been formed, and it was not possible for Christ and the Holy Spirit, who were brought forth by Nous and Truth, to remain outside the Pleroma, Christ and the Holy Spirit hastened away from her who had been given form and back to Nous and Truth, and within the Limit celebrated the Father along with the other aeons.

32, 1. Since then there was one single peace and harmony of all the aeons within the Pleroma, they decided not only to have celebrated him* in conjugal union, but also to magnify (him) through the offering of fruits which were suitable for the Father. So all the thirty aeons decided to bring forth *one* aeon as a joint fruit of the Pleroma, in order that he might be the proof of their unity, agreement and peace. 2. And that single one brought forth by all the aeons for the Father is he who is called among them 'Joint Fruit of the Pleroma'. This is what took place within the Pleroma. And the 'Joint Fruit of the Pleroma' was produced, Jesus—for so he is called—the 'great High Priest'.

The Sophia outside the Pleroma sought Christ who had given her form and the Holy Spirit, and fell into a state of great terror because she got lost when he who gave her form and security was separated (from her). 3. She experienced grief and great distress when she recalled who had given her form, who the Holy Spirit was, whither he had gone, who it was that hindered them from being together, and who had been envious of that good and blessed sight. In the midst of these sufferings, she turns herself to fervent pleading with him who had departed from her. 4. Christ, who was inside the Pleroma, had compassion on her prayer, and all the rest of the aeons as well, and they sent forth from the Pleroma the Joint Fruit of the Pleroma as a marriage-partner for Sophia outside, that he might rectify the sufferings (or: passions) which she experienced whilst she sought for Christ.

5. When the Joint Fruit of the Pleroma came forth from the Pleroma and found her involved in the four primary passions—fear, sorrow, distress, and entreaty—he set her to rights from her passions; but as he did so, he saw that it would not be right to destroy them, since they were eternal and exclusive to Sophia, but, on the other hand, that Sophia could not continue with such passions, fear, sorrow, entreaty, and distress. 6. Being an aeon so great, and the offspring of the entire Pleroma, he caused the passions to depart from her, and he made them into substance-possessing essences: the fear he made into a psychic essence, the sorrow into a material one, the distress into a demonic, but the conversion, the entreaty, and supplication for ascent he made into repentance and the power of the psychic substance, which is called 'the right'.

* Greek: 'the Son'.

7. The Demiurge is (made) from the fear; and that, he says, is what Scripture affirms: 'The fear of the Lord is the beginning of wisdom' (Ps. 111 (110): 10; Prov. 1 : 7; 9: 10). For this is the beginning of the passions of Sophia. She feared first, then was involved in sorrow, then in distress, and so took refuge in entreaty and supplication. But the psychic essence, he says, is fiery, and is also called by them Topos (of the Middle), the Hebdomad, and 'the Ancient of Days' (Dan. 7: 9). And whatever they say in respect of this is said with reference to the psychic one who, he says, is the creator of the world. 8. But he is fiery in appearance, as Moses (he says) also affirms: 'The Lord thy God is a burning and devouring fire' (Exod. 24: 17; Deut. 4: 24)—for this in their view is how it stands written. But the power of the fire is twofold. It is an all-consuming fire which cannot be quenched. (Lacuna.) In this respect the soul is mortal, for it is the Middle; it is in fact Hebdomad and rest. 9. For it is beneath the Ogdoad, where the Sophia which was given form and the Joint Fruit of the Pleroma are, but above matter, of which it is the Demiurge. If it (the soul) becomes like those above, namely, the Ogdoad, then is it immortal and it comes into the Ogdoad, which (he asserts) is 'the heavenly Jerusalem' (Heb. 12: 22): but if it becomes like matter, that is, the corporeal passions, then is it perishable and goes to destruction.

33. As the first and greatest power of the psychic essence has become an image of the Father, likewise the power of the material essence is an image of the Demiurge, and he is the Devil, the ruler of this world, and an image of the Devil is the ruler of the essence of the demons who are derived from the distress, and that is Beelzebul.[1] Sophia works from above, from the Ogdoad, as far as the Hebdomad. The Demiurge, they say, knows nothing whatsoever, but is, in their view, without understanding and silly, and he does not know what he is doing or bringing to pass. In him, who does not know what he is doing, Sophia was active and operative, and when she was active he believed that he was bringing about by himself the creation of the world. Therefore he began to say: 'I am God, and apart from me there is no other' (Isa. 45: 5).

34, 1. The Valentinian Tetrad then is a source of the eternal nature which has roots, and Sophia is (the one) from whom the

---

[1] This passage because of lacunae is difficult to understand.

psychic and material creation derives its present condition. Sophia is called Pneuma, the Demiurge Psyche, the Devil (is) the ruler of the world, and Beelzebul is the ruler of the demons. 2. This is what they say. Beyond this, they make their entire system arithmetical, as I have already mentioned: the thirty aeons within the Pleroma have, by analogy, brought forth for themselves other aeons in order that the Pleroma may be brought together to reach (in total) a perfect number. 3. . . . Subdivisions are also made in the Ogdoad, and Sophia, who, according to him, is 'the mother of all living creatures' (Gen. 3: 20), and the Joint Fruit of the Pleroma brought forth seventy Logoi, which are heavenly angels who live in the Jerusalem above, which is in Heaven. 4. This Jerusalem is Sophia outside (the Pleroma), and her bridegroom is the Joint Fruit of the Pleroma.

The Demiurge also brought forth souls, and this is the essence of the souls. According to them, he (the Demiurge) is Abraham, and these (souls) are the children of Abraham. From the material and devilish essence the Demiurge made bodies for the souls. 5. This is what is stated: 'And God formed man, taking dust from the earth, and breathed into his countenance the breath of life. And man became a living soul' (Gen. 2: 7). This, according to them, is the inner man, the psychic one which resides in the material body, the material (man) which is perishable, wholly formed from the devilish essence. 6. This material man, in their view, is like an inn, or residence, either of the soul alone, or of the soul and demons, or even of the soul and Logoi—which Logoi have been sown from above, from the Joint Fruit of the Pleroma and from Sophia, into this world and they dwell in an earthly body if no demons reside with the soul.

7. This, he affirms, is what stands written in Scripture: 'For this reason I bow my knees to the God and Father and Lord of our Lord Jesus Christ, that God may grant to you that Christ may dwell in the inner man'—that is, the psychic, not the corporeal man—'that you may be able to understand what is the depth'—that is, the Father of all—'and the breadth'— which is the Cross, the limit of the Pleroma—or 'what is the height' (Eph. 3: 14, 16–18), that is, the Pleroma of the aeons. 8. Therefore, he says, 'a psychic man does not receive what belongs to the Spirit of God, for it is foolishness to him' (1 Cor.

2: 14). Foolishness, he says, is the power of the Demiurge. For he was foolish and without understanding, and believed that he himself was creating the world, unaware that Sophia, the mother, the Ogdoad, was accomplishing everything for the creation of the world, without his knowledge.

35, 1. All the prophets and the law spoke from the Demiurge, a silly god (in his view), and they were foolish and knew nothing. That is why, he says, the Saviour declares: 'All who have come before me are thieves and robbers' (John 10:8), and the apostle: 'The mystery which was not made known to former generations' (Eph. 3: 4 f.). 2. For none of the prophets, he maintains, said anything at all concerning the things of which we speak. For everything was unknown because it was spoken by the Demiurge alone.

When the creation had been completed and when, finally, there ought to have taken place 'the revelation of the sons of God' (Rom. 8: 19)—that is, of the Demiurge—which was concealed and in which the psychic man was hidden and had 'a veil upon his heart' (2 Cor. 3: 15)—3. when the veil was to be taken away and these mysteries revealed, then Jesus was born through Mary the virgin, according to that which is declared: 'The Holy Spirit will come upon thee'—the Spirit is Sophia—'and the power of the Most High will overshadow thee'—the Most High is the Demiurge—'wherefore that which is born of thee shall be called holy' (Luke 1: 35). 4. For he has been born not from the Most High alone, as those created in the likeness of Adam were created by the Most High alone, that is, by the Demiurge. Rather, Jesus is the 'New Man' (Eph. 2: 15; 4: 24), (created) by the Holy Spirit and by the Most High, that is, by Sophia and the Demiurge, in order that the Demiurge might complete the formation and equipment of his body, but the Holy Spirit provide his essence, and a heavenly Logos proceed from the Ogdoad, born through Mary.

5. Concerning this there is a great dispute among them—a cause of dissension and division. Consequently, their teaching is divided and the one is called among them the eastern doctrine, the other the Italian. 6. Those from Italy—and to this group Heracleon and Ptolemaeus belong—say that the body of Jesus was psychic and that because of this at his baptism the Spirit came upon him like a dove—that is, the Logos of Sophia,

the mother from above—and entered into his psychic body, and (also) raised him from the dead. This, he says, is what has been declared: 'He who raised Christ from the dead will also make alive your mortal bodies' (Rom. 8: 11)—the psychic ones. The dust (*chus*) is under the curse. 'For dust thou art', he says, 'and to dust thou shalt return' (Gen. 3: 19). 7. Those from the east—to whom Axionicus and Ardesianes belong—affirm that the body of the Saviour was pneumatic. For there came upon Mary the Holy Spirit, that is, Sophia, and the power of the Most High, the creative art, in order that that which was given to Mary by the Spirit might be formed.

36, 1. . . . He adds: Just as the trespasses pertaining to the aeons within had been set right, so also were those pertaining to the Ogdoad, the Sophia outside, and likewise those pertaining to the Hebdomad. 2. For the Demiurge was instructed by Sophia to the effect that he is not God alone, as he imagined, with no other existing apart from him; but taught by Sophia, he recognized the higher (deity); for he was instructed, initiated, and indoctrinated into the great mystery of the Father and of the aeons, and he disclosed it to no one. This, as he says, is what he (the Demiurge) declares to Moses: 'I am the God of Abraham, the God of Isaac, and the God of Jacob, and the name of God have I not communicated to them' (Exod. 6: 3), that is, I have not declared the mystery, and I have not explained who God is, but I have preserved the mystery which I heard from Sophia in secrecy with myself.

3. When the realm above had been set right, it was necessary, as a consequence, that the things here (below) should be rectified as well. Therefore, Jesus the Saviour was born through Mary in order that he might set right the things here, as Christ, who had been additionally produced from above by Nous and Truth, had rectified the passions of the Sophia outside, that is, the abortion. And again the Saviour who was born through Mary came to set right the passions of the soul.

4. There are thus, according to them, three Christs: the one brought forth by Nous and Truth along with the Holy Spirit; the Joint Fruit of the Pleroma, the husband of the Sophia outside, who is also called Holy Spirit, but inferior to the first; and, thirdly, the one born through Mary for the purpose of rectifying this creation of ours.

11

VALENTINIANISM IV
MARCUS AND OTHERS

To begin with, Irenaeus provides us with information on Valentinus and some of his disciples. In so doing he mentions only a few names, among others Ptolemaeus. What he says of Valentinus' disciples is indeed difficult to correlate with what we have come to recognize as his system. Nevertheless, the reports render us a service in that they show how easily and quickly variations appear.

Irenaeus, *Adv. Haer.* I 11, 1–12, 3 (Selection)

11, 1. Let us now consider the inconsistent teaching of these men, for although there are only two or three of them they do not speak with one voice on the same points, but with reference to the subject-matter and the names put forward opposing views. Now the first of the so-called gnostic sect, the one who adapted the basic doctrines to his own individualistic brand of teaching, is Valentinus, who expressed the following opinions: he laid it down that there is a Dyad which is unnameable, of which one part is called Ineffable, and the other Sige (Silence). Then there was brought forth from this Dyad another Dyad, of which he calls one part Father, and the other Truth. From this Tetrad there derive Logos and Life, Man and Church. These constitute the first Ogdoad. From Logos and Life there were produced, according to him, ten powers, as we have previously mentioned, and from Man and Church twelve, one of which fell away and was reduced to a state of need and gave rise to the rest of what took place. But he also assumed two Limits (Horoi), one between Primal Cause and the remainder of the Pleroma, which separates the created aeons from the uncreated Father, while the other separates the mother from the Pleroma. Christ also was not produced from the aeons in the Pleroma, but was brought forth by the mother who was outside the Pleroma, with a certain shadow, in accordance with the remembrance of higher things. And he, being male, cut away the shadow from himself and hastened back into the Pleroma. But the mother, left alone with the shadow and emptied of her spiritual substance, brought forth another son, and this is the Demiurge, whom he also styles the supreme ruler over all that is subject to him. There was brought forth along with him, he asserts, a left-hand ruler; and in teaching this he is in agreement with those who are termed by us 'false gnostics'.

Jesus is now said to have been brought forth by him who withdrew from the mother and was united with those in the totality, that is, by Desired (Theletos), or again by him who returned into the Pleroma, that is, by Christ; and yet again, by Man and Church. The Holy Spirit, he maintains, was produced by Truth (or the Church) for the inspection and fructifying of the aeons, entering invisibly into them, and hence the aeons also caused the plants of truth to grow.

2. Secundus says that the first Ogdoad consists of a right-hand and a left-hand Tetrad, the one being Light and the other Darkness. In his opinion, the power which fell away and was lost did not derive from the thirty aeons, but from their fruits.

3. But another prominent teacher among them, who aspires to greater heights and to a more sublime knowledge, with reference to the primary Tetrad speaks as follows: There is before all things a Pre-beginning, of which one can form no conception, give no description or name, which I call Unity (*Monotes*). Together with this Unity there exists a power which I call Oneness (*Henotes*). This Oneness and the Unity, being one, sent forth, without doing so intentionally (or: without sending forth anything from themselves), an intelligible beginning for all things, unbegotten and invisible, and this beginning the word calls Monad. With this Monad there coexists a power of the same essence, which I term the One (*to Hen*). These powers—Unity, Oneness, Monad, and the One—produced the rest of the origins of the aeons. . . .

4. Others of them, however, have called the primary and first-begotten Ogdoad by the following names: first of all, Proarchon, then the Inconceivable, thirdly, the Ineffable, and fourth, the Invisible. From the first, Proarchon, there was

brought forth, in the first and fifth place, Beginning; from the Inconceivable, in the second and sixth place, the Incomprehensible; from the Ineffable, in the third and seventh place, the Unnameable; and from the Invisible, in the fourth and eighth place, the Unbegotten. This is the Pleroma of the first Ogdoad. These powers are said to have come into being before Bythos (Primal Cause) and Sige (Silence), and therefore they are more perfect than the perfect and more gnostic than the gnostics. . . .

5. Concerning even Bythos himself there are many different opinions among them. Some say that he is without a partner, neither male nor female, nor anything at all, whereas others say that he is male-female. . . . Others again allot to him Sige as a consort so that the first conjunction (syzygy) may be formed.

12, 1. But those who are followers of Ptolemaeus and wish to know more say that Bythos has two consorts, which they call dispositions, namely Ennoia (Thought) and Thelesis (Willing). For he first thought what he wanted to produce and then he willed it. Wherefore, when these two dispositions or powers, Thought and Willing, became united with one another, the production took place, through a kind of marriage relation, of the Only-begotten and Truth. These were produced as types and images of the two dispositions of the Father—visible representations of things invisible—Nous from Will, and Truth from Thought. And, accordingly, the masculine is an image of the adventitious Willing, and the feminine (an image) of the unbegotten Thought. Thus Willing became as it were a faculty of Thought. For Thought continually yearned after offspring, but was not able of herself to bring forth what she desired. But when the power of Willing came upon her, then she brought forth that which she yearned for. . . .

2. But those who are thought to be more prudent than these say that the first Ogdoad was not brought forth gradually, one aeon by another; but rather, they assert—as confidently as if they had been midwives at their birth—that the six aeons were brought into existence together and at the same time by the Forefather and Ennoia (Thought). So he and his followers claim that Man and Church were not produced from Logos and Life, but that Logos and Life were derived from Man and

Church, and this they express in the following way: What the Forefather had in mind to produce, that became known as Father. But then, because what he brought forth was true, it was called Truth. But when he then wished to reveal himself, that became known as Man; but what he had previously thought of, when he actually created it, that was called Church; and Man named the Logos, which is the first-born son. But Life followed upon Logos, and thus the first Ogdoad was completed.

3. There is great contention among them about the Saviour as well. Some say that he came into being out of all, and for that reason is called the Well-pleasing, since it pleased the entire Pleroma to praise the Father through him. Others maintain that he (was created) out of the ten aeons which were brought forth by Logos and Life, and that on this account he is called Logos and Life, thus preserving the parental names. Others again say that he derived his being from the twelve aeons which were produced by Man and Church, and on this account he designates himself Son of Man, being, as it were, a descendant of Man. Still others maintain that he was created by Christ and the Holy Spirit, who were sent forth to make the Pleroma firm and secure, and on this account, they say, he is called Christ, thus preserving the designation of his Father, by whom he was produced. And there are others who assert that the Forefather of all things himself, the Pre-beginning and the Pre-unthinkable, is called 'Man', and that this is the great and hidden mystery, namely, that the power which is above all and which embraces all is termed Man. And because of this the Saviour designates himself Son of Man.

From this it follows, as far as Valentinus himself is concerned, that he does indeed define differently the name of Bythos and also assumes two Limits, but otherwise presents the same view of the thirty aeons as did Ptolemaeus, according to Irenaeus' account. The real difference is first that the Christ was not brought forth within the Pleroma, but by the mother, who is called in Irenaeus Achamoth, and in Hippolytus the Sophia outside: that he was produced with a shadow, but that after he had divested himself of this, he hastened back into the Pleroma. The mother brought forth not only the Demiurge, but also a left-hand ruler. By this is intended the figure of the 'Devil' or the 'world-ruler'. Ptolemaeus, Heracleon, and the system which Hippolytus offers us have adapted this in various ways, or toned it down. On the origin of the Saviour known as 'Jesus', Valentinus, and perhaps his comrades as well, had different ideas; and likewise on the origin of the Holy Spirit.

As far as Secundus is concerned, we know no more than is narrated here. Another unknown teacher sets before the beginning of the aeons four abstract entities, others even eight; Primal Cause and Silence seemed to them still not abstract enough.

Members of Ptolemaeus' circle had different ideas, and still others partly rearranged the order of the highest aeons. Without mentioning names, Irenaeus gives an account of different views on what according to Ptolemaeus is termed 'fruit': finally, at the end, mention is made of the opinion that the Forefather of all things was called 'Man'.

MARCUS THE MAGICIAN

If we leave aside for the moment *Adv. Haer.* I 13 and 21, it is particularly on Marcus' numerical speculations that Irenaeus provides information.

It should be noted, in the first place, that the Greeks had no special signs for numbers, but employed the twenty-four letters of the Greek alphabet to designate the numbers as well. In addition, there are three ancient signs which were no longer used as letters but which were employed in their ancient role as numerical signs. The only one of interest to us in this connection is the sign for six, the 'special sign'. Furthermore, it must be said that the transcription of the Greek word does not always produce the same number of letters as in the Greek, for ph, th, ch, and ps are each written as *one* Greek letter; and, on the other hand, in Greek the 'u' and occasionally also the 'i' are written with two letters. Accordingly, 'Christos' in Greek may have seven or eight letters, and 'arche' (beginning) has four letters instead of five.

All kinds of details of the system are read off from the letters, which are at the same time numerical symbols. The first word which the Father spoke had four letters (beginning = 'arche'), the second also four, the third ten, and the fourth had twelve letters, that is, thirty letters altogether, and these stand for the thirty aeons and are interpreted as the secret name of the incomprehensible Father. Then, there is an echo in this world of one of them, the last letter, which is said to indicate the last aeon, Sophia; this world is set in order by it, and this is supposed to point to the action of Achamoth. The twenty-four letters are arranged in correspondence in such a way that when the first and the last, the second and the penultimate, and so on, are arranged together they are said to produce the form of 'Truth'. The twenty-four letters are further divided into nine mute letters (which recall the Father, since he is unutterable), eight semi-vowels, and seven vowels: a mute letter was added to the seven vowels with the result that numerical similarity prevails, and this is the symbol of the 'fruit'. The double letters, xi, psi, and zeta, are counted twice and added to the twenty-four letters (among which, of course, they already are!) and that makes again a total of thirty. Likewise, when reckoning with the numerical symbol for six, six and twenty-four again make thirty. The numerical value of the name 'Jesus', that is, the number arrived at when one counts up the letters, interpreting them as numerical signs, is 888: this number is obtained on the basis of other speculative views as well.

In this connection, it is significant that here also, in the midst of speculation on numbers, the part played by ignorance and error appears. The final sentences of I 15, 2 reveal ideas like those which come to expression in the Gospel of Truth. Moreover, Jesus proclaimed to men the unknown Father, and that is his saving work (I 15, 3; 20, 2). With reference to the remaining numerical speculations of Chapter 16, where it is possible that Marcus himself is not speaking, it should be observed that the Romans counted the numbers up to ninety-nine with the fingers of the left hand, but used the right hand for numbers from a hundred upwards.[1] As to the following chapters, it should be noted, in connection with 20, 1, that in the extant apocryphal Infancy Gospels something similar is related concerning Jesus.

The system of Marcus and his disciples is differentiated from the system which Irenaeus recounts for us by the fact that Marcus places another tetrad before the thirty aeons, with the names Unity, Oneness, Monad, and One, which agrees with what Irenaeus I 11, 2 narrates about disciples of Valentinus. Moreover, Logos and Truth are produced *after* Man and Church—which Irenaeus I 12, 2 also affirms; and Jesus was created 'through the Logos', as Irenaeus I 12, 3 reports. And if Christ and the 'seed' descended and ascended, that harmonizes with Valentinus himself, Irenaeus I 11, 1.

In Chapter 13 of *Adv. Haer.* I, Irenaeus tells something about the tricks of this man, Marcus. He passed himself off as a prophet who was able to give to others the prophetic gifts. 'Prophet' here is the designation not of one who has the power to see into the future, but, in general, of anyone who is filled with knowledge and power from the supernatural sphere. The angel whom the Father beholds

[1] H. I. Marrou, *History of Education in Antiquity*, ET London, 1964, 219.

continually (13, 3) is perhaps the angel of the male seed who even now unites himself to the faithful; consequently, anyone to whom this happens becomes what Marcus is, a prophet or a prophetess. The prayer to the 'one who sits beside God', narrated in 13, 6, is related to the formula which the Ophians used with reference to the archontic powers. At this point the feeling that these powers can actually have an influence is particularly striking, since the formula is offered only if the need arises. As far as the content of the prayer is concerned, it is just as remarkable as the formula of the Ophians and just as difficult to explain. The 'daring, bold one' is probably Achamoth, and those who 'draw back upwards' are probably the 'great ones', that is, the angels, the companions of the Saviour; 'their forms' are probably the pneumatics, 'we' who are one with them. But it is hard to say to whom the prayer is directed: one thinks of Sophia, consort of the 'Desired', but elsewhere she plays no special part, let alone being known as 'one who sits beside God'. Is it perhaps Truth, whose beauty Marcus claims to have seen? or should one read 'O thou who sittest beside God, thou mystical, eternal Silence', so that the prayer would be directed to Silence?

In Chapter 21 Irenaeus has given us some information on the sacraments of the gnostics, but whether it was actually the Marcosians who employed them is improbable, for the patristic author has assembled at this point (as he himself makes clear) material from many quarters. The matters dealt with are, first, baptism, then the rites for redemption, and finally, prayers with the dying.

Irenaeus, *Adv. Haer.* I 13, 1–21, 5 (Selection) = Epiphanius *Panarion*, XXXIV 2, 1–20, 12

13, 1. There is another of those among them who prides himself on being an improver of his master's teaching. His name is Marcus, and he is knowledgeable in magical deceit, by means of which he has led astray many men and not a few women and has induced them to turn to him as to one possessed of great skill and who has received a great power from the invisible and ineffable regions, an actual precursor of the Antichrist. . . .

2. Over a cup mixed with wine he pretends to pray and, whilst greatly prolonging the invocation, he contrives that it should appear purple and red so that Grace, who belongs to the company of those who are superior to all things, may seem to be dropping her blood into that cup by means of his invocation, and that those present should fervently desire to taste of that cup in order that the Grace called hither by that magician

may let (her blood) flow into them. Again, he gives to women cups already mixed and full, and bids them offer thanks in his presence. When this is done, he produces another cup much larger than the one over which the deluded woman has given thanks, and he then pours from the smaller one over which she has given thanks into the one which he has brought forward— which was much larger—and at the same time he speaks as follows: 'May "Grace"[2] who is before all things, who is beyond thought and description, fill thine inner man and multiply in thee her knowledge, sowing the mustard seed in good soil.' By saying such things and by making the wretched woman deranged, he appears as a wonder-worker, when the larger cup is filled from the smaller one to such an extent that it actually overflows. By doing other things like this he has deceived many and drawn them into following him.

3. It is clearly recognizable that he has a demon too residing in him, by means of which he appears to be able to prophesy and to enable the (women) whom he counts worthy to be partakers of his Grace to prophesy as well. He concerns himself in particular with women, especially with those of high rank, the elegantly attired and wealthy, whom he frequently attempts to lead astray by flattering them and saying, 'I desire to make thee a partaker of my Grace, since the Father of all doth continually behold thy angel before his face (Matt. 18:10). The place of thy greatness* is ever in us: we must come together. First, receive from me and through me Grace. Adorn thyself as a bride who expects her bridegroom, that thou mayest be what I am, and I what thou art. Receive in thy bride-chamber the seed of light. Receive from me the bridegroom, and give him a place, and have a place in him. Behold, Grace has descended upon thee; open thy mouth and prophesy.' But if the woman replies, 'I have never prophesied before, nor can I prophesy', then, for the second time, he offers some prayers to bewilder the deluded woman, and says to her, 'Open thy mouth and speak whatever comes to thee, and thou shalt prophesy.' And the woman, deluded and puffed up by what has been said, and excited by the expectation that she is about to prophesy, takes

---

[2] Charis, one of the names of Sige, Silence.

---

* In this system *megethos* ('greatness') = angel.

the risk, and with her heart pounding abnormally she utters ridiculous nonsense, anything that happens to come into her head, idly and audaciously, for she is stimulated by a vain spirit . . ., henceforth considers herself as a prophetess, and thanks Marcus who has shared with her his Grace. She tries to repay him, not only with the gift of her possessions—by which means he has collected a great amount of money—but also by physical intercourse, prepared as she is to be united with him in everything in order that she, with him, may enter into the One. . . .

5. Moreover, that this man Marcus, with the intention of degrading their bodies, administers love-potions and aphrodisiacs to some of these women, even if not to all of them, they have frequently confessed after they have returned to the church of God, and that they were physically abused by him, and that they had loved him with violent passion.

6. And disciples of his, who concern themselves with the same things, have deceived and led astray many women, passing themselves off as perfect, as if none could equal the extent of their knowledge, not even if you were to mention Paul or Peter, or any other of the apostles.[3] They claim that they have more knowledge than all others, and that they alone have attained the greatness of the knowledge of the ineffable power. They claim that they are in the heights beyond every power, and as a result are free to do anything, for they have no fear whatever of anything. By reason of the 'redemption' they claim that they are unassailable by and invisible to the judge. If one should lay hold on them, they step up to him, along with the 'redemption', and say: 'O thou that sittest beside God and the eternal, mystical Silence, through whom the great ones ever behold the face of the Father (Matt. 18: 10), using thee as guide and introducer (into the Pleroma) they draw back upwards their forms, which that daring, bold one imagined, and by the goodness of the Father produced us, their images, at the time when she had, like a dream, the mental picture of the (things) above: Behold, the judge is at hand, and the herald bids me make my defence; but do thou—thou who knowest the affairs of both—give account to the judge for us both, inasmuch as we are one.' No sooner has the mother heard this than she puts upon them the Homeric helmet of Hades, so that

[3] Cf. Carpocrates, Ir. I 25, 2.

they can escape from the judge without being seen, and immediately she carries them upwards, conducts them into the bride-chamber, and hands them over to their consorts. 7. By means of words and actions like these they have led astray many women in our district of the Rhône.

14, 1. This Marcus, who passed himself off as being the sole womb and receptacle of the Sige of Colorbasus, as being the only begotten, gave forth from himself in the following manner that which the 'deficiency' had deposited in him. That Tetrad, which is in the highest, invisible and indescribable places, descended upon him in female form because, as he maintains, the world could not endure its male form, and it revealed to him its nature and disclosed to him alone the origin of all things, which it never before had revealed to anyone, either of the gods or of men. It spoke as follows: when first the inconceivable and non-material Father, who is without paternity and who is neither male nor female, willed to make utterable that of him which was ineffable and to give form to that which was invisible, he opened his mouth and sent forth a word which was similar to himself. This stood by and showed him who and what he was: a form, appearing from the invisible. The enunciation of this name took place as follows: He uttered the first word of his name, which was 'beginning' (*Arche*)[4] and this word was made up of four letters or elements (*Stoicheion*). He added the second word and it too consisted of four elements. He then spoke the next one, and it was made up of ten elements; and then he uttered another, and it consisted of twelve elements. The enunciation of the whole name consisted of thirty letters or elements, and of four distinct utterances (or: syllables). Each element has its own letters, its own form, its own pronunciation, appearance, and images, and no one of them perceives the form of that whereof it is only an element. It does not even perceive or know the pronunciation of its neighbour, but believes that that which it expresses itself names the whole, as if it expressed the whole. Each (element) of them is a part of the whole and has its own sound to designate the whole, and it does not stop sounding until it reaches the last letter of each element, enunciating it particularly (?). But the restitution of all things will take place, he declares, when the whole has reached the one

---

[4] Cf. Ir. I 1, 1: beginning of the All.

letter and one and the same expression is sounded. The image of that utterance is considered to be the 'Amen' spoken by us all together. The sounds, however, are those which have given form to the immaterial and unbegotten aeon, and these in fact are the forms which the Lord has called angels who continually behold the face of the Father (Matt. 18: 10). 2. The utterable and customary names of the elements he called aeons, words, roots, seeds, fullnesses (*pleromata*), and fruits. The particulars of each one of them and the peculiarity of every particular, he affirms, is to be understood as being contained in the name 'Church'.

The last letter of the last element lifted up its voice and its sound went forth and produced its own elements, after the image of the (other) elements: on the basis of these (so he asserts) the things here were arranged in order and the things which preceded them brought into existence. The letter itself, whose echo followed the echo below, was received up again by its own syllable, for the sake of the completion of the whole. But the echo remained below, as though cast off outside. But the element from which the letter with its own pronunciation descended is said by him to have comprised thirty letters, and each one of the thirty letters contains in itself other letters by means of which the name of the letter is expressed, and again the other letters are in turn indicated by means of other letters, and the others by still others, so that the number of the letters extends to infinity.

You may more clearly understand what is said from the following example. The word (lit. element) Delta[5] contains five letters: D, E, L, T, A, and these letters in turn are designated by other letters (e.g. D by delta, E by epsilon, etc.) and these others by still others. If then the total composition of DELTA stretches to infinity, letters constantly producing other letters and following one another in succession, how much greater is the ocean of letters from that single (original) element. And if the one letter is infinite, consider the immensity of the letters of that entire name out of which the Sige of Marcus declared the Forefather to be composed. Accordingly, because he knew that he was incomprehensible, the Father has bestowed on the

---

[5] The letter delta as a numeral designates 4; was it, therefore, perhaps chosen as an example to suggest the (higher) tetrad?

elements—which he also calls aeons—the power by which each may utter its own enunciation, because one of them was not capable by itself of enunciating the whole.

3. After explaining this, the Tetrad said to him: 'I desire to show thee also Truth herself. I have brought her down from the dwellings above that thou mayest see her uncovered and understand her beauty, hear her speak and admire her understanding. Behold her head on high: Alpha and Omega; her neck: Beta and Psi; her shoulders and hands: Gamma and Chi; her breast: Delta and Phi; her diaphragm: Epsilon and Upsilon; her back: Zeta and Tau; her stomach: Eta and Sigma; her thighs: Theta and Rho; her knees: Iota and Pi; her shins: Kappa and Omicron; her ankles: Lambda and Xi; her feet: Mu and Nu. This is the body of Truth, according to the magician. This is the form of the element, this the character of the letter. And this element he calls "Man", and says it is the source of all speech, the beginning of every sound, the expression of all that is unspeakable, and the mouth of the silent Sige. So much, then, on her body. But do thou lift up on high the thought of thine understanding and listen to the self-begotten Word, given by the Father, from out of the mouth of Truth.'

4. When she had said this, Truth looked at him, opened her mouth and uttered a word. The word became a name, and the name became the one we know and speak of, Christ Jesus. This she uttered and immediately fell silent. But whilst Marcus was expecting that she would say something more, the Tetrad came forward again and said: 'Thou hast regarded as trivial the word which thou hast heard from the mouth of Truth. It is not, as thou imaginest, an ancient name; thou knowest only its sound but thou art not acquainted with its power. Jesus is a special name, with six letters, which is known by all those who belong to the calling. The (name) among the aeons of the Pleroma consists of many parts, has another form and another appearance, and is known by those akin to him, whose greatnesses are always present with him. 5. Understand the twenty-four letters that you have as symbolic emanations of the three powers which contain the entire number of the elements above. The nine consonants (mutes) belong to the Father and Truth because they are voiceless, that is, inexpressible and unutterable. The eight semi-vowels belong to Logos and Life, since

they occupy, as it were, the middle position between the un-
voiced and the voiced; and they receive the outflowing of those
above them and elevate those which are beneath them. The
vowels, seven in number, belong to Man and Church, since a
voice went forth from Man and formed all things. For the echo
of the voice gave them form. Thus, Logos and Life have eight
(letters), Man and Church seven, and the Father and Truth
nine. On account of the one which was deficient, that which
was extra in the Father came down, being sent to the one from
whom he was separated, in order to set matters right, so that the
unity of the aeons might possess equality and might produce
in all the one power which is from all. And thus the seven
achieved the power of eight, and the three groups became the
same numerically, that is, eights. These three, when added
together, produce the number twenty-four. These three elements—from which flowed the twenty-four letters (lit. elements)
—exist, according to him, in conjunctions of the (three) powers,
thus forming six, and being multiplied by the number of the
ineffable Tetrad give rise to the same number, and these are
said to belong to the Ineffable one. These are borne by the
three powers, after the likeness of the Invisible: the images of
these elements are the three double-letters, and if one adds these
to the twenty-four letters, by the force of analogy, one arrives
at the number thirty.

6. The fruit of this calculation and arrangement is said by
him to have appeared in the likeness of an image, namely him
who after six days ascended into the mountain with three others,
and became the sixth (Matt. 17: 1 ff. par.),[6] who descended
and was contained in the Hebdomad,[7] who himself was an
illustrious Ogdoad and contained in himself the entire number
of the elements, who, on the occasion of his baptism, was
revealed by the descent of the dove (Matt. 3: 16 par.)—which
is Alpha and Omega, for its number is 801.[8] For this reason
also Moses declared that man had been created on the sixth
day (Gen. 1: 31); and the dispensation of salvation (manifested
itself) on the sixth day, the day of preparation, for on that day

---

[6] The thought is of the transfiguration story (Matt. 17: 1 ff.); Jesus ascends the
mountain with three of his disciples and is thus the fourth. Then come Moses and
Elias, making six in all.

[7] The Hebdomad is a symbol of our present world.

[8] The Greek word for dove (*peristerá*) has the numerical value 801.

the last man appeared for the regeneration of the first man, and of this dispensation both the beginning and the ending are at the sixth hour, at which time he was nailed to the tree.[9] For the perfect Nous, knowing that the number six has the power of creation and regeneration, is said to have revealed to the children of light that regeneration which took place through him who appeared as the 'special' one in that (special)[10] number. For this reason it is also affirmed that the double letters contain the special number, that is, the number six, for this special number, when added to the twenty-four letters, makes the thirty letters complete.

7. They use as an instrument (so the Sige of Marcus says) the greatness of the number seven[11] in order that the fruit of the independent purpose may become manifest. This special number is now related to the one who was given form through the special (number), who was, as it were, divided or cut in parts and remained outside, who by his own power and intelligence, through his own offspring,[12] gave life to the world of the seven powers, in imitation of the power of the Hebdomad, and made it the soul of all that is seen. He performs this work as though it were being done by him of his own resolve; he performs this service of making imitations of what cannot be imitated, the 'thought' (*enthumesis*) of the mother (?).

The first heaven utters the Alpha, the one after it Epsilon, the third Eta, the fourth, which is in the middle of the seven, utters the force (or: sound) of Iota, the fifth Omicron, the sixth Upsilon, and the seventh, which is the fourth from the middle, expresses the Omega, as the Sige of Marcus . . . asserts. All these powers, he says, when linked to one another, sound forth the praises of him by whom they were brought forth. The glory of this sound is sent up again to the Forefather. The echo of this utterance of praise is brought down to earth, according to him, and becomes the shaper and parent of the things on the earth.

8. The proof of this he evinces from new-born children, whose soul, as soon as it comes forth from the womb, declaims the sound of every one of these elements. Just as the seven powers

---

9 According to John 19: 14, in contrast to Mark 15: 25.

10 The number six is the 'special number' six, written with a special sign.

11 'Truth' in Greek has seven letters.

12 His 'offspring' is Ialdabaoth, who created the world in imitation of the higher world (Ir. I 5, 3).

extol the Logos, so also does the soul in infants, as it weeps and cries, glorify Marcus. For this reason, too, David said, 'Out of the mouths of babes and sucklings thou hast established praise' (Ps. 8: 3), and again, 'The heavens declare the glory of God' (Ps. 19 (18): 2). Hence the soul also, when for its purification it is in need and distress, exclaims Omega (Oh!), as a sign of praise, so that the soul above may recognize its kinship with it and may send down to it a helper.

15, 1. The all-wise Sige announced to him the creation of the twenty-four elements as follows. Along with Unity (*Monotes*) there was Oneness (*Henotes*), from which, as mentioned above, two (entities) were produced. Monad and One, when added to the other two, make four, for two and two are four. Again, the two and the four, when added together, exhibit the number six. And six multiplied by four produces the twenty-four forms. And the names of the first Tetrad, which are regarded like the holy of holies and which cannot be expressed, are discerned only by the Son, whilst the Father knows what they are. Those things which require respect, which are to be named with reverence and faith, are as follows: Ineffable and Sige, Father and Truth. Of this Tetrad the entire sum amounts to twenty-four letters. For Ineffable (*arretos*) has seven letters, Sige contains five, Father (*pater*) five, and Truth (*aletheia*) seven: when taken together, twice five and twice seven make up the number twenty-four. In like manner, the second Tetrad, Logos and Life, Man and Church, makes up the same number of elements or letters. The name of the Saviour that can be uttered (Jesus) has six letters (i.e. in Greek), but his unutterable name has twenty-four; Christ (the) Son contains twelve letters (in Greek), but the unutterable name for Christ has thirty letters. Consequently, he calls him Alpha and Omega in order to indicate the dove, for this bird has that number.[13]

2. Jesus has the following unspeakable origin. From the mother of all things, the first Tetrad, there came forth, after the manner of a daughter, the second Tetrad, and that made up an Ogdoad, from which a Decad proceeded. Thus a Decad and an Ogdoad came into being. The Decad combined with the Ogdoad and multiplied it ten times and produced the

---

[13] Alpha and Omega have the numerical value 801, like the Greek word for dove (see p. 206 n. 8).

number 80, and again 80 being multiplied ten times produced
the number 800, so that the entire number that proceeds from
the eight and the ten is 888, and this is Jesus. For the name
Jesus, when calculated by the numerical value of the letters,
amounts to 888.[14] Thus, in their opinion, you have a clear
account of the supernatural origin of Jesus. For this reason the
alphabet of the Greeks has eight (letters) for units, eight to
denote tens, and eight for hundreds;[15] the number 888 signifies
Jesus, who is formed from them all. And he is indicated too by
Alpha and Omega, for he has his origin from all. And again
(they explain) as follows: the first Tetrad adds up to ten, when
the numbers are taken together; for one, two, three, and four,
when counted up, give ten, and this is said to indicate Jesus—
for the letter Iota with which the name Jesus begins (in Greek)
has a numerical value of ten! Moreover, the word Christ, he
says, made up (in Greek) of eight letters, signifies the first
Ogdoad, which, when multiplied by ten, gives birth to Jesus.
But he is also called Christ (the) Son, that is, the Duodecad:
Son (in Greek) has four letters, and Christ eight, and these,
when added together, signify the greatness of the Duodecad.

But, he affirms, before the specialty (*episemon*) of the name
appeared, that is, Jesus, the Son, men were in great ignorance
and error. But when the name with six letters appeared,[16] which
assumed flesh so as to be perceived by men, the one who
contained in himself the six and the twenty-four, then they
recognized him, laid aside their ignorance, and passed from
death to life, and this name was for them a path to the Father
of truth. For the Father of all desired to remove ignorance and
to abolish death. The abolishing of ignorance was the knowledge
of him. And on this account the Man was chosen who, according to his will, was formed after the image of the power above.

3. The aeons proceeded from the Tetrad. In the Tetrad were
Man and Church, Logos and Life.[17] The powers which emanated from these four (Man, Church, Logos, and Life) generated
the Jesus who appeared on earth. The angel Gabriel took the
place of Logos, the Holy Spirit that of Life, the power of the

---

[14] Ἰησοῦς = 10+8+200+70+400+200 = 888.

[15] Here the three signs, without which the writing of the numbers as letters
could not be accomplished, are not included; see the introduction to this chapter.

[16] 'Jesus' in Greek has six letters.　　　　　[17] See Ir. I 12, 2.

Most High that of Man, and the Virgin demonstrated the place of the Church (allusion to Luke 1: 26–35). And thus, according to him, there was born through Mary the man in accordance with the divine dispensation, whom, as he passed through the womb, the Father of all chose, through the Logos,[18] to receive the knowledge of himself. And when he came to the water (of baptism) there descended upon him in the form of a dove the one who had ascended on high and who completed the number twelve.[19] In him there existed the seed of those who had been generated with him, and who had descended and ascended along with him. He asserts that the power which descended was the seed of the Father, containing in itself both the Father and the Son and also that inexpressible power of Sige which is known by means of them, and all the aeons as well. And this is the Spirit which spoke through Jesus, who confessed that he was Son of Man and that he revealed the Father, who came upon Jesus and was made one with him. And Jesus, the Saviour by divine dispensation, destroyed death, he says, and Christ made known the Father.[20] Jesus is said to be the name of the man formed by the dispensation and charged with expressing the likeness and formation of the man who was about to descend upon him, who contained him in himself. He possessed (in himself) Man, Logos, Father, the Ineffable,[21] Sige, Truth, Church, and Life. . . .

16, 1. They combine the generation of the aeons with the straying of the sheep and its recovery (Luke 15:4–6) and attempt to set it forth in a mystical fashion, these men who relate everything to numbers and assert that the whole (universe) derives its existence from a Monad and a Dyad, and by counting from the Monad to the Tetrad they produce the Decad. For one, two, three, and four added together produce the number of the ten aeons. Furthermore, the Dyad, advancing from itself by twos, as far as the special (numerical sign)—two, four, six—

[18] Cf. Ir. I 12, 3.

[19] Thus 'Christ', son of the fallen Sophia, as in Valentinus himself (Ir. I 11, 1) and like Cl. Al. (*Exc.* § 23, 2 and 32, 2.).

[20] The destruction of death is here ascribed to the Saviour 'Jesus' and related to the psychic (from the Oikonomia), while 'Christ' 'makes the Father known' for the pneumatics. Thus here the appellation 'the Saviour' is used for Jesus and that is also an appropriate designation for him in relation to the psychic (see pp. 15, 126 f.).

[21] Father = Nous, Ineffable = the Primal Cause.

produces the Duodecad. And, if we count in the same way from the two up to ten, then the number thirty appears, in which (also) eight plus ten plus twelve (are contained). Since it contains the special sign and because the special sign follows (it), they call the Duodecad passion. And therefore, since the accident took place in connection with the twelfth number, the sheep wantonly went astray, since, as they claim, the defection took place from the Duodecad. Likewise, in prophetic fashion, they say that by reason of the defection from the Duodecad *one* power has been lost, and this is the woman who lost the drachma, lit a lamp, and found it (Luke 15: 8). So also they combine the remaining numbers—in the case of the drachmae nine, and in the case of the sheep eleven[22]—and these, if multiplied, give the number ninety-nine, for nine times eleven makes ninety-nine. Wherefore, the Amen is said to contain this number.[23]

2. I will not hesitate to inform you of what they have discovered by other interpretations in order that you may know from every point of view what results they achieve. They want the letter Eta, when taken together with the special letter, to produce the Ogdoad, since it occupies the eighth place from Alpha. Again, leaving out the special (symbol), they count the numerical values of the letters and add them up as far as Eta and that produces the number thirty. For if one commences with the Alpha and ends with the Eta, but misses out the special number, and adds together the numbers as they increase, he will find that he has reached the number thirty. For up to Epsilon there are fifteen; then, one adds to that the number seven, which makes twenty-two; then, one adds on the Eta, that is, eight, and the wonder number thirty is complete! On the basis of this they proclaim that the Ogdoad is the mother of the thirty aeons. Since the number thirty is composed of the three 'powers',[24] if multiplied by three, it gives ninety, for three times thirty is ninety. The three when multiplied by itself (three) gives nine. Thus, the Ogdoad has produced the number ninety-nine. Because the twelfth aeon defected and left the

---

[22] The sheep represents Sophia who abandoned her eleven fellow aeons. If, however, one were to combine the nine drachmae with the number of the sheep left behind the result would be 9×99!

[23] The numerical value of Amen is 99.

[24] From eight and ten and twelve; see above.

eleven above, they claim that the form of the letters corresponds to the method of their calculation; for Lambda is the eleventh letter and has a numerical value of thirty, and stands as an image of the dispensation above. From Alpha up to Lambda, with the omission of the special letter, one has (counting the Lambda) the number ninety-nine. The Lambda, which in the series holds eleventh place, descended to seek the one like to itself, in order to make complete the number twelve, and when it found it became complete: this is clear from the form of the letter: for Lambda, being engaged in the search for an equal, found it, grasped it to itself, and filled the place of the twelfth, the sign for Mu being made up of two Lambdas.[25] Therefore, by reason of their knowledge, they avoid the place of ninety-nine, that is, of the defection, an image of the left hand: they seek the one, which, when added to the ninety-nine, enables them to change (it) to the right hand. . . .

17, 1. I wish to explain to you how, in their opinion, the creation itself was brought about through the mother by the Demiurge, without his being aware of it, after the image of things invisible. First of all, they assert that the four elements, fire, water, earth, and air, were produced as images of the Tetrad above. If their characteristic effects—hot and cold, dry and moist—are added, then they form an exact image of the Ogdoad. Next, they count up ten powers in the following way: there are seven spherical bodies which they call heavens, then the sphere which contains them, and which they call the eighth heaven, and then the sun and the moon. These, numbering ten in all, are said to be images of the invisible Decad which proceeded from Logos and Life. They claim to see the Duodecad represented in the zodiac: for the twelve signs of the zodiac are considered by them to image forth very clearly the daughter of Man and Church, namely the Duodecad. Since the topmost heaven is linked with the revolution of the whole system, which is very rapid, and presses upon the (hollow) sphere, thus providing a counter-balance to its speed by means of its own slowness, so that it completes in thirty years the cycle from one (zodiacal) sign to the next—they affirm that it is the image of Horos (Limit) which encircles the mother with the name of thirty. The moon, too, which travels through her heaven in

[25] The Greek sign for *M* is apparently composed from two *l*'s ($\Lambda + \Lambda = M$).

thirty days, provides by means of these days an image of the number of the thirty aeons. The sun which makes its cycle in twelve months and completes its orbit by returning to the same point expresses the Duodecad by means of the twelve months. And the days as well, each having twelve hours, are a type of the invisible Duodecad. Even the hour, the twelfth part of a day, is made up of thirty parts in order to be, in their view, the image of the Triacontad. And the zodiacal circle itself has a circumference of 360 degrees, each sign having thirty degrees. So they say that by means of this circle the image of the connection between the Duodecad and the Triacontad is preserved. The earth too, being divided, in their opinion, into twelve zones, receives in each zone a power from the heaven according to the perpendicular (that is, from the part of heaven which lies perpendicularly above) and brings forth productions which are like to the one who sends down the power as an influence—this, according to their firm assurance, is a type of the Duodecad and its offspring.

2. In addition, they declare that the Demiurge wished to imitate the infinitude, the eternity, the limitlessness, and the timelessness of the Ogdoad above. But he could not express its permanence and eternity because he was the offspring of deficiency; consequently he spread out its eternity into long periods of time, seasons, and vast numbers of years, thinking to imitate its infinitude by means of the multitude of these times. They add that, because the truth escaped him, he followed falsehood, and as a result, when the times are fulfilled, his work will perish.

18, 1. . . . For Moses, they declare, when he began his account of creation, pointed out at the very beginning the mother of all things, in the words, 'In the beginning God created the heaven and the earth' (Gen. 1: 1). He names four things here: God, beginning, heaven, and earth, and thereby, as they say, sets forth their Tetrad. And he indicates that it (the Tetrad) was invisible and hidden by saying, 'But the earth was invisible and unformed' (Gen. 1: 2 LXX). They claim that he made mention of the second Tetrad, the offspring of the first, in the following way—by naming the abyss and the darkness, and the water in them, and the spirit which hovered over the water (Gen. 1: 2). Then he mentions the Decad by naming light, day, night, the firmament, evening, morning, dry land and the sea, plants, and, in the tenth place, the tree. By means of these ten names he indicates the ten aeons. The power of the Duodecad was imaged forth by him as follows: he names the sun and the moon, the stars and the seasons, years, and whales, fish, reptiles, birds, cattle, and wild beasts, and then, in the twelfth place, man. Thus they teach that the Triacontad is spoken of by the Spirit through Moses. And further the man formed after the image of the power above has in himself the power from the one source. This is situated in the region of the brain. From it there proceed four faculties, after the image of the Tetrad above, and these are called sight, hearing, smell, and taste. The Ogdoad is indicated by means of man in the following way: he has two ears, the same number of eyes, two nostrils, and a two-fold taste, of what is bitter and of what is sweet. Moreover, they teach that the whole man contains the total image of the Triacontad as follows: in his hands he bears, by means of the fingers, the Decad; in his whole body, which is divided into twelve members, (he bears) the Duodecad, for they portion out the body, just as they divide up the body of truth, on which matter we have already spoken. The Ogdoad, being unspeakable and invisible, is understood as hidden in the viscera.

2. The sun, the great light, was created on the fourth day, for the sake of the number four (Gen. 1: 16–19). The courts of the tabernacle which was constructed by Moses were made out of linen, blue, purple, and scarlet (Exod. 26: 1; 36: 8) to point, in their view, to the same image. They maintain that the robe of the high priest, which was adorned with four rows of precious stones (Exod. 28: 17–20), indicates the Tetrad. And if anything else is discovered in Scripture which can be traced back to the number four, then they say that it had its origin with a view to representing the Tetrad. Again, the Ogdoad was indicated as follows: on the eighth day, according to them, man was formed. Sometimes, however, they want to have him formed on the sixth day, and at other times, on the eighth, unless they wish to imply that the earthly man was formed on the sixth, and the fleshly man on the eighth.[26] There are differences among them here. Some claim that the one who was formed after the image and likeness of God (Gen. 1: 27) was masculine-feminine, and

[26] Cf. Ir. I 5, 5.

that he was the spiritual man, whereas the other one was formed out of the earth.

3. Further, the dispensation of the ark in the time of the flood, by means of which eight persons were saved (Gen. 7: 7) points most clearly to the saving Ogdoad. David, who was the eighth of the brothers from the point of view of age, demonstrates the same thing (1 Sam. 16: 6–12). Finally, circumcision, which takes place on the eighth day (Gen. 17: 12), points to the separation from the Ogdoad above. In short, whatever is found in Scripture that can be brought into relation to the number eight is said to fulfil the mystery of the Ogdoad. Then again, in connection with the Decad: in their view, it is indicated by the ten peoples which God gave to Abraham for a possession (Gen. 15: 18 f.); and the event concerning Sarah, whereby after ten years she gave to him her handmaid that he might acquire a son by her (Gen. 16: 3), is said to disclose the same point. And Abraham's servant who was sent to seek Rebekah and gave her, by the spring, ten gold bracelets, and her brothers who detained her for ten days (Gen. 24: 22, 55): Jeroboam, too, who received the ten sceptres (1 Kgs. 11: 30 f.), and the ten curtains of the tabernacle (Exod. 26: 1; 36: 8), the columns which were ten cubits high (Exod. 36: 21), the ten sons of Jacob who were sent first to Egypt to buy corn (Gen. 42: 3), and the ten apostles to whom the Lord revealed himself after the resurrection, when Thomas was not present (John 20: 24)—(all these), according to them, were types of the invisible Decad.

4. But the Duodecad, in connection with which the mystery of the passion of the defect took place, from which passion what is visible is said to have been formed, is clearly and plainly present everywhere, according to them: for instance, the twelve sons of Jacob (Gen. 35: 22), from whom the twelve tribes took their origin, and the artistic breastplate which contained twelve precious stones, and the twelve little bells (Exod. 28: 17–20; 39: 10–13, 25), and the twelve stones laid by Moses at the foot of the mountain (Exod. 24: 4), likewise those which Joshua placed in the river, and the others on the other side (Josh. 4: 3, 8 f.), the bearers of the ark of the covenant (Josh. 3: 12), and the (stones which) Elijah set up when he brought the burnt-offering of the calf (1 Kgs. 18: 31), the number of the apostles (Matt. 10: 1 ff. par.)—in short, everything

that provides the number twelve is said by them to set forth the Duodecad. The Triacontad, which is the name given to the union of all these things, (is indicated) by the thirty cubits' height of Noah's ark (Gen. 6: 15), by Samuel who allowed Saul to have the first place among thirty guests (1 Sam. 9: 22), by David, when he concealed himself for thirty days in the field (1 Sam. 20: 5), and by those who went with him into the cave (2 Sam. 23: 13), and, again, by the fact that the tabernacle was thirty cubits long (Exod. 26: 8); and if they discover anything which has the same number, then they think it right and proper to indicate their number thirty by means of such (figures).

19, 1. I have considered it necessary to add to this what they select from the Scriptures concerning their Forefather who was totally unknown before the advent of Christ, attempting to prove that they state that our Lord announced another Father than the creator of this universe. Him they impiously call, as we have said earlier, an offspring of the 'deficiency'.[27] When the prophet Isaiah says, 'Israel has not known me and my people have not understood me' (Isa. 1: 3), they alter this in such a way as to suggest that (the prophet) was speaking about ignorance of the invisible Primal Cause. And that which was said by Hosea, 'There is in them no truth, nor knowledge of God' (Hos. 4: 1), they forcibly apply to the same thing. And 'There is no one who understands or seeks after God; all are gone astray, they have become altogether unprofitable' (Ps. 14 (13): 2 f. = Rom. 3: 10 f.) is referred by them to lack of knowledge of the Primal Cause. And what was said by Moses, 'No man shall see God and remain alive' (Exod. 33: 20), is said to refer to that as well.

2. For they falsely claim that the creator was seen by the prophets, but the saying 'No one shall see God and remain alive' is supposed by them to have been uttered with reference to the invisible 'Greatness', unknown to all. . . . And Daniel is said to have indicated the same thing by asking the angel for the explanation of the images, since he did not understand them; but the angel concealed from him the great mystery of Bythos and said to him, 'Go thy way, Daniel, for these sayings are closed up until those who have understanding understand and those who are white become white' (Dan. 12: 9 f. LXX?). They

[27] See p. 210 n. 19.

themselves claim to be those who are white and who understand.

20, 1. In addition they bring forward an innumerable quantity of apocryphal and spurious writings, which they themselves have forged, in order to bewilder the foolish who do not understand the Scriptures of truth. They adduce even that fable which tells that when the Lord was a child and was learning the alphabet, the teacher said to him, as is usual, 'Say Alpha', and he replied, 'Alpha'. When the teacher again told him to say Beta, the Lord answered, 'Tell me first what Alpha is, and then I will tell you what Beta is.'[28] They deduce from this that he alone understood the Unknown, which he revealed under the type of the Alpha.

2. Some parts of what appears in the Gospels they alter to suit this kind of interpretation: for example, the answer given to his mother when he was twelve years old, 'Do you not know that I must be concerned with the affairs of my Father?' (Luke 2: 49), on which they comment that he announced to them the Father whom they did not know; for this reason too he sent out his disciples to the twelve tribes preaching the God who was unknown to them. And to the man who said to him, 'Good Master' he made known the God who is really good by saying, 'Why do you call me good? One there is who is good, the Father in heaven' (Mark 10: 17 f. par.). Heaven, they affirm at this point, means the aeons. And from the fact that he did not reply to those who said to him, 'By what power do you do this?', but by a counter-question put them in confusion (Matt. 21: 23 ff. par.), they deduce that he showed to them the unknown nature of the Father, through his not speaking. But concerning even the saying, 'Often have I desired to hear one of these words, and I had no one to utter it' (apocryphal), they say that it was (the word) of one who by means of the word 'one' made known the one true God, whom they did not know. Furthermore, when he drew near to Jerusalem and wept over it saying, 'If thou hadst known, even thou, today, what belongs to thy peace, but it is hidden from thee' (Luke 19: 42), by the words 'it is hidden' he reveals the hidden nature of Bythos. And again when he said, 'Come to me all you who

---

[28] Cf. Arabic Gospel of the Infancy 48 f.; Gospel of Thomas, Greek A 6: B 7, in C. v. Tischendorf, *Evangelia apocrypha*, 1876.

are labouring and heavy-laden: I will refresh you; learn of me!'
(Matt. 11 : 28 f.), he announced the 'Father of truth'. What
they knew not he promised to teach them. As the chief witness
to and a kind of crown for their teaching, they adduce the
following: 'I thank thee, Father, Lord of heaven and earth,
that thou hast hidden these things from the wise and understanding and hast revealed them to babes. Yea, Father, for so
it was well pleasing to thee. All things have been delivered to
me by my Father, and no one knows the Father except the son,
or the son except the Father, and he to whom the son reveals
(discloses) him' (Matt. 11 : 25–7 par.). In these words, they say,
he expressly showed that the 'Father of truth', discovered by
them, was known to no one before his advent; and they want
to prove that the maker and creator of this world was always
known by all, whereas the Lord said this about the Father,
unknown to all, whom they themselves proclaim.

21. 1. The tradition about their redemption is invisible and
incomprehensible, since it is the mother of things incomprehensible and invisible. Because it is fluctuating and changeable,
it cannot be explained simply or in a word. Therefore each
individual hands down the tradition concerning it, as he himself
wishes. So there are as many systems of redemption as there are
mystical teachers of this doctrine. . . .

2. They affirm that it is necessary for those who have attained
to perfect knowledge, that they may be regenerated into the
power which is above all. Otherwise, it is impossible to enter into
the Pleroma, for it is this (redemption) which leads them down
into the profundities of Bythos. For the baptism of (that is,
instituted by) the visible Jesus took place for the remission of
sins, but the redemption by the Christ who descended upon
him for perfection. They allege that the former is psychic and
the latter spiritual. The baptism is regarded as having been
proclaimed by John unto repentance (Mark 1 : 4), but the
redemption by the Christ who is in him (Jesus?) was brought
in with a view to perfection. And it is to this that he refers when
he says, 'And I have another baptism to be baptized with, and
I am strongly urged towards it' (Luke 12 : 50). But the Lord is
said to have added this redemption to the sons of Zebedee,
when their mother asked that they might sit on the right hand
and on the left in his kingdom, saying, 'Can you be baptized

with the baptism with which I am to be baptized?' (Matt. 20: 20 ff.). And they say Paul often clearly set forth the 'redemption' in Christ Jesus and that it is this that is handed down by them in various and discordant ways.

3. Some of them prepare a bridal chamber and perform a mystic rite, with certain invocations, for those who are being consecrated, and they claim that what they are effecting is a spiritual marriage, after the image of the conjunctions (syzygies) above. Others bring to the water and baptize saying, 'In(to) the name of the unknown Father of all things, into Truth, the mother of all, into him who descended on Jesus, into union, into redemption, into the communion of the powers.' Others employ Hebrew words in order to baffle even more those who are being consecrated: 'Basema chamosse baaianora mistadia rouada kousta babophor kalachthei.' The interpretation of this is: 'I call upon that which is above every power of the Father, which is called Light, and the good spirit, and life; for thou hast reigned in the body.'[29] Others refer to the redemption as follows: 'The name which is hidden from every deity, dominion, and power,[30] which Jesus of Nazareth put on in the spheres of light, (the name) of Christ, the Christ who lives through the Holy Spirit for the angelic redemption.' The name of the restitution (*apokatastasis*) is as follows: 'Messia ufareg namempsaiman chaldaian mosomedaea akfranai psaoua, Jesu Nazaria.' And the translation of these words is: 'I do not divide the spirit, the heart, and the super-celestial power which shows mercy. May I enjoy thy name, Saviour of truth.' This is what those who are initiating say; but the initiate answers, 'I am established, I am redeemed, and I redeem my soul from this age and from all that comes from it, in the name of Iao, who redeemed his soul unto the redemption in Christ, the living one.' Then the bystanders add, 'Peace be with all on whom this name rests.' Then they anoint the initiate with oil from the balsam tree. This oil is said to be a type of the sweet savour which is above all terrestrial things.

4. But some say that it is superfluous to bring people to the water, but they mix oil and water together and pour it on the

---

[29] This is not a translation of the Aramaic text. Possibilities of translation in K. Rudolph, *Die Mandäer*, II: *Der Kult*, Göttingen, 1961, 388 n. 1.

[30] For 'truth', the reading of the manuscripts, 'power' should be read.

heads of those to be initiated, with expressions like those which we have just mentioned: this is regarded as being the redemption. They also anoint with balsam. But others reject all this and say that one ought not to celebrate the mystery of the ineffable and invisible power by means of visible and corruptible created things, the inconceivable and incorporeal by means of what is sensually tangible and corporeal. The perfect redemption is said to be the knowledge of the ineffable 'Greatness'. From ignorance both deficiency and passion derived: through 'knowledge' will the entire substance derived from ignorance be destroyed. Therefore, this 'knowledge' is redemption of the inner man. And this is not corporeal, since the body perishes, nor psychic, because the soul also derives from the deficiency and is like a habitation of the spirit (*pneuma*): the redemption must therefore be spiritual. The inner, spiritual man is redeemed through knowledge: sufficient for them is the knowledge of all things, and this is the true redemption.

5. Still others there are who redeem the dying up to the point of their departure by pouring on their heads oil and water, or the aforementioned ointment with water, together with the above-named invocations, in order that they may become unassailable by and invisible to the powers and authorities, and that their inner man may ascend above the realm of the invisible, whilst their body remains behind in the created world, and their soul is delivered to the Demiurge. And they instruct them to speak as follows when, after death, they come to the powers: 'I am a son of the Father, the pre-existent Father, and now a son in the pre-existent Father. I have come to behold all things, both what is strange and what belongs to me. But they are by no means totally strange, but belong to Achamoth, who is female and who has made these things for herself. I derive my being from him who was pre-existent, and I go again to that which is my own, whence I came forth.' And, according to them, when he says this, he eludes and escapes from the powers. He then comes to those who are about the Demiurge and says, 'I am a precious vessel, more precious than the female which made you. If your mother does not know her origin, I know myself and am aware whence I am, and I invoke the incorruptible Sophia, who is in the Father, mother of your mother, who has no father nor any male consort. A female

sprung from a female made you, and she did not know her mother, but believed that she existed all alone. But I call upon her mother.' When those around the Demiurge hear this, they become greatly confused and pass judgement on their origin and the race of their mother. But he proceeds to his own, after casting away his chain, the soul. This is all that has come down to us concerning the redemption. But since in relation to doctrine and tradition they diverge from one another, and since those who are considered more modern among them endeavour to discover and invent day after day some new thing which no one ever thought of before, it is difficult to describe all their opinions.

12

VALENTINIANISM V
THE *EXCERPTA EX THEODOTO* AND
THE ACCOUNT OF EPIPHANIUS

THE *EXCERPTA EX THEODOTO*

The *Excerpta ex Theodoto* of Clement is a collection of sayings from various Valentinians: Theodotus, after whom the collection is named, is but one of a larger number. Comments of Clement are inserted here and there as well. We have already acquainted ourselves with that section of it which is most closely related to the great account by Irenaeus. The remaining parts do not form so consistent a whole. So, in what follows, we shall reproduce the text of the fragments and make some observations in connection with them, and these, because they are arranged under various themes, provide some explanations. The text is translated according to the edition of Sagnard. The sections which Sagnard attributes to Clement himself are omitted, as are also Chapters 69–77 and 81–4, which are perhaps also Clement's own remarks.

Clement of Alexandria, *Excerpta ex Theodoto*, 1, 1–80, 3 (Selection)

1, 1. 'Father', he says, 'into thy hands I commit my spirit' (Luke 23: 46). What Sophia brought forth as 'flesh' for the Logos, (he says), namely, the spiritual seed, that the Saviour put on and descended. 2. Therefore at his passion he commits the Sophia (outside) to the Father in order that he may receive it back from the Father, and that she may not be held back here by those who have the power to plunder her. So he commits the entire spiritual seed, the elect, through the word already mentioned. . . .

2, 1. The Valentinians say that when the psychic body had been formed a male seed was implanted by the Logos in the elect soul while it slept, which (seed) is the effluence deriving from the angels, in order that there may be no deficiency. 2. And this operated like leaven, in that it unified what appeared to be separated, namely, the soul and the flesh, which had in fact been brought forth separately by Sophia. Sleep was for Adam the oblivion of the soul, which the spiritual seed, implanted by the Saviour in the soul, held together in order that it should not be dissolved. The seed was an effluence of the male and angelic. Therefore the Saviour said: 'Save thyself and thy soul' (Gen. 19:17).

3, 1. So when the Saviour came, he awakened the soul, but kindled the spark. For the words of the Lord are power. Therefore he said: 'Let your light shine before men' (Matt. 5:16). 2. And after the resurrection, when he breathed the Spirit into the apostles, he blew away the (choic) dust like ashes and removed it, but he kindled and made alive the spark. . . .

6, 1. 'In the beginning was the Word, and the Word was with God, and the Word was God' (John 1:1) is expounded by the Valentinians in the following way: 2. 'Beginning' they say is the 'Only-begotten', whom they also call God, just as he (John) immediately calls him God in what follows: 'The only-begotten God, who is in the bosom of the Father, he has made him known' (John 1:18). 3. The Logos, which was 'in the beginning' —that is, in the Only-begotten, namely, in Nous and in Truth —he makes known as the Christ, that is, as the Logos and the Life. Therefore he appropriately calls God him who is in the god Nous. 4. 'That which was made in him, the Logos, was life' (John 1:3 f.), (refers to) the consort; therefore the Lord also says, 'I am the life' (John 11:25; 14:6).[1]

7, 1. Because the Father was unknown, he desired to become known to the aeons. And through his own 'thought' (*enthumesis*), as the one who knew himself, he brought forth the spirit of knowledge, which is in knowledge, the Only-begotten. He who came forth from knowledge, that is, from the Father's thought, became himself knowledge, that is, the Son, because 'through the Son is the Father known' (Matt. 11:27 par.). 2. The Spirit of love has been combined with that of knowledge, as the Father is with the Son, and thought with truth, proceeding from the truth, just as knowledge proceeds from thought. 3. The one who remained 'only-begotten Son in the bosom of the Father' (John 1:18) is he who through knowledge explains the thought to the aeons, as though he had indeed gone forth from

[1] Cf. Ir. I 8, 5 and Heracleon Fragm. 1.

his bosom. He who appeared here is no longer called 'only-begotten' by the apostle, but 'as an only-begotten'—'(a) glory as of the only-begotten' (John 1: 14). . . . 5. They call the Demiurge an image of the Only-begotten. Therefore the works of the 'image' are transitory. Therefore also the Lord, forming an image of the spiritual resurrection, raised the dead whom he raised, not incorruptible so far as the flesh was concerned, but as if they were going to die again. . . .

16, 1. And the dove—which some call the Holy Spirit (Matt. 3: 16 par.), the followers of Basilides the servant, the Valentinians the spirit of the 'thought' of the Father—also appeared as a body, when it came down upon the flesh of the Logos.

17, 1. According to the Valentinians, Jesus, the 'Church', and Sophia form a complete and powerful mixture (union) of the bodies. . . .

21, 1. By the statement 'In the image of God he created them, male and female he created them' (Gen. 1 : 27) the Valentinians say that the finest production of Sophia is meant, of which the male denotes the 'election', and the female the 'calling'. And the male (beings) they call angelic, while the female are themselves, the superior seed. 2. So also in the case of Adam: the male remained in him, but the entire female seed was taken from him and became Eve, from whom the female beings (derive), as do the males from him (Adam). 3. The males were drawn together with the Logos, but the female, having become male, unites itself with the angels and enters into the Pleroma. Therefore it is said that the woman is changed into a man[2] and the Church here below into angels.

22, 1. And when the apostle says, 'What are they doing who are baptized for the dead?' (1 Cor. 15: 29), what he is actually saying is that for us the angels of whom we are part were baptized. 2. We are the dead, who have been put to death through this condition. The living are the males who did not share in this condition. 3. 'If the dead are not raised, why, then, are people baptized?' (1 Cor. 15: 29). So then we are raised equal to angels, restored to the males, member to member, to form a unity. 4. 'Those who are baptized for the dead' (1 Cor. 15: 29), they say, are the angels who are baptized for us, in

---

[2] Cf. Heracleon Fragm. 5.

order that we too, possessing the name, may not be held back and prevented by Horos (Limit) and the Cross from entering into the Pleroma. 5. Hence also at the laying on of hands they say at the end, 'for the angelic redemption', that is, the one which the angels also have, in order that he who has received the redemption may be baptized in the same name as that in which his angel was baptized before him. 6. In the beginning the angels were baptized through the 'redemption' of the name which came down upon Jesus in the dove and redeemed him. 7. 'Redemption' was necessary even for Jesus, in order that he might not be detained by the Ennoia of the deficiency[3] in which he was placed, though conducted (thereto) through Sophia, as Theodotus says.

23, 1. The Valentinians call Jesus the 'Paraclete' because he came forth, full of the aeons, as one who proceeded from the Whole. 2. For Christ, leaving behind (the) Sophia which brought him forth and entering into the Pleroma, sought help on behalf of the Sophia who had been left outside, and by the good pleasure of the aeons Jesus was brought forth, a Paraclete for the aeon which had transgressed. As a type of the Paraclete, Paul became the apostle of the resurrection. 3. Immediately after the Passion of the Lord, he was sent to preach. Therefore he proclaimed the Saviour in both fashions: as begotten and capable of suffering for the sake of those on the left, because they feared him, since they were able to know him as regards his 'place';[4] and according to the spiritual (understanding did he proclaim him) as (coming into being) from the Holy Spirit and the virgin (Luke 1: 35), as the angels on the right know him. . . .

24, 1. The Valentinians say that the spirit which each of the prophets received specially for his ministry is poured out upon all in the Church: therefore the signs of the Spirit—healings and prophesyings—are accomplished through the Church.

25, 1. The Valentinians defined the angel as a Logos having a message from Him who is. And using the same name as the Logos, they call the aeons Logoi. 2. The apostles, he says, were associated with the twelve signs of the zodiac. For just as birth is regulated by them, so the rebirth is directed by the apostles.

---

[3] In Irenaeus, she is called 'Achamoth'.
[4] 'Place' is the abode of the Demiurge.

26, 1. The visible part of Jesus was (the) Wisdom and the church of the superior seed, which he put on through the flesh, as Theodotus says: but the invisible part was the Name, which is the only-begotten Son. 2. Therefore, when he says, 'I am the door' (John 10: 7), he means 'up to the Horos (Limit), where I am, you will come, you who belong to the superior seed.' 3. But when he himself enters (into the Pleroma), then the seed also enters with him, united and introduced through the 'door'.[5] . . .

28. The statement 'God recompenses the disobedient unto the third and fourth generation' is understood by the followers of Basilides as referring to the (re-)incarnations. The Valentinians (say that) the three places on the left are thereby indicated, while the fourth generation is their own seed. 'He shows mercy unto thousands' (Exod. 20: 5 f.) (alludes, according to the Valentinians,) to those on the right.

29. Sige, they say, who is the mother of all those brought forth by 'Depth', kept silence on that which she could not express of the ineffable; but what she understood, this she expressed as incomprehensible.

30, 1. [Then, forgetting the glory of God, they say, impiously, that he (God) suffered.[6]] For in that the Father shared in suffering—though he is by nature rigid, Theodotus says, and does not submit—showing himself submissive in order that Sige might understand it (him), [that is a suffering. 2. For sharing in suffering is a suffering of one through the suffering of the other.] Yes, indeed. And when the Passion took place, the Whole shared in suffering in order to bring to correction the being which suffered.

31, 1. But if he who came down was the good-pleasure of the Whole—for 'in him was the entire Pleroma in bodily form' (Col. 2: 9)—and himself suffered, [then it is clear that the seed which was in him also shared in the suffering, and therefore it follows that the Whole and the All suffered.] 2. But, as a result of the fall of the twelfth aeon, the Whole in which it was trained, as they say, suffered. 3. For then they recognized that what they are, they are by the grace of the Father, an inexpressible

---

[5] Cf. the speculations of the Naassenes on the 'gate' (Hipp. V 8, 18 ff. 44; 9, 21).

[6] In §§ 30 and 31, the words which Clement (polemically) speaks are placed in square brackets [ ].

name, form, and knowledge. The aeon which desired to grasp that which is beyond knowledge fell into ignorance and formlessness. 4. Therefore he brought about a 'void' of 'knowledge' (that is, an emptiness for knowledge) which is a shadow of the name, which is the Son, the form of the aeons. Thus, the partial name of the aeons is the loss of the name.

32, 1. In the Pleroma, then, where there is a unity, each of the aeons has his own pleroma (complement), the syzygy. What proceeds from a syzygy, they say, are pleromas, and what (proceeds) from one are images. 2. Therefore Theodotus called the Christ who proceeded from the 'thought' of Sophia an image of the Pleroma. 3. But he left behind his mother, entered into the Pleroma, and was mingled, as with the Whole, so also with the Paraclete.

33, 1. Christ thus was adopted as a Son, since in relation to pleromas he became 'elect' and 'first-born' of the things there. . . . 3. When Christ abandoned what was foreign to him and had been drawn back into the Pleroma, having been born from the mother's thought, then the mother again brought forth the ruler of the Oikonomia (dispensation), as an image of him who had left her, according to her longing for him who was indeed stronger, for he was an image (type) of the Father of all. 4. Therefore he (the Demiurge) was weaker, for he was composed of the suffering of desire. She was disgusted at him when she saw his roughness—so they say.

34, 1. But the powers on the left, brought forth by her earlier than those on the right, were not formed by the advent of the light; those on the left were left to be formed by the Topos. 2. When, however, the mother, with the son and the seeds, has entered into the Pleroma, then Topos will obtain the authority and the rank which the mother has at present.

35, 1. Jesus, our light, as the apostle says, 'emptied himself' (Phil. 2: 7), that is, according to Theodotus, he went forth outside Horos (Limit) and, being an angel of the Pleroma, he brought forth with him the angels of the superior seed. 2. And since he had proceeded from the Pleroma, he himself had the redemption, but he brought the angels (with him) for the correction of the seed. 3. They entreat and supplicate (for us), as if for a part (of them), and, being restrained for our sake in their haste to enter, they plead for forgiveness for us, in order that we may enter in with them. 4. For they virtually have need of us that they may enter, since without us it is not permitted to them—for this reason, they say, even the mother did not enter without us—but justifiably they plead for us.

36, 1. Our angels were of course brought forth in unity, they say, being one because they came forth from one. 2. But since we were divided, Jesus was baptized, that the undivided might be divided, until he unites us with them in the Pleroma, in order that we, the many become one, may all of us be united with the One which for our sakes was divided.

37. Those who came forth from Adam: of these the righteous, making their way through things created, were detained in the Topos, according to the Valentinians, but the others (remain) in the creation of darkness, among those on the left, and there have experience of the fire.

38, 1. 'A stream of fire issues from under the throne' (Dan. 7: 10) of Topos and flows into the void of what is created, which is hell, and is not filled from the creation of the fire that flows. Topos itself is fiery. 2. Therefore, he says, it has a curtain, in order that the spirits may not be devoured by the sight of it. Only the archangel goes into it, according to the likeness of whom the high priest enters once a year into the Holy of Holies (Heb. 9: 7). 3. Summoned thence, Jesus seated himself beside the Topos in order that the spirits might remain and not rise before him, and that he might subdue Topos and secure for the seeds a pathway into the Pleroma.

39. After the mother had brought forth the Christ complete and had been abandoned by him, she no more brought forth in the future anything complete, but she retained by her what was possible for her. So, when she has brought forth the angels[7] of the Topos and of the called, she keeps them by her, whereas the angels of the elect had been brought forth still earlier by the male.

40. Now those on the right were brought forth by the mother before she requested the light, but the seed of the Church after she had requested the light, when the angels of the seed were put forth by the male.

41, 1. The superior seeds, he says, were brought forth neither as passions, on the dissolution of which the seeds also would

[7] In §§ 39 and 40, the original text is literally 'the angelic' instead of 'angels'.

have perished, nor as creation—for when the creation was brought to completion, the seeds also would have been brought to completion—2. but as children. Therefore they have an affinity with the light which the Christ who entreated the aeons brought forth first, namely, Jesus. In him the seeds were potentially purified, as they entered with him into the Pleroma.[8] Consequently, it is rightly said of the Church that it was chosen before the foundation of the world. In the beginning, they say, we were united and made manifest. 3. Therefore the Saviour says, 'Let your light shine' (Matt. 5: 16), referring to the light which appeared and gave form, and of which the apostle says, 'which lightens every man who comes into the world' (John 1: 9), (namely) the men of the superior seed. 4. For when man was illumined, then he came into the world, that is, he brought himself into order (word-play on *kosmos*), in that he separated from himself the passions which were blinding him and were mixed with him. And the Demiurge, who beforehand held Adam in (his) thought, (first) brought him forth at the end of creation.

42, 1. The Cross is a symbol of Limit (Horos) in the Pleroma, for it divides the unfaithful from the faithful, just as the latter separates the world from the Pleroma. 2. Therefore Jesus, by the sign of the Cross, also carries the seeds on his shoulders, and leads them into the Pleroma. For Jesus is called 'the shoulders of the seed', but the head (is called) Christ. 3. Wherefore it is said, 'Whoever does not take up his cross and follow me is not my brother' (cf. Matt. 10: 38 par.). He (Christ) took up the body of Jesus which was of the same substance as the Church.

43, 1. They also say: those on the right knew the names of Jesus and of the Christ, even before the advent, but the power of the sign they did not know. 43. 2–65 (see pp. 146–53).

66. The Saviour taught the apostles, first in a figurative and mystical way, then in parables and riddles, and thirdly, clearly and directly in private.

67, 1. 'When we were in the flesh' (Rom. 7: 5) says the apostle, as though he was speaking already from outside the body. He says that 'flesh' denotes that weakness, the offspring of the woman above. 2. And when the Saviour says to Salome

---

[8] The (grains of) seed are thus brought upwards by the son of the outer Sophia, Christ, in order to be purified!

that death reigns as long as women give birth,[9] he is not saying this to make child-bearing reproachful, since it is indispensable for the salvation of those who believe 3.—for this child-bearing is essential until the previously reckoned seed is brought forth— 4. rather he is speaking enigmatically of the woman above, whose passions became creation and who brought forth the unformed substances, and on whose account also the Saviour came down to tear us away from the passions and bring us into union with himself.

68. As long as we were children of the female only, as of a dishonourable union, we were incomplete, childish, without understanding, weak, and without form, brought forth like abortions, in short, we were children of the woman. But having been given form by the Saviour, we are the children of the man (husband) and of the bride-chamber.[10]

78, 1. Until baptism, they say, Fate is effective, but after it the astrologers no longer speak the truth. 2. It is not the bath (washing) alone that makes us free, but also the knowledge: who were we? what have we become? where were we? into what place have we been cast? whither are we hastening? from what are we delivered? what is birth? what is rebirth?

79. So long as the seed is still unformed, they say, it is a child of the female. But when it is formed, it is changed into a man and becomes a son of the bridegroom. No longer is it weak and subjected to the cosmic (powers), visible and invisible, but, having become a man, it becomes a male fruit.[11]

80, 1. He to whom the mother gives birth is led into death and into the world. But he to whom Christ gives second birth is translated into Life, into the Ogdoad. 2. And they die indeed to the world, but live to God in order that death may be destroyed by death, and corruption by the resurrection. 3. For he who has been sealed by the Father and the Son and the Holy Spirit is unassailable by every other power, and by the three names he is released from the entire Triad which consists in corruption. 'Having borne the image of the (man from) earth (or: dust), he will then bear the image of the heavenly' (cf. 1 Cor. 15: 49).[12]

---

[9] Gospel of the Egyptians, see Hennecke and Schneemelcher (eds.), *N.T. Apocrypha*, I 166.

[10] Cf. Ir. I 21, 5.   [11] Cf. Heracleon Fragm. 5 and note there.

[12] Is Clement perhaps already speaking at 80, 3?

The supreme god is called 'Father' in 1, 1 and 7, 1, or 'Depth' in 29. The term 'Father' for the supreme god appears to have been coined by Valentinus himself, according to Irenaeus II 4, 1. Silence, which is also called Ennoia, is termed 'Thought' (*enthumesis*) in 7, 1 f. It is from 'Truth'—and this is a special feature—that Love appears to have proceeded; but see the diagram of the Ophians (Origen, *Contra Celsum* VI 38). Jesus, the fruit, is merely called 'as (like) an only-begotten son' (7, 3).

If the Father showed himself 'submissive' (30, 1 f.), then this is explained in Epiphanius' account of Valentinus (XXXI 5, 5), where the expression 'to wheedle' occurs with reference to the 'Greatness'. Clement employs this idea with a view to ascribing to the Father a 'sharing in suffering'; even the Whole, even the 'fruit' suffered in sympathy. In 31, 2 there occurs the expression 'to train', which is probably intended to indicate the 'formation according to knowledge': this and the remainder of the chapter agrees with the account of Irenaeus I 1–8.

In 23, 2 and 32, 2—in the latter passage it is expressly referred to as the view of Theodotus—Christ is represented as brought forth by the fallen Sophia, and that accords with the view of the founder of the sect (Irenaeus I 11, 1). Together with him the seeds, which go into the Pleroma with him, are purified, 41, 1–3. With that there also coheres the view that the 'mother' (Irenaeus I 5, 3, etc.) loathed the Demiurge, whom she had just brought forth, when she saw his roughness (33, 4).

The 'seed' is a subject for fertile speculation. Sophia produced as flesh for the Logos (that is, the 'Saviour') the spiritual seed, which he put on and which, in the passion, he committed to the Father (1, 1–2). The spirit of the Thought of the Father came down upon Jesus, and therefore upon his flesh as well (the spiritual seed, 1, 1). More precise, or at any rate different is 21: Sophia brought forth 'male and female' (according to Gen. 1:27), that is, the 'election', the angelic beings, and the 'calling', which means the superior (or special) seed, the pneumatics. Here the two terms 'election' and 'calling' are in a different relationship from elsewhere: usually the 'calling' denotes the psychics, and the 'election' the pneumatics. The female, on becoming male, is united with the angels and so enters into the Pleroma, and to this the formula 'The woman is changed into a man' is expressly applied in 21, 3; similarly in 79, 'having become a man, it (the pneumatic) becomes a male fruit', and likewise in 68. The same use of the image is to be found in Heracleon, Fragment 5.

Here in the *Excerpta* 22, 1–7 the enigmatic passage from Paul in 1 Cor. 15:29 on baptism for the dead is related to the angels who are baptized for 'us dead', in order that we may be 'restored to them'. In 35 and 36 a similar speculation is introduced: the angels are brought forth 'in unity', Jesus is baptized in order that the undivided, the angels, may be divided, until Jesus unites us, the divided, in the Pleroma, and we thus, become one, are united with the One: cf. Heracleon, Fragments 33 and 34. Again, in 67, 4 there occurs the phrase 'to bring into union with himself'. Here is a different view of things from that in Irenaeus' account, in which there stands as the final phase 'rest in the marriage', that is, the uniting of the pneumatics, as brides, with the angels.

On the other hand, according to 2, 1 and 2, the implanting of the seed in the soul is something which operated like leaven, for it unified soul and flesh, which had been produced separately by Sophia. Frequently speculations occur concerning the Name: in 26, 1 f. the (inferior?) Sophia and the Church of the superior seed is the visible part of Jesus which according to 1, 1 he put on and descended; the invisible part was the 'name', the only-begotten Son, 26, 1—a speculation which Clement attributes to Theodotus.

The difference in the activity of the 'Saviour' in relation to the pneumatics and the psychics comes to expression in 3, 1 and 2. The soul he awakens; the spark, that is, the spiritual part in man, he kindles: only in relation to the spiritual is it said, 'He blew away the evil'—the psychic must itself get rid of the evil. Jesus is also called 'the Paraclete', and is sent out from the Pleroma with the 'aeons'— that is, with the purified seeds (41, 1–3)—to the assistance of the aeon which had fallen into error. Paul proclaims the Saviour in two ways: on the one hand, for the sake of 'those on the left'—here they are the psychics, as begotten and capable of suffering; if they have recognized him, they must fear him: this is indeed the characteristic feature of the psychics. And he whom they know is the psychic Christ; their fear of him in fact controls their conduct; they are not 'saved by nature', but only if they do good works. But the pneumatic recognizes him, the Saviour, as the 'angels of the right', the 'fruit', know him, namely without fear, as 'children', as 41, 1 and 2 affirm.

Their relation to the Saviour is an 'affinity', and according to 41, 2 one might assume that these seeds went with him first of all into the aeon and were purified along with him, with Christ who laid aside the shadow and so entered into the aeon. Hence the 'Church', the community of the pneumatics, was created before the foundation of the world—and that indeed potentially, but probably also in principle—in contrast to the gnostic training and purification which took place only when the seed was sown in the world, as 41, 3–4 states.

In 22, 7 Jesus is represented as requiring 'redemption' in order that he might not be detained by the '*ennoia* of deficiency': this is striking, even if 'Jesus' is not synonymous with 'Christ'. According to 24, 1 the Holy Spirit was given to the prophets of the Old Testament only for their special ministry. Whether the assertion which follows—that it is poured out upon all in the 'Church'—is supposed to hold for the gnostics, or for the entire Christian church, is not clear: it could be true of the whole Church, to which Valentinianism then concedes that miracles took place in it.

It is characteristic of the *Excerpta* that the Demiurge is often represented as being hostilely disposed to the pneumatics. As early as 1, 2 mention is made of those who could plunder Sophia: it is particularly clear in 38. In 22, 4 it is said of the 'Limit' that, if necessary, it could prevent the pneumatics from entering into the Pleroma.

In sections 34 to 39 there is discussion of the Topos (the Place). Here the Demiurge himself is meant, whereas elsewhere the 'Place' is only a designation of the region of the Demiurge. According to 37 f. the Demiurge is fiery and has a curtain in order that the 'spirits', that is, the pneumatics, may not be consumed by the sight of him. Hence, 'Jesus' has taken his seat with him in order that he may subdue him, Topos, and secure for the seeds access into the Pleroma. This appears to be a further testimony from Theodotus, and probably agrees with Fragment 1 from Valentinus himself, so that at this point also Theodotus has preserved the position of the master more faithfully than Ptolemaeus and Heracleon.[13]

The relation to the power of the astrologically understood Fate is the theme of the last section of the *Excerpta*. There in the foreground stand baptism, eucharist, and anointing (with oil). It is a question whether 69–77 and perhaps also 81–6 reproduce gnostic thought at all, and not rather statements of Clement himself. In any case, however, 78, 1–80, 3 is gnostic. Baptism—here called the 'bath'— is not the only saving agency, but knowledge is added as well. According to what we said at the beginning, a sacrament does not belong indispensably to Gnosis: but here we see how the sacramental and the gnostic are drawn together in an alliance in which the sacramental may even be predominant.

In 80, 1 it is striking that as the final goal 'Life' is identified with existence in the Ogdoad. The section 80, 2 recalls Valentinus himself. In 80, 3 the two triads, and especially that of corruption, are difficult to explain in detail, but perhaps this passage as well belongs to Clement.

[13] A trace of it occurs in Ir. I 7, 1: 'without being held or seen'.

THE ACCOUNT OF EPIPHANIUS CONCERNING VALENTINUS

The first point to take note of here is the introductory formula, which is, however, mutilated. It is the writing of an 'indestructible one', and it is addressed to 'indestructible ones'; and this recalls the fourth fragment from Valentinus. The expression 'to wheedle' makes us think of *Excerpta ex Theodoto* 30, 1. The composition of the Pleroma is, at the outset, parallel to that which Irenaeus offers, save that the Father of Truth, who is elsewhere called the Only-begotten and Nous, is here termed 'Man'. This recalls Irenaeus I 12, 3 where the supreme God is actually styled in this way. But then the creation of a further thirty aeons is mentioned, the production of lights in even greater numbers, and finally a Pentad of male aeons is referred to as well. The meaning of these conceptions cannot be found out, for Epiphanius breaks off at this point.

The statement Epiphanius makes (7, 11)—no longer in quotation —to the effect that the psychics are delivered over to the angels of the Saviour and become their brides in the Pleroma can in this form scarcely be the intention of a Valentinian system.

Whether or not this piece is one of the oldest fragments of Valentinianism[14] is a question which cannot be decided here: the different names which are given to the highest powers and which actually appear in other Valentinian systems make a later date for its origin probable.

Epiphanius, *Panarion* XXXI 5, 1–8, 3 (Selection)

5, 1. But again I shall leave these things aside and, following the order of their books, I shall set out here, word for word as it is written, what is read among them, that is, the book (current) among them, and this is what it says: 'In the midst of the intelligent, the psychics, the fleshly, the worldlings, the Greatness . . . indestructible Nous greets the indestructible ones. 2. Unknown and unspeakable transcendent mysteries I make known to you, which can be conceived neither by powers nor authorities nor those subordinate to them, nor by any commixture, (mysteries which) are manifest only to the Ennoia (Thought) of the unmoved one. 3. For when in the beginning the self-engendered contained in himself everything, which was with him in unawareness—he whom some call an aeon which

[14] K. Holl in his edition of Epiphanius considers it one of the oldest pieces from Valentinianism; O. Dibelius, on the other hand, in his 'Studien zur Geschichte der Valentinianer II', *ZNW* 9 (1908), 329–40, regards it as a later piece.

grows not old, eternally young, male-female, who contains in himself all things and is himself not contained (in anything)—then Ennoia within him willed—4. she whom some call Ennoia, others Charis (Grace), and rightly, for she presents treasures of the Greatness to those who derive from the Greatness, but those who spoke the truth have named her Sige (Silence), because the Greatness brought everything to completion by means of Thought (*enthumesis*) and without a word—5. as I have already said, the imperishable Ennoia wished to break the eternal chains, and therefore she wheedled the Greatness into longing for his repose. And she was united with him and produced the Father of Truth whom the perfect ones rightly call 'Man' because he is an antitype of the pre-existent unbegotten one. 6. Thereafter Sige (Silence), when she had brought about a natural unity of the light with the man—their coming together is desire—produced Truth. And Truth is rightly so named by the perfect, for she was truly like her own mother Sige (Silence); for Silence desired that the luminous part both of the male and of the female should be equal in order that through them even their Unity(?) might be revealed to those from them who were divided up into visible lights. 7. After this, Truth produced maternal desire and wheedled the Father to herself, and they came together in an imperishable bond and an eternal union, and they brought forth a spiritual, male-female, Tetrad, the antitype of the original Tetrad which was Primal Cause, Silence, Father, and Truth. This is the Tetrad derived from the Father and Truth: Man, Church, Logos, and Life. 8. Then, in accordance with the will of Primal Cause who embraces all things, Man and Church came together, mindful of the Father's words, and they brought forth a Duodecad of male-female procreative powers. Now the male are—Paraclete, Paternal, Maternal, everlasting Nous (Mind), Desired—that is, Light—and Churchly: the female are—Faith, Hope, Love, Intelligence, Blessedness, and Wisdom. 9. Then Logos and Life, after forming again the gift of unity, were joined together—their communion was desire—and, on coming together, they produced a Decad of procreative desires, and these were male-female too. The male are—Deep, Never-ageing, Spontaneously created, Only-begotten, Motionless: these assumed their designations to the glory of him who embraces all things: the female are—Mingling, Uniting, Blending, Unity, Desire, and these took names to the glory of Sige.

6, 1. When the Triacontad of Truth had been completed in conformity with the Father—(the Triacontad) which earthly men who are not intelligent enumerate, and when they come up to that number (the Triacontad) they find no further number, and they repeat the action, by counting it up all over again—and it is . . . (list of the names), 2. then he who embraces all things decided, in his unsurpassable wisdom and with determination, to raise up another Ogdoad in place of the original, fundamental Ogdoad, which might remain within the number of the Triacontad—for it was not the intention of the Greatness to be counted up—and he set the males in place of the males, the first, third, fifth, and seventh; and the females: Dyad, Tetrad, Hexad, and Ogdoad. 3. Now this Ogdoad, which had been called forth to take the place of the original Ogdoad (Primal Cause, Father, Man, Logos, and Silence, Truth, Church, and Life) united itself with the lights and the number thirty was completed. 4. The original Ogdoad, however, rested. But Primal Cause went forth in order that with the stability of the Greatness he might be made one with the Triacontad. For he joined himself to Truth, and the Father of Truth to the Church, Maternal had Life, the Paraclete had Unity, and Unity joined herself to the Father of Truth, and the Father of Truth came (together) with Silence, the spiritual Logos entered into union with . . . (some name has dropped out) in a spiritual fusion and imperishable mingling, achieving the goal of the self-generated, his own undivided repose. 5. Because the Triacontad had now completed the unfathomable mysteries, in that they had consummated marriage in the realm of the immortal, they brought forth imperishable lights, which were called children of the unity (Middle?) and were not imprinted: because that which is intellectual was not in them, they remain, without Ennoia, outside the thinking process. For if a man does not completely comprehend that with which he concerns himself he achieves nothing. 6. Then the lights came into being, the multitude of which need not be expressed numerically, but one ought to recognize it. Each light had allotted to it its own particular name, by reason of knowledge of unspeakable mysteries. 7. Silence then, out of the desire to save everything for the choice of knowledge, joined (herself?) to the second, counterpart Ogdoad in an imperishable union, in an intellectual desire. Her intellectual desire was the Holy Spirit, which is in the midst of the holy churches. This she sent to the second Ogdoad and persuaded it also to become joined to her. 8. So a marriage was consummated among the members of the Ogdoad, in that the Holy Spirit was united with the One, the Dyad with the third, the third with the Hexad, and the Ogdoad with the seventh, and the seventh with the Dyad, and the sixth with the fifth. 9. The entire Ogdoad came together with everlasting joy and imperishable intercourse—for there was no separation of one from the other, but there was a uniting with undefiled pleasure—and brought forth a Pentad of Non-Females ready to procreate, whose names are—Deliverer, Limit-setter, Grateful (Agreeable?), Released, Leader-across (*Metagogeus*). These are called sons of the Middle. 10. But you must know . . . (list of unintelligible names).' . . .

7, 3. He and his followers call our Lord Jesus Christ (as I said) Saviour, Christ, Logos, Cross, Leader-across, Limit-setter, and Limit as well. 4. But they say that his body was brought down from above, and passed through the virgin Mary like water through a pipe, without having received anything from the virgin's womb, but he had a body from above, as I have already said.[15] 5. But he was not (they maintain) the first Logos, nor the Christ after the Logos, who remained above among the aeons above, but they say that he was brought forth for no other reason than to come and save the spiritual race from above. 6. They deny the resurrection of the dead, saying something mysterious and ridiculous, that it is not this body which rises, but another one rises from it, which they call spiritual. Only those who are called pneumatics by them, and the others who are called the psychics, will be saved, provided that the psychics behave correctly. The hylics, who are called fleshly and choic, perish utterly and will not be saved at all. 7. Each substance returns to its own parents; the material is given back to matter, and the fleshly and earthly to the earth. 8. There are three classes of men, pneumatics, psychics, and fleshy (*sarkikoi*). The class of the pneumatics is made up of themselves, inasmuch as they are also called gnostics, and they need no exertion but

[15] Cf. Cl. Al., *Exc.* § 60.

only knowledge (*gnosis*) and what was said thereon in the mysteries. Each one of them does anything whatever without fear, and does not worry. Their class, being spiritual, will be saved entirely, they say. 9. The second class of men in the world, which they call psychic, cannot be saved of itself unless they save themselves by effort and good behaviour. The material (hylic) class of men in the world can neither understand knowledge nor receive it, they say, and even if one of this class desires it and strives for it, he will perish in soul and in body. 10. Their own class, the spiritual, is saved with another body, one that is within, which they in their fanciful imagination call a 'spiritual body'. 11. The psychics who have made great efforts and proceeded beyond the Demiurge will be delivered above to the angels who came simultaneously with Christ, but they carry away nothing at all from the body; rather, only the souls, which are found in the Pleroma of their knowledge and which have passed beyond the Demiurge, are given over as brides to the angels with Christ.

8, 1–3. There is still more to say, but Epiphanius has stated only as much as is necessary on the questions, whence, at what time, and from whom the Valentinians are derived. As for the rest, he will introduce the account from Irenaeus, which then follows.

Epiphanius, *Panarion* XXXI 35, 4

For there stood before him (the twelfth aeon) the Leader-across (*Metagogeus*) or Limit-setter, who said to him 'Iao', as they say, and thus he (the twelfth aeon) was established.[16]

[16] Cf. Ir. I 4, 1, where 'Iao' is spoken against Achamoth.

13

VALENTINIANISM VI
VALENTINUS

INTRODUCTION

Now we come to the fragments which are preserved from the founder
of the sect himself. It would be futile to wish to form from them a
picture of the entire system, for the fragments are too few in number,
too short, and have to do with different points. All we can do is to
examine the individual fragments to find out whether they fit in
with what has been transmitted elsewhere in tradition about
Valentinus and his disciples.

Fragment 9 provides only the name of a document. Fragment 8,
the text of which is not quite certain, offers merely a general sketch
of the world-view into which many systems of thought could be
incorporated. Fragment 7 professes to set out the origin of the entire
Valentinian system, but we can draw no conclusions from it.

Fragment 4 agrees both with the beginning of Epiphanius' account
of the Valentinians and with the *Excerpta ex Theodoto* (80, 2). The
prevailing note is the sublime assurance that in themselves they have
abolished death.

The third fragment agrees with what Hippolytus says about the
Anatolian school, namely, that the body of the Saviour was spiritual.
By reason of his having a spiritual body it is understood that he
cannot 'digest' food, because he can destroy nothing whatsoever.
Fragment 2 again appears in the account of Hippolytus, who also
compares man to an inn (Hippol. VI 34, 6).

Fragment 5 sets out to illustrate the relation of the 'living aeon'
to the world by the relation of a man to his painted picture. The
'painter' is so gripped by the majesty of the figure that he ventures
upon its portrayal, which naturally remains only a poor copy.
According to Clement's explanation, Valentinus had in view in the
painter Sophia, and in the picture the Demiurge.

Fragment 1 is the most remarkable. It affirms that Man is a work
of angels—which need not absolutely exclude the view that he is a
work of the Demiurge—into whom, invisibly, seed of the substance
above is introduced and who thereupon expresses himself freely:

what he expresses is not stated, but since it is said that Adam instilled in the angels fear before the 'pre-existent man', he must also have openly expressed something from the world above. That Adam was fashioned in the name of Man is not remarkable, but it is striking that he inspired in the angels fear before the pre-existent man. Towards the end of Irenaeus I 12, 3 there is the statement that some call the Forefather of all things 'Man'. Whether it is in accordance with, or apart from, or even against the wishes of Ialdabaoth, the angels here must be evil powers. The 'pre-existent man' certainly cannot be the Primal Cause—if indeed the speculation on the aeons goes back to Valentinus himself—but only the (male) partner of the Church.

At all events, Valentinus must have had a lot more speculative opinions than appears to be the case from his followers Ptolemaeus and Heracleon. The fragments of Valentinus, the account about him, and what was reported from Theodotus seem to justify the conjecture that Valentinus was inclined towards strongly mythological ideas. No other system has such a plethora of divine beings, 'aeons', neither Basilides nor the Baruch-gnosis, nor the Ophites and the Apocryphon of John, nor the systems to be adduced later. In this connection one can see that the total of thirty aeons is an additional feature: only the eight aeons have real significance, for the ten and the twelve aeons bear utterly artificial names (with the exception of Sophia). Since the thirty aeons are a feature common to all Valentinians, the hand of Valentinus himself may perhaps be detected at this point.

That Sophia falls corresponds to the 'female' type of Gnosis, and it is precisely so among the Ophites and in Barbelo-gnosis. The theme is parallel to that in the Apocryphon of John: if this was the original theme of Valentinianism, then Ptolemaeus has introduced a modification, whilst the system of Hippolytus has preserved better the position of the master. Ptolemaeus would then have discovered a more intellectual motif.

Ptolemaeus and whoever stands behind Hippolytus' account have again brought in a significant alteration as compared with the Ophites and Barbelo-gnosis: it is not through that which was inserted by the 'mother' as mother in Ialdabaoth that the spiritual element entered into man, but only through the seed which, fertilized by the 'fruit', she intentionally introduced into men. Fragment 1 of Valentinus is more consistent with the system of the Ophites, for in this fragment the demiurgic powers are astonished and terrified when man expresses something greater than that which they have placed in him: this is also the case with the Ophites and the Barbelo-gnostics. Even the hostility of the Demiurge, which emerges from this fragment, is more clearly expressed in the *Excerpta ex Theodoto* (apart from the section which corresponds with Irenaeus) and can still be traced in the system of Hippolytus. In the main, the system of Irenaeus and that of Hippolytus clearly show a more kindly attitude on the part of the Demiurge, and that does not at all agree with the first fragment from Valentinus.

So one might assume that the 'older teaching' which Valentinus is reputed to have 'discovered'[1] was a system which was akin to that of the Ophites or the Barbelo-gnostics. How this hypothesis accords with the conjectured Valentinian origin of the 'Gospel of Truth' is quite another matter.

Fragment 1. Clement of Alexandria, *Strom.* II 8 = § 36, 2–4

2. Valentinus also seems to have had something of this sort in mind in a letter when he writes as follows: 'Just as fear fell on the angels in the presence of this creature when it emitted greater (sounds) than his creation (justified), because of the one who had invisibly deposited in him seed of the substance above, and expressed himself freely, 3. so also among the generations of men of this world the works of men become objects of fear to those who make them, as in the case of statues, images and everything which hands fashion in the name of a "god". 4. For Adam, being fashioned in the name of "Man", inspired fear of the pre-existent man, because he was in him: they (the angels) were terrified and quickly concealed their work.'

Fragment 2. Clement of Alexandria, *Strom.* II 20 = § 114, 3–6

3. But Valentinus also writes in a letter to someone about the appendages: 'One is good, whose manifestation through the Son (gives) confidence, and through him alone is it possible for the heart to become pure when every evil spirit is banished from the heart. 4. For many spirits dwell in it and do not permit it to be pure; each of them brings to fruition its own works, and they treat it abusively by means of unseemly desires. 5. To me it seems that the heart suffers in much the same way as an inn: for it (an inn) has holes and trenches dug in it and is often filled with filth by men who live there licentiously and have no regard for the place because it belongs to another. 6. Likewise, the heart, so long as it is not cared for, is unclean

---

[1] See p. 122 n. 9.

and the abode of many demons. But when the Father, who alone is good, visits it, it is sanctified and becomes bright with light; and he who has such a heart will be proclaimed blessed, for he will see God' (Matt. 5: 8).

Fragment 3. Clement of Alexandria, *Strom.* III 7 = § 59, 3

In the letter to Agathopus Valentinus says: 'Whilst enduring everything he was continent. Jesus realized divinity: he ate and drank in a special way, without evacuating the food. So great was his power of continence that the food was not corrupted in him, for he did not possess corruptibility.'

Fragment 4. Clement of Alexandria, *Strom.* IV 13 = § 89, 2–3

2. Valentinus writes in a homily: 'From the beginning you are immortal and children of eternal life. You wished to take death to yourselves as your portion in order that you might destroy it and annihilate it utterly, and that death might die in you and through you. 3. For when you destroy the world and yourselves are not destroyed, then you are lords over the whole creation and over all decay.'

Fragment 5. Clement of Alexandria, *Strom.* IV 13 = § 89, 6–90, 2

6. Concerning this god he speaks as follows, in a rather obscure way, writing thus: 'The world is as much inferior to the living aeon as the picture is inferior to the living figure. 90, 1. What then is the reason for the picture? It is the majesty of the living figure, which presents the example for the painter so that it may be honoured through his name. For the form was not found to correspond to the actuality, but the name filled up what was lacking in the image. But the invisible power of God works for the authenticity of the image.' 2. Then Valentinus designates the creator of the world, in so far as he was called God and Father, as the likeness of the true God and as his herald, but Sophia as the painter whose work the likeness is, for the glorification of the invisible one. . . .

Fragment 6. Clement of Alexandria, *Strom.* V 16 = § 52, 3–4

3. . . . The leader Valentinus, in his homily 'On friends', speaks as follows: 4. 'Much that is written in the generally available books is found written also in the church of God. That which is common is this: the words which come from the

heart, the law which is written in the heart. This is the people of the Beloved, who are loved by him and who love him.'

Fragment 7. Hippolytus, *Ref.* VI 42, 2

For Valentinus says (that) he saw a small child, newly born, and asked him who he was, and he answered that he was the Logos. Then he added to this an imposing myth and on this he wants to base the 'sect' that was founded by him.

Fragment 8. Hippolytus, *Ref.* VI 37, 6–8

6. . . . Valentinus has set it (the arrangement) out concisely in a psalm . . . as follows: 7. 'Harvest(?)

> I see that all is suspended on spirit,
> I perceive that all is wafted upon spirit.
> Flesh is suspended on soul,
> And soul depends on the air,
> Air is suspended from ether,
> From the depths come forth fruits,
> From the womb comes forth a child.'

8. And this he understands as follows: flesh for them is matter, which is suspended from the soul of the Demiurge. The soul depends on the air, that is, the Demiurge depends on the spirit of the external Sophia; air is suspended from ether, that is, the Sophia outside depends upon her who is within Horos and on the entire Pleroma. From the depths come forth fruits: the entire procession of the aeons from the Father.

Fragment 9. Anthimus, *De Sancta Ecclesia* 9

. . . and they teach three hypostases, just as Valentinus the heresiarch himself first conceived it in that book of his which bears the title 'On the three natures'. For he was the first to conceive of three hypostases and three persons, the Father, the Son, and the Holy Spirit.

14

SYSTEMS INVOLVING THREE PRINCIPLES I
GENERAL INTRODUCTION AND MONOIMUS

INTRODUCTION TO CHAPTERS 14-19

The following systems, which except for the Sethians are noticed only by Hippolytus, have the peculiarity that they all operate expressly with three principles. The *Megale Apophasis* (or *'Great Exposition'*) says explicitly: 'There are three that stand, and without there being three that stand, the unoriginate ... is not set in order.'[1] The Naassenes say 'He who says that the universe proceeds from one (principle) is mistaken; he who says that it is from three, speaks the truth.'[2] The Peratae speak of a threefold division of the world into the 'perfect good', the 'self-originated', consisting of a multitude of powers, and the 'particular'. The self-originated moves to and fro between the Good, which is the unoriginate, and the particular, which is matter. It has the nature of a serpent which takes upon its face the powers deriving from the Good, that is the Father, and then turns itself toward matter, which is without form and without qualities, and impresses upon it the powers of the Father.[3] In this process nothing is taken from the Father; he remains what he is;[4] nevertheless, the 'characteristics of the Father' are transferred to the world, as if by a portrait-painter. Similarly, these characteristics of the Father are carried up again to God. Thus there seems to be an eternal coming and going, downwards from above and upwards from below. This is also the case with the Naassenes, where the ocean flows now upwards, now downwards; the downward flow signifies the origin of mankind, the upward that of the 'gods', i.e. the 'pneumatikoi' or spirit-born.[5] The Naassenes teach that every element, the intellectual, the psychic, and the earth-born ('choic'), has come together in Jesus, and that these three men who are united in Jesus have each spoken to their own;[6] the Peratae, following a similar

---

[1] Hipp. VI 17, 2.   [2] Hipp. V 8, 1.   [3] Hipp. V 17, 2.
[4] Hipp. VIII 13, 4; V 17, 5.   [5] Hipp. V 7, 38.
[6] Hipp. V 6, 7; 8, 12.

speculation, hold that through the descent of Christ 'all that is divided into three' will be 'saved';[7] and Monoimus says that everything is contained in the 'One', that is 'Father and Mother, the two immortal names'; this interpretation is also used by the Naassenes.[8] If the divinity in men becomes great 'through its own insight', according to a passage in the Naassene sermon in which the *Megale Apophasis* is cited,[9] no redeemer is needed; the whole appears to be a unitary philosophical scheme.

But this interpretation is not adequate. None of the systems envisages a purely cyclical process; on the contrary, these systems, like the others, aim at 'no longer entering the changing world'.[10] Even though the world is called 'most beautiful', it is none the less permeated by a mysterious opposition to the divinity, as is shown by the quotation from Isa. 1: 2 in the *Megale Apophasis*;[11] and if the Father's characteristics are brought back again to the upper world, this is nevertheless not a self-evident and automatic process, either in the *Megale Apophasis*, where the possibility is seriously envisaged that the 'seventh power' will not be formed, or with the Peratae, whose 'rods by the drinking-troughs' can become either white or speckled, and 'only we' escape corruption, or again with the Naassenes.[12] Accordingly the Naassene sermon speaks of a fourth power, which is evil.[13] So besides the three principles, and the movement downwards from above and upwards from below, we must recognize a fourth principle, which is seldom clearly formulated in the systems already mentioned and which forms the resistance to a simple cyclical process. It then becomes clear that only his 'calling' sets a man free from this resistance. This principle operates in the *Megale Apophasis* in its application of 'learning from the imparted word'. For the Naassenes the 'pneumatikoi' must be 'born again' through 'Jesus' and enter through the 'third door'. For the Sethians the Son, Jesus, plays a part which is not altogether clear, but in any case salvation can only be gained by those who (through him, perhaps?) have recognized the necessity of the world-process and the way by which to escape it. Yet there remains a tension between the unitary pronouncements and those which are specifically gnostic.

Here it may be advantageous to glance at the two systems which have not yet been described, that of the Docetists and that of the Sethians. According to the Docetists, three Aeons have come into being from a single originative principle, differing in their extent but otherwise similar. The third Aeon provided chaos with archetypal forms. This chaos, presupposed as something already existing, (now)

[7] Hipp. V 12, 6.   [8] Hipp. VIII 12, 5; V 6, 5.   [9] Hipp. V 9, 5.
[10] Hipp. VI 14, 6.   [11] Hipp. VI 13.
[12] Hipp. V 17, 4–7; 16, 1; 8, 29; 9, 21 f.   [13] Hipp. V 7, 30; 8, 5.

acquires fixity. The ruler of the world, i.e. of chaos, has darkness as his substance. The whole intelligible realm is formed by the three Aeons and is good and beautiful; it is only the descent of the archetypal forms into chaos that troubles them, and makes them require the salvation that Jesus brings; previously there was no process of salvation. All men can acknowledge Jesus, and do so in their own fashion, but only the Docetists know him completely.

The three powers conceived by the Docetists must not be equated with (e.g.) the Naassenes' three. But there is this possibility: in the attempt to come to terms with Greek thought, the material world and the world informed by archetypal forms may have coalesced. This seems to be still to some extent clearly discernible in the case of the Peratae. Through Christ 'all that is divided in three' is to be saved, since 'all that came down from above will ascend through him'. But in the very next sentence we have, 'But (all) that conspires against what came down from above is abandoned and consigned to punishment.'[14] There is a violent conflict between the two sets of ideas. It is probable that the pronouncements concerning the threefold man Jesus or Christ, and the salvation of the three kinds of men, can be explained, as with the Basilidians, as meaning that each group goes to its own sphere, which is nevertheless not the sphere of matter.

The Sethians pursued a different course. They also started with three principles. But the lowest of these is bad, and also endowed with intelligence, from the very beginning. The conflict of the three worlds gives rise to the earthly world. The darkness then seeks to retain the portions of light and spirit which it gained through this conflict, and therefore the Saviour must set out on his mission. Here there is no question of a unitary world-view.

MONOIMUS THE ARABIAN

Monoimus the Arabian has left us only a comparatively short extract, preserved by Hippolytus, which is not detailed enough for us to grasp the conceptions which he enunciated in their proper connection. However, this account exhibits a number of expressions and conceptions which reappear in the descriptions that follow; so this extract is recorded here. The extract starts with 'Man' and the 'Son of Man', as with the Naassenes; the first is the origin of all things, the second derives from him as, for instance, light comes from fire. 'Man' is a unity, both indivisible and divisible, containing all within himself, producing all;[15] he is both Father and Mother, 'the two immortal names', as with the Naassenes.[16] The beauty of

[14] Hipp. V 12, 6. [15] Hipp. VI 14, 4 = *Megale Apophasis.*
[16] Hipp. V 6, 5.

this 'Oneness' is indescribable, as the Naassenes also say.[17] Everything is in things, and also nothing, as the Peratae also say.[18] The
world was made in six days, the seventh day has a special significance; this is reminiscent of the 'Great Exposition' (*Megale Apophasis*)
and its 'seventh power', and also of the six days' work of creation
and the day of rest. All this gives the appearance of a monistic
scheme; nevertheless the 'God of Creation' is also mentioned, who
rejoices in change, just as if he were a wicked god (as it would
seem); such a god does indeed make his appearance with the
Naassenes, and is found also with the Peratae. The whole universe
is explained by reference to the single stroke of the iota, to which
there is a lengthy allusion: the Greek iota, written with a single
stroke, is also a numeral and signifies the number 10, and so
figuratively contains all numbers within itself. A passage is cited
from a letter of Monoimus which makes the demand that one should
look within oneself, which seems to indicate a mystical piety. The
passage is too short to allow firm conclusions to be drawn; however,
the Son of Man seems to be 'passible', which permits us to conclude
that 'Jesus' also was introduced into these speculations.

Hippolytus, *Ref.* VIII 12, 1–15, 2

12, 1. Monoimus the Arabian utterly departed from the
thought of the sublime poet when he thought that man had
such a character as the poet gave to Ocean, when he said, 2.
'Ocean, the origin of gods, and the origin of men' (cf. Hom. *Il.*
XIV 201). He changes this to a different wording and says that
Man is the All, that is the beginning of all things, without
origin, incorruptible, eternal, and that the Son of this Man is
originate and passible, having his origin without time, without
will, without forethought. 3. For such is the power of that Man,
as he says; and since he is so powerful, the Son came into being
quicker than thought or will.[19] 4. And this, he says, is what is
written in the Scriptures: 'He was, and he became what he is';
there was Man, and his Son came into being, as one might say,
there was fire and light came into being, without lapse of time,
without will, without forethought, along with the existence of
the fire.

5. This Man is a single unity, incomposite and indivisible,
composite and divisible; wholly friendly, wholly peaceable,
wholly hostile, wholly at enmity with itself, dissimilar and

---

[17] Hipp. V 9, 14. [18] Hipp. V 17, 5.
[19] Cf. Basilides in Hipp. VII 21, 1; 22, 8.

similar, like some musical harmony, which contains within itself everything which one might name or leave unnoticed, producing all things, generating all things. This (unity) is Mother, this is Father, the two immortal names.[20] 6. By way of an example, he says, consider as the greatest image of the perfect Man an Iota, the 'single stroke', namely the stroke which is one, incomposite, simple, a pure unity, which is not composed of anything at all, (and yet is) composite, having many forms, many divisions, many parts. 7. That single undivided stroke, he says, is the many-faced, many-eyed, many-named single stroke of the letter Iota, which is an image of that perfect invisible Man.

13, 1. Now unity, the single stroke, he says, is also the number ten: for this power of the single stroke, the letter Iota, is also the number two, and three, and four, and five, and six, and seven, and eight, and nine, and so up to ten; for these, he says, are the numbers, so many ways divided, that reside in that simple, incomposite, single stroke of the letter Iota. 2. This is (the meaning of) the saying 'For the whole fullness was pleased to reside in the Son of Man in bodily form' (Col. 2: 9). For, he says, these compositions of numbers (deriving) from the simple incomposite single stroke of the Iota have become bodily substances. 3. And so, he says, from the perfect Man has come the Son of Man, whom no one knows; but the whole creation, he says, in its ignorance of the Son, pictures him as one born of woman; and from this Son come rays, though dim ones to be sure, which in their approach to this world contain and control the process of change, the world-process. 4. Now the splendour of that Son of Man is incomprehensible till now to all men who are misled by thinking of one born of a woman. Nothing in this world has come, or ever will come, from that Man (of whom I spoke before);[21] but what comes to pass has come from —not the whole, but some part of—the Son of Man. For, he says, the Son of Man is that single Iota, the single stroke, which runs down from above, which is full and which fills all things, having in itself everything that belongs to the Man, that is, the Father of the Son of Man.

14, 1. Now the world was made, as Moses says, in six days, that is, in the six powers contained in the single stroke of the

[20] Cf. the Naassenes, Hipp. V 6, 5.   [21] Cf. the Naassenes, Hipp. V 7, 25.

Iota. The seventh (day) is the (day of) rest and the sabbath (Gen. 1: 3 ff.; 2: 3). From that (series of) seven was made (the substance) of earth and water and fire and air, out of which the world was made from the single stroke. 2. For cubes, octahedra, pyramids, and all the figures like these, of which fire, air, water, and earth are composed, come from the numbers that are contained in that simple stroke of the Iota, which is the Son of Man, perfect (Son) of perfect (Man). 3. So then, he says, when Moses speaks of a rod that turns itself in various ways to make the plagues upon Egypt, which, he says, are allegories symbolizing the Creation (Exod. 7: 1–11: 10; 12: 29 ff.), he forms ten plagues and no more from his staff, which is the single stroke. Double, he says, and multiform is this tenfold plague,* the world's creation. 4. For all things engender and bear fruit by being beaten,* as do the vines. 'Man leaps forth from man' he says 'and is separated, being parted by a blow'* (Democritus, fr. 32 Diels), so that he may come into being. And if you speak of the Law which Moses laid down, receiving it from God, the Law conforms to that single stroke, it being the Ten Commandments, which are allegories of the divine mysteries of the Words.[22] For all knowledge of the universe is based on ten impulsions (lit. 'blows') and ten words, this knowledge which is not known by any of those who mistakenly think of one who is born of woman. And if you say that the whole law is a Pentateuch (i.e. comprises five books), this derives from the number five which is contained in the single stroke.

6. Now the whole (world), he says, for those who are not completely disabled in mind, is a mystery, a festival which is new and never grows old, 'lawful and eternally enduring to' our 'generations', 'the Passover of the Lord God', 'observed' by those who are able to see 'at the beginning of the' tenth, which, he says, is the origin of the number ten by which men count. For the number one rising to fourteen is the sum of the single stroke, the perfect number; for from one plus two plus three plus 'four, ten' results, which is the single stroke.† 7. But

---

[22] The Ten Commandments are called 'The Ten Words'.

* 'Plague' and 'blow' render the same Greek word, and 'beaten' a related one.

† I have modified the German version. Monoimus argues that 'beginning the fourteenth day' in Exodus 12: 8 really means 'tenth'; for since $1+2+3+4 = 10$, the final unit is 'fourth and tenth', which in Greek suggests 'fourteenth'.

from the fourteenth to the twenty-first, he says, (Moses) speaks of seven (days) which are in the single stroke, namely the creation of the world which is unleavened among all these (Exod. 12: 19?). For why, he says, should the single stroke require some substance from outside like leaven for the Lord's Passover, the eternal festival which is given for (all) generations? For the whole world and all the causes of creation are the Passover, the festival of the Lord. 8. For the God of creation rejoices at the transformation which is wrought by the ten blows (or 'plagues') of the single stroke, which is the rod of Moses, given by God, with which he plagues the land of the Egyptians, and changes the bodies, given into the hand of Moses,* changing water into blood (Exod. 7: 14–25) and the others likewise; the locusts (Exod. 10: 1–20), which refers to 'grass', he explains as the change of the elements into flesh; for 'all flesh is grass' (Isa. 40: 6). 9. Indeed these men expound the whole Law in some such fashion as this; perhaps, as I suppose, they are following those among the Greeks who maintain that there are (ten categories, namely) substance, quality, quantity, relation, place, time, position, action, possession, and affection.

15, 1. Accordingly Monoimus himself writes as follows in his letter to Theophrastus: 'Cease to seek after God and creation and things like these, and seek after yourself of yourself, and learn who it is who appropriates all things within you without exception and says, "*My* God, *my* mind, *my* thought, *my* soul, *my* body", and learn whence comes grief and rejoicing and love and hatred, and waking without intention, and sleeping without intention, and anger without intention, and love without intention. And if you carefully consider these things', he says, 'you will find yourself within yourself, being both one and many like that stroke, and will find the outcome of yourself.'

* Or possibly, 'as he does the hand of Moses', cf. Exod. 4: 6.

15

SYSTEMS INVOLVING THREE PRINCIPLES II
THE *MEGALE APOPHASIS*

INTRODUCTION

The *Megale Apophasis* was ascribed to Simon of Gitta; but nothing can be ascertained to justify this ascription. It is largely a philosophical work, which attempts to buttress its assertions with allegories based on the Bible and Homer and with speculations about the human embryo and the human brain. It begins on a note of monism. The cause of everything is fire, a Stoic view. But this fire has a double nature, it is both unseen and apparent. The apparent aspect of fire is that which is visible, the unseen aspect is that on which it depends, and is spiritual. At the beginning of the world six powers were in operation, which took their origin from fire, namely mind and thought, voice and name, reflection and conception; each of them a spiritual capacity and the result of its activity. The number six, which also appears in Monoimus, is of course derived from the six days' work of the Creation.

Furthermore, within these six powers there is a seventh power, often called Logos, which 'stands, took his stand, and will stand', which came into being before all the Aeons, the spirit that hovered over the waters (Gen. 1: 2), which contains, creates, and forms all things. The six powers, but especially the first two, which are identified with the 'heaven and earth' of the creation story, are now also exhibited, in an allegorical exposition of the narrative of Eden, as describing the formation of the embryo in its mother's womb. The twofold nature of fire is again interpreted as the transformation of blood into semen in the man, and into milk in the woman. The meaning of the seventh power's being 'he that stands, took his stand, and will stand' is that the way which leads from the unoriginate power on to the origin of the world, and thence again upwards to the blessed power, this way which is also seen in the twirling fiery sword of the fall story, is indispensible if the world is to achieve its goal. But the seventh power is also 'self-generating, self-increasing, self-seeking, self-finding, its own mother, its own father, its own sister, its own consort, its own daughter, its own son, father, mother, unity, the root of all things'. What is intended can be discerned in yet another speculation, on the relationship between mind and thought: mind does not exist without thought, mind can only be known through its thought. To use another image, these are the two offshoots of the whole which 'exhibit the space between them, the intangible air which has neither beginning nor end'. The twofold aspect of the act of creation thus permeates the created order, the male and the female, and leaves room for the peculiar 'seventh' power on which it depends.

This power on which it depends has also a significance for soteriology. All men possess the seventh power within themselves, but only as a potentiality. It must be 'fully formed' and made actual, in which case it becomes an infinite power, in no respect inferior to the infinite power itself. The whole world and the world-process is staged with the sole intention that this 'fruit' be fully formed and escape from the process of becoming, while the visible component of the fire will finally be destroyed by this fire. What then is the seventh power? It has no resemblance to the geometrical talent which men possess, which is merely introduced as a comparison. It is the 'unoriginate' element residing in men, that element in men which is divine; however, it needs the instruction, the teaching of the Word which comes to it, or else it perishes (17, 7). The interpretation of the story of Circe from the *Odyssey* signifies that the 'world' can turn men into a 'beast', and that a 'miraculous herb' is needed to let him become 'man' again. This teaching, which in other respects has a markedly philosophical tone, is distinguished from (genuine) philosophy by the fact that it desiderates a word, a teaching, and this teaching addresses itself, not to rational thinking, but to intuition. A single word, for instance a verse from Homer, is in principle sufficient to declare the essential point. Further, this teaching has a single objective, namely 'to escape from the process of becoming'. The elevated and obscure language of the opening passage is also gnostic.

Hippolytus, *Ref.* VI 9, 4–18, 7

9, 4. Simon describes the beginning of all things as an infinite power. He writes as follows: 'This is the text of the exposition (*Apophasis*) of the voice and name that come from the thought of the great power which is infinite. Hence it shall be sealed, covered, veiled, stored up in the dwelling-place where the root of all things has its foundation.' 'Dwelling-place' is his name for this man who is generated from blood; and there dwells in him the infinite power, which he calls the root of all things. Now the infinite power, which is fire, is in Simon's view not a simple thing, as people generally say that the four elements are simple, and accordingly regard fire as simple; but rather, he holds that the nature of fire is in some way double; and one part of this double (nature) he calls hidden, the other apparent. 6. The hidden (aspects) of fire, he says, lie hidden in those which are apparent, and its apparent (aspects) were made by the hidden ones. . . . 7. And the apparent (part) of the fire contains in itself everything that one could perceive or even inadvertently ignore, among visible things; but the hidden (part contains) everything that one can conceive and that eludes sensation, or again what one could ignore and fail to envisage. 8. To sum up, one may say that all realities, both perceptible and intelligible—which he terms hidden and apparent—are treasured up in the fire that is above the heavens, like the great tree which appeared to Nebuchadnezzar in a dream (Dan. 4: 7 ff.) from which all flesh takes its nourishment. 9. Now the apparent (part) of the fire he takes to be the stem, the branches, the leaves, and the bark which surrounds it outside; all these parts of the great tree, he says, are to be burnt by the all-devouring flame of the fire and disappear. 10. But the fruit of the tree, if it be fully formed and receive its proper shape, is to be put into the store-house, not into the fire. For the fruit, he says, has come into being in order to be put into the store-house, but the chaff in order to be consigned to the fire (cf. Matt. 3: 10)—meaning the stem, which came into being not for its own sake, but for the sake of the fruit.[1]

10, 1. And this, he says, is what is written in the scripture: 'For the vineyard of the Lord Sabaoth is the house of Israel, and the man of Judah the new plant which he loved' (Isa. 5: 7). But if the man of Judah is the new plant which he loved, then, he says, it is proved that the tree is nothing else than a man. 2. But as to the separating and selecting, he says that the scripture has declared it clearly enough, and this text is sufficient to instruct those who are 'fully formed': 'All flesh is grass, and all the glory of the flesh is like the flower of grass. The grass withered and its flower fell; but the word of the Lord abides for eternity' (Isa. 40: 6–8). Now 'the word of the Lord', he says, means the

[1] Cf. the Naassenes, Hipp. V 8, 28.

Word and Logos of the Lord who proceeds from his mouth; apart from him there is no place where things come to be.

11, 1. Such then, in brief, is the fire in Simon's view, and all things that have being, both visible and invisible, which he himself in his Great Exposition calls sounding and unsounding, numerable and innumerable, perfect, intelligible, just as each one of those things which in infinite repetition can be infinitely conceived can also speak and think and work, just as Empedocles says: 'For with earth do we see earth, with water water, with air (bright) air, with fire consuming fire; with love do we see love, strife also with dread strife.'[2]

12, 1. For, he says, he considered that all parts of the fire, both visible and invisible, have equal thought and judgement. So the world which is generated took its being from the fire which is ingenerate. But it came into being in this manner, as he says. The world which is generated took six roots which were prior to the beginning of its generation from the beginning of that fire. 2. He says that the roots came into being in pairs from the fire; and he calls these roots mind and thought, voice and name, reflection and conception; and in these six roots there is present the infinite power, potentially but not actually. 3. This infinite power he calls 'him that stands, took his stand, and will stand'. If he be fully formed when he is present in the six powers, he will be in substance, in power, in greatness, and in effective action one and the same with the ingenerate and infinite power, being in no way inferior to that ingenerate, unalterable, infinite power; 4. but if he remain only as a potentiality in the six powers and be not fully formed, then he disappears (he says) and is lost, like the power of doing grammar or geometry in the human soul; for if this power acquires (the necessary) skill, it illuminates what comes to pass; but if it fails to acquire it, unskilfulness and obscurity result, and just as if it never existed, it perishes with the man at his death.

13, 1. Now of these six powers, and of the seventh that is (associated) with these six, he calls the first pair mind and thought, (or) heaven and earth; and the male (partner) looks down and cares for his consort, while the earth below receives her kindred intelligible fruits brought down to earth from heaven. On this account, he says, the Word often refers to the

---

[2] Empedocles, Fragm. 109 Diels; the sentence is not complete.

things which are generated from mind and thought, that is from heaven and earth, and says 'Hear, O heaven, and give ear, O earth, for the Lord hath spoken: "I have begotten sons and made them great, but they have despised me"' (Isa. 1: 2). But he who says this, Simon states, is the seventh power, he who stands, took his stand, and will stand; for he is the cause of these good things, which Moses commended and called 'very good' (Gen. 1: 31). But 'voice' and 'name' mean sun and moon, 'reflection' and 'conception' mean air and water. And in all these, as I said, there is mixed and infused the great and infinite power, he who stands.

14, 1. Now whereas Moses said 'Six days (there were) in which God made heaven and earth, and on the seventh he rested from all his works' (Gen. 2: 2), Simon adapts (the passage) in the manner I have described and makes himself a god. 2. So when they say that there are three days which come into being before the sun and moon, they signify mind and thought, that is, heaven and earth, and the seventh power which is infinite, for these are the three powers which came into being before all the rest. 3. But when they say 'Before all the ages he begets me' (Prov. 8: 23, 25) these words, he says, are meant to refer to the seventh power. Now this seventh power is that which existed as a power in the infinite power, and which came into being before all the ages. 4. It is this, he says, the seventh power, of which Moses says, 'and the spirit of God hovered over the water' (Gen. 1: 2), that is, he says, the spirit who contains all things in himself, the image of the infinite power, which Simon describes as 'an image of an incorruptible form, which alone gives order to all things'. 5. For this power which hovered over the water, he says, which came into being from an incorruptible form, alone gives order to all things.

Now after the formation of the world they describe had come about in this form or the like, 'God moulded man', he says 'taking clay from the earth' (Gen. 2: 7); and his moulding was not simple but double, 'in the image and in the likeness' (Gen. 1: 26). 6. 'Image' means the spirit that hovered above the water; which if it be not fully formed will perish with the world, since it remains only as a potentiality and does not come to be in actuality; this, he says, is (the meaning of) the text 'lest we be condemned along with the world' (1 Cor. 11: 32); but if it be fully formed and comes into being from an indivisible point, as it is written in the Exposition, then what is little will become great; but this great thing will become the infinite and unalterable Aeon, which no longer enters into becoming. 7. How then and in what manner does God mould men? In the Garden (Gk. 'paradise'), he maintains. The Garden, he says, must be the womb; and scripture will teach us that this is true when it says, 'I am he that moulded thee in thy mother's womb' (Isa. 44: 2), for this is how he makes the text run. The Garden, he says, is Moses' allegorical term for the womb, if one is to believe the text. 8. But if God moulds man in his mother's womb, that is, in the Garden, as I said, the Garden must be the womb, and Eden the placenta, and 'the river which comes out of Eden to water the Garden' (Gen. 2: 10) the navel. This navel, he says, 'is divided into four sources' (ibid.); for on either side of the navel there extend two arteries, which are air-channels (or 'spirit-channels') and two veins, which are blood-channels. 9. But, he says, when the navel, proceeding from Eden, the placenta, begins to grow on the unborn (child) upon the region of the belly, which people generally call the navel . . .[3] But the two veins, through which the blood flows and makes its way from Eden, the placenta, to the so-called gates of the liver, these are they which nourish the unborn child. 10. The arteries, which we said were air-channels, surround the bladder on either side by the pelvis and join up at the great artery near the spine which is called the aorta, and so the air (spirit) making its way through the side-entries into the heart imparts motion to the embryos. 11. For while the infant is being moulded in the 'Garden', it neither takes nourishment with the mouth nor breathes with its nostrils; for since it is surrounded by fluid there would be instant death if it drew breath; for it would draw in some of the fluid and so perish. But it is completely enclosed by what is called the amnion and it is nourished through the navel; and through the aorta that is by the backbone, as I said, it obtains the substance of its breath (or 'spirit').

15, 1. The river which comes out of Eden, he says, is divided into four sources, four channels, that is, the four senses of the unborn child, sight, smell, taste, and touch. For the child that is being moulded in the 'Garden' has only these senses. This, he

---

[3] There is a lacuna in the text.

says, is the Law which Moses laid down, and each of the books is written about this same law, as their titles make clear. 2. The first book is Genesis; the title of this book, he says, should be sufficient for the knowledge of the universe. For, he says, this Genesis means sight, the first section into which the river is divided; for the universe was contemplated by sight. 3. The title of the second book is Exodus, for the (child that is) born must pass through the Red Sea and come into the desert—and the Red Sea, they say, is the blood—and taste bitter water. For bitter, he says, is the water which comes after the Red Sea, which is the way we tread of the knowledge of the bitter and painful things in our life. 4. But when changed by Moses, that is by the Word, that bitter (substance) becomes sweet. And that this is the case, one may hear from all men generally when they repeat the poet's words: 'It was black at the root, but its flower was like milk; and the gods call it moly; and it is difficult to dig for mortal men; but the gods can do all things' (Homer, *Od.* X 304–6).

16, 1. What is said by the Gentiles, he says, is sufficient to give knowledge of the universe to those who have ears to hear: for, he says, only the man who tasted of this fruit escaped being turned into a beast by Circe; indeed by using the power of such a fruit he (restored) those who were already turned into beasts—remoulded, re-formed, and recalled them to their own proper shape. 2. And the man is found faithful and beloved by that witch, he says, because of that milky divine fruit. Similarly, the third book is Leviticus, which means smelling or breathing. For the whole of that book is concerned with sacrifices and offerings; but where there is a sacrifice, there comes a smell of fragrance from the sacrifice because of the incense; and of this fragrance the sense of smell must be the judge. 3. The fourth of these books is Numbers; it means taste, (in the place) where the Word is at work; since he speaks of all things, he is called by the designation 'Number'. But Deuteronomy is given its title because of the feeling of the child that is moulded. 4. For just as feeling by its contact recapitulates and confirms the things seen by the other senses, testing what is hard or warm or sticky, so the fifth book of the Law is a recapitulation of the four that were written before it.

5. So all unoriginate things, he says, are within us potentially,

not actually, like grammar or geometry. So if they obtain the appropriate word and teaching and the bitter is turned into sweet, that is, 'spears into sickles and swords into ploughshares' (Isa. 2: 4) the child will not be chaff and wood, which are consumed by fire, but perfect fruit fully formed, as I said, equalling and resembling the unoriginate and infinite power. 6. But if it remain merely as a tree bearing no fruit, then being not fully formed it is consumed. 'For the axe is near the roots of the tree' he says; 'every tree', he says, 'that does not bear good fruit is cut down and cast into the fire' (Matt. 3: 10 par.).

17, 1. According to Simon, then, that blessed and incorruptible being lies hidden in every being potentially, not actually, that is he who stands, took his stand, and will stand; who stands on high in the unoriginate power, who took his stand below in the chaos of waters when he was begotten in the image, who will stand on high with the blessed infinite power if he be fully formed. 2. For, he says, there are three that stand, and without there being three that stand, the [un]originate being, who (they say) hovers over the water, is not set in order, the perfect heavenly being who is re-created according to the likeness, who becomes in no respect inferior to the unoriginate power. This is (the meaning of) their saying, 'I and thou are one, thou art before me, I am after thee.'[4] 3. This, he says, is one power, divided as being above and below, self-generating, self-increasing, self-seeking, self-finding, its own mother, its own father, its own sister, its own consort, its own daughter, its own son, father, mother, unity, the root of all things.

4. And that fire is the first principle of being in all things that are generated, you may realize, he says, in some such fashion as this. In all things that come into being, the desire for their being originates from fire. Therefore the desire for the generation of things that change is said to be 'burning'. Now the fire, being one, is turned by change into two. For, he says, the blood, which is both hot and bright red in appearance like fire, is turned in the man into seed, but in the woman this very same (substance is turned) into milk. And this change in the man produces the generative power, but in the woman it produces nourishment for what is generated. This, he says, is the 'flaming sword which turned itself about to guard the way to the tree

---

[4] Cf. Epiph. XXVI 3, 1.

of life' (Gen. 3: 24). For the blood is turned into seed and milk, and this power becomes (both) mother and father, father of the things that come into being and increase of those that are nourished, needing nothing, self-sufficient. And the tree of life is 'guarded', he says, by the flaming sword which turns itself about, as we have said, the seventh power which comes from itself, which contains all, which resides in the six powers. 7. For if the flaming sword does not turn, then that good tree will perish and come to nothing; but if it is turned into seed and milk, then that which potentially resides in these, obtaining the appropriate word and place of the Lord* in which the Word is generated, beginning as it were from a tiny spark, will be enlarged and increase and will be an infinite power, unvarying, equal, and alike to the unvarying Aeon that never enters into being for the aeon without end.

18, 1. By this account, then, Simon has undeniably made himself a god for those who lack understanding . . . being originate and capable of suffering, when he exists in potentiality, but (transformed) from an originate being (into) one incapable of suffering, when he is fully formed and becomes perfect and so departs from the two principal powers, namely heaven and earth. 2. For Simon himself explains this in so many words in his Exposition, as follows: 'To you then I say what I say and write what I write, this writing (that follows): there are two offshoots of all the Aeons, which neither begin nor end, proceeding from a single root, the power which is silence, invisible, incomprehensible. 3. One of these appears on high, namely the great power which is the mind of the universe, which governs all things, (which is) male; and the other below, a great conception, which is female, which generates all things. Therefore being each other's counterparts they form a pair and exhibit the space between them, the intangible air which has neither beginning nor end. 4. Within it is the Father who upholds all things and nourishes the things that begin and end. This is he who stands, took his stand and will stand, being a male-and-female power like the pre-existing infinite power which neither begins nor ends, existing in unity; for from this proceeded the conception which is in unity, and became two. 5. Now he was one; for having this (conception) in himself

* Word-play: the Greek can mean both 'place of the Lord' and 'proper place'.

he existed by himself; but he was not the first, although pre-existing; but by appearing to himself from himself he became second. Nor again was he called Father, before that (conception) called him Father. 6. So then just as he, by bringing himself forth from himself, disclosed to himself his own conception, so the conception that appeared did not make (him), but on seeing him concealed the Father within herself, that is the (aforesaid) power. So there is a bisexual power and conception. Hence they are each other's counterparts—for power does not differ at all from conception—and are (also) one; 7. from the things on high it is discovered as power, from those below as conception. And so also is that which appeared from them; being one it is found to be two, a male-and-female being having the female within it. So mind exists in conception, as things inseparable from one another; being one they are found to be two.'

16

SYSTEMS INVOLVING THREE PRINCIPLES III
THE NAASSENES

INTRODUCTION

The Naassenes are mentioned only by Hippolytus in his *Refutatio* V 6, 3–11, 1, which is repeated in summary form at X 9, 1–3. The Naassenes derive their name from the Serpent, the Hebrew word for which is rendered in Greek as 'Naas'.[1] The main part of this account is an extract from an allegorical treatise dealing *inter alia* with a hymn in which Attis, a deity of the mystery cults of Asia Minor, is equated with a series of other divine figures; this section is known to scholars as the 'Naassene Sermon'. Before and after it Hippolytus presents accounts of the sect, which have so many points of contact with the Sermon that they can be regarded as dependent on it.

In this case also the starting-point is that the world arises out of three principles, the pre-existent, the self-originate, and the out-poured chaos. The self-originate, who is called Adamas, is bisexual, and as a consequence the hymn in 6, 5 is addressed to the *one* Adamas.[2] He is also compared with the seed, the water, the serpent, and the soul; he is that which makes everything, but is not identical with anything that he makes.[3] Every 'nature', i.e. every species of being in nature, seeks after this water, or after this soul; without it nothing, whether immortal or mortal, whether living or lifeless, can exist. It is also compared with the great 'Ocean', which flows 'downwards' and 'upwards'. Its downward flow means that men come into being, referring to their natural birth, its upward flow means that 'gods' come into being, referring to the divine element in men as returning to its true home. Since this beginning resembles the *Megale Apophasis*, it is not surprising that a section of it is reproduced (9, 5), while the sentence, 'He who says that the universe proceeds from one (principle) is mistaken; he who says that it is from

---

[1] Hebrew: *nahash.*   [2] Cf. Monoimus, Hipp. VIII 12, 5.
[3] Cf. Hipp. V 17, 15.

three, speaks the truth' also seems to resemble it. These three powers are also discovered in the three words taken from Isa. 28: 10: Caulacau, Saulasau, and Zeesar.

But in this case we can see, more clearly than with the *Megale Apophasis*, that the sect was not content with these three principles and their interaction. This is made clear in the first place by the treatment of the 'soul', which is sought after by the three parts of the world, the terrestrial, the infernal, and the celestial (but not the super-celestial!) but which is castrated by the 'mother of the gods', that is to say the 'masculine power' of the soul is drawn up to the super-celestial region and withdrawn from the process of generation;[4] and a similar treatment of the water, from which each nature selects its own proper product, as with the olive-tree and its oil, and so on, 'but we, the spiritual men, are selected by the living water. . . .'[5] But furthermore there appears a fourth power called Esaldaeus (7, 30) to which a further allusion is made in 8, 5; this is 'the fiery god', the creator of this world, who enslaves mankind. Again, mankind has fallen in among the 'images of clay', as the material world is called, and consequently (is here) without the knowledge and consent of Adamas (even though we are told that 'they are sown into it' [by Adamas], 8, 28. 32). The spiritual men must undergo some experience, if they are to reattain their spiritual home; they must not only awake, but also 'be born again'. The spiritual element in man, which lies (hidden) in him like the leaven in the three bushels of meal, can also be called Christ, or 'the great Man from on high'. Distinct from him there is the Redeemer who releases men from their captivity to the material world; he is 'Jesus' or 'the Saviour'. Men must 'enter through the third door' which is Jesus. Probably this alludes to a sacrament which imparts salvation.

Other passages in Hippolytus' account also provide evidence of more extensive speculations, as for instance when the man, before he is animated (Gen. 2: 7) is said to have 'been made by the many powers', or when he 'goes through all realms and regions' (8, 13 f.). The only ethical point which is made clear is that men must carefully abstain from intercourse with women (7, 18; 8, 33; 9, 11).

Those same problems which are posed by the *Megale Apophasis* and which arise also in the case of the Peratae are also traceable here. The Ocean first turns itself to bring men into being, then to bring gods into being, which gives the impression of a cyclical process. But all those who do not 'enter through the third door' remain dead. This indicates a distinction in men's destinies. And what happens to 'those who have fallen from above'? Do they

---

[4] Hipp. V 7, 11–13.　　　[5] Hipp. V 9, 21.

necessarily return to the higher sphere? On the other hand, the being called 'Papas' confers peace upon the spiritual and upon the material and earthy; how can this be the case, if all who are not spiritual are 'dead'? Hippolytus' account asserts that the intellectual, the psychic, and the earthly ('choic') elements all descend upon Jesus, the Son of Man, and that 'these three men' each speak according to their 'substances'. What is to be thought of this? Admittedly, we must observe that this is all based on artificial allegories which are only fabricated to conform to a pagan hymn and which do not present the whole system; nevertheless, some of the difficulties could be resolved by a supposition such as was indicated in the opening section (p. 245 f.). On the other hand, it is to be noted that the allegory speaks not only of the 'primal man' who is called Adamas; the reference may be to the 'inner man', as in 7, 36, or to 'Jesus' as indicated in 8, 22, where it is Papas who puts an end to the conflict. Immediately afterwards there is a reference to the man who rests in the body as in a tomb, that is, to Christ. The Being without form, Adamas, the Man, must indeed be distinguished from the 'Son of Man', the 'Great Man'; but occasionally the allegory switches from one to the other without indicating the fact. It does so particularly in its interpretation of Hermes as the Logos.

Hippolytus, *Ref.* V 6, 3–11, 1

6, 3. Now the time has come for us to proceed to investigate the matters that lie before us, and to begin with those who have had the effrontery to praise the serpent, who was the cause of temptation, as a result of certain arguments invented through his inspiration. The priests and advocates of this doctrine were first of all those who are called the 'Naassenes', who are so called after the Hebrew language, in which 'naas' is the word for the serpent. 4. But after this they called themselves gnostics, alleging that they alone 'knew the deep things' (Rev. 2: 24). Many (others) have split off from them and divided the heresy into many factions, though it is really one, by presenting the same (story) under different names. . . .

These men, according to their own doctrine, reverence beyond all others Man and the Son of Man. 5. Now this Man is bisexual and is called by them Adamas. A great many hymns of various kinds have been composed for him; and the hymns, to put it briefly, are worded by them in some such fashion as this: 'From thee, Father, and through thee, Mother, the two immortal names, parents of the Aeons, thou citizen of heaven,

Man of the mighty name.'[6] They divide him, like Geryon, in three; for one part of him is intellectual,[7] another psychic, another earthly; and they think that knowledge of him is the beginning of the power to know God, in that they say, 'The beginning of perfection is the knowledge of Man, but the knowledge of God is complete perfection.' 7. All these (elements), he says, the intellectual, the psychic, and the earthly, have passed over and descended together into one man, Jesus who was born of Mary; and accordingly, he says, these three men spoke together, each out of his own substance and each to his own. For there are three classes of being in the universe, in their view, angelic, psychic, and earthly; and three communities (or 'churches'), angelic, psychic, and earthly; and their names are, the chosen, the called, and the enslaved.

7, 1. These are the principal points out of a great number of discourses which James the Lord's brother is said to have delivered to Mariamne. . . . 2. The basis of their system is the Man Adamas, and they say that he is the subject of the text, 'His generation, who shall declare it?' (Isa. 53: 8). . . . 3. The earth it was, according to the Greeks, that first produced man, bearing a noble gift; for she desired to be the mother, not of senseless plants nor of brute beasts but of a tractable and God-loving creature. 4. But it is hard to discover, he says, whether with the Boeotians beyond Lake Cephisis Alalcomeneus appeared as the first of mankind, or whether it was the Curetes of Mount Ida, that divine race, or the Phrygian Corybantes, whom first the sun beheld springing up like trees; or did Arcadia (see) Pelasgus, a man older than the moon, or Eleusis (see) Diaulus who dwelt in Raria; or did Lemnos engender the fair child Cabirus in an unspeakable ecstasy, or Pellene the Phlegræan Alcyoneus, the eldest of the giants? 5. But the Libyans say that Garamas was the first-born, who arose from the desert lands, and began upon the sweet acorn of Zeus. And in Egypt the Nile enriching her silt to this very day, he says, brings to life (creatures) clothed in flesh by her moist warmth and bears living beings. 6. The Assyrians say that Oannes the fish-eater came from them, the Chaldaeans speak (likewise) of Adam. And they say that he was the man whom the earth produced by herself; and he lay without breath, without motion, without

---

[6] Cf. Monoimus, Hipp. VIII 12, 5. [7] Greek *noeros*, cognate with Nous.

a tremor, like a statue, being an image of that celestial being praised in song, the Man Adamas; and he was made by the many powers, who are severally described at length.

7. Now in order that the great Man from on high should be completely held fast, 'from whom', as they say, 'every family that is named on earth and in heaven' (Eph. 3: 15) originates, there was given to him also a soul, so that through his soul suffering and punishment in slavery might come upon the creation of that great and most noble and perfect Man; for that is what they call him. 8. So they inqurie again, what is the soul, and whence comes it, and what is its nature, that by coming into man and quickening him it should enslave and punish the creation of the perfect Man; and they make this inquiry, not from the scriptures, but once again from the secret writings. And they say that the soul is most hard to discover and hard to conceive; for it does not remain in the same form or shape all the time, or in one condition, so that one could describe its character or conceive its substance. 9. These manifold alterations they have set down in the Gospel entitled According to the Egyptians. And they wonder, like all the other Gentiles, whether it comes from the Pre-existent or from the Self-originate or from the outpoured chaos.

And first, since they envisage the threefold division of mankind, they take refuge in the rites of the Assyrians. For the Assyrians are the first who have held that the soul is divided in three, (yet) also one. 10. For, they say, every species seeks after soul, but in different ways. For the soul is the cause of everything that comes into being; for, he says, everything that takes nourishment and grows requires a soul. For nothing, he says, is able to obtain either nourishment or growth if a soul is not present. Even the stones, he says, have souls; for they possess the power of growth. And growth could never take place without nourishment; for the things that grow, grow by adding (to themselves); and the addition is the nourishment of the thing that takes nourishment. 11. So every species, he says, 'of things in heaven and things on earth and things under the earth' (Phil. 2: 10) seeks after soul. And the Assyrians call this Adonis or Endymion. And when it is called Adonis, he says, then Aphrodite loves and desires the soul of this name; and Aphrodite for them means generation. 12. But when Persephone, who is also called Corè, loves Adonis, then, he says, the soul is something mortal, separated from the generation that belongs to Aphrodite. And if Selena (the Moon-goddess) comes to desire of Endymion and to love of form (or, formation), the higher creation, he says, also requires soul. 13. But if, he says, the mother of the gods castrates Attis, though she too is in love with him, then, he says, the sublime and blessed nature of the super-celestial and eternal (realities) recalls the masculine power of the soul to herself.

14. For Man, they say, is bisexual. So in accordance with this thought of theirs, the intercourse of woman with man is in their teaching shown to be most wicked and prohibited.

15. For, he says, Attis was castrated, that is, (cut off) from the earthly parts of the creation (here) below, and has gone over to the eternal substance above where, he says, there is neither female nor male, but a new creature, 'a new man' (Eph. 2: 15; 4: 24; 2 Cor. 5: 17), who is bisexual. . . .

16. And, they say, their thought is confirmed not only by Rhea alone, but by practically the whole creation. And, they explain, this is what is meant by the text, 'For his invisible things have been discerned since the creation of the world, being known through his works, namely his eternal power and glory, so that those men have no excuse; because although they knew God they did not glorify him as God nor render him thanks, but their senseless heart was made futile. 17. For though they said they were wise, they became fools, and exchanged the glory of the incorruptible God for likenesses of the form of corruptible man and of birds, beasts, and creeping things. Therefore God has given them over to shameful passions; for their women have exchanged natural intercourse for unnatural' —18. and what natural intercourse is in their view we shall describe in due course—'and likewise the men, giving up natural intercourse with women, have been inflamed with passion for one another; men behaving shamelessly with men'—and shame-lessness for them is (lack of form, the) primal, blessed, formless substance,[8] which is the cause of all forms in the things that are formed—'and receiving in themselves the due reward for their error'. (Rom. 1: 20–7) 19. For these words spoken by Paul, they

---

[8] A word-play in the Greek: 'not formed' means not subjected to an individual 'formation'.

say, contain the whole secret and unspeakable mystery of blessed enjoyment. For the promise of the washing (in baptism) is, they say, nothing less than the introduction into unfading enjoyment of him who in their fashion is washed in living water and anointed with unutterable anointing.

20. And not only the mysteries of the Assyrians and Phrygians but also those of the Egyptians, they say, confirm their thought about the blessed nature, concealed and yet disclosed, of what has come to pass and comes to pass and will come to pass, which he says is the kingdom of heaven within man (Luke 17: 21) which is sought after, concerning which they clearly deliver (their teaching) in the Gospel entitled 'According to Thomas', in these words, 'He who seeks will find me in children from seven years onwards; for there I am found, who am hidden, in the fourteenth age (Aeon).' 21. . . . . Hence they locate the generative nature of the universe in the generative seed and say . . . that a child of seven years is half a father, that he reveals himself at fourteen years, according to Thomas. This is the unutterable and mystical doctrine that they hold.

22. They say indeed that the Egyptians, who next to the Phrygians are the oldest (race) of all mankind, and admittedly were the first to teach all other men after them the rites and orgies of all the gods and their forms and activities, possess the holy and venerable mysteries of Isis that must not be disclosed to the uninitiate. 23. And these are nothing else than that which was stolen and was sought by the lady of the seven robes and the sable clothing, the 'shame' (i.e. genital part) of Osiris. Now Osiris is their name for water. And nature has seven robes, since it wears and is robed in seven ethereal robes—for thus they refer to the planets by their allegory, and call them ethereal; and through these, they say, the process of change is displayed by the ineffable, unimaginable, inconceivable, formless being, transforming creation. 24. And this is what is meant by the text, 'Seven times the righteous one shall fall and shall arise' (Prov. 24: 16); for these 'falls', they say, are the changing positions of the stars as they are moved by him who moves all things.

25. As to the nature of the seed, which is the cause of all that comes into being, they say that it *is* none of these, but it generates and produces all that comes into being; their text is, 'I become what I will, and I am what I am.' Therefore they say

that the being which moves everything does not move; for while it produces everything it remains what it is, without coming to be any of the things that come into being.⁹ 26. Him (!) alone he calls good, and of him was said the Saviour's saying, 'Why do you call me good? There is one who is good, my Father in heaven, who makes his sun rise upon the just and the unjust, and sends rain upon the righteous and the sinners' (Mark 10: 18; Matt. 5: 45). . . . 27. And this is said to be the great and secret mystery, unknown to all, that is concealed and revealed among the Egyptians. For there is no temple, he says, which has not standing before its entrance the hidden thing unclothed, looking up from below and crowned with all its fruits of things that come to be.

28. But this thing, they say, not only stands in the most holy temples in front of the statues, but also (it is there) for all to know, like a light which is placed not under a bushel but on a candlestick (Matt. 5: 15), a proclamation proclaimed upon the house-tops, in every street, and in every alley (cf. Matt. 10: 27; Luke 14: 21) and by the houses themselves, set up before them as a boundary and limit of the house; and this is what is called 'good' by all; for they call it 'the bringer of good', without knowing what they are saying. And this mystical (observance) the Greeks have adopted from the Egyptians and observe it to this very day. 29. For we see, he says, that the (figures of) Hermes are honoured among them in this form. The Cyllenians especially honour the Logos; for, he says, 'Hermes is the Logos'; being the interpreter (*hermeneus*) and artificer of what has come to be and comes to be and will come to be, he stands among them as an honoured figure, portrayed in a form like this, namely a human phallus, pointing upwards from below.

30. He is the guide of souls, he says—meaning this Hermes— and the sender of souls and the cause of souls, as even the poets of the Gentiles observe, who say 'Cyllenian Hermes called out the souls of the suitors' (Hom. *Od.* XXIV 1 f.)—not those of Penelope's suitors, you poor (fools), he says, but (the souls) of those who are awakened, 'in pursuit of'* 'what honour and

---

⁹ Cf. Monoimus, Hipp. VIII 13, 4.

---

* Lit. 'remembering': the word *mnēstēr* 'suitor', suggests Plato's concept of *anamnēsis*, 'remembrance' of a higher world.

what mass of wealth' (Empedocles, fr. 119 Diels), that is of that blessed (being) on high, Man or Primal Man or Adamas, as they suppose, from whom they were brought down into this moulded figure of clay to serve the artificer of this creation, Esaldaeus, the fiery god, the fourth in number—31. for this is the name they give to the Demiurge, the artificer, the father of the particular world. 'But he (Hermes) had in his hands the fair golden rod with which he soothes the eyes of men, as he pleases, and others again he wakes from sleep' (Hom., *Od.* XXIV 2–4). 32. He it is, he says, who alone has power over life and death; of him, he says, it is written, 'thou shalt shepherd them with a rod of iron' (Ps. 2: 9). But the poet, he says, wishing to dignify the incomprehensible character of the blessed nature of the Logos, equipped him not with an iron but with a golden rod. And he 'soothes the eyes' of the dead, he says, 'and others again he wakes from sleep', that is those who have awakened and become 'suitors'. 33. These, he says, are told in Scripture, 'Awake, thou that sleepest, and arise, and Christ shall give thee light' (Eph. 5: 14). This is the Christ, he says, who among all those who (*or*, those things which) come into being is characterized as Son of Man from the uncharacterized Word. 34. This, he says, is the great unutterable mystery of the Eleusinians, 'Give rain, give life' (*Hye, Cye*).

And, he says, that 'all things are subjected to him' (1 Cor. 15: 27) is also (proved by) the text 'Their sound has gone out over all the earth' (Rom. 10: 18); like Hermes who swings the staff he carries, and the souls pressing close 'follow him crying', as the poet has shown in his image, where he says, 'As when bats in a corner of a mysterious cave squeak as they fly if one of the swarm falls from the rock, and keep close together' (Hom., *Od.* XXIV 5–8). 35. The Rock, he says, means Adamas, 'the corner-stone, who is become the head of the corner' (Isa. 28: 16, Ps. 118 (117): 22; cf. Matt. 21: 42, etc.); for in the head is located the brain[10] that gives character, the being 'from which all fatherhood' takes its character (Eph. 3: 15)—'whom', he says, 'I lay down as adamant at the foundations of Zion'; speaking allegorically, he says, of the creation of mankind. 36. Now he that is laid down is Adamas, 'the inner man' (2 Cor. 4: 16), and the foundations of Zion are the teeth, as

[10] Word-play: head = *kephale*, brain = *enkephalos*.

Homer speaks of the 'fence of the teeth' (e.g. *Il.* IV 350), meaning a wall and rampart, within which is the inner man, who has fallen down from there, from Adamas, the primal Man on high 'who was cut out without hands' to cut him (cf. Dan. 2: 45) and brought down to the creature of forgetfulness, the earthly, the 'potsherd' (ibid.). 37. And he says that the souls followed 'squeaking' after the Logos: 'As they went squeaking, ruled' (that is, 'led') by good Hermes along the mouldering paths', that is, he says, into the eternal realms removed from all evil.

For where, he says, did they go? 'They went by the streams of Ocean and the Leucadian rock, by the gates of the sun and the land of dreams' (Hom., *Od.* XXIV 9–12). 38. This is the Ocean, 'the origin of gods and the origin of men', he says, turning always in its ebb and flow, now upwards, now downwards. But when Ocean flows downwards, he says, this means the origin of man, but when it flows upwards to the wall and the rampart and the Leucadian rock, this is the origin of gods. 39. This, he says, is the meaning of the text, 'I said, you are gods, you are all sons of the Most High' (Ps. 82 (81): 6), if you hasten to escape from Egypt and go across the Red Sea into the desert, that is to escape from earthly intercourse to the heavenly Jerusalem (Gal. 4: 26), which is 'the mother of the living' (Gen. 3: 20); but if you return again to Egypt, that is, to earthly intercourse, 'you must die like men' (Ps. 82 (81): 7).

40. For all earthly birth ('origin'), he says, is mortal, but that which originates in heaven is immortal. For from water alone, and the spirit, the spiritual man is born, not the man of the flesh; but the earthly man is of the flesh. So it is written, he says: 'That which is born of the flesh is flesh, but that which is born of the spirit is spirit' (John 3: 6). This is the spiritual birth, as they suppose. 41. This, he says, is the great Jordan, which flowed down and prevented the children of Israel from coming out of Egypt, i.e. away from earthly intercourse; for Egypt, they hold, is the body; but Jesus (Joshua) checked it and made it flow upwards (cf. Josh. 3: 16).

8, 1. . . . They say, 'He who says that the universe proceeds from one (principle) is mistaken; he who says that it is from three, speaks the truth and will give the description (or, proof?) of all things. 2. For one, he says, is the blessed nature of the blessed Man on high, Adamas; and one the mortal (nature) here below; and one is the undominated race that ascends to that place where, he says, is Miriam who was sought after and Jethro, the great sage, Zipporah the seer, and Moses, whose generation is not in Egypt; for there were born to him children in Midian. 3. And this, he says, is not unknown to the poets either: 'The whole is divided in three, each one partaking of honour' (Hom., *Il.* XV 189).[11] For, he says, the great things must be told, but told in such a way by all men everywhere 'that hearing they may not hear and seeing they may not see' (Matt. 13: 13, etc.). For if the great things were not told, he says, the world could not continue.[12] 4. These are the three portentous words 'Caulacau, Saulasau, Zeesar' (Isa. 28: 10), Caulacau (denoting) the being on high, Adamas, Saulasau the mortal here below, Zeesar the Jordan that flows upwards. This, he says is the bisexual Man who is in all (men), whom the ignorant call three-bodied Geryon, Geryon as if 'flowing from earth' (*Gē-rheōn*), but the Greeks in general call the 'heavenly crescent moon', because it has 'mingled' and 'crushed' all together. 5. For 'all things were made by him, and without him was nothing made. That which was made in him is life' (John 1: 3 f.). This life, he says, is the unutterable generation of perfect men, which 'was not known to the former generations' (Eph. 3: 5); and the 'nothing', which was made without him, is the particular world; for it was made without him by the third (being) and the fourth.

6. This, he says, is the drinking-cup, 'the goblet with which the king makes divination when he drinks' (Gen. 44: 2, 4 f., 12). This, he says, was hidden and was found in the good seed of Benjamin. And the Greeks confirm this, he says, with their ecstatic speech:

> Bring (me) water, boy, bring wine,
> make me drunken, make me sleepy;
> for my drinking-cup informs me
> of the kind of man I must be,
> speaking without speech in silence.

7. This drinking-cup of Anacreon's, he says, which speaks without speech of the unutterable mystery should be enough for

---

[11] Cf. Hipp. V 20, 8, the Sethians.
[12] Cf. *Megale Apophasis*, Hipp. VI 17, 2.

men if it be merely conceived. For it is without speech, he says—
this cup of Anacreon's, which (Anacreon says) speaks to him in
utterance without speech, (telling him) of the kind of man he
must be, that is spiritual, not carnal, if he hear the hidden
mystery in silence. And this is the water which at that glorious
marriage Jesus turned and made into wine. This, he says, is the
great and true 'beginning of the signs' which Jesus performed
'in Cana of Galilee and manifested' the kingdom of heaven
(John 2: 1–11). 8. This, he says, is 'the kingdom of heaven
which lies in' us like a treasure (Luke 17: 21), like leaven hidden
'in three measures of meal' (Matt. 13: 33). 9. This, he says, is
the great and unutterable mystery of the Samothracians, which
can be known only by the perfect, he says, namely ourselves.
For the Samothracians clearly commemorate that same Adam,
the primal man, in the mysteries performed among them. 10.
And there are two statues standing in the Samothracians' temple,
statues of naked men, having both hands stretched upwards
towards heaven and their male members turned upwards, like
the statue of Hermes in Cyllene. And these statues which I have
described are images of the primal man and of the spiritual
man who is reborn, essentially the same in all respects with that
(primal) man.

11. This, he says, is what the Saviour said: 'Unless you drink
my blood and eat my flesh, you shall not enter the kingdom of
heaven; but even if you drink the cup which I drink,' he says,
'you cannot enter into the place where I am going' (John 6: 53;
Matt. 20:22 f., etc.; John 8: 21; 13: 33). 12. For he says, he
knew of what nature each of his disciples is, and that each of
them is bound to go to his own nature. For he chose twelve
disciples, he says, out of the twelve tribes, and through them he
spoke to each tribe; for this reason, he says, not all men have
heard the preaching of the twelve disciples, or, if they hear, can
receive them. For the things that are not according to their
nature are against (their) nature.

13. He is called Corybas, he says, by the Thracians who live
around Mount Haemus, and by the Phrygians just like the
Thracians, because from the 'crown' (*coryphe*) above and from
the brain that is without character he takes the beginning of his
descent and passes through the realms of all the subordinate
(powers); but how and in what way he comes down, we do not

understand. 14. This, he says, is the saying, 'We have heard his voice, but have not seen his form' (Deut. 4: 12). For when he is extended and given character, a voice is heard, but as to the form which comes down from above from the uncharacterized being, no one knows what it is like. But it is in the creature moulded from the earth, but no one knows it. 15. He is 'the God who inhabits the great flood', he says, according to the Psalter, who also gives utterance and cries aloud from 'many waters' (Ps. 29 (28): 3, 10).[13] The 'many waters', he says, are the manifold origin of mortal man, from which he shouts and cries aloud to the uncharacterized Man, saying, 'Save my first-born from the lions' (Ps. 22 (21): 21 f.; 35 (34): 17). 16. To him, he says, is addressed the saying, 'Thou art my son, Israel, fear not; if thou passest through the rivers, they shall not over-whelm thee, if thou passest through the fire, it shall not consume thee' (Isa. 43: 1 f.). 'Rivers', he says, means the moist substance of generation, and 'fire' is the urge and desire that leads to generation. 'Thou art mine, fear not' (Isa. 41: 9 f.). 17. And again, he says, 'If a mother will forget her children so as to have no pity nor give (them) the breast, then will I forget you'—this, he says, is spoken by Adamas to the men who are his; 'but even if a woman will forget them, yet I will not forget you. I have engraved you upon my hands' (Isa. 49: 15 f.). 18. And as to his ascent, that is, the regeneration, so that a man becomes spiritual, not carnal, on this, he says, the Scripture says 'Lift up the gates, your (!) rulers, and be ye lifted up, ye everlasting gates, and the king of glory shall come in' (Ps. 24 (23): 9 f.). This is a marvel of marvels. For 'who', he says, 'is this king of glory?'. 'A worm and no man, a reproach of man and an outcast of the people' (Ps. 22 (21): 7).[14] 'He is the king of glory, he who is mighty in warfare' (Ps. 24 (23): 8). 19. By 'warfare' he means that which occurs in the body, seeing that the moulded creature is moulded out of hostile elements, as it is written (he says) 'Remember the warfare that takes place in the body' (Job 40: 32 (27), English versions 41: 8). This entrance, he says, and this 'gate' was seen by Jacob when he travelled into Mesopotamia, that is, when he was already turning from a child into a youth and a man; that is to say, it was made known to him who was travelling into Mesopotamia.

---

[13] Cf. the Sethians, Hipp. V 19, 16.   [14] Cf. Hipp. V 9, 21 and VIII 10, 5.

20. But Mesopotamia ('amid the rivers'), he says, is the stream of the great Ocean that flows out from the middle of the perfect Man (or 'of the full-grown man').[15] And he marvelled at the heavenly gate, saying, 'How fearful is this place. This is none other than the house of God, and this is the gate of heaven' (Gen. 28: 17). For this reason, he says, Jesus says, 'I am the true gate' (John 10: 9). 21. And he who says this (he says) is the perfect man who is fully characterized (proceeding) from the uncharacterized being above. For, he says, the perfect (*or* 'full-grown'?) man cannot be saved unless he be regenerated by entering through this gate.

22. This same being, he says, is also called 'Papas' by the Phrygians, because he 'put a pause' to all things that were in disorderly and faulty motion before his own appearance. For the name Papas, he says, is (given him) by all things alike 'in heaven and on earth and under the earth' (Phil. 2: 10) who say, (*Paue, paue,* that is,) Stay, stay, the disorder of the world, and make 'peace to those far off', that is, to the material and earthy (men) and 'peace to those who are near by' (Eph. 2: 17), that is, to the spiritual and intellectual perfect men.

And the Phrygians call this same being 'the Dead', since he is buried in the body as if in a tomb and a sepulchre. 23. This, he says, is the saying, 'You are whited sepulchres, which are filled', he says, 'with dead men's bones' (Matt. 23: 27), because there is not in you the man who lives; and again, he says, 'the dead shall leap up from the grave' (John 5: 28?), that is, from their earthly bodies, being regenerated as spiritual men, not carnal. 24. This, he says, is the resurrection which comes to pass through the gate of heaven, and those who do not enter by it, he says, all remain dead.

And these same Phrygians, he says, call this same being by the opposite title of 'god'. For he becomes god, he says, when he has risen from the dead and enters through this gate into heaven. 25. This gate, he says, was known to Paul the Apostle, who partly disclosed it in a mystery and said that he had been caught up by an angel and attained to the second and the third heaven, to paradise itself, and had seen what he saw and 'had heard unutterable words which it is not possible for man to speak' (2 Cor. 12:4).

[15] Word-play on 'Mesopotamia'.

26. These, he says, are the mysteries which all men declare to be unutterable, 'which also we speak, not in words taught by human wisdom, but in those taught by the spirit, comparing spiritual things with spiritual. But the psychic (i.e. unspiritual) man does not accept what belongs to the spirit of God; for these things to him are foolishness' (1 Cor. 2: 13 f.). These things, he says, are the unutterable mysteries of the spirit, which we alone know. 27. Of these, he says, the Saviour said, 'No man can come to me, unless my heavenly Father draw him' (John 6: 44). For, he says, it is most difficult to accept and receive this great and unutterable mystery. Moreover, he says, the Saviour said, 'Not everyone that says to me, Lord, Lord, shall enter into the kingdom of heaven, but he who does the will of my Father in heaven' (Matt. 7: 21). 28. Men must do this, not merely hear it, and so enter into the kingdom of heaven. And again, says he, he has said, 'The publicans and whores enter into the kingdom of heaven before you' (Matt. 21: 31); for 'publicans' (*telonai*) he says, are those who achieve the fulfilment (*telē*) of all things; and we, he says, are the 'publicans', 'for whom the fulfilment (*telē*) of the ages has arrived' (1 Cor. 10: 11). For 'fulfilment', he says, means the seeds that are sown from the uncharacterized being into the world, through which the whole world is fulfilled; 29. since through these it also took its beginning.[16]

And this, he says, is what is written: 'The sower went out to sow; and some fell by the wayside and was trodden down; and some on the rocky ground, and it sprang up', he says, 'and because it had no depth, it withered and perished; but some, he says, fell on the ground that was fair and good, and it brought forth fruit, some a hundred(-fold), some sixty, some thirty. He who has ears to hear', he says, 'let him hear' (Matt. 13: 3–9, etc.). That means, he says: No one has become a hearer of these mysteries saving only the gnostics who are 'fulfilled' (or 'perfect'). 30. This, he says, is the fair and good (land), of which Moses says, 'I will bring you into a land which is fair and good, a land flowing with milk and honey' (Deut. 31: 20). Now the milk and honey, he says, are that whose taste makes the perfect become undominated and attain the pleroma (or 'fullness'). The pleroma, he says, is that through which all originate beings

[16] Cf. Hipp. VI 9, 10.

that come into being, come to be, and are filled from that which is unoriginate.

31. This same being is also called 'the unfruitful' by the Phrygians. For he is unfruitful when he is carnal and executes 'the desire of the flesh' (Gal. 5: 16). This, he says, is the saying, 'Every tree that does not bear good fruit is cut down and cast into the fire' (Matt. 3: 10, etc.). For these fruits, he says, are nothing but the rational, the living men, those who enter through the third gate. 32. So they say, 'If you ate dead things and made them living, what will you do if you eat living things?' (Cf. Gospel of Thomas, 11.) By 'living' they mean reasons and minds and men, the pearls belonging to that uncharacterized being that are thrown down into the moulded creature. 33. This is the saying, 'Do not throw what is holy to the dogs, nor pearls to the pigs' (Matt. 7: 6) for they say that this is pigs' and dogs' business, the intercourse of women with men.

34. This same being, he says, the Phrygians call Aipolos (the Goatherd), not, he says, because he pastured goats and kids, as the psychic (unenlightened) men name him, but, he says, because he is *aeipolos*, that is, he who 'always pulls'* round and turns and rotates the whole universe in a circle. For 'pulling' means turning and altering things. 35. For this reason, he says, the two centres of the heavens are always called 'poles'. And the poet says, 'Here turneth in (*pōleitai*) a sage old merman, the immortal Proteus of Egypt' (Hom. *Od.* IV 384 f.); he does not mean that he is on sale (= *pōleitai*) but that he turns in his place and as it were goes round. And the cities in which we live are called cities (*poleis*) because we turn around and circulate (*poloumen*) in them. 36. So, he says, the Phrygians call him Aipolos, who always everywhere turns all things round and changes them to his own.

And, he says, the Phrygians also call him 'the Fruitful one', because, he says, 'the deserted wife has more children than she that keeps her husband' (Isa. 54: 1), that is, many are those who are reborn, who are immortal and last for ever, even if those who are born are few; what is carnal, he says, is always corruptible, even if there are very many who are born. 37. For this reason, he says, 'Rachel wept for her children, and would

---

* The Greek means 'turns', but I have attempted to reproduce the word-play.

not be comforted as she wept over them; for she knew', he says, 'that they are not' (Jer. 31: 15). And Jeremiah also laments for the earthly Jerusalem, (meaning) not the city in Phoenicia, but the corruptible earthly generation; for, he says, Jeremiah knew the perfect man who is regenerated 'by water and the spirit' (John 3: 5), not the carnal one. 38. Indeed Jeremiah himself said, 'He is a man, and who shall know him?' (Jer. 17: 9 LXX). This (shows), he says, how very deep and incomprehensible is the knowledge of the perfect man: for, he says, the beginning of perfection is the knowledge of man, but complete perfection is the knowledge of God.

39. But the Phrygians, he says, also call him 'the green ear that is harvested', and the Athenians also, following the Phrygians, when they make the initiations of Eleusis and display to the beholders that great and wondrous and most perfect mystery which is to be beheld there in silence, a harvested ear. 40. Now this ear is for the Athenians too the great and perfect Illuminator coming from the uncharacterized one; likewise the hierophant himself, who is not indeed castrated, like Attis, but is made a eunuch with hemlock and is separated from all carnal generation, when he celebrates the great and unutterable mysteries by night at Eleusis under a brilliant light, calls out and proclaims these words: 'A holy child is born to the Lady Brimo, Brimos'—that is, to the Strong one, the Strong. 41. Lady, he says, means the spiritual birth, the heavenly, higher (birth); and strong is the man who is born in this fashion. And the mystery aforesaid is called Eleusis and Anactoreum; Eleusis, he says, because we have come, we who are spiritual, flowing down from above, from Adamas—for *eleusesthai*, he says, means 'to come'—and Anactoreum because of our ascent on high (*anō*). 42. This, he says, is what the devotees of the Eleusinian cult call the great mysteries; for it is the custom that those who have been initiated into the lesser should again be initiated into the great ones; for 'greater dooms gain greater destinies' (Heraclitus, fr. 25 Diels). 43. For the lesser mysteries, he says, are those of Persephone here below; and of these mysteries and the road that leads there, which is 'broad and wide' (Matt. 7: 13) and leads those who are perishing to Persephone, the poet also says: 'But beneath it is an awesome pathway, cavernous and clayey; but this is the best that leads to the

pleasant grove of glorious Aphrodite' (Parmenides, fr. 20 Diels). 44. This means, he says, the lesser mysteries of birth in the flesh; and when men have been initiated into these they must wait a little before they are initiated into the great, heavenly ones. For those who are allotted those dooms, he says, receive greater destinies. For this, he says, is 'the gate of heaven', and this is 'the house of God' (Gen. 28: 17), where the good God dwells alone, where no unclean person, he says, shall enter, no psychic (unspiritual), no carnal man, but it is reserved for the spiritual alone; and when men come there they must lay down their clothing[17] and all become bridegrooms, being rendered wholly male through the virgin spirit (cf. Gospel of Thomas, 114). 45. For she is the virgin who is with child and conceives and bears a son (cf. Isa. 7: 14), who is not psychic, not bodily, but a blessed Aeon of Aeons. Concerning this, he says, the Saviour has said clearly that 'strait and narrow is the way that leads to life, and few there are that enter upon it; but wide and broad is the way that leads to destruction, and many there are who pass over it' (Matt. 7: 13 f.).

9, 1. The Phrygians also say that the Father of the universe is Amygdalus, an almond(-tree); it is not a tree that is amygdalus, he says, but it is that pre-existent being, who having within himself the perfect fruit, which was so to say stirring and moving deep within him, opened his heart and begot that invisible, unnameable, and unutterable Son of his, of whom we are speaking. 2. For (the word) *amyxai* means to break and cut open, as in the case of bodies which are inflamed, he says, and have in them a sort of gathering such as doctors call *amychai* when they cut them open. So, he says, the Phrygians call the pre-existent being Amygdalus, from whom there came forth and was begotten the invisible one through whom 'all things were made and without him nothing was made' (John 1: 3). And the Phrygians call that offspring of his a 'flute-player', because that offspring is a spirit in harmony. For 'God is a spirit', he says, 'and therefore it is neither in this mountain nor in Jerusalem that the true worshippers offer worship, but in the spirit' (John 4: 21, 23). 4. For the worship of the perfect, he says, is spiritual, not carnal. And the spirit, he says, is there wherever the Father is named together with the Son

---

[17] That is, the souls, cf. Ir. I 7, 1.

who was begotten there from this same Father. This, he says, is the being with many names, the thousand-eyed, the incomprehensible, after whom every nature strives in its own fashion.

5. This, he says, is the word of God, namely the word of the Exposition (*apophasis*) of the Great Power; 'hence it shall be sealed and covered and veiled, stored up in the dwelling-place where the root of all things has its foundation'—(the root) of Aeons, powers, conceptions, of gods, angels, and courier spirits, of (all) that are and that are not, originate and unoriginate, incomprehensible and comprehensible, of years, months, days, and hours, of the indivisible point from which the smallest thing gradually begins to grow; for the indivisible point, he says, which is nothing and consists of nothing, will by its conception of itself become an inconceivable magnitude. 6. This, he says, is the kingdom of heaven, the mustard-seed (Matt. 13: 31, etc.), the indivisible point existing in the body which, he says, no man knows but the spiritual only. This, he says, is what is written, 'There are no words nor speeches, whose voices are not heard' (Ps. 19 (18): 4). 7. So they ramble on, adapting everything that was said or done by anyone to their own theory, saying that everything is spiritual. Hence they say that even the performers in the theatre do not speak or act without providence. Therefore, he says, when the community assembles in the theatre and there enters one clothed in a peculiar dress carrying a lyre and singing to it, then in his hymn he declares the great mysteries without knowing what he says:

8. Be it the race of Cronos, or the blessed child of Zeus or of
     great Rhea,
   Hail to thee, Attis, sad message of Rhea;
   Assyrians call thee thrice-desired Adonis, all Egypt, Osiris,
   The wisdom of the Greeks, the heavenly crescent moon,
   The Samothracians, venerable Adamas,
   The men of Haemus, Corybas,
   The Phrygians, sometimes Papas, or again the Dead, or God,
     Or the Unfruitful, the Goatherd, or the green Ear that is
     harvested,
     Or the Man, the Flute-player, born of the fruitful
     Almond.

9. This being, he says, is the many-formed Attis, whom they describe as follows in their hymns:

> I will sing of Attis, the son of Rhea,
> Not with the clang of bells nor with the flute
>   or with the bellowing of the Curetes of Ida
> But I will tune it to the muse of Phoebus' lyre.
> All hail! All hail! — as Pan, as Bacchus,
>   as shepherd of the shining stars.

10. Because of these words, and others like them, they attend the so-called mysteries of the Great Mother, thinking that through those (sacred) actions they will best understand the universal mystery. For these men have nothing (to offer) beyond what is done there, except that they are not castrated, they only perform the functions of those who are castrated. 11. For they urge most severely and carefully that one should abstain, as those men do, from intercourse with women; their behaviour otherwise, as we have fully explained, is like that of the castrated.

These men venerate nothing else than the serpent (*naas*), being called Naassenes. 12. But Naas is the serpent, from whom, they say, all the temples in the world get their name of *naos*, namely from *naas*; and for this *naas* alone is established every shrine, every rite, and every mystery. And no rite can be found in the world which does not involve a temple (*naos*) and the serpent (*naas*) in it, from which its name of *naos* is derived. 13. And they say that the serpent is liquid substance . . . and that nothing at all that exists, be it immortal or mortal, animate or inanimate, can consist without it. 14. All things are subject to it, and it is good, and it has the goodness of everything else within it[18] as in the horn of the unicorn and gives to all that exists its beauty, according to the nature and peculiar form of each thing, as it were passing through all things, as 'coming out of Eden and dividing into four sources' (Gen. 2: 10–14).

15. Eden they say is the brain, being as it were 'bounden' and enfolded in the membranes which surround it, like the heavens; and paradise they think is man, to the extent of his head alone. Now this river that comes out of Eden, that is, from the brain, 'is divided into four sources, and the name of the

---

[18] Cf. *Megale Apophasis*, Hipp. VI 13: What was created by the seventh power is 'very good'.

first river is called Pheison; it is this which surrounds the whole
land of Euilat; and there is gold there; and the gold of that
land is good; and there is the fire-ruby and the green stone'.
16. This, he says, is the eye, which through its value and its
colours confirms what is said. 'And the name of the second
river is Geon; it is this which surrounds the whole land of
Ethiopia.' This, he says, is the ear, with its labyrinth (of passages). 'And the name of the third is Tigris (the Tiger); it is this
flows opposite Assyria.' 17. This, he says, is the (sense of) smell,
because of the powerful flow of its current; and it flows opposite
Assyria, because when the breath is breathed out, at its in-
drawing there is sucked in (*syr*-omenon) from the air a more
powerful and stronger breath; for this, he says, is the nature of
the breath. 'And the fourth river is Euphrates'; 18. this, they
say, is the mouth, through which prayer goes forth and nourishment comes in, which gladdens (*euphrainei*) and nourishes and
characterizes the spiritual, perfect man.

This, he says, is the water above the firmament (Gen. 1: 7),
concerning which, he says, the Saviour said: 'If thou knewest
who it is that asketh thee, thou wouldest have asked of him,
and he would have given thee to drink of living water that
springeth up' (John 4: 10, 14). To this water, he says, every
natural species comes and selects its own substance, and for
each natural species there comes from this water what is
appropriate for it, he says, more than the iron comes to the
magnet or gold to the sea-ray's sting or chaff to amber.[19] 20.
But, he says, if any man is blind from birth, who has not beheld
'the true light, which lighteth every man who cometh into the
world' (John 1: 9), let him through us recover his sight and
see how, as if through some garden of paradise which contains
all plants and variety of seeds, (there is) water which passes
through all plants and all seeds; and he will see that from one
and the same water (each plant) selects and draws out (its own
product), the olive its oil, the vine its wine, and each of the
other plants according to its kind.

21. But that man, he says, is without honour in the world
and yet has great honour (in heaven; but he is surrendered)[20]
by those who do not know him to those who do not know him
and is considered as 'a drop from the bucket' (Isa. 40: 15). But

[19] The same comparison often occurs.   [20] Completed.

we, he says, are the spiritual men, who were chosen as his own possession by the living water, the Euphrates who flows through the midst of Babylon; for we enter in through the true gate, which is Jesus the blessed one, 22. and out of all men we are the only true Christians, who complete the mystery at the third gate and are there anointed with an unutterable ointment from a horn, as was David, not from an earthen flask, he says, as was Saul who conversed with the wicked spirit of the desire of the flesh.

10, 1. We have produced this as a brief (example) out of a great mass (of teaching) . . . They have strung together this psalm, through which they suppose they are celebrating all the mysteries of their error:

First-born Nous was the law that engendered all,
Next (masc.!) to the first-born was the outpoured chaos,
Thirdly the soul received a law as it worked [? as it was made].
Hence clad in the form of a stag (?)
It labours, captive, as a spoil for death.
Now with royal (honour) it sees the light,
Now cast out into misery, it weeps.
Now it is wept for, it rejoices,
Now it weeps, it is judged,
Now it is judged, it dies,
. . . and without escape the wretched (soul)
    enters a labyrinth of evils in its wanderings.[21]
But Jesus said, 'Father, behold:
Pursued by evils here upon the earth
There roams the (work) of thine own breath;
It seeks to escape the bitter chaos
But knows not how it shall win through.
Therefore send me, Father;
Bearing the seals I will descend,
I will pass through all the Aeons,
I will disclose all mysteries,
I will show the forms of the Gods
And the hidden things of the holy way,
Awaking knowledge (*gnosis*), I will impart.'

11, 1. These are the efforts of the Naassenes, who call themselves Gnostics.

[21] Text uncertain.

17

SYSTEMS INVOLVING THREE PRINCIPLES IV THE PERATAE

INTRODUCTION

The Peratae are another sect who adopt a division into three. The highest principle is 'the perfect Good', without origin; the second is the self-generated, full of powers, the third is the originate being, namely matter. The intermediate power in this system is that which first turns itself towards the supreme God, the Father, and receives from him the ideas, and then turns itself towards matter and expresses them in it. From matter again it receives the 'Father's imprints' and carries them up to the Father. This intermediate power is appropriately called 'the serpent', since this title aptly symbolizes the passage to and fro, descending from above to the lower world and returning thence to the upper. It therefore plays the crucial part in production and also in restoration.

Similar use is made of the story of the Israelites' deliverance from the plague of serpents in their journey through the desert, Num. 21: 4 ff. But at this point evil powers are suddenly introduced, namely the stars, which determine the destinies of the changing world. In general the Peratae seem to have been much concerned with the stars, as a passage quoted by Hippolytus makes clear. The stars are also pictured in the image of the serpents who bit the Israelites in the desert, which Moses countered by exhibiting 'the perfect serpent, full of fullness'; everyone who believed in him was not bitten by the 'powers'—an alternative name for the beings who control the processes of change and dissolution. This serpent resembles the 'Son' (John 3: 14) who appeared in human form in the last days in the time of Herod; but there is no clear explanation of *how* he saves. If a man wishes to escape from change and dissolution, this depends upon his awakening and coming to know the paths by which man has passed into the world.

Clearly, therefore, the system does not depend upon an eternal cyclical process of change and dissolution. The third part of the world, which like the Naassenes they call 'the particular', has certainly come into being through an 'outflow' from above, but the 'things here below' are governed by the stars and subject to change and dissolution. The fact that everything is formed from above is also indicated by the fact that the serpent is held to be the 'wise word of Eve', who is the 'mother of all that live' (Gen. 3: 20), and so, because of the word 'all', the mother of gods and angels, of immortals and mortals, of irrational and rational beings. But the stars enslave mankind so that they do not escape the process of dissolution —except for the Peratae. Here then it is the stars who hold men captive, as Esaldaeus does in the Naassenes' view. As in the *Megale Apophasis* not all mankind is saved. It is indeed said that what comes down from above will also return there; but 'all that conspires against what is come from above will be cast out for punishment'; so a selection takes place among mankind, as is also shown by the sentence that only the Peratae can escape the destiny of the world.

Christ is held to have descended into this world in the time of Herod, having in himself all the powers of the three parts of the world; he is a threefold man with three bodies and three powers.[1]

Hippolytus, *Ref.* V 12, 1–17, 13

12, 1. There is yet another (heresy), that of the Peratae, whose slanders against Christ have remained hidden for many years; it is now resolved to publish their secret mysteries. These men declare that the universe is one, having three parts. 2. One part of their threefold partition is as it were a single principle like a great source, which can be divided by the word into an infinite number of divisions. The first and most important division in their view is a trinity, and is called 'perfect goodness', a paternal power;* but the second part of their trinity is like an infinite number of powers which have originated from themselves; the third is the particular. 3. And the first is unoriginate and is good, the second good (and) self-originate, the third is originate; hence they explicitly speak of three gods, three words, three minds, three men. For to each part of the world, in virtue of their distinction, they attribute both gods and words and minds and men, and so on.

4. And they say there came down from on high, from the unoriginate being, the first division of the world, when the

---

[1] Cf. the Naassenes, Hipp. V 6, 7 and the Apocryphon of John 27, 19 ff.

---

* Or possibly, with a different punctuation, 'divisions (but the first . . . in their view is a trinity) and is called', etc., thus identifying 'perfect goodness' with the 'single source' rather than with the 'trinity'.

world was otherwise complete,—(there came down) in the time of Herod, for reasons which we shall presently describe, a three-natured man called Christ, having three bodies and three powers, possessing in himself the complexities and powers proceeding from the three parts of the world. 5. And this, he says, is the meaning of the saying: 'The whole fullness determined to dwell in him in bodily form' (Col. 2: 9) and in him is all the godhead of the trinity divided as aforesaid. For he says there were brought down from the two superior worlds, the unoriginate and the self-originate, into this world in which we are, the seeds of every kind of power. 6. Now the manner of their descent we shall presently describe.

He says therefore that Christ came down from on high, from the unoriginate being, in order that by his descent all the threefold division might be saved. For, he says, the things that were brought down from on high will ascend through him; but the things that conspired against what was brought down from on high are abandoned, punished, and rejected. 7. This, he says, is (the meaning of) the saying, 'For the Son of Man came not into the world to destroy the world, but that the world through him might be saved' (John 3: 17). By 'world', he says, he means the two superior parts, the unoriginate and the self-originate. But, he says, when the Scripture says 'lest we be condemned with the world' (1 Cor. 11: 32), it means the third part of the world, the particular. For the third part must be destroyed, which he calls 'world', but the two superior parts become free from corruption.

13, 1. So we will first learn how they have taken over this teaching from the astrologers and insult Christ. . . . 9. These things and their comments on them we have carefully set out in the preceding book, from which the student can learn how the leaders of the Peratic heresy, Euphrates the Perate and Celbes of Carystia, have adopted them, changing only the name but teaching essentially similar doctrine. . . . 12. This system and this distinction of the stars, which are really Chaldaean, have been drawn in by the aforementioned (teachers), who falsify the name of truth, and have given out as a word of Christ the position of the Aeons, and the defection of good powers to the bad, and alliances of good ones and bad. They spoke also of 'toparchs' and 'proastii', and invented innumerable other names for themselves which are not real objects; they simply elaborated the whole delusion of the astrologers concerning the stars; and as they have laid the foundation of a serious error, they shall be refuted through our own diligence. I will set out some of the compositions of the Peratae for comparison with the Chaldaean practice of the astrologers which I have described; this will enable those who compare them to understand how the doctrines of the Peratae are undeniably those of the astrologers, not those of Christ.

14, 1. I propose, therefore, to quote one of the books which are approved among them, where it says: 'I am the voice of awakening in the age (Aeon) of night; now I begin to expose the power that comes from chaos. The power of the abysmal darkness, which supports the silt of the imperishable watery void, the whole power of the convulsion, coloured like water, which is ever-moving, bearing up what holds fast, consolidating what is unstable, resolving what is to come, lightening what holds fast, cleansing what increases; the faithful treasurer of the path of the vapours, which enjoys what wells up from the twelve "eyes" (sources) of the Law,* showing the seal to the power that governs with those unseen waters that hover above, its name was Thalassa (the Sea). To this power ignorance gave the name of Cronos, guarded with chains, since he bound together the complication of the dense and cloudy dim dark Tartarus. There were born after his image Cepheus, Prometheus, Iapetus . . .'

(The rest of c. 14 is not translated; it presents further astrological statements which introduce divine names and legendary characters without contributing material essentially relevant to gnosticism.)

15, 1. It has been easily demonstrated to all that the heresy of the Peratae is derived from the astrologers with merely verbal adaptations; and their other books contain the same style of writing, in case anyone cared to go through them all. 2. For, as I said, they consider that the original causes of all originate beings are those that are unoriginate and superior;

---

* The German has 'Law of the twelve eyes'. I prefer Legge's version. 'Eye' in Hebrew can mean 'well', and Exod. 15: 25–7 contains a reference to a law-giving and to twelve wells. Cf. the reference to 'twelve mouths' in 14, 3, omitted in this version.

and this world of ours, which they call 'the particular', came into being by emanation; and all these stars together which are visible in heaven were the causes of this world—they merely change their name, as can be seen by comparison in the case of the Proastii. 3. Secondly and similarly, just as the world has come into being by emanation from above, so they say the things within it take their beginning and end and are directed by the emanation of the stars. For since the astrologers recognize the horoscope (i.e. rising) and the zenith and the setting and the nadir, and realize that as these stars undergo their different motions at different times through the perpetual revolution of the whole universe there are different declinations from the pole at different times and approximations to the poles—so (these men), by allegorizing the system of the astrologers, present the pole as God and monad and Lord of the whole world-process, and the declination they call the left, and the approximation the right. 5. So when anyone reading their writings finds a power which they call right or left, let him refer to the centre and the declination and the approximation, and he will clearly perceive that their whole system is an astrological doctrine.

16, 1. They call themselves Peratae, holding that nothing belonging to the world of becoming can escape the destiny laid down for things that come into being from their (moment of) coming into being. For he says, 'Whatever comes into being is also completely destroyed', as the Sibyl has it.[2] But we alone, he says, who have realized the necessity of coming-into-being and the routes by which man has entered the world, are exactly instructed and are the only ones who can pass through and cross over (*perāsai*) destruction. 2. Now destruction, he says, is water, and nothing else brings quicker destruction on the world than water. Now water is that which encircles the Proastii, they say, namely Cronos; for he says it is a power of the colour of water; and this power, namely Cronos, cannot be escaped by anything belonging to the world of becoming; 3. for Cronos presides over the whole process of becoming, so as to make it subject to destruction; and there is no coming-into-being without the interference of Cronos. This he says, is what the poets also describe, which alarms even the gods: he says,

2 *Die Oracula Sibyllina*, ed. J. Geffcken, Leipzig, 1902, Fragm. 3 V. 1.

> Let earth be witness, and broad heaven above
> And the down-rushing stream of Styx, the oath
> Most great and dreadful for the blessed gods.[3]
>
> (Hom. *Il.* XV 36–8.)

4. And not only the poets say this, he says, but also the wisest of the Greeks have done so, one of whom is Heraclitus, who said, 'It is death for souls to become water' (fr. 36 Diels); this, he says, is the death which overtakes the Egyptians in the Red Sea together with their chariots (Exod. 14); and all the ignorant, he says, are Egyptians. 5. And departing from Egypt, he says, means departing from the body—for they consider the body a miniature Egypt—and crossing over the Red Sea, that is, the water of destruction, namely Cronos, and crossing over beyond the Red Sea, that is, beyond the process of becoming, and arriving in the desert, that is, escaping from the process of becoming (to the place) where there are (collected) together all the gods of destruction and the god of salvation. 6. Now, he says, the gods of destruction are the stars which bring upon those who come into being the necessity which belongs to changeable generation. And these, he says, Moses called the serpents of the desert (Num. 21: 6) which bit and destroyed those who thought they had crossed over the Red Sea. 7. Now when the children of Israel were being bitten in the desert, he says, Moses showed them the true perfect serpent; and those who believed in him were not bitten in the desert, that is, by the powers. Therefore, he says, there is no one who can save and deliver those who depart from Egypt, that is, from the body and from this world, except only the perfect serpent who is filled with (all) fullness. 8. The man who sets his hope on him, he says, will not be destroyed by the serpents in the desert, that is, by the gods of generation. It is written, he says, in the book of Moses; this serpent, he says, is the power that accompanied Moses, the rod that turned itself into a serpent. But, he says, the power of Moses was opposed in Egypt by the serpents of the magicians, the gods of destruction; but the rod of Moses subdued and destroyed them all (Exod. 7: 10–12).

The universal serpent, he says, is the wise word of Eve. 9. This, he says, is the mystery of Eden, this is the river (that

---

[3] Cf. the Sethians, Hipp. V 20, 10.

flowed) out of Eden (Gen. 2: 10–14), this is the sign that was marked on Cain so that anyone who found him should not kill him (Gen. 4: 15). This, he says, is (that) Cain whose sacrifice was not accepted by the god of this world; but he received the bloody sacrifice of Abel (Gen. 4: 3–5); for the lord of this world delights in blood. 10. This, he says, is he who appeared in the last days in a human form, in the time of Herod, being made in the image of Joseph who was sold by the hands of his brothers, who alone wore a many-coloured garment (Gen. 37: 3). He it is, he says, who is in the image of Esau, whose garment was blessed even when he was not present (Gen. 27: 27 ff.), who, he says, did not receive the dim-sighted blessing but became rich from elsewhere, taking nothing from the dim-sighted man; whose face Jacob saw 'as a man might see the face of God' (Gen. 33: 10). 11. Of him, he says, it is written, 'Like Nimrod, a mighty hunter before the Lord' (Gen. 10: 9). But, he says, there are many imitators of him, as many as appeared to the children of Israel in the desert and bit them; but those who were bitten were delivered from them by that perfect serpent that Moses set up. This, he says, is what is written, 'And as Moses lifted up the serpent in the desert, even so must the Son of Man be lifted up' (John 3: 14). 12. In his image was made the brazen serpent in the desert that Moses set up. His likeness, and his alone, he says, remains in heaven perpetually to be seen in light. He is the great Beginning, he says, of which Scripture tells. To him, he says, applies the saying, 'In the beginning was the Word, and the Word was with God, and the Word was God. He was in the beginning with God. All things were made by him, and without him nothing was made. What was made in him, is life' (John 1: 1–4). And in him, he says, Eve was made, the Eve (who is) life. 13. And she, he says, is Eve 'the mother of all that live' (Gen. 3: 20), universal nature, that is (the nature) of gods and angels, of immortals and mortals, of irrational and rational beings; for, he says, he who said 'all' meant all. 14. And if anyone has 'eyes that are blessed', he says, that man will see when he looks up to heaven the fair image of the serpent in the great beginning of the heavens turning about and becoming the beginning of all movement in all things that come into being, and will understand that without him nothing of the things in heaven or of those on earth or of those beneath the earth remains in being, neither night, nor moon, nor fruits, nor birth, nor riches, nor travel, nor any at all of the things that exist, exists without his giving the sign. 15. In him, he says, is that 'great wonder' to be seen in heaven for those who can see. For, he says, upon this crown of his head—an utterly incredible fact for those who have no knowledge—the setting and rising (i.e. west and east) mingle with each other. This is what ignorance describes as follows: in heaven 'The Dragon winds, great wonder dread to see' (Aratus, V 46). 16. And on either side of him are ranged the Crown and the Lyre, and just above his head is to be seen a wretched man, the Kneeler 'Holding the twisted Dragon's right foot's tip' (ibid. 70). And at the Kneeler's back there is an imperfect serpent held fast in both hands by the serpent-holder, Ophiuchus, and prevented from touching the crown that lies beside the perfect serpent.

17, 1. This is the exceedingly subtle wisdom of the Peratic sect, which it is difficult to describe in full, so twisted is it through its evident dependence on astrology. As far as possible in a few words we have set out its whole content.

But in order to exhibit their whole teaching in outline we may add the following. According to them the universe is Father, Son, and matter; each one of these three has innumerable powers in himself. 2. Midway between matter and the Father there sits his Son, the Word, the serpent who is always moving towards the immovable Father and towards the movable matter. And at one time he turns toward the Father and receives the powers in his own person (lit. 'face'), and when he has received the powers he turns himself towards matter, and the matter which is without quality or configuration is imprinted with the forms (or ideas) from the Son, which the Son printed off from the Father. 3. And the Son is imprinted from the Father unutterably, inexpressibly, and unalterably, in the way that Moses says the colours of those (sheep) that conceived flowed from the rods set up by the drinking-troughs (Gen. 30: 37). 4. In the same way also the powers flow from the Son into matter, just as the conception (through) the power that passed from the rods into those that conceived; and the difference of the colours, and their unlikeness, which flowed from the rods through the water into the sheep is a difference, he says, between corruptible and incorruptible generation.

Corrigenda: Aratus v. 46 (70)

5. Or rather, just as a painter takes nothing away from the creatures (he paints) with his brush, yet transfers their forms to his board as he draws them, in the same way the Son by his own power transfers the characters of the Father to matter. For all that belongs to the Father is here, and (yet) nothing is.[4] 6. For, he says, if anyone of those here below has the strength even to comprehend that he is a character of the Father brought down from above and put into a body in this world, then just as a conception coming from the rod (he) becomes white, essentially the same in all respects with the Father in heaven, and ascends to that place; but if he does not gain this teaching nor recognize the necessity that belongs to generation, then like an abortion born by night he shall perish by night. 7. So, he says, when the Saviour says, 'Your Father in heaven' (Matt. 7: 11, etc.), he means the One from whom the Son takes over the characters and has transferred them to his world; but when he says, 'Your father is a murderer (and has been) from the beginning' (John 8: 44) he means the ruler and artificer of matter, who taking up the characters distributed by the Son has reproduced them in this world, who is a murderer from the beginning; for his work makes for corruption and death. 8. So, he says, no one can be saved apart from the Son, or ascend (without him); who is the serpent. For as he has brought down from above the Father's characters, so again he brings up from this world those who are awakened and have become characters of the Father, bringing them across to that world from this as real beings out of unreality. 9. This, he says, is the saying, 'I am the door' (John 10: 7). And he brings them across, he says . . .[5] like the naphtha that attracts fire to itself from every side, or rather as the magnet (draws) iron and nothing else, 10. or as the sea-ray's sting (draws) gold and nothing else; or as chaff is drawn by amber,[6] so, he says, by the serpent there is drawn back again from the world the fully formed perfect race which is essentially the same, but nothing else, just as it was sent down by him. 11. As proof of this they bring in the anatomy of the brain, comparing the brain itself to the Father because of its immobility, and the cerebellum with the Son, since it moves and has a serpentine shape; 12. and this, they say, without

---

[4] Cf. Monoimus, Hipp. VIII 13, 4 and Basilides, Hipp. VII 25, 6.
[5] Text here unintelligible.   [6] Cf. the Sethians, Hipp. V 21, 8.

speech or sign draws up through the pineal gland the spiritual and life-giving substance that flows out from the arch (of the brain), which the cerebellum receives, in the same manner as the Son without speech imparts the forms (ideas) to matter, that is to say, down the marrow of the backbone there flow the seeds and the genera of those who are generated according to the flesh.

13. By the use of this comparison they think they can introduce in an attractive form their unspeakable mysteries which are to be handed on in silence.

18

SYSTEMS INVOLVING THREE PRINCIPLES V
THE SETHIANS AND THE ARCHONTICS

THE SETHIANS ACCORDING TO EPIPHANIUS

The Sethians, like Basilides, are known to us through two different accounts, but in their case the discrepancy is less marked than in that of Basilides. One account is found in Tertullian[1] and Epiphanius, the other in Hippolytus. The former gives a convincing explanation of the name 'Sethians'; it deals with the originative power, the 'Mother', with Abel and Cain, and it tells how, after the sin of Cain and the murder of Abel, the Mother gave birth to Seth, the perfect one, and subsequently, because sin persisted, brought on the Flood, so that only the pure seed of Seth might be preserved. This plan was frustrated by the cunning of the angels. After this Christ appeared from the line of Seth.

Epiphanius, *Panarion* XXXIX, 1–5, 3 (in part)

1, 1. The Sethians, again, are another sect, which goes by this name but is not to be found in every place . . . 2. I believe that I encountered this sect also in Egypt; I do not remember exactly in which country I met them. We have discovered some things about it by (personal) investigation with our own eyes, and have learnt some more from written accounts. 3. The Sethians boast that they trace their descent from Seth the son of Adam, and glorify him and ascribe to him everything that seems virtuous and the proofs of virtue and justice and everything else of this kind. Indeed they even call him Christ and assert that he is Jesus. 4. And their teaching is such as to say that the universe derives from angels and not from the power on high.

2, 1. In this respect what they say agrees with the former heresy of the Cainites: that in the beginning two men first

---

[1] *Adv. Omnes Haer.* 2.

originated, and from these two were derived Cain and Abel, and over these two the angels fell out and made war on each other, and so caused Abel to be killed by Cain (Gen. 4: 1–8). 2. For the quarrel among the angels who contended concerned the races of men and involved those two, the one who had begotten Cain and the one who had begotten Abel. 3. But the power on high prevailed (over them), the one they call the Mother, and Female; for they think that there are mothers in the higher world, and females and males—they almost talk of family relations and paternal authorities. 4. Now when the one called Mother and Female prevailed, they say, since she knew that Abel had been killed she took thought and caused Seth to be born and put into him her own power, implanting in him a seed of the power from on high and the spark that was sent from on high for the first foundation of the seed and of the institution (of the world). 5. And this was the institution of justice and the election of the (elect) seed and race, so that through this institution and this seed destruction should come upon the powers of the angels who made the world and (made) the two men in the beginning. 6. For this reason, then, the race of Seth is set apart and taken up from this world, since it is an elect (race) and separated from the other race.

7. For as the times went past, they say, and the two races were together, the race of Cain and that of Abel, and came together because of their great wickedness and were mixed with one another, the Mother of all took notice and resolved to purify the seed of men, as I said before, since Abel had been killed. And she chose this Seth and displayed him in purity and in him alone she put the seed of her power and purity.

3, 1. But again, seeing the great confusion and the disorderly passion of angels and men, through which the two races inter-mingled, and uprisings of the races introduced by their dis-order, the same Mother and female (deity) went and brought on a flood and destroyed every insurrection of all men of the opposing race (Gen. 6: 9 ff.), in order, of course, that the pure and just race deriving from Seth should alone remain in the world, for the institution of the higher race and of the spark of justice. 2. But the angels again evaded her and brought Ham into the ark, who was of their seed. For when eight souls were saved in Noah's ark at that time, they say that seven belonged to the pure race, but one of them was Ham who belonged to the other power, who went in, evading the Mother on high. 3. Now this plan contrived by the angels was effected in this way; when (as they say) the angels learnt that all their seed was to be wiped out in the flood, they cunningly introduced the aforesaid Ham to preserve the race of wickedness created by them. 4. From this there arose forgetfulness and error among men and disorderly impulsions to sin and wicked promiscuity in the world; and so the world returned again to its original state of disorder and was filled with wickedness as it was in the beginning before the flood.

5. But from Seth, from his seed and descending from his race there came the Christ himself, Jesus, not by (human) birth but miraculously appearing in the world; and he is Seth himself, who both then and now visits the human race, being sent from the Mother on high . . .

5, 1. They write certain books under the names of great men; they say there are seven books named after Seth, and some other different books they call Allogeneis; another which they call a Revelation (Apocalypse) takes its name from Abraham and is full of all manner of wickedness; others are named after Moses, others again after other men. 2. And submitting their minds to great foolishness, they say that Seth had a wife named Horaea* (? Norea). . . . 3. For there are other heresies which say there is a power to which they give the name (?) Norea; and this power which the others recognize and call (?) Norea, is said by these men to be the wife of Seth.

THE ARCHONTICS ACCORDING TO EPIPHANIUS

This late form of Gnosis is described by Epiphanius. The books which he reports these men as possessing are in part the same as those of the Sethians. The doctrines are certainly rather different, but are basically similar to those ascribed by Epiphanius to the Sethians. They certainly reject the Christian sacraments, and it is not made clear whether and in what form Christ is recognized in their doctrines. In this case the report of a single Father of the Church

---

* This means 'beautiful', but is probably a mistake for 'Norea', who is mentioned elsewhere as Seth's wife.

indicates how the same direction of thought could lead some to practise libertinism, others asceticism.

Epiphanius, *Panarion* XL 1, 1–8, 2 (in part)

After these there comes the heresy of the Archontics; however, this is not current in many places, but only in the province of Palestine; but they have already conveyed their poison from there as far as Greater Armenia, indeed 2. Lesser Armenia too has been sown with this noxious weed ('tare'; Matt. 13: 25) by an Armenian who visited Palestine in the time of Constantine, shortly before his death; this man was called Eutactus ('orderly'), but was really Atactus ('disorderly') in his way of life; and he learnt this false teaching and then returned home and taught it. 3. In Palestine, as I said, he acquired this snake poison from an old man named Peter . . . who lived in the region of Eleutheropolis and Jerusalem, three miles from Hebron; they call the village Capharbaricha . . . (4–7 omitted).

8. To this old man there came the aforesaid Eutactus (if indeed Eutactus is his right name) who was travelling through from Egypt; he acquired the old man's false teaching, and taking up this harmful stuff as if it were a valuable cargo he brought it to his own native land; for, as I said, he came from Lesser Armenia, from the neighbourhood of Satale. 9. And when he returned to his native land he infected many of the inhabitants of Lesser Armenia and corrupted several rich men and a senator and other respected figures; and through these eminent men he destroyed many in that region. . . .

2, 1. These men likewise have fabricated some apocryphal books for themselves, whose names are as follows: one book they call the Little Symphony, forsooth, another the Great Symphony. And they pile up other books for themselves, being accustomed to add to the pile whatever they read, so as to suggest that all these (books) help to confirm their own error. 2. They also use the books called Allogeneis—for there are books bearing that name. And they take advantage of the Ascension of Isaiah and also some other apocrypha.

3. The whole system can be understood from the book entitled *The Symphony*, in which they say there is an eightfold series (Ogdoad) of heavens, and also a sevenfold one (Hebdomad), and in each heaven there are archons (ruling powers).

One group belongs to the seven heavens, one archon for each heaven, and each archon has ranks (of subordinates), and the radiant Mother is highest of all in the eighth (heaven), as the other heresies also teach.

4. And some of them have polluted their bodies by licentiousness, but others pretend to an affected abstinence and deceive the simpler sort of men by making a show of withdrawal from the world in imitation of the monks.

5. And, as I said before, they say that in each heaven there is an authority, a power, and services of angels, since each archon produced and made a service for himself. And there is no resurrection of the flesh, but only of the soul.

6. They condemn baptism, even though some of them were previously baptized; and they reject participation in the sacraments and (deny) their value, as extraneous and introduced in the name of Sabaoth;[2] for like some of the other heresies they think that it is he who is the dominant power in the seventh heaven and overpowers the others. 7. And they say that the soul is food for the authorities and powers, without which they cannot live, since it derives from the dew which comes from above and gives them strength. 8. And when it acquires knowledge (*gnosis*) and shuns the baptism of the Church and the name of Sabaoth who has given men the Law, it ascends from heaven to heaven and speaks its defence before each power and so attains to the higher (power), the Mother and (to the?) Father of all, from whom it has come down into this world. . . .

5, 1. Now these men say, as I have demonstrated above, that the Devil is the son of the seventh power, namely Sabaoth. And Sabaoth they say is the god of the Jews, but the Devil is an evil son of his, and being from the earth he opposes his own father. 2. And his father is not like him, nor again is he the incomprehensible god whom they call the Father, but he belongs to the left-hand power. 3. Another myth is related by these folk; the Devil, it says, came to Eve and had intercourse with her as a man does with a woman, and begot with her Cain and Abel. 4. On this account one rose up against the other, because of the jealousy they felt for one another, not because Abel pleased God at all, as the truth relates, but they invent

---

[2] Sabaoth = Zebaoth.

another tale which they tell; it says, since they both were in love with their own sister, for this reason Cain rose up against Abel and killed him. For they say that they were natural offspring of the Devil's seed, as I said before. 5. And when they wish to deceive men, they produce evidence from the Holy Scriptures, as I have described in the case of another heresy: the Saviour said to the Jews, 'You are from Satan' and 'When he speaks a lie, he speaks from his own, for his father also was a liar'—in order, of course, to show that Cain came from the Devil, since he has said, 'He has been a murderer from the beginning' and 'He is a liar, for his father was a liar' (John 8: 44), in order to show that his father was the Devil, and the Devil's father is the archon who is a liar, whom the foolish ones, bringing blasphemies upon their own heads, identify with Sabaoth . . .

7, 1. Again, the same persons say that Adam had intercourse with his own wife Eve and begot Seth, his own natural son. And then they say that the power from on high came down together with the angels who serve the good god 2. and caught up Seth, whom they also call Allogenes, and carried him up to some higher sphere and cared for him for some time, so that he should not be killed; and after a long time they carried him back again to this world and made him spiritual and invisible (?), so that the Demiurge had no power over him, nor yet the powers and authorities of the (same) god who made the world. 3. And they say that he no longer served the maker, the Demiurge, but had knowledge of the unnameable power, the good God who is above, and served him and gave many revelations discrediting the maker of the world and the authorities and powers. 4. Hence they have composed books written in the name of Seth, saying that these were given them by him, and others bearing the name of Seth and of his seven sons. 5. For they say that he begot seven sons called Allogeneis, as we have described in the case of other sects, namely the gnostics and Sethians. 6. And these men also say that there are other prophets, one Martiades, one Marsianus, who were caught up into heaven and three days later came down. . . .

8, 2. The body (of Christ) which was not real, but merely was seen as an appearance, as these men again affirm . . .

THE SETHIANS ACCORDING TO HIPPOLYTUS

A completely different account of the Sethians is set down in Hippolytus. Like that of the Naassenes and of the Peratae, its point of departure is a threefold system of light, darkness, and pure spirit in between. The spirit is not conceived as a gentle current of air, as might be suggested by the Greek word, which means 'blowing' or 'breathing', but is to be conceived as a fragrance which, apparently, has nothing material about it. These three powers are at rest so long as they remain by themselves. But they collide; and from the collision there arise heaven and earth and the manifold living creatures. In this process the darkness, realizing that without light and spirit she would remain alone and powerless, keeps fast hold of the sparks of light and of spirit that she received in the collision. The fact that darkness is active and cunning, and not merely a material substance without qualities, distinguishes this system from those just described. The Sethians therefore have no need of a 'fourth being'; on the other hand, they cannot speak of the pneumatic, psychic, and earthly (choic) elements descending upon a single man. The darkness, which in further speculations is identified with the water and the serpent, produces a son who as regards his essential nature is not her son, namely Nous (mind), who is a small separated particle of the light and the spirit. He cannot win salvation for himself. To deliver him, the Logos of the light makes himself like Nous, that is to say, like him he is born of a virgin in the uncleanliness of the maternal womb and 'looses the pangs of darkness'. Yet he must still drink 'the cup of living water'.

An allusion to Seth, however, is to be found in this presentation also, as evidenced by the biblical triads, which are introduced here as a proof of the triadic structure on which the system is based; and these include a reference to Cain, Abel, and Seth.

Every element of a mixture has its own proper place, and seeks to separate from the mixture and return to it. So the adherent of this system must first study its doctrine of mixture and intermingling, which the Sethians explain with a variety of examples. This is a point of contact between their system and that of Basilides.

This is Gnosis in the full sense of the term, dominated by a strict dualism of light and darkness, and with the fall of the 'particles of light' based on the spatial proximity of light and darkness. The particles of light cannot deliver themselves; a figure from the world of light, who is indeed connected with it but has an individual name, must descend in order to bring salvation. Numerous images are used to explain and confirm this doctrine; and there is probably some allusion to a sacrament.

Hippolytus, *Ref.* V 19, 1–22, 1

19, 1. Let us now see what the Sethians say. They think that the universe has three clearly defined principles, and each principle has an infinite number of powers. When they speak of 'powers' the listener may reckon that their meaning is this: everything that you conceive by thinking, or fail to conceive and ignore, is something that each principle is naturally able to become, as is the case in the human soul with every single art that is taught; 2. for example, he says, this child will become a flute-player if he spends time with a flute-player, or a geometer, if he (attends) a geometer, a grammarian, if a grammarian, a mason, if a mason; and the like will happen with any of the other arts if he has contact with them. But the essential natures of the principles, he says, are light and darkness; and in between these is a pure spirit. 3. But the spirit, which is placed in between the darkness which is below and the light which is above, is not a spirit like a puff of wind or a gentle breeze that can be observed, but it is like a scent of myrrh or of compounded incense, a subtle power which penetrates with inconceivable fragrance better than words can describe. 4. But since the light is above and the darkness below, and between them, as I said, the spirit which is of this kind, and since the light, like a ray of the sun, was such as to shine from above on the darkness below, and again the fragrance of the spirit, which is situated between them, extends and diffuses everywhere, just as we have experienced the fragrance of incense-offerings on the fire diffusing everywhere 5. — since this is the power of the (elements) divided into three, the power of the spirit and of the light is present together in the darkness that is situated below them. But the darkness is a dreadful water, into which the light, together with the spirit, is drawn down and transferred into this element. 6. Now the darkness is not without intelligence, but cunning in all respects, and it knows that if the light is taken away from the darkness, the darkness remains deserted, dark, without light, without power, inert, and feeble. So it exerts itself with all its cunning and intelligence to keep in its possession the brilliance and the spark of light with the fragrance of the spirit.

7. A natural image of all this can be seen in the human face: the pupil of the eye, which is dark from the waters that underlie

it, but illuminated by the spirit. So as the darkness seeks to possess the brilliant light, so that it may have the spark (of light) at its service and (be able to) see, in the same way the light and the spirit seek to possess their own power; and they hasten to remove and recover for themselves their own powers that have been mingled with the dark and dreadful water that lies beneath. 8. And all the powers of the three principles, which are infinitely infinite in number, are each of them rational and intelligent as regards their own essential nature. And being innumerable in quantity and rational and intelligent, when they remain by themselves they all are at rest; 9. but if one power approaches another, the unlikeness of the contact produces a movement and an energy which takes its form from the movement according to the impact of the converging powers. 10. For the impact of the powers takes place like the stamp of a seal which is struck out by impact so as to resemble the man who (or, 'stamp which') stamps out the substances presented. So since the powers of the three principles are infinite in number, and innumerable impacts result from the innumerable powers, there have necessarily come into being the images of innumerable seals. These images are the forms ('ideas') of the different living creatures. 11. So from the first great impact of the three principles there has come a great form of a seal, namely that of heaven and earth. Heaven and earth are shaped like a womb having the navel in the middle. And, he says, if anyone wishes to visualize this shape, let him carefully examine a pregnant womb belonging to any animal he wishes, and he will find the design of heaven and earth and everything in between exactly laid out. 12. Now the shape of heaven and earth came to resemble a womb at the first impact; but further, in between heaven and earth innumerable impacts of powers have occurred; and each impact produced and stamped out nothing else but the seal of heaven and earth resembling a womb; and in it there sprang to life, from the innumerable different seals, the innumerable multitudes of living creatures. 13. And into all this infinite number which exists under heaven in the different living creatures there is inseminated and distributed, together with the light, the fragrance of the spirit.

Now from the water there has come, as a first derivative principle, a fierce and violent wind which is the cause of all generation. For by making a turbulence in the waters it raises swelling waves from them; 14. and the generation of the waves, as if it were some urge to swell in pregnancy, is the origin of man or of the mind, whenever it is stirred to excitement by the urging of the spirit. But when this swelling wave, which is aroused from the water by the wind and made nature swell in pregnancy, receives in itself the offspring of a female being, it holds fast the light which is inseminated from above with the fragrance of the spirit; 15. and this is the mind which takes form in its different patterns. And it is (a) perfect god, brought down from the unbegotten light above and from the spirit, (and put) into human nature as into a temple which is begotten from water by the impulse of nature and by the movement of the wind, and which is compounded and intermingled with bodies, being like salt among changing things and like light in darkness (cf. Matt. 5: 13–15), which impatiently seeks to be freed from its bodies and cannot find its release or its escape. 16. For a tiny spark, a detached fragment from the ray of light from above, is intermingled in the variously compounded bodies, and calls out of many waters as—he says—it is said in the Psalms (Ps. 29 (28): 3).[3] So the whole thought and care of the light from above is, how and by what means the mind may be freed from the death of the wicked and benighted body, (and) from the father who is below, who is the wind which in roaring confusion stirred up swelling waves and begot perfect mind as his son, although it is not his own son in its essential nature. 17. For there was a ray coming from above from that perfect light held fast in the dark, dreadful, bitter, filthy water, which is the spirit of light 'rushing' over the water (Gen. 1: 2) . . . (more than two lines are damaged and unintelligible), as can be seen with all living creatures. 18. But the violent and dreadful rush of wind sweeps along like a serpent, borne on wings. From this wind, that is, from the serpent, has come the beginning of generation in the aforesaid manner, when all beings received the beginning of their generation at the same time. 19. Now since the light and the spirit, he says, are imprisoned in the unclean and hurtful womb of disorder, into which the serpent enters, the wind of darkness, the first-born of the waters, and produces man, the unclean womb neither loves nor recognizes any other form.

[3] Cf. the Naassenes, Hipp. V 8,15.

20. So the perfect word of the light on high taking the likeness of that beast, the snake, entered into the unclean womb, deceiving it by his likeness with the beast, in order to undo the bonds which are laid upon the perfect mind which is begotten in the uncleanness of the womb by the first-born of the water, by the serpent, the wind, the beast. 21. This, he says, is the 'form of a servant' (Phil. 2: 7), and this is the reason that compelled the Word of God to come down into a virgin's womb. 22. But, he says, it is not enough that the perfect man, the Word, entered a virgin's womb and 'loosed the pangs' that were in that darkness (cf. Acts 2: 24); but after he entered into the foul mysteries of the womb he washed himself and drank the cup of living, springing water, which everyone must needs drink who is to put off the form of the servant and put on the heavenly apparel.

20, 1. This, in brief, is what is said by the champions of the Sethian doctrines. . . . But they say that Moses too confirms their doctrine, when he speaks of 'darkness and murk and storm' (Exod. 10: 22; Deut. 5: 22)[4]—these, he says, are the three words; 2. or when he says that there were three in paradise, Adam, Eve, and the serpent; or when he speaks of the three, Cain, Abel, and Seth, and again of three, Shem, Ham, Japheth (Gen. 6: 10); or when he speaks of three patriarchs, Abraham, Isaac, and Jacob; or when he says there were three days before the (creation of) the sun and moon (Gen. 1: 5–13);[5] or when he speaks of three laws, the prohibitive, the permissive, and the punitive. 3. A prohibitive law is: 'Of every tree in the garden (paradise) you may freely eat, but of the tree of knowledge of good and evil you shall not eat' (Gen. 2: 16 f.). When it says, 'Go out from your land and from your family and come to a land which I will show you' (Gen. 12: 1) this law, he says, is a permissive one; for the man who chooses can go out, the man who does not choose to, can remain. And a punitive law is the one which says, 'Thou shalt not commit adultery, thou shalt not kill, thou shalt not steal' (Exod. 20: 13–15): for each of these misdeeds is assigned a penalty.

4–6. The whole content of their teaching comes from the ancient theologians, Musaeus, Linus, and Orpheus, who especially made known the rites and mysteries . . . (In Phlius

---

[4] Cf. the Docetists, Hipp. VIII 8, 15.
[5] Cf. *Megale Apophasis*, Hipp. VI 14, 2.

there is upon the gates an old man with wings, having his phallus erect, and a woman fleeing from him; the former is entitled *phaos rhyentes*).

7. . . . They say that the name *phaos rhyentes* means the downward flow of light from above. 8. . . . The threefold division seems to be confirmed by the poet, who says, 'The whole is divided in three, each one partaking of honour' (Hom., *Il.* XV 189),[6] meaning that each member of the threefold division has acquired power.

9. And the descent of the light into the underlying dark water here below, and the need to recover and take up from it the spark that was brought down, these things the ingenious Sethians seem to have borrowed from Homer, who says,

Let earth be witness, and broad heaven above
And the down-rushing stream of Styx, the oath
Most great and dreadful for the blessed gods.

(Hom., *Il.* XV 36–8.)[7]

that is to say, the gods according to Homer think water to be something ill-omened and frightful, whereas the Sethians' doctrine says it is dreadful for Nous, the mind.

21, 1. This and the like is what they say in innumerable books. And they persuade those who become their disciples to study the doctrine of infusion and mixture, which has been elaborated by many (writers) including Andronicus the Peripatetic. 2. Now the Sethians say that the doctrine of infusion and mixture is constituted as follows: the ray of light has been infused from above and the tiny spark is finely intermixed with the dark waters below and united with them and turned into a single mass, like a single perfume arising from the many spices thrown upon the fire; 3. and the expert, who has a keen sense of smell, must acutely distinguish from the single perfume each of the spices which are mixed together upon the fire, such as storax, myrrh, frankincense, or whatever else is mixed in. 4. And they make use of other illustrations, saying that bronze is mixed with gold, and that a method has been invented for separating bronze from gold. Similarly if tin or bronze or the like is found to be mixed with silver, these too can be separated by a method which overcomes the mixture. 5. Someone indeed

[6] Cf. the Naassenes, Hipp. V 8, 3.   [7] Cf. the Peratae, Hipp. V 16, 3.

actually separates water which is mixed with wine. In the same way, they say, everything that has been compounded is separated. Indeed, he says, you may realize this from animals. For when an animal is dead all (its elements) are separated, and at their parting the animal disappears. This, he says, is the saying, 'I came not to bring peace on earth, but a sword' (Matt. 10: 34), that is, to divide and put apart what is compounded. 6. For everything that has been compounded is divided and separated, finding its own place. For just as there is a single place for all animals where they are compounded, so there is a single one fixed for their dissolution, which no one knows, he says, except only ourselves, the regenerate, who are spiritual, not carnal, whose 'citizenship is in heaven' above (Phil. 3: 20). . . . 8. For, he says, everything that is compounded, as aforesaid, has its own place and runs to its proper (counterpart), as iron does to the magnet, or chaff that is near amber, or gold (drawn) by the sea-ray's sting.[8] 9. So the ray of light that is mixed with the water, when it receives its proper place by instruction and learning, presses towards the Word that came from above in the form of a servant, and with the Word becomes a Word in that place where the Word is, more than the iron does to the magnet. And to prove that this is so, and that all compounded things are separated in their proper places, attend to this: 10. There is in Persia, in the city of Ampe on the Tigris, a well; and next to the well there is built up a cistern with three outlets from it. A man draws from the well with a bucket, raises what is drawn from the well, whatever it is, and pours it into the nearby cistern; and when what is poured in comes to the outlets, (though it was) drawn up in a single vessel, it is separated; 11. and at one (outlet) rock-salt appears, at another outlet asphalt, and at the third oil. And the oil is black, as (he says) Herodotus reports, and gives off an acrid smell; and the Persians call it rhadinace. 12. This illustration of the well, say the Sethians, would suffice to prove their case better than anything that has been mentioned.

22, 1. The Sethians' doctrine, we think, has been adequately explained. But if anyone wishes to acquaint himself with the whole of their system, let him read the book entitled *The Paraphrasis of Seth*; for there he will find all their secrets set down. . . .

---

[8] Cf. the Peratae, Hipp. V 17, 9 f.

19

SYSTEMS INVOLVING THREE PRINCIPLES VI THE DOCETISTS

INTRODUCTION

In the case of the Docetists, once more it is only Hippolytus who provides any information. The initial point, involving the seed of a fig-tree, is not really clear; but in any case three Aeons are derived from the seed of the fig-tree, each of which perfected himself through ten Aeons, so that in all there are thirty Aeons in existence. They are different in power, but not in essence. The first, whose place was nearest to God, drew his measure ten times, the second six times, the third, who was at an infinite distance from the other two, drew his own measure only three times.[1] All three are bisexual Aeons who combined to beget the Saviour from the Virgin Mary as their joint offspring. All the Aeons have innumerable prototypes of living creatures within them; all of them are light.

Now the light shone upon the chaos that lay below it. This has not been previously described; it is something that has no substantial reality. However, chaos received the prototypes by way of the third Aeon, held them fast below, and set fast herself. The third Aeon did not long allow the darkness to hold fast the characters of light, but laid down a firmament, the vault of heaven, beneath the Aeons, so that not all the characters of the Aeons would be held fast by the darkness. From the pattern of the Aeons themselves there came into being a 'living fire', from which came the 'Great Archon', the Lord of the Old Testament, who being without substance has darkness as his substance and insults the characters, prototypes, or ideas of the light that have come from above. The Son created by the Aeons now made himself small, so as not to alarm the prototypes or ideas, assumed the body formed from the Virgin Mary, and received in baptism the replica of that body, so that when the Archon condemned his own creation to death on the cross, he might put off this second body and yet not be found naked.

[1] Plutarch (*De Iside et Osiride* 47) reports that Oromazdes expanded himself to thrice his original size.

All possible prototypes or ideas deriving from the thirty Aeons of the three (original) Aeons are kept in this world, and each according to his own nature can understand Jesus, who derives from all the Aeons; but each of them can only understand him in part, until the time of the Docetists, who derive from the central and supreme Ogdoad, and understand him entirely. However, this Ogdoad, or 'eightfold series', is evidence of a separate line of speculation.

This is a 'Gnosis' resembling that of the Sethians with the exception that chaos is expressly said to be outside the three light-Aeons, and its origin and consistency remain obscure. It seems that it has no substantial reality. Yet it received the 'prototypes' from the three Aeons and thereby 'set fast'—does that mean that it obtains substantial reality through this process? The prototypes or ideas are held fast here (in this world) by the God of the Old Testament through reincarnation. It is not clear how the redeeming work of the Saviour is achieved in detail. At all events this sect also maintains that each soul is predestined by nature as regards the extent of its awareness of him. The majority have only a partial awareness of him, and only the Docetists possess it in full. The souls' full or partial awareness of the 'Son' is apparently the fact on which their eternal destiny depends.

Hippolytus, *Ref.* VIII 8, 2–10, 11

8, 2. . . . Those who called themselves Docetists, laying down the following doctrines: 3. The first God is like the seed of a fig-tree, which is extremely small in size, but infinitely great in power, innumerable in number, self-sufficient for generation, the refuge of the fearful, the shelter for the naked, the covering of shame, the looked-for fruit, for which, he says, the man who looked for it came three times and did not find it; for which reason he cursed the fig-tree, he says, because he did not find that sweet fruit upon it, the looked-for fruit (Matt. 21: 18 f., etc.). 4. Now since, in their view, God is of such a kind, as far as images describe him, and of such a magnitude, both minute and extremely large, the world, as they suppose, came into being in the following manner: when the branches of the fig-tree became tender there came forth leaves, as can be seen, and there followed the fruit, in which the infinite and innumerable seed of the fig-tree is stored up and preserved. 5. We hold that there are three things that were first produced by the seed of the fig-tree; the trunk, namely the fig-tree, the leaves, and the fruit, the fig (itself), as we have already related. So, he says, three

Aeons have come into being, three principles of the universe deriving from the first principle. And this, he says, was not left unremarked by Moses either when he said that the words of God are three, 'darkness, murk and storm, and he added no more' (Exod. 10: 22; Deut. 5: 22).[2] 6. For, he says, God added nothing to the three Aeons, but they provided everything for all that came into being, and do provide it. But God himself remains by himself, being far removed from the three Aeons.

When these Aeons began to come into being, he says, as has been described, (each one) gradually increased and became great and grew perfect. 7. But perfection, they think, is the number ten. So when the Aeons had become equal in number and perfection, as they suppose, thirty Aeons came into being in all,[3] each one of them being complete in a decad (*or* 'ten'). Now they are distinct from one another, and the three have the self-same honour among themselves, (but) differ only in position, in that one of them is first, another second, another third. 8. But their position produced in them a difference in power; for the one who had his position nearest the first God, the seed as it were, obtained a more fertile power than the others, since he, who is unmeasurable, measured himself ten times in magnitude. But the one who was placed second after the first, comprehended himself, the incomprehensible, six times. And the one who came third in position, removed by an infinite distance through the increase of his brothers, conceived himself three times and bound himself as a sort of eternal bond of unity. 9, 1. And this, they think, is what the Saviour said: 'The sower went out to sow, and that which fell on the fair and good land made, one a hundred, one sixty, one thirty.' And, he says, this is the reason why he said, 'He who has ears to hear, let him hear' (Matt. 13: 3, 8 f.), since these things are not (fit) hearing for all. 2. All these Aeons, both the three and the infinitely infinite (number which derive) from them, are all bisexual Aeons. So when they increased and became great, and all of them, from that one first seed which is their harmony and unity, all became a single Aeon together at their own centre, they all begot as their joint offspring from the Virgin Mary the Saviour of all who is in the middle region,[4] who in all respects has the same power as the

[2] Cf. the Sethians, Hipp. V 20, 1.   [3] Cf. Valentinianism.
[4] Cf. Valentinianism: the 'common fruit'.

'seed of the fig-tree', except that he is begotten, whereas that first seed from which the fig-tree came is unbegotten.

3. Now when those three Aeons were equipped with all virtue and all sanctity, as these men in their teaching suppose, and that child—the only-begotten, for he alone was born to the three infinite Aeons of a three-fold (stock); for three immeasurable Aeons begot him in harmony of will—the whole intelligible nature was equipped with nothing lacking, and all those intelligible and eternal beings were light, but a light that was not formless or inactive or, so to speak, in need of some further agent; but it contained—according to the number of the infinitely infinite (Aeons?), as the example of the fig-tree (suggests)— an infinity of patterns ('ideas') of the multifarious living creatures that are there, and it shone from above upon the chaos that lay below. But this (chaos), being illuminated and given form by those multifarious patterns from above, set fast and received all the patterns from above from the third Aeon, the one who tripled himself. But this third Aeon, seeing his own characters all held fast together in the underlying darkness below, and knowing well the power of the darkness and the simplicity and generosity of the light, did not for long allow the characters of light from above to be drawn down by the darkness below, 5. but he laid down beneath the Aeons a firmament of heaven below and 'made a division between darkness and light, and he called the light day, that (light) which was above the firmament, and the darkness he called night' (Gen. 1: 4f., 7).

6. Now as all the infinite patterns of the third Aeon, as I said, were held fast in this lowest darkness, there is also the imprint of this Aeon impressed upon it with the rest, (that is,) living fire coming from light;[5] and from this there came the great Archon (ruler), of whom Moses says, 'In the beginning (or "with authority"?) God made heaven and earth' (Gen. 1: 1). 7. Moses calls him a fiery God who spoke from the bush (Exod. 3: 2), that is, from the murky air—for *bátos* (bush) means all the air that is subjected to darkness; and Moses, he says, called it *bátos* because all the patterns of light from above crossed over it making the air their crossing-place (*batós*). 8. And the Word, equally, is recognized by us from the bush; for the sound which

---

[5] Fire as an antithesis to light: see Poimandres, and Valentinus in Hipp. VI 32, 8, also Cl. Al., *Exc.* § 38, 1.

signifies the word is reverberating air, and without it a human word is not perceived. And not only does the Word legislate for us from the bush, that is the air, and accompany us, but also scents and colours display to us their own powers through the air. 10, 1. Now this fiery God, the fire that came from light, has made the world just as Moses describes; who is himself without solid reality, having darkness as his substance, and always insults (or 'maltreats') the eternal characters of light which (have come) from above (and) are held fast here below. Therefore until the manifestation of the Saviour, there proceeds from the God of fiery light, the Demiurge, great error among the souls; for the ideas are called souls because they have cooled down from their higher forms[6] and continue in darkness, passing from one body to another and guarded by the Demiurge. 2. The truth of this, he says, can be proved from Job, who says, 'I am a wanderer, passing from place to place and from house to house' (Job 2: 9d LXX, not in English versions) and from the Saviour, who says, 'And if you will receive it, this is Elijah who is to come. He who has ears to hear, let him hear' (Matt. 11: 14 f.). But from the Saviour onwards reincarnation has been brought to an end, and faith is proclaimed for the remission of sins, in some such manner as follows.

3. That only-begotten Son, seeing the patterns of the Aeons above coming from above and being passed about among the dark bodies, willed to come down and save them. And knowing that not even the Aeons can endure to behold in its entirety the fullness (plērōma) of all the Aeons, but they, the incorruptible ones,* in terror succumb to corruption, being overcome by the grandeur and glory of (the) power, he contracted himself like a lightning-flash in a minute body, or rather as the light of the eye, enclosed beneath the eyelids, reaches as far as heaven and when it has touched the stars which are there† contracts itself again beneath the eyelids when it wills; 4. and the light of the eye, though it does this and goes everywhere and becomes all things, is invisible to us, and all we see is the eyelids, the white

---

[6] Play on words: soul = *psychē*, cold = *psychrós*.

---

* Or, as MS., 'whereas corruptible beings', etc.
† German: 'heaven and the stars, when it has touched all that, contracts', etc.

corners, the membranes, the iris with its many folds and many layers, the hornlike outer coat, and beneath this the pupil which is shaped like a berry, net-shaped, disc-shaped, and whatever other outer coats there are for the light of the eye in which it is clothed and hidden. 5. So, he says, the eternal only-begotten Son from on high clothed himself with each Aeon of the third Aeon and taking the number of thirty Aeons he came into this world, being so great* as we have said, invisible, unknowable, without honour, without credit.⁷ 6. So then, say the Docetists, in order that he should clothe himself with the outer darkness— meaning the flesh—an angel who accompanied him from above brought the gospel (i.e. good news) to Mary, he says, as it is written (Luke 1: 26 ff.). 7. And her offspring was born, as it is written; and when it was born, then he who came from on high clothed himself with it, and did everything as it is described in the Gospels. He washed himself in Jordan: he washed himself receiving the type and imprint in the water of the body born from the Virgin, so that when the Archon condemned his own creation to death, to the Cross, that soul which had been trained within the body should put off the body and nail it to the Cross, and through it should triumph over authorities and powers (Col. 2: 14 f.); and (yet) should not be found naked, but should put on the body which was imprinted in the water, when he was baptized, instead of that flesh. 8. This, he says, is what the Saviour says, 'Unless a man be born of water and spirit, he shall not enter the kingdom of heaven; for what is born of the flesh is flesh' (John 3: 5 f.). And from the thirty Aeons he put on thirty forms ('ideas'); for this reason that eternal one was thirty years on the earth, each Aeon being disclosed in a form (for each) year.

9. But from each of the thirty Aeons all the forms are held fast here below as souls, and each of them possesses a nature so as to know Jesus who is according to (their) nature, namely he whom the eternal Only-begotten (coming) from the eternal places put on. But these (places?) are different. 10. This is the reason why so many sects contentiously seek after Jesus, and he belongs to them all, but appears as different to the different

---

⁷ Cf. Hipp. V 8, 18; 9, 21, the Naassenes.

---

* Or 'of such an age', viz. 30; cf. 8.

sects from the different places towards which, he says, each heresy tends, and presses on, thinking that this alone is he who is her own kinsman and fellow citizen, whom alone when she saw him first she recognized as her own brother, but the rest are spurious. 11. Now those who derive their nature from the places below cannot see the forms of the Saviour that are above them, but those (who derive) from above, he says, from the Decad that lies midway and from the Ogdoad that is supreme—from which we ourselves come, they say—these men understand Jesus the Saviour not in part but in full, and they alone are the perfect ones from above: but all the rest (understand him only) in part.

20

LIBERTINE GNOSTICS

We have omitted an important section of Irenaeus' long account of Valentinus, namely the one in which he describes the libertinism of the Valentinians. The reason for this was that the account of it given by this Father of the Church does not correspond with the rest of his account of Valentinus' brand of Gnosis. For (according to this) the man who is 'harnessed in change' with the psychics cannot do and omit whatever he likes. Nor can any libertinism be recognized in the Letter of Ptolemaeus to Flora, in the central section of the *Excerpta ex Theodoto*, or in the fragments of Heracleon's Commentary on John. Irenaeus himself allows us to infer that he is not simply describing the common doctrines of ordinary Valentinians, for he refers to the 'most perfect among them', and so to a mere group, and also mentions some who initially lived with their wives as with sisters, and so provides evidence also of ascetic modes of life. It is indeed not at all certain whether he himself has Valentinians exclusively in view, or whether he is here speaking more generally. But he undoubtedly does revert to Valentinian doctrines in conclusion, in order to proceed from them to his other pronouncements about Valentinus.

Irenaeus, *Adv. Haer.* I 6, 3 f. (continuation of the passage translated on p. 139)

For this reason the most perfect among them freely practise everything that is forbidden. . . . For they eat food that was offered to idols with indifference, and they are the first to arrive at any festival party of the gentiles that takes place in honour of the idols, while some of them do not even avoid the murderous spectacle of fights with beasts and single combats, which are hateful to God and man. And some, who are immoderately given over to the desires of the flesh, say that they are repaying to the flesh what belongs to the flesh, and to the spirit what belongs to the spirit. And some of them secretly seduce women who are taught this teaching by them; since frequently women who were deceived by some of them and then returned to the Church of God confessed this fact along with the rest of their error. And some, openly parading their shameless conduct, seduced any women they fell in love with away from their husbands and treated them as their own wives. Others again who initially made an impressive pretence of living with (women) as with sisters were convicted in course of time, when the 'sister' became pregnant by the 'brother'. 4. And while they carry on many other foul and impious practices they slander us, who through fear of God guard ourselves against sins even of thought and word, saying we are simple-minded and know nothing; while they give themselves a superior dignity and call themselves 'perfect' and 'an elect seed'. For they say that we receive grace on loan, and for this reason it will be taken away; but they have grace as their own possession, which has come down from above with them from the unutterable and unnameable Conjunction (*syzygy*); and for this reason it will be increased for them (Mark 4: 24 f.). Therefore they must always in every possible way practise the mystery of Conjunction. And they persuade the simple folk of this, pronouncing these very words: 'Whoever is in the world and has not loved a woman so as to possess her, is not of the truth, and will not attain truth; but he who comes from the world and is possessed by a woman will not attain truth because he was possessed with passion for (*or* "by") a woman.' For this reason they call us 'psychics' and say that we are from the world, and that continence and virtuous conduct are necessary for us, so that by means of them we may arrive at the 'middle region'; but by no means (necessary) for themselves whom they call 'spiritual' (*pneumatikos*) and 'perfect'; for it is not conduct that brings men into the plērōma (fullness, heaven) but the seed which was sent out from it in its infancy and is made perfect in this world.

Clement of Alexandria, *Strom.* VII 17 = § 108, 2 says

Others get their names . . . from the unlawful actions they practice and venture (to perform), like the so-called Entychites of the Simonians.

In another passage, *Strom.* III 4 = §34, 3 f., he says: some others, whom we call Antitactae, say that God is by nature the

Father of us all, and everything that he has made is good. But one of his creatures sowed tares (Matt. 13: 25) by creating the nature of evil, with which he has entangled us all and made us oppose (*antitaxas*) the Father. 4. For this reason we also oppose him in order to avenge the Father, by resisting the will of this second (power). So since he has said 'Thou shalt not commit adultery' (Exod. 20: 14), let us commit adultery, they say, in order to nullify his commandment.

In several passages he has occasion to speak of a certain Prodicus; he says of him (*Strom.* I 15 = §69, 6): The Persian Zoroaster, the Magian, was emulated by Pythagoras, and those who follow the heresy of Prodicus boast that they possess apocryphal books written by this man.

A further account is given in *Strom.* III 4 = §30, 1:

Similar teaching is given by the (adherents) of Prodicus, who falsely style themselves gnostics and say that they are by nature sons of the first God; and profiting by their noble descent and their freedom they live as they will; and their will is to be rid of domination, and in their love of pleasure they consider that they are Lords of the Sabbath and superior to every race of men as Kings' children; and unwritten law, they say, is King . . . 2. What they do, they do as wretched slaves, for they commit adultery only in secret.

A little later Clement discloses that they feel themselves to be in the world that is 'strange' to them (*Strom.* III 4 = §31, 3), and in *Strom.* VII 7 = §41, 1 he says:

At this point I am reminded of the doctrines introduced by certain heterodox teachers, namely those who belong to the sect of Prodicus, (who say) that one must not pray.

THE GNOSTICS DESCRIBED BY EPIPHANIUS

Epiphanius traces the 'gnostics' whom he has often encountered in Egypt to Nicolas, whom he identifies with the almoner of that name (Acts 6: 1 ff.). Before passing to a detailed description of their practices he mentions certain speculations connected with them. He refers to Barbelo, who is in the eighth heaven, which is probably the highest heaven, in which are also the 'Father of the Universe' and Christ, from whom Jesus Christ descended. Whether Barbelo and Prunicus denote the same figure under different names, or whether Prunicus assumes the role enacted by Achamoth or the fallen Sophia in the Valentinian system, cannot now be discovered.[1] The names of the Aeons partly remind one of the Ophites, partly of of the Apocryphon of John and of the Sethians; probably these are names which were taken over from different systems. The gnostics intend to be Christians, for in their view Jesus Christ descended and revealed to men the Gnosis which this sect puts into practice; this, however, is a different form of it from those we have previously examined. Epiphanius introduces two word-for-word quotations, both of which express the same idea: One must collect oneself from every quarter. For the 'soul' is dispersed everywhere; it is in plants and animals exactly as it is in men. The collecting is accomplished by eating. Human beings especially embody the soul in the male semen and the woman's monthly periods; if a child is born, the soul-energy passes over into a new body and is not redeemed. Therefore the semen and the menstrual blood of the female must be consumed; this is the explanation of their perverse practices and 'sacraments'.

Epiphanius, *Panarion* XXV 2, 7—XXVI 13, 7 (Selection)

XXV 2. 1. From this source the (advocates) of Gnosis falsely so called have begun their evil growth upon the world, namely the so-called gnostics and Phibionites and the followers of Epiphanes, and the Stratiotici and Levitici and Borborians and the rest. For each of these has contrived his own sect to suit his own passions and has devised thousands of ways of evil. 2. For some of them glorify a certain Barbelo who they say is above in the eighth heaven, and they say she was produced by the Father; and she is the mother of Ialdabaoth, according to some, of Sabaoth according to others.[2] 3. And her son violently and tyrannously possessed himself of the seventh heaven, and says to those below 'I am the first', he says, 'and he who comes after, and apart from me there is no other god' (Combination of Isa. 45: 5 and 21). 4. And Barbelo heard this saying and wept. And she always appears to the Archons in beauty and takes from them their seed through pleasure (causing) its emission, in order that by so doing she may recover again her own power that was inseminated into those various beings. 5. And so from this basis he has introduced with the world the secret of his own indecent talk . . .

3, 2. Others honour a certain Prunicus and, like the former,

---

[1] See below (XXVI 10, 4) and the Acts of Thomas p. 342.
[2] Cf. Ir. I 29, 1 f. and the Apocryphon of John.

when they indulge their passions have recourse to a myth to give this pretext of their shameful deeds; they say, 'We are collecting the power of Prunicus from bodies by their fluids'— which means the semen and the periods . . . 4. And others glorify the aforesaid Ialdabaoth, saying that he is the first son of Barbelo, as I said; and he (!) says, one must give honour to him, because he made many revelations.[3] 5. Therefore they compose some books in the name of Ialdabaoth, and invent innumerable outlandish names of Archons, as they say, and authorities who in each heaven oppose the human soul . . . 6. Others glorify Caulacau (Isa. 28: 10)[4] in the same manner, giving this name to an Archon . . .

5, 1. Others among them invent new names and say that there was darkness and abyss and water, and the spirit was between them and made a division between them (cf. Gen. 1: 1). But the darkness was hostile and jealous of the spirit; and this darkness ran up and embraced the spirit and engendered, as he says, a so-called Womb[5] which when it was engendered became pregnant by that same spirit (?). 2. And from the Womb four Aeons were produced, and from the four Aeons another fourteen, and there came into being the right (side) and the left, light and darkness. 3. And afterwards after all these there was produced a loathsome Aeon, and he had intercourse with the Womb formerly described; and from this loathsome Aeon and the Womb there originated gods and angels and demons and seven spirits . . .

XXVI 1, 3. These men who are in alliance with Nicolas . . . produce for us certain names without meaning and forge books, one of which they call Noria . . . 4. This Noria is supposed to be the wife of Noah . . . 7. Next, those who profess to us Philistion's doctrines, give us the reason. She often desired to enter the ark with Noah, but was not allowed to, because, he says, the Archon who created the world wished to destroy her with all the others in the flood. 8. And they say she took her seat upon the chest (i.e. ark) and burnt it, both once and again and a third time. Therefore the building of the chest by Noah himself took many years, because it was often burnt by her.[6] 9. For,

---

[3] This is not said of Ialdabaoth elsewhere.
[4] Cf. Hipp. V 8, 4, the Naassenes, and Ir. I 24, 5, Basilides.
[5] Cf. Ir. I 31, 2, the Cainites. [6] Cf. Ir. I 30, 10, the Ophites.

he says, Noah was obedient to the Archon, but Noria revealed the powers on high and Barbelo who came from the powers, who was opposed to the Archon as were also the other powers, and showed that what was taken from the Mother on high through the Archon who made the world and the other gods and angels and demons who were with him must be collected from the power that is in bodies, through the emissions of men and of women.

2, 2. Others of them (the gnostics) . . . introduce a prophet named Barcabbas[7] . . . 4. They bring us a shameful story derived from this extraordinary prophet, so that we may be persuaded to associate with corruptible bodies* . . . 5. Others of them introduce a spurious, paltry work, a composition which they call (the) Gospel of Perfection . . . 6. Others are not ashamed to speak of a Gospel of Eve, calling it after her because she found the food of knowledge through a revelation (given by) the serpent who spoke with her (cf. Gen. 3:1–6).

3, 1. They base their teaching on (lit. 'start from') foolish visions and testimonies in the Gospel which they profess. For they say, 'I stood upon a high mountain and saw a tall man and another (who was) short. And I heard as it were a sound of thunder, and I drew near in order to hear, and he spoke to me and said, "I am thou and thou I, and where thou art, there am I, and I am sown within all things. Whencesoever thou wilt thou collectest me, and collecting me thou collectest thyself."' . . . 3, 6. So that by some they are aptly named Borborians (i.e. muddy, dirty), and others call them Coddians . . . 7. . . . And the same people are called Stratiotici in Egypt, and Phibionites . . . but some call them Zacchaeans, others Barbelites.

4, 1. . . . First, they have their women in common. 2. And if a visitor comes to them who holds the same opinion, there is a sign in use among them, the men for the women and the women for the men; when they stretch out their hand, by way of a greeting of course, they make a tickling stroke beneath the palm of the hand, indicating by this means that the new arrival belongs to their cult. 3. After this recognition of each other they

---

[7] Cf. Eus. *H.E.* IV 7, 7, Basilides.

---

* German: 'To approach (God?) with corruptible bodies.'

proceed at once to a feast; and they serve up lavish helpings of meat and wine, even if they are poor. Then, when they have had their drinking-party and so to speak filled their veins to satiety, they give themselves over to passion. 4. For the husband withdraws from his wife, and says these words to his own wife: 'Rise up, make the love (feast) with the brother.' And when the wretches have had intercourse with each other . . . 5. When they have had intercourse out of the passion of fornication, then, holding up their own blasphemy before heaven, the woman and the man take the man's emission in their own hands, and stand there looking up towards heaven. 6. And while they have uncleanness in their hands they (profess to) pray, the so-called Stratiotici and gnostics, offering to the natural Father of the Universe that which is in their hands, and saying 'We offer thee this gift, the body of Christ.' 7. And so they eat it, partaking of their own shame and saying, 'This is the body of Christ, and this is the Passover; hence our bodies are given over to passion and compelled to confess the passion of Christ.' 8. Similarly with the woman's emission at her period; they collect the menstrual blood which is unclean, take it and eat it together, and say 'This is the blood of Christ.'

5, 1. For this reason when they read in the apocryphal writings: 'I saw a tree which bears twelve fruits each year, and he said to me, "This is the tree of life"' (cf. Rev. 22: 2), they allegorize this to refer to the woman's monthly emission. 2. And while they have intercourse with each other they forbid the bearing of children. For this shameful conduct is pursued by them not for the bearing of children but for the sake of pleasure . . . 3. They have their pleasure, and take for themselves their seed which is unclean, not implanting it for the bearing of children, but themselves eating the shameful thing. 4. But if one of them mistakenly (?) implants the natural emission and the woman becomes pregnant, attend to the further outrage that these men perform. 5. They extract the embryo when they can lay hands on it and take this aborted infant and smash it with a pestle in a mortar, and when they have mixed in honey and pepper and other condiments and spices to prevent them from vomiting, then they all assemble, every member of this troop of swine and dogs, and each one with his fingers takes a piece of the mangled child. 6. And so when they have finished their feast of human flesh, they pray to God and say, 'We have not been deceived by the Archon of lust, but we have retrieved our brother's transgression.' And this they consider the perfect Passover. 7. And they have other outrageous practices. When they are excited to madness they moisten their own hands with the shamefulness of their own emissions and get up and with their own hands thus polluted they pray with their whole bodies naked, as if by such a practice they could gain free access to God. 8. And they tend their bodies night and day, the contemptible objects, both women and men; they anoint themselves, wash themselves, feast themselves, devoting themselves to bedding and drinking. And they curse the man who fasts, saying that it is wrong to fast; for fasting belongs to this Archon who made the world (lit. 'Aeon'). But it is right to take food so that the body may be strong, so that it may bring forth its fruit in due season.

6, 1. They use the Old and the New Testament, but they reject Him who has spoken in the Old Testament. And when they find any saying whose sense can be contrary to them, they say that this was spoken by the spirit of (this) world 2. But if any text can be adapted to make a pattern for their lust . . . they alter it according to their lust and say that it was spoken by the spirit of truth. 3. And this, he says, is what the Lord said about John: 'What went ye out into the wilderness to see? A reed shaken by the wind?' (Matt. 11: 7, etc.). For John, he says, was not perfect; for he was blown upon by many 'spirits' (or 'winds') like the reed that is moved by every wind. 4. And when the spirit of the Archon came, he preached Judaism; but when the Holy Spirit (came), he spoke of Christ. And this, he says, is why 'He that is least in the kingdom of heaven' and so on (Matt. 11: 11, etc.); he spoke of us, he says, because the least among us is greater than he. . . .

8, 1. They possess many books. For they publish certain 'Questions of Mary', and others issue a number of books on the aforesaid Ialdabaoth or in the name of Seth. There are others which they call Revelations of Adam, and they have dared to compose other gospels in the name of the disciples; and they are not ashamed to say that our Saviour and Lord Jesus Christ himself revealed this shameful practice. 2. For in the so-called 'Great Questions of Mary'—for they have composed lesser ones also—they pretend that he gave her a revelation; that he took her to the mountain and prayed and took out a woman from his side and began to have intercourse with her, and so took up his emission and showed it (to her, saying) 3. 'We must do this, that we may live', and as Mary was overcome and sank to the ground, he raised her up again and said to her, 'Why didst thou doubt, O thou of little faith?' (Matt. 14: 31) 4. — and they say that this is what is spoken in the Gospel: 'If I told you earthly things and yet believe not, how shall ye believe the heavenly things?' (John 3: 12). And the text, 'When ye see the Son of Man going up where he was before' (John 6: 62) means the emission which is taken up to the place from which it came, 5. and the saying, 'Unless ye eat my flesh and drink my blood' (John 6: 53), when the disciples were perplexed and said, 'Who can hear this?' (John 6: 60)—they quote this as if the saying referred to indecency, 6. this being the reason why they were overcome and 'went backward' (John 6: 66); for, he says, they were not yet established in the Pleroma (i.e. fullness of life). 7. And when David says, 'He shall be as a tree that is planted by the springs of the waters, which shall give forth its fruit in due season' (Ps. 1: 3), he refers, he says, to the male member (lit. 'shame'). 'By the water-springs' and 'which shall give forth its fruit' refers, he says, to the emission with its pleasure; and 'his leaf shall not fall', because, he says, we do not allow it to drop upon the ground, but eat it ourselves . . .

9, 2. When it says that Rahab fastened a scarlet cord in the window (Josh. 2: 18), he says, this was not a scarlet cord, but the parts of the female nature; and the scarlet cord, he says, is the blood of the periods; and the saying, 'Drink water out of thine own vessels' (Prov. 5: 15) refers to the same. 3. They say that the flesh is to perish and is not to be raised up, but it belongs to the Archon. 4. And the power which resides in the periods and in the semen, they say, is the soul, which we collect and eat. And whatever we eat, be it meat, vegetables, bread, or anything else, we are doing a kindness to created things, in that we collect the soul from all things and transmit it with ourselves to the heavenly world. For this reason they take meat of every kind, saying that it is in order that we may show mercy to our race. 5. And they say that it is the same soul which is implanted in living creatures, —beasts, fishes, serpents, and men, as well as in plants, trees, and fruits. 6. And those of them who are called Phibionites offer the shameful sacrifices of their immorality, which we have already described here, to 365 names which they themselves invented, belonging supposedly to Archons; and they delude their wretched womenfolk, saying, 'Be one with me, that I may present you to the Archon'; 7. and at each union they pronounce the outlandish name of one of their inventions and make as if to pray, saying 'To thee, O X, I present (my offering), that thou mayest present it to Y.' And at the next union he pretends to present (her) likewise to another, in order that he may present (her) to yet another. 8. And until he ascends, or rather descends through 365 falls into immorality, in each case the man who does this invokes a name. And then he begins to come down again through the same (series of names), doing the same shameful actions and deluding the women who are seduced. 9. So when he arrives at the enormous total of 730 falls, that is of immoral unions and of names that they have invented, then the man in question dares to say, 'I am Christ, for I have descended from above through the names of the 365 Archons.'

10, 1. The names of their great Archons they say are as follows, for there are many that they name. In the first heaven is the Archon Iao, in the second he says is Saclas the Archon of fornication, in the third the Archon Seth, in the fourth, he says, is Davides.[8] 2. For they suppose that there is a third and a fourth heaven; and another fifth heaven, in which is Eloaeus, who is also called Adonaeus. In the sixth heaven is, some say Ialdabaoth, but others Elilaeus. 3. And they suppose that there is another, seventh, heaven, in which, they say, is Sabaoth; but others say, No; but Ialdabaoth is in the seventh. 4. In the eighth heaven is the female (power) who is called Barbelo[9] and the Father of the Universe, its Lord, who is also called Autopater ('Self-father'); and another one, Christ, who brought himself to birth, and this Christ is the one who descended and showed men this knowledge, whom they also call Jesus. 5. And he was not born from Mary, but was manifested through Mary. And he has not assumed flesh, unless it be a mere appearance. 6. And some say that Sabaoth has the face of an ass,[10] others, that

---

[8] Cf. the Apocryphon of John 33, 18 and Ir. I 29, 2.

[9] Barbelo also among the Barbelognostics and in the Apocryphon of John.

[10] Cf. the Ophians, Origen, *C. Cels.* VI 26, 30.

of a swine; for this reason, he says, he commanded the Jews not to eat swine. And he is the maker of heaven and earth and of the heavens after him and of his own angels. 7. And the soul as it leaves this (world) passes by these Archons but cannot pass through unless it is in full possession (*pleroma*) of this knowledge, or rather condemnation (*katagnosis*), and being carried (past) escapes the hands of the Archons and authorities. 8. And the Archon who possesses this world has the form of a serpent, and he devours the souls which are not in a state of knowledge and brings them again into the world through his tail, where they are sent into swine and other beasts and brought back up again by the same means. 9. But if, he says, a man attains this knowledge and collects himself from the world through the periods and the flowing-out of desire, he is no longer held fast in this world, but passes beyond the aforesaid Archons. 10. And they say that he comes to Sabaoth and tramples upon his head—such are their impudent blasphemies! —and so passes over into the higher region, where is the Mother of the Living, Barbero or Barbelo, and so the soul is saved. 11. And the wretches say that Sabaoth has hair like a woman, believing that the name Sabaoth denotes a particular Archon . . .

11, 1. . . . Some of them do not consort with women but corrupt themselves with their own hands, and they take their own corruption in their hands 2. and so eat it, using a falsified proof-text, namely, 'These hands were sufficient, not only for me but for those with me' (Acts 20: 34), and again: 'Working with your own hands, so that you may have something to share with those who have nothing' (Eph. 4: 28) . . . 8. For those who corrupt themselves with their own hands, and not only they, but also those who consort with women, since they are not satiated with their promiscuous intercourse with women, are inflamed towards one another, men with men, as it is written (Rom. 1: 27) . . . For these, who are utterly abandoned, congratulate each other, as if they had received the choicest distinction. 9. But those too who seduce the female sex to their obedience . . . say to those who are seduced by them, 'So-and-so is a virgin', one who for so many years has been corrupted and is corrupted every day. For there is no satisfying their licentiousness, but the more infamous a man is in his conduct among them, the more he is honoured among them. 10. And they give the name of 'virgins' to women who have never proceeded with natural intercourse in marriage in physical union so far as to conceive seed, but are constantly copulating and fornicating, but before their pleasure finds its natural outcome let go the wicked corrupter of their intercourse and take the aforesaid indecency to be eaten . . . 11. But from (the time of) their virginity they have practised this art of being corrupted, but not accepting the (full) union and the emission from their corruption.

12, 1. Innumerable other spurious writings have been put up by them. For they say there is a book called 'The Birth of Mary' into which they made outrageous and depraved interpolations, and then say they derive them from it. 2. It was for this reason, it says, that Zacharias was put to death in the temple, because, it says, he saw a vision, and when in his fright he tried to disclose the vision, his mouth was stopped. For, it says, at the time of the incense-offering he saw, as he offered it, a man standing, having the form of an ass. 3. And as he went out and tried to say 'Alas for you, who is it that you worship?', the man who appeared to him inside the temple stopped his mouth to prevent him from speaking. But when his mouth was opened so that he should speak, then he revealed it to them and they put him to death. And so, says, Zacharias met his death (cf. Luke 1 : 5 ff.).* 4. For this is the reason, it says, why the high priest was commanded by the law-giver himself to wear bells (Exod. 28: 33–5) so that when he went in to officiate as priest, the one who was worshipped should hear the sound (lit. 'noise') and hide himself, so that this suppositious† likeness of his form should not be disclosed . . .

13, 1. Those among them who are called Levites do not have intercourse with women, but with each other. And it is these who are actually distinguished and honoured among them. And they deride those who are occupied with civil life and purity and virginity as if they undertook their labour to no purpose. 2. They produce a spurious gospel composed in the name of the holy disciple Philip, saying that 'The Lord revealed to me what the soul must say as it ascends into heaven, and how it must answer each of the higher powers; "I have known

---

* Cf. also Matt. 23: 35.

† German 'the real'; this version substituted after discussion.

myself"'', it says, '"and I have collected myself from every side; I have sowed no children for the Archon, but I have uprooted his roots and I have collected the members that were scattered, and I know who thou art. For I"'', it says, '"am one of those from on high"; and so', it says, 'it is allowed to go'. 3. But, it says, if it is found to have begotten a son, it is held fast here below until it can recover its own children and restore them to itself. 4. And such are their fantasies and romances that they even dare to insult the holy Elias and say that when he was taken up (into heaven) he was cast down again into the world. 5. For there came a (female) demon, it says, and seized him and said to him, 'Where are you going? For I have children of yours, and you cannot ascend and leave your children here.' And (Elias), it says, replied, 'How did you get children of mine, when I lived in purity?' It answered him—it says—'Why, when you were dreaming dreams and often discharged an emission of the body, it was I who received the seed from you and bore you sons.' . . . 7. . . . . For they wish to apply to themselves even more the testimony given against them in the Epistle of Jude when he said, 'These dreamers defile the flesh and despise authority and speak evil of dignities' (Jude 8).

In 17, 4 ff. Epiphanius describes his personal acquaintance with heretics, whom he finally reported to the Bishop; and he expelled them from the city, to the number of some eighty souls.

21

POIMANDRES

INTRODUCTION

Poimandres is a pagan gnostic writing. Jesus does not appear in it as redeemer, but neither does any other redeemer-figure. The 'system' reveals how the tragic situation arose that Man, 'who is immortal and has power over all things, suffers the fate of death, because he lies under Fate'. This system is the call from the other world, and it shows the way to salvation. The whole Tractate as far as § 26 consists of a revelation, bestowed during a state of ecstasy, of the god Poimandres, Nous, the Mind or Thought of the Absolute.

The Tractate begins with a vision of light, which is followed shortly after by a vision of darkness. This darkness is not to be regarded as created by the light; rather it is there, simply later and younger than the light. A 'holy Word' descends upon 'Nature' and divides fire and air from water and earth, which remain undivided. It is noteworthy that this Logos is 'like that in you which sees and hears', but it is not peculiarly gnostic; this thought is later allowed to drop. The seer then sees the light divided into innumerable powers; the divine world consists of 'powers'. The fire is contained by a very great power. What is this? It is the Original Form. Valentinianism also spoke of a Demiurge who formed everything in accordance with the Pleroma, but the point of view here remains somewhat different. The seer then asks where the constituents of Nature came from, and receives the reply: 'From the will of God, who with the Logos . . . copied the beautiful world.' This introduction of a figure feminine in Greek is surprising. The place of this thought in the whole is disputed.

Be that as it may, the God Nous brings forth another Nous, the God of the fire and the Spirit,* and he creates seven Administrators who encircle the visible world, and their activity is called Fate. Neither the creator of these Administrators nor Fate is characterized by any word as evil, again in contrast to gnosticism. Then the first Logos springs up from the lower elements into the pure construction of Nature and is united with the Demiurge-Nous. The lower elements of Nature, that is, water and earth, thus become

* Or: wind (Gk. πνεῦμα).

Logosless. Then the Demiurge-Nous rotated the world, and from the elements of Nature this rotation produced birds and beasts. The Father-Nous then created a Man, who bore his image, and handed over to him his whole creation. The man comes into the sphere of his brother, the Creator-Nous, and obtains a share of what each of the seven Administrators appoints.* Because he wanted to break through the periphery of the circle and learn the power that is over the fire, he stooped through the Harmony of the spheres, and the Nature below smiled when it saw him, and he, when he saw his own image in the water, wanted to stay there; Nature took him, and they were united in love. Because of this Man is divided, mortal because of the body, immortal because of the 'essential Man'. This is the 'fall' of the 'primal man'. It could be called a tragic mistake.

Nature then bore seven men according to the pattern of the seven Administrators, formed from the four parts of Nature. Man from life and light became soul and Nous. Then in accordance with God's will the bond of all things is loosed, male and female are separated from each other, God calls with a holy word, 'Be fruitful and multiply' (Gen. 1 : 28), and Man, who has the Nous, must recognize himself as immortal, and the eros which is the cause of death.

The reason for this appears from §§ 20 and 21: He who loves the body loves what derives from the odious darkness, and goes downwards, while he who recognizes himself (that is, the essential Man) recognizes the Father of the universe from whom the Man arose, and goes upwards.

Not all men have the Nous. He is near the pious and pitiful, but wicked and foolish men are tormented by the demon of vengeance.

Then Poimandres explains how the ascent takes place. The body dissolves into its elements, the individual form disappears, the character is handed over to the demon, and the bodily senses go together with passion and lust into the irrational Nature. Then the ascent through the seven circles is described, circles which formerly were not evil; to each circle what corresponds with it is given back unused. The series of circles corresponds to the Greek arrangement of the corresponding planets. Then the deceased arrives in the Ogdoad and there praises the Father; then they go up to the Father, become 'powers', and come to be 'in God'.

Then when the vision is over and Poimandres has merged with the powers above, the Seer begins a preaching of repentance, with the result that some mock him, while others beg to be instructed. And he becomes guide of the race. In the evening he recites a thanksgiving to Poimandres.

* What each appoints = τῆς τάξεως αὐτοῦ, Ch. 13, pp. 330 f.

Should we here continue to speak at all of Gnosis in the sense in which the term has been used so far? In § 6 the will of God is made responsible for the origin of the world and the soul. But even if we take this passage as an interpolation or as a view accepted by the author which cannot be reconciled with his general viewpoint, and if we thus set this passage aside and depend upon the fact that Nature and God are opposed to each other, a number of striking points still remain. Only two of the elements, water and earth, are reasonless, while the other two elements, at any rate within the seven Administrators, are indeed 'Fate', but this Fate does not enslave, rather is it the destiny of the world; consequently only the bodily love, eros, is evil. The divine in man is 'soul' and 'Nous' and not Nous only (§ 17). The differentiation between sexes in the world, including that of humans, is narrated without comment. The condemnation of the deceitfulness of lust in § 25 is not enough to indicate definite sexual asceticism, and there is no mention of the end of the world.

But account must also be taken of the other side. For one thing, the world goes back to a dualism between God and visible things, which exists without causation at the beginning. It should next be noted that the dominion of the seven powers of Fate over the reasonless 'Nature' is represented as lawful, while the dominion of the circles over men has the consequences described in § 25. A fall of Man brings about the movement of cosmic history; whether therefore the fall is already seen in the acceptance of the gifts of the seven Administrators or only when the Man sees and loves his own image in the water and on the ground, it is certainly a matter of life and death, and knowledge brings salvation, which is the 'essential Man' and the corresponding conduct. Love of the body is not sin, but error and ignorance (§ 28). Poimandres is, moreover, a vision, and the vision is really only the form of the call which teaches Man how he fell and how he can be saved. This call is given in a myth.

More distinct, and less involved with other motifs, is the waking call presented in the seventh Tractate of the *Corpus Hermeticum*, to which the short sentences in Poimandres § 28 offer a clear parallel, so clear that one might postulate a single author. Thus Poimandres and the seventh Tractate of the *Corpus Hermeticum* certainly stand within Gnosis; its hard contours, however, are definitely softened.

Poimandres, *Corp. Herm.* I 1–32

1. Once, when an insight was imparted to me about what is, and my mind was very elevated, my bodily senses being restrained as (with) those who through overeating or hard physical work are in a deep sleep, I thought that a giant of

immense size called me by name and said to me, 'What do you wish to hear and to see and by understanding to learn and know?' 2. I said, 'Who are you?' He said, 'I am Poimandres, the Mind (Nous) of the Absolute. I know what you wish, and I am with you everywhere.' 3. I said, 'I wish to learn what is, and to understand its nature, and to know God. How much', I said, 'I want to hear it!' He in turn said to me, 'Keep in your mind the things you wish to hear, and I will teach you all.'

4. After these words he changed in aspect, and immediately everything became instantaneously clear to me. I saw an immeasurable view, everything is light, (a light) serene and gay, and I loved the sight. Shortly after there was a darkness, tending downwards, following in its turn, frightful and horrible, wound in a coil; it appeared to me like a snake. Then the darkness changed into something moist, unspeakably confused, giving off smoke as from a fire, and uttering an inexpressibly doleful sound. Then an inarticulate cry issued from it, such that I supposed it came from the fire. 5. And from the light a holy Logos (Word) came upon the Nature, and pure fire shot up from the moist Nature to the height. For it was light, quick and vigorous all at once, and the air, being light, followed the spirit, as it ascended from earth and water up to the fire, so that it seemed to me to be hanging from it. But earth and water remained mixed together by themselves, so that I did not see the earth for water. But they were stirred through the spiritual Logos which stirred upon them (Gen. 1 : 2?), so that it became audible (?).

6. Poimandres said to me, 'Have you perceived what this vision means?' And I said, 'I shall (soon) know.' 'That light', he said, 'is I, the Nous, your God, who (was there) before the moisture which appeared from the darkness. The luminous Logos which came forth from the Nous is the Son of God.' 'How?' said I. 'Understand it in this way: What sees and hears in you is the Logos of the Lord, but the Nous is the Father-God. For they are not separated from each other; their union is life.' 'I thank you,' said I. 'Then attend to the light and apprehend it.'

7. When he had said this, he looked at me for a long time, so that I trembled at his aspect. When I looked up, I see in my Nous that the light consists of innumerable powers, and that an immeasurable world had come to be, and that the fire was being

contained with very great power and was held under control.
I perceived this in thought through the word of Poimandres.
8. But while I was still frightened, he again said to me: 'Have
you seen in the Nous the Original Form, which existed before
the boundless beginning?' This is what Poimandres said to me.
'Whence (then)', said I, 'did the elements of Nature come into
existence?' To this he again replied: 'From the will of God,
which took the Logos and saw the beautiful world and copied
it, and it became the world through its own elements and
through the generation of souls.

9. Nous the God, being bisexual and life and light, brought
forth through the Word another Nous, the Demiurge, who as
God of the fire and the spirit created seven Administrators, who
encompass the visible world in circles; their administration is
called Fate.

10. The Logos of God sprang at once out of the lower elements into the pure creation of Nature and united with the
Creator-Nous. For it was like him. And the lower elements were
left without Logos, so that they were mere matter. 11. Together
with the Logos the Demiurge-Nous who encompasses the
circles and swings (spins) them whirring round, set his creatures
turning, and let them turn from an infinite beginning to a
boundless end. For they begin where they cease. Their circling
motion, as the Nous intended, brought forth from the lower
elements irrational beasts—for they did not have the Logos
(any more)—the air produced birds and the water aquatic
animals. For earth and water were separated from each other,
as the Nous had intended, and the earth brought forth from
itself what it had, quadrupeds and reptiles, wild and tame
beasts.

12. The Father of all, the Nous, who is life and light, bore
a Man who was like him, whom he loved as his own child. For
he was exceedingly beautiful, and wore his father's image.
Even God actually loved his own form and handed over to him
all his creatures. 13. And when he observed what the Demiurge
created in the fire,[1] he himself also wanted to create, and his
Father allowed him. Since he was in the demiurgic sphere, he
who was to have all the power, he observed the creatures of his
brother. And they fell in love with him, and each gave him

[1] Or: 'in the father', as the manuscripts have.

(something) of what he appoints. And having learned their essence and partaken of their nature he wanted to break through the periphery of the circles and apprehend the power of him who is above the fire. 14. And he who had full authority over the world of the mortals and the irrational beasts stooped (down) through the Harmony, breaking open the hollow, and he showed to the Nature below the beautiful form of God. She saw him in his inexhaustible beauty, having in himself the whole power of the Administrators and the form of God, (and) smiled at him in love, inasmuch as she saw the image of the beautiful form of the Man in the water, and his shadow on the ground. But when he saw in her (in the Physis) the form that was like him in the water, he loved it and wanted to inhabit it. At the same time as the will came execution, and he inhabited the irrational form, and Nature took her lover and enfolded him in her embrace, and they were united, for they were in love (with each other)

15. That is why man, unlike all the living things on earth, is twofold: mortal because of the body, immortal because of the essential Man. For he who is immortal and has authority over all things experiences mortality, being subject to fate. He who is up above the Harmony (of the spheres) has become a slave inside the Harmony. Bisexual from a bisexual Father, and unsleeping from an unsleeping Father, he is ruled (by love [eros] and sleep).'

16. Thereafter (I said), 'My Nous, (teach me all), for I love the word.' And Poimandres said: 'This is the secret hidden until this day. For the Nature which was joined to the man produced a wonderful marvel. For whereas he had the nature of the Harmony of the Seven, which I told you are of fire and spirit, Nature did not wait, but immediately gave birth to seven men in accordance with the nature of the Seven Administrators, bisexual and sublime.'

After that (I said), 'O Poimandres, I am now in a great passion and I long to hear; do not desist.' And Poimandres said, 'Be quiet; I have not yet unfolded the first tale.' 'See, I am quiet', said I. 17. 'The origin of these seven took place, as I said, in the following manner. The earth was female, the water male, what came from fire was maturity, from the aether it got the spirit, and so Nature produced bodies in the shape of the Man.

From life and light man became soul and mind, from life the soul, from light the mind. And all the beings of the visible world remained just so until the end of a period and until the beginning of the kinds. 18. 'Hear then the account which you desire to hear. When the period was completed the bond of all things was undone by God's decree. All the beasts, which were bisexual, were together with the man divided, and they became on the one hand male and on the other hand female. And straight away God spoke with a holy word: "Increase and multiply (Gen. 1 : 28) all you things that are created and made. And let Man who has Nous recognize himself as immortal, and the love (eros) which is the cause of death, and everything that is." 19. When he had said this, Providence made the unions through Fate and the Harmony of the spheres and brought about the births, and the universe was filled according to (distinct) kinds; and he that recognizes himself has attained the essential good, but he who loves the body from the seduction of love remains in the darkness, wandering about, sensibly suffering what belongs to death.'

20. 'What great sin do those who are ignorant commit', I said, 'such that they are deprived of immortality?' 'You appear, sir, to have paid no attention to what you have heard. Did I not tell you to take note?' 'I am taking note and remembering and I am also thankful.' 'If you have been taking note, then tell me, why do those who are in death deserve death?' 'Because before their own body there exists the horrible darkness, and from it the moist Nature, and from that the body is constituted in the visible world, and from that death drinks.' 21. 'You have taken good note, sir; but why does he who has recognized himself go to him, as the divine word has it?' I replied, 'Because the Father of the universe consists of light and life, and from him has come the Man.' 'What you say is right. God the Father, from whom the Man came, is light and life. If then you learn that you consist of life and light and that you come from these, you will go back to life.' That is what Poimandres said.

'But still tell me this', said I; 'how I will go back to life, my Nous? For God says, "Let Man who has Nous recognize himself." 22. For do not all men have the Nous?' 'Be quiet, sir. I, the Nous, am near the pious, good, pure, pitiful, reverent ones, and my presence becomes aid, and at once they perceive everything, they propitiate the Father by love, and they thank him with praises and hymns directed towards him in love. Before they hand over the body to its death they abominate the sensations, because they know their effects. Rather I, the Nous, will not allow the bodily activities which press upon them to be fulfilled. Like a good door-keeper I shut the entrances of evil and shameful actions by cutting off the thoughts (of them). 23. But from the foolish, bad, and wicked, the envious, self-seeking, murderers, and impious, I am far away, and make way for the avenging demon, who applies the sharpness of the fire to them and perceptibly tosses about him (who so behaves) and drives him more and more to lawless acts, so that he may get more punishment; and he continually suffers the craving of insatiable desires, incessantly fighting in the dark—he torments this man and heaps fire upon him.'

24. 'You have taught me everything I wished, Nous; but tell me also how the ascent takes place.' To this Poimandres replied: 'First, at the dissolution of the material body you surrender the body to change, and the form you have disappears, and you surrender your character to the demon as ineffectual. And the bodily senses return to their sources; they become separate parts and are compounded again for effectiveness. And passion and desire go into the irrational nature. 25. And so he then goes upwards through the Harmony, and to the first circle he gives the capacity to grow or to diminish, to the second his evil machinations, guile, unexercised, to the third the deceit of lust, unexercised, to the fourth the ostentation of command (?) not exploited, and to the fifth impious boldness and the rashness of audacity, to the sixth the evil urges for riches, unexercised, and to the seventh circle the lurking lie. 26. And then, freed (stripped) of all the activities of the Harmony, he reaches the nature of the Ogdoad with his own power, and with those who are there he praises the Father. Those who are present rejoice together that this one has come, and becoming like those with him he hears also certain powers above the nature of the Ogdoad praising God with a sweet sound. And then in order they go up to the Father, change themselves into powers, and having become powers they come to be in God. This is the good end of those who have obtained knowledge, to

become God. What then are you waiting for? Will you not, as one who has received everything, become a guide to the worthy, so that the human race may by means of you be saved by God?'

27. With these words Poimandres was for me mingled with the powers. But I, giving thanks and praise to the Father of the universe, was sent by him, empowered and instructed about the nature of the universe and about the great vision. And I began to proclaim to men the beauty of piety and knowledge: 'You peoples, earth-born men, who have given yourselves up to drunkenness and sleep and to ignorance of God, sober up, stop being drunk, bewitched by unreasoning sleep.'

28. They heard, and came with one accord. And I said: 'Why, earth-born men, have you given yourselves up to death, when you have power to share in immortality? Repent, you who have travelled in company with error and have made common cause with ignorance. Separate yourselves from the dark light, forsake corruption and partake of immortality.'

29. Some of them made fun (of me) and went away, and (so) gave themselves up to the way of death, but the others threw themselves at my feet and begged to be instructed. But I made them stand up, and became a guide of the (human) race, and taught them how and in what way they will be saved. I sowed in them the words of wisdom, and they were nourished by ambrosial water. And when evening came and the radiance of the sun was beginning to set entirely, I exhorted them to thank God; and when they had completed their thanksgiving they went each to his bed.

30. And I wrote down the benefit done to me by Poimandres, and I rejoiced, being filled with what I desired. For bodily sleep had become a vigil of the soul, the slumber of the eyes a true vision, my silence had become pregnant with good, and the utterance of the word (had brought) new growths of good things. This happened to me because I had received (it) from my Nous, that is, from Poimandres, the Logos of the Absolute. I have come, filled with truth by God's Spirit. Therefore with all my soul and strength I give praise to God the Father.

31. Holy is God, the Father of the universe.
Holy is God, whose will is performed by his powers.
Holy is God, who wishes to be known and is known by his own.

Holy art thou, who by thy word hast constituted what
   exists.
Holy art thou, of whom all Nature became the image.
Holy art thou, whom Nature has not formed.
Holy art thou, who art stronger than every power.
Holy art thou, who art greater than every eminence.
Holy art thou, who art higher than all praise.

Receive rational, pure offerings from soul and heart which
stretch out to thee, thou unutterable, ineffable one whom
silence names. 32. To me, who pray that I may not fall from
the knowledge which accords with our being, grant it and give
me power. With this grace I will enlighten those who are in
ignorance of their origin, my brothers, thy sons. Therefore I
believe and testify: I go to life and into light. Blessed art thou,
Father. Thy Man wishes together with thee to sanctify, as thou
hast granted him all authority.'

Corp. Herm. VII 1–3

1. You men, where are you rushing in your drunkenness, you
who have drained the undiluted doctrine of ignorance, which
you cannot contain, but are already spewing out? Be sober and
stop, look up with the eyes of your heart! And if all of you
cannot, then at least those who can. For the evil of ignorance
is flooding the whole earth and corrupting also the soul
imprisoned in the body, and not letting it reach port in the
havens of salvation. 2. Therefore do not let yourselves be swept
on by the great flood, but use an eddy, you who can reach the
haven of salvation, make port there, seek a guide who will lead
you to the gates of knowledge, where the bright light is, uncon-
taminated by darkness, where not one is drunk, but all are
sober, because they look with their heart at him who wishes
to be seen. For he cannot be heard or spoken of, he cannot be
seen with the eyes, but only with the Nous and the heart.

But first you (singular) must tear up the garment you are
wearing, the fabric of ignorance, the base of evil, the bond of
corruption, the dark wall, the living death, the perceptible
corpse, the grave you carry around with you, the robber
within you, who hates through what he loves and envies
through what he hates. 3. Such is the enemy whom you have
put on (as) a robe, who drags you by the throat downwards

towards himself, so that you may not look up and see the beauty of the truth and the good that lies therein, and hate his own wickedness and perceive his plot which he has laid against you, he who makes insensitive the organs of sense, which are such but are not held to be such, blocking them with much matter and filling them with filthy desire, so that you neither hear what you ought to hear nor see what you ought to see.

22

THE ACTS OF THOMAS

INTRODUCTION

A good example of the gnostic acts of apostles is the Acts of Thomas, probably composed originally in Syriac, though far more manuscripts are preserved of the Greek version. The textual tradition is far from unanimous. Not only do the Syriac and Greek texts show considerable differences, but within both recensions themselves there are great diversities, in part going back to later revisions of the Acts in the interests of ecclesiastical Christianity.

The Acts of Thomas contain no narratives which derive merely from the desire to tell stories, nor are they pure representations of the gnostic myth; rather they are both at once, legend and myth. Moreover, they penetrated wide areas of the Great Church.

Judas Thomas the Twin is the name of the apostle from whom the Acts of Thomas gets its name. The Johannine surname 'the Twin' is interpreted as 'the Twin of Christ'. Thus the foundation is laid for Thomas, while retaining his character as an apostle, to be able to portray the gnostic drama of redemption.

The opening depicts the distribution of the lands between the apostles by lot, and in this way Thomas finds himself directed to India. At first he refuses, but is sold by the Lord Christ to Abbanes, a merchant of King Gundafor (first century A.D.), for three pounds of unminted silver as a slave craftsman. In the second Act both reach India, and Thomas is commissioned to build a palace for the king in a wooded place, for which he is entrusted with money. But he gives it away to all the poor of the neighbourhood. When the king becomes aware of this and wants to put him to a cruel death, the king's brother dies; angels lead him to heaven, where there stands a great building, in which he would like to live, but it is the house that Thomas has built for his brother, the king Gundafor. The brother asks whether he might be allowed to go to the earth to ask the king for permission to live there. This he does, and thereupon the king 'repents', and he asks for and receives the sacrament of 'sealing'. This Act in its first half here outlined is based on the contrast between the visible and perishable and the invisible and imperishable, and ends up as glorification of the life of poverty, free from whoredom, gluttony, and covetousness (§ 28). This transparent allegory of the house-building could also have been framed by a Churchman or *mutatis mutandis* by a cynic-stoic philosopher.

But we have given only a preliminary account of the first Act. Thomas, in company with the merchant, does not immediately reach the royal court, but comes first to a city called Andrapolis, that is, Mancity. From this it is clear that what follows can happen and does happen anywhere and everywhere in the 'world'. Andrapolis, the Mancity, the world, is just keeping a festival, to which all are invited and have to come; he who does not come will be punished by the king (not called Gundafor). So Thomas and the merchant Abbanes go in. He who is in the 'world' must participate in its doings. But how? Thomas, who has come as a stranger, a Hebrew, takes no nourishment; he does not participate in the pleasures of the world. He anoints his nostrils, ears, teeth, and especially his heart, and thereby protects himself from the 'world'. Only a female flute-player, which means according to ancient views a prostitute, was like Thomas a Hebrew, that is, she did not belong to the 'world'. Thomas sings a song in the Hebrew language, a bridal song. A miracle happens, and then the flute-player breaks up her flute; she gives up her career as a prostitute.

Thomas, at the king's invitation, prays for the bridal couple, and then all leave the bridal chamber. But suddenly Jesus himself is present there in the form of Thomas, and recites a speech to the two newly weds in which he speaks of the 'sordid intercourse' and invites them to keep their souls pure for God; then they will as companions of the bridegroom enter the immortal, bright bridal chamber of the world beyond. The recital would set the 'bridal chamber' of the world beyond and its splendour before the eyes, not surely of the newly weds, who could not have understood it, but rather of the readers. The newly weds follow Christ's words, and the king finds them next morning sitting facing each other and the bride with her face unveiled. Questioned about this, she replies that shame and shyness have been taken far away from her. The bridegroom says among other things in a prayer of thanksgiving: 'I thank thee, Lord, . . . who . . . hast shown me how to seek myself and to know who I was and who and how I now am, so that I may again become what I was. . . .' Thus the foundation of Gnosis, as it was explained at the beginning, is expressly stated. The only decision required of the bridal couple is that of continence, for which thoroughly familiar arguments are asserted, and faith in the Lord; in the following passages, too, continence plays the decisive part, and next to it the turning away from wealth and self-seeking.

The third Act is devoted to the raising of a youth whom a dragon has killed. The dragon introduces himself as the son of Satan, as the one who once seduced Eve in Paradise and taught Cain fratricide, who appointed Judas to his work, etc. He is ordered by Thomas to suck out the venom which he had injected into the lad. This happens, and the youth comes to life again, while the dragon dies, and the earth is split with a great fissure, in which the dragon is swallowed up. Thomas, however, orders this fissure to be filled in again and houses to be built over it, so that it may become an abode for 'strangers'. This is a 'type' of the Devil, who will some time come to an end, when he sucks up what he has 'spread' over the creation. But in this way a faith not otherwise represented in Gnosis, in the original and finally restored good of this world, finds expression; it comes to light also in the fact that the snake acknowledges himself as son of the Devil, who hurt and struck the 'four standing brothers'. That cannot refer to anything but the four elements. The youth then gives an account of his experiences in the world of the dead. With emphatic contrast he describes how he was delivered from the darkness and met the light.

With the third Act the Thomas–Abbanes–Gundafor narrative ends.

In the fourth Act an ass's colt carries Thomas as far as the gates of the city, going whithersoever he desires, and then falls down dead, without the apostle raising him again. The event is a figure for the body, which carries man as far as the gates of the heavenly city; then its task is finished, and it is not raised again—a gnostic estimate of the body.

In the fifth Act a woman is afflicted against her will by a demon. He appears to her as a youth, but to her serving-maid as an old man. She asks the apostle to drive away the demon, 'so that I may be free, and collected together in my ancient nature',[1] a prayer that is again gnostic. The demon then gives way, but intends to return when the apostle is no longer near. But the woman asks for the 'sealing', which will protect her from the demon, and she receives it.

In the sixth Act both hands of a youth wither as he receives the eucharist, because he has killed his sweetheart because she was not willing to live together 'purely' with him. The youth has to wash his hands in water over which the apostle has prayed, and then lay them on the one he had killed. She rises from the dead and recounts her journey through the underworld, with its five places where men are punished for their various bad deeds. In view of this the apostle admonishes the people to put off the old man and put on the new man.

With the seventh Act a coherent series of accounts begins, the second part of the Acts, which centres on a king's army commander,

§ 43 = p. 161, 9 f. Bonnet.

his wife, and a series of other persons culminating in the king's consort and her son, all of whom are won over by the apostle. The king is here called without further clarification Misdaios, not Gundafor, an indication that the Acts of Thomas are not from one source. We have here a story of demons and an incident with wild asses, related to the events of the first part and surpassing them. It is a question of the conversion of a number of people to the pure and simple life and the bestowal on them of the sacraments. Only the king Misdaios remains unconverted, and finally arranges that Judas, as Judas Thomas the apostle is called in the second part, should be pierced with their lances by four soldiers, symbols of the four elements. A long time after his death a son of king Misdaios is possessed by a demon and healed by dust from the apostle's grave, whereat the king also repents.

Of special significance are the two hymns which are inserted in two 'Acts', in the first Act the wedding hymn, in the ninth the celebrated song of the Pearl. The former is so worked into the course of events in the first Act that it cannot be removed without extensive reconstruction of the whole story. The song is indeed very beautiful, but the poetic language resists precise interpretation. By reference to the maiden it deals with the (fallen) Sophia, who with the 'Eternals', the pneumatics, goes to the heavenly wedding which Christ has made possible for her. Who the twice seven and the twelve are is scarcely in doubt; they are the seven planets and the twelve signs of the zodiac. That the gnostic understanding of the evil nature of the world, which stands under fate, is thus broken through, we have already seen earlier in the Acts of Thomas.

With the song that is reported in the ninth Act the position is different from the position with that in the first Act. It is possible— apart from the introductory sentence—to separate it from its context without disruption. It is, however, not entirely inappropriate in its setting, in so far as Thomas has there been cast into prison and in the song he describes the homecoming of the king's son, who comes back with the pearl he has won to his father's house; similarly he himself also as the twin of Christ enters the father's house with many redeemed souls. The song celebrates the king's son, who is sent from the world of light in the east to the land of darkness, Egypt, to fetch the pearl which is there beside the devouring dragon. Thus the descent of the Redeemer is described, since he intends to deceive the Egyptians by his unkingly clothing—a thought that also occurs elsewhere in the Acts of Thomas.[2] But nowhere else in the whole Acts of Thomas is it said that the king's son eats the food of the world,

___
[2] § 45 and similarly § 143.

falls asleep, and forgets his mission, and that it is a cry from his homeland which first reminds him of his mission. That is the thought, which in Gnosis is only rarely attested, of the 'redeemed redeemer', the redeemer who himself suffers the fate which those who are to be redeemed have suffered. Manichaeism further enlarged this feature. The boy in Egypt who is 'related' to the king's son is of course Jesus, on whom Christ descends. The shining robe, which he acquires again on his return, and which resembles him, is himself in his deeds. —Does the 'Second', with whom the king's son is to reign in the kingdom after his return, correspond to the 'Living Spirit' in Manichaeism?

It remains to mention—since we cannot here go through the whole Acts of Thomas—certain separate individual passages. These are the passages in which the evil power gives a description of himself and in which the work of Jesus is discussed, and some other scenes in which the sacraments are mentioned and the procedure for celebrating them described with the appropriate prayers, which exhibit more or less clear gnostic characteristics.

In § 31 the 'dragon' is at the same time the place through which one can pass; in § 45 (as already in § 33) 'the enemy' says that he still has time left to carry out his evil will. That time will be over only at the end of the world. In § 167 the 'tax-gatherers'[3] stand at the service of the evil one, as do the 'creditors' or the Devil himself with his children the demons; even if Judas Thomas prays only for the sake of those who are to hear, and in the whole Acts appears as absolutely superior to the power of the enemy, yet this prayer is evidence that the powers whom the ascending one must pass are not simply a nonentity. The prayers of ascent used by the Ophians and the Valentinian Marcus indicate still more clearly the dread of these powers.

The Acts also bring the sacraments to our notice. Three are mentioned: unction, baptism, and eucharist, which apparently follow in that order. The unction and the baptism are unrepeatable; the baptism seems to be merely peripheral, and is apparently of secondary status, which agrees with the absence of any account of separate prayers for it. One may well ask whether it has not been added because of the Great Church. Most important apparently is the seal, through which those who receive it become unassailable by the power of the evil one.[4] In the prayers, the humiliation and contemptibility of Jesus are mentioned, and at the same time his perfect power. Directly gnostic are the three secret words which he is

---

[3] The same image also in Mandeism.
[4] § 46 = p. 163, 8–13 and § 49 = p. 165, 12–17 Bonnet.

supposed to have said to Thomas,[5] and the fact that he came forth from the 'perfect compassion' (that is, from the 'mother'), and that he is called multiform.[6] Further, in both the invocations of the 'mother', §§ 27 and 50, something is also said about Jesus which is typically gnostic. In § 27 'ambassador of the five members' is a formula reminiscent of Manichaeism.[7] In § 50 the 'noble contestant' is reminiscent of a similar formula in the *Excerpta ex Theodoto* § 58, 1. The 'mother of the seven houses, so that thy rest may enter into the eighth house' is no doubt reminiscent of Valentinian speculation, but according to Irenaeus the fallen Sophia first finds the final rest in the Pleroma.[8] The one addressed is the mother who knows the highest mysteries. The holy dove, who hatches the twin chicks, is a speculation which can no longer be understood.

Next to gnostic features others appear which are not gnostic, especially when reference is made to remission of sins.

It is scarcely possible to construct a total system from the Acts of Thomas. But they are important, first because of the form of their narrative, but also because of their numerous allusions to gnostic thought, and probably also because they are a connecting link between Gnosis and Manichaeism.

THE FIRST ACT

1. At that time all of us apostles were in Jerusalem, Simon who is called Peter, and Andrew his brother, James the son of Zebedee, and John his brother, Philip and Bartholomew, Thomas and the tax-gatherer Matthew, James the son of Alphaeus and Simon the Cananaean, and Judas the son of James (Luke 6: 14 f.; Matt. 10: 2–4. Only the names accord with Luke, the characteristics with Matthew), and we divided the regions of the world, so that each one of us should go to the territory which fell to him by lot, and to the people to whom the Lord sent him. In the lot India fell to Judas Thomas, who is also called Twin (John 11: 16, etc.). But he would not go, saying that he was not capable and could not go because of the weakness of the flesh, and, 'I am a Hebrew; how can I go to preach the truth among the Indians?' While he was meditating and saying this, the Saviour appeared to him during the night and

---

[5] § 47 = p. 164, 3 Bonnet, see Gospel of Thomas 13 = 83, 8.

[6] § 48 = p. 164, 15 Bonnet.

[7] The Greek text admittedly has 'elder' but this is a confusion with the similar word for 'emissary'. See W. Bousset, *ZNW* 18 (1917/18), 1–3.

[8] Cf., however, Epiph. XXXI 7, 11 and especially XXVI 10, 4.

said to him, 'Do not be afraid, Thomas; go to India and preach the word there. For my grace is with you.' But he did not obey, but said, 'Send me wherever you want to send me, (but) somewhere else; for I will not go to the Indians.'

2. While he was saying and thinking this, it chanced that a merchant was there, one who had come from India, by name Abbanes, who had been sent by king Gundafor and had received orders from him to buy and bring to him a craftsman. Now the Lord saw him walking in the market-place at midday and said to him, 'Do you want to buy a craftsman?' He said to him, 'Yes.' And the Lord said to him, 'I have a slave who is a craftsman, and I wish to sell him.' And when he had said this he pointed out Thomas to him from far off, agreed a price with him of three pounds of unminted (silver), and wrote a (deed of) sale in these terms: 'I Jesus, son of the carpenter Joseph, declare that I have sold a slave of mine, Judas by name, to you Abbanes, merchant of Gundafor King of the Indians.' As soon as the sale was completed, the Saviour took Judas, who is also called Thomas, and led him to Abbanes the merchant. And when Abbanes saw him, he said to him, 'Is this your master?' And the apostle answered and said, 'Yes, he is my Lord.' But he said, 'I have bought you from him.' And the apostle kept silent.

3. The next day early in the morning the apostle called upon the Lord, prayed to him, and said, 'I go where you will, Lord Jesus. Your will be done.' He went to Abbanes the merchant, and took nothing whatever with him except his purchase price alone. For the Lord had given (it) to him and said, 'With my grace may your purchase price also be with you, wherever you may go.' And the apostle came upon Abbanes as he was carrying his luggage aboard the ship. So he also began to carry (it) with him. But when they had embarked and sat down, Abbanes questioned the apostle and said, 'What work are you skilled in?' And he said: 'In wood, ploughs and yokes, balances, ships and ships' oars, masts, and small wheels; in stone, pillars, temples, and royal palaces.' And the merchant Abbanes said to him, 'We need just such a craftsman.' Thus they began their voyage. They had a favourable wind and sailed in good heart until they reached Andrapolis, a royal city.

4. But when they had disembarked from the ship, they entered the city. And behold, the sounds of flutes (Gk. flute-players),

water-organs, and trumpets sounded round about them. And the apostle inquired and said, 'What is this feast in this city?' The inhabitants said to him: 'The gods have led you also here to be well entertained in this city. For the king has an only daughter, and is now giving her to a husband in marriage. Because of the wedding, therefore, joy prevails, and this popular festival which you have seen is taking place. And the king has sent out heralds to proclaim everywhere that all are to attend the wedding, both rich and poor, slaves and free, foreigners and citizens. And if anyone makes excuses and does not attend the wedding, he will be answerable to the king.' But when Abbanes heard that, he said to the apostle, 'Then let us go, too, so that we give no offence to the king, especially as we are foreigners.' And he said, 'Let us go.' And when they had put up at the inn and rested a little, they went to the wedding. And when the apostle saw that they were all reclining at table, he also took his place among them. And they all looked at him as one who was a stranger and had come from a foreign land. But the merchant Abbanes, as being master, went and reclined in another place.

5. When they ate and drank, the apostle took nothing. Those who were around him therefore said to him, 'Why have you come here, and eat and drink nothing?' But he answered them and said: 'I came here for something greater than food or drink, and in order to fulfil the king's command. For the heralds are proclaiming the king's (orders), and whoever does not listen to the heralds will be liable to the king's judgement.'

As they ate and drank, therefore, and garlands and ointments were brought, they each took ointment and one anointed his face, another his chin, and another other parts of his body. But the apostle anointed the top of his head, and smeared a little on his nostrils, put some drops also into his ears, touched also his teeth, and carefully anointed the parts round his heart. And the garland also which was brought to him, woven of myrtle and other flowers, he took and put on his head, and he took a stick of reed in his hand and held (it) firmly.

But the flute-girl, holding her flutes in her hand, went round everybody and played. But when she came to the place where the apostle was, she stood above him and played her flute over his head for a long time. And that flute-girl was by race a

Hebrew. 6. But while the apostle was looking at the ground, one of the wine-waiters put out his hand and boxed his ear. And the apostle raised his eyes and fixed (them) on the one who had hit and him, said, 'My God will forgive you this wrong in the future world, but in this world he will display his wonders, and I shall presently see that hand which hit me dragged away by dogs.'

And when he had said this, he began to sing and to utter this song:

'The girl (is) a daughter of light; on her rests and abides the proud image of the kings, and pleasing is her aspect, radiating serene beauty. Her robes are like spring flowers, scented fragrance is spread abroad from them. And on her crest sits the King, feeding with his ambrosia (German: *Götterspeise*) those who sit beneath him. Truth rests upon her head, and she makes bliss appear with her feet. Her mouth is opened and (it is) becoming to her. There are thirty-two who sing her praise. Her tongue is like the curtain of a door that is swept aside for those who enter. Her neck lies there as the model of the steps which the first Demiurge created. And her two hands sign and point, proclaiming the chorus of the fortunate aeons, and her fingers point to the gates of the city. Her bride-chamber is light, smelling of balsam and every spice, and giving off a sweet perfume of myrrh and leaves. Spread out within are myrtle twigs and very (many fragrant flowers), and the entrances are adorned with wands of reed. 7. Her (male) bridal attendants have her encircled, seven in number, whom she has herself chosen. And her bridesmaids are seven, who dance before her in chorus. But twelve in number are those who serve before her and obey her, marking and gazing on the Bridegroom, that by his aspect they may be enlightened. And for eternity they will be with him in that eternal bliss, and they will be at that wedding at which the great ones are assembled, and they will attend the banquet of which the eternals are deemed worthy. And they will put on royal robes and dress in bright garments, and both will be in joy and exultation, and they will glorify the Father of all things. His proud light they have received, and they were enlightened by the vision of their Master, and his ambrosial food which never fails they have received. And they drank also of the wine that causes them no thirst and no desire; and they glorified and praised with the living Spirit the Father of truth and the Mother of wisdom.'

8. And when he had sung and finished this song, all those who were present gazed at him. And he was silent. And they also saw his face changed. But they did not understand the things that were said by him, because he was a Hebrew, and what was said by him was said in Hebrew. The flute-player alone understood everything, for she was Hebrew by race. And she went away from him and played for the others, but many times she looked and gazed at him. For she loved him very much, as being a man of the same nation as herself. And he was in appearance more beautiful than all those who were there. And when the flute-player had finished with them all and had played, she sat down opposite him, looking and staring at him. But he looked at no one at all and paid attention to none, but kept his eyes fixed only on the ground, and waited till he might leave.

But that wine-waiter who had punched him went down to the well to draw water. It happened that there was a lion there, which killed him, tore him to pieces, and left him lying there. And dogs straight away took the pieces of him, among them one, a black dog, which seized his right hand with its mouth and carried it into the place of the banquet.

9. When they saw it they were all terrified, inquiring which of them had left. But when it became clear that it was the right hand of the wine-waiter who had struck the apostle, the flute-player broke her flutes and threw them away, and went and sat at the feet of the apostle saying: 'This man is either a god or God's apostle; for I heard him say to the wine-waiter in Hebrew, "I shall presently see the hand that hit me dragged by dogs", which you also have just seen. For as he said, so it has also come about.' And some believed her, while others did not.

But when the king heard these things, he approached and said to the apostle, 'Get up and come with me, and pray for my daughter, for she is the only one I have, and I am giving her away today.' But the apostle refused to go with him, for the Lord had not yet been revealed to him there. But the king led him against his will to the bridal chamber so that he might pray for them. 10. And the apostle stepped forward, and began to pray, and spoke thus: 'My Lord and my God, the companion of his servants, who leads and guides those who believe in him; refuge and rest of the oppressed, hope of the poor and liberator of prisoners, physician of souls that lie sick, and saviour of all creation, who gives life to the world and empowers souls; thou knowest the future things, and dost accomplish them through us. Thou, Lord, art he that discloses hidden mysteries and reveals words that are unutterable; thou, Lord, art he that has planted the good tree, and by thine hands are all good works created. Thou, Lord, art he that is in all things and penetrates through all things; who art present in all thy works and revealed in the activity of all things, Jesus Christ, Son of Compassion[9] and perfect saviour, Christ, Son of the living God, undaunted power that overthrew the foe, and the voice that was heard by the archons, that shook all their powers, ambassador that was sent from the height and reached Hades, thou who hast also opened the doors and led up thence those who were for long times shut up in the treasury of darkness, and hast shown them the ascent that leads up to the height; I pray thee, Lord Jesus, and present to thee a supplication for these young people, that thou do what is helpful to them and profitable and beneficial.' And he laid his hands on them and said, 'The Lord shall be with you.' Then he left them there and went away.

11. But the king asked the bridal companions to come out of the bridal chamber. And when they had all gone and the doors were shut, the bridegroom drew up the curtain of the bridal chamber in order to bring the bride to himself. And he saw the Lord Jesus, who had the appearance of Judas Thomas and was conversing with the bride, (the appearance) of the apostle, who shortly before had blessed them and gone away from them, and he said to him: 'Did you not go out first of all? How did you now come to be here?' And the Lord said to him, 'I am not Judas who (is) also (called) Thomas, but I am his brother.' And the Lord sat down on the bed, and told them also to sit down on the chairs, and began to speak to them:

12. 'Remember, my children, what my brother said to you and to whom he entrusted you. And know this, that if you abstain from this sordid intercourse, you become holy temples, pure and free from afflictions and pains both visible and hidden,

---

[9] i.e. the mother.

and you will not be burdened with cares about life and children, the end of which is destruction. But if you do have many children, for their sakes you become thieves and frauds, beating orphans and getting rich at the expense of widows, and by doing these things you expose yourselves to the severest punishments. For most children become foolish, molested by demons, some openly, and others secretly. For they become either lunatics or half-withered or crippled or deaf or dumb or paralytic or mentally defective. And even if they are healthy, they will again be unprofitable, inasmuch as they do foolish and abominable deeds. For they are caught at adultery or murder or theft or whoredom, and you will be worn out with anxiety by all these things. But if you obey, and keep your souls holy for God, then living children will belong to you, whom these hurts do not touch, you will be free from care, leading an untroubled life without sorrow and care, expecting to enjoy that uncorrupt and true wedding, and at it you will enter together as bridal companions into that bride-chamber full of immortality and light.'

13. But when the young people heard these things they believed the Lord and gave themselves up to him, and refrained from the sordid lust, and remained thus, passing the night in the place. But the Lord had gone out from their presence, after saying to them, 'The grace of the Lord be with you.'

But when morning came the king arrived, laid the table, and brought it in before the bridegroom and the bride. And he found them sitting opposite each other, and he found the bride's face unveiled, and the bridegroom was entirely serene. But when her mother came near, she said to the bride, 'Why are you sitting like that, child, and are not ashamed, but are behaving as though you had (already) lived a long time with your husband?' And her father said, 'Is it because of your great love for your husband that you do not even cover yourself?'

14. But the bride answered and said: 'Truly, father, I am in great love, and pray my Lord that this love which I have felt this night may stay with me, and I may obtain this husband whom I have perceived today. That is why I shall no longer veil myself, since the mirror of disgrace has been taken away from me. And no longer do I feel disgrace or shame, since the work of disgrace and of shame has been far removed from me. And I am not terrified, because terror has not stayed with me.

And I am in gladness and joy, because the day of joy has not been shaken. And I have held of no account this husband and this marriage which are passing before my eyes, since I have been joined together in another marriage. And I have not had intercourse with a transient husband, the consequence of which is lust and bitterness of soul, since I have been linked together with a true husband.'

15. While the bride would have said even more than this, the bridegroom replied and said: 'I thank thee, Lord, who wast proclaimed by the strange man and found by us; who hast removed me from corruption and sown in me life; who hast separated me from this disease, which is hard to heal and hard to relieve and stays for ever, and hast set rational sanity in me; who hast shown thyself to me and revealed to me the whole condition in which I find myself; who hast redeemed me from perdition and led me to the better, and hast freed me from the transient and deemed me worthy of that which is immortal and always exists; who hast humbled thyself to me and my littleness, to set me beside the Majesty and unite me with thee; who hast not withheld thy compassion from me, who was perishing, but hast shown me how to seek myself and to know who I was and who and how I now am, so that I may again become what I was; whom I indeed did not know, but thyself hast sought (me) out; of whom I was ignorant, but thyself hast laid hold of me; whom I have perceived and whom I cannot now forget; whose love wells up in me, and I cannot tell it as I ought; but what I am capable of saying about it is brief and all too little and not comparable with his glory. But he does not blame me if I am (so) rash as to speak to him even of what I do not understand. For it is for love of him that I say even these things.'

16. But when the king heard these things from the bridegroom and the bride, he tore his robe and said to those who stood nearby him: 'Go out quickly and comb the whole city and arrest that sorcerer and bring him to me, for his presence in this city is unlucky. For I led him with my own hands into my house, and I told him to pray for my unhappy daughter. And whoever finds him and brings him to me, I will give him everything he may ask of me.' They went and ran about looking for him, and did not find him; for he had sailed.

But they went also to the inn where he had put up, and found there the flute-girl weeping and afflicted, because he had not taken her with him. And when they explained to her the event which had taken place in connection with the young people, she was overjoyed when she heard, set aside her sorrow, and said, 'Now I too have found rest here.' And she got up and went to them, and was with them a long time, until they reported it also to the king. And many also of the brothers used to assemble there, until they heard the news of the apostle that he had landed in India and was teaching there. And they went off and joined him.

THE THIRD ACT

30. And the apostle went out to go where the Lord had commanded him. And as he approached the second mile and had turned aside a little from the road, he saw the corpse of a handsome youth lying there, and said: 'Lord, was it for this reason that you led me out to come here, that I might see this testing? Let your will be done, then, as you wish.' And he began to pray and say: 'Lord, Judge of the living and the dead, (Acts 10: 42), of the living who stand by and of those who lie dead, and Lord over all and Father, but Father not of the souls that are in bodies, but of the departed; for of those which are still in defilement thou art the Lord and Judge. Come at this hour when I call, and show thy majesty to this one who lies here.' And turning to those who followed him he said: 'This deed has not been done for nothing, but the enemy has been active and has brought this about so that he may use it to attack. And you see that he has not used another form nor operated through any other animal than the one that obeys him.'

31. And when he had said this, a great dragon came out of a cave, thrusting out his head and beating his tail on the ground, and he said in a loud voice to the apostle, 'I will say in front of you the reason why I killed this man, since you have come for the purpose of proving my deeds wrong.' And the apostle said, 'Yes, speak.' And the dragon: 'A beautiful woman lives in that place opposite. And as she went past me I saw her and desired her, and I followed her and watched her. And I found

this youth kissing her, and he was intimate with her and did other disgraceful things with her. It was easy for me to expose these things in front of you, for I know that you are a twin of Christ and always bring our kind to nought. But not wishing to terrify her I did not kill him at the very hour, but I watched him, and when he came by in the evening I struck and killed him; especially because he had the insolence to do this on the Lord's day.' And the apostle examined him and said, 'Tell me what ancestry and what stock you are of.'

32. And he said to him: 'I am a crawler of a crawling kind and a pest from a pest. I am a son of him who hurt and struck the four standing brothers; I am the son of him who sits on a throne over what is under heaven; (the son) of him who takes his own from those who borrow. I am the son of him who girds the circle. And I am akin to him who is outside the Ocean, whose tail lies in his mouth. I am he that entered through the fence in the Paradise and spoke with Eve as my father had commanded me to speak with her (Gen. 3: 1 ff.). I am he who inflamed and fired Cain to kill his brother (Gen. 4: 5–8), and because of me thorns and thistles grew on the earth (Gen. 3: 18). I am he who threw down the angels from above and bound them by their lusts for women (Gen. 6: 1 f.), so that earth-born sons might spring from them and I might accomplish my purpose by them. I am he that hardened Pharaoh's heart, so that he might kill Israel's children and enslave them in a yoke of hardship (Exod. 1: 10–16). I am he that led astray the masses in the wilderness, when they made the (golden) calf (Exod. 32: 1–4). I am he that inflamed Herod (Matt. 2: 16 or Luke 23: 6–11) and fired Caiaphas to false lies before Pilate; for these things suited me. I am he who inflamed Judas and bought him, so that he would hand over Christ to death (Matt. 26: 14–16, 47–50 par.). I am he that inhabits and holds the pit of Tartarus; but the Son of God did me injustice against my will, and chose his own from me. I am akin to him who is to come from the East,[10] to whom also authority is given to do what he himself wills upon the earth.'

33. And when that dragon had said this and all the crowd had heard, the apostle raised his voice high and said: 'Stop now, most shameless one, and be ashamed, you who are utterly

[10] The Antichrist.

dead; for the end, your destruction, has arrived. And do not dare to speak of what you have achieved through those who became subject to you. I command you in the name of that Jesus, who till now has fought against you (plur.) through his own men, to suck out and draw up and remove from him your venom which you put into this man.' But the dragon said: 'The moment of our end has not yet arrived as you said. Why do you compel me to take what I have injected into this man, and to die before the time? For even my father, when he draws up and sucks out what he has cast over the world, will then come to his end.'

But the apostle said to him, 'Then show now your father's nature.' And the dragon approached, put its mouth on the young man's wound and sucked the gall out of him. And in a short while the young man's skin, which was purplish, turned white, but the dragon swelled up. And when the dragon had sucked all the gall into himself, the young man leaped up and stood upright, and ran and fell at the feet of the apostle. But the dragon swelled up, burst, and died; and its venom and gall spilled out. And in the place where its venom spilled a great chasm appeared, and that dragon was swallowed up. And the apostle said to the king and his brother, 'Fetch workmen and fill up that place, lay foundations, and build houses on them, so that there may be a residence for strangers.'

34. But the young man said to the apostle amid many tears: 'What wrong have I done you? For you are a man of two forms, and wherever you like you are to be found, and are restrained by no one, as I perceive. For I saw that man as he stood beside you, and he said to you: "I have many wonders to show through you and great deeds to perform through you, for which you will be rewarded. And you will bring it about that many will live, and will be at rest in eternal light as God's children. Bring to life then", he said, speaking to you about me, "this youth laid low by the enemy, and be at all times his keeper." It is good that you have come here, and it is good that you should go to him again, for he never parts from you. But I became free from anxiety and reproach. And light shone on me far from the anxiety of the night, and I rested from the toil of the day. But I was also separated from him who impelled me to do these things; I sinned against that one who taught me the opposite.

And I lost that kinsman of night who by his own deeds compelled me to sin, and I found that brilliant one as my kinsman. I lost him who darkens and obscures his subjects, so that they may not know what they are doing and become ashamed of their deeds and desist from them, and their practices cease. And I have found him whose deeds are light and his practices truth, which if anyone performs he does not regret. And I have also been freed from him whose lie persists, who is also preceded by darkness as his veil; shame also follows (him) behind, immodest in intemperance. And I have found him who showed me good things for me to grasp them, the son of truth, the kinsman of concord, who clears away the mist and illuminates his own creation, and heals its wounds and overthrows its enemies. But I pray you, man of God, make me behold him again, and see this one who has become hidden to me now, so that I may also hear his voice, the wonder of which I cannot describe; for it is not of the nature of this bodily instrument.'

35. And the apostle answered him and said: 'If you free yourself from these things of which you have obtained knowledge, as indeed you have said, and if you know who he is who accomplished these things in you, and you learn and become obedient to him whom you now desire with your fervent love, you will see him and be with him for eternity, and you will rest in his resting-place and be in his joy. But if you are indifferently disposed towards him and you turn back again to your earlier practices, and you overlook beauty and that bright face which has now been shown to you, and you forget the radiance of his light, which you now long for, (then) you will be deprived not only of this life, but also of the one to come, and you will go to him whom you said you had lost, and you will no longer see him whom you said you had found.'

36. And when the apostle had said this, he went into the city holding the hand of that young man and saying to him: 'What you have seen, child, are a few of the many (things) which God has. For he does not proclaim to us good news about these visible (things), but greater than these he promises to us. As long as we are in the body, we cannot say or express what he is going to give to our souls. If we say that he gives us light, that is something seen and we have it; if (we say) wealth, which exists and appears in this world, then we name it and do not need it,

since it is said, "With difficulty will a rich man enter the kingdom of heaven" (Matt. 19: 23 par.). But if we speak of (fine)
clothes, which the indulgent in this life put on, its name is
spoken and it is said (of it), "Those who wear fine things are
in king's houses" (Matt. 11: 8 par.). But if of sumptuous
banquets, we have received a command about these that we
should avoid them, so as not to be burdened with debauchery
and intoxication and anxieties about earthly life (Luke 21: 34)—
he said what is (so)—and it is said, "Do not be anxious about
your life, what you are to eat or what you are to drink, nor
about your body, what you are to put on; life is more than food
and the body than clothing" (Matt. 6: 25 par.). But if we speak
also of this transitory repose, a judgement is laid down for that,
too. We speak, however, of the world above, of God and angels,
of the vigilant and holy, of the ambrosial food and the drink
from the true vine, of lasting clothes that do not grow old, of
what eye has not seen nor ear heard, nor has it risen up in the
heart of sinful men, what God has prepared for those who
love him (1 Cor. 2: 9). Of these things we speak, and about
these things we preach the good news.

'Believe in him, then, yourself so that you may live, and put
your trust in him and you will never die. For he is not persuaded
by gifts so that you may offer them, nor does he need sacrifices
so that you should sacrifice to him. Rather, look to him and he
will not overlook you; and turn to him, and he will not forsake
you. For his worth and beauty will make you full of longing so
that you love him; but it will also not allow you to turn away
from him.'

37. And when the apostle had said this, a large crowd gathered
about that youth. And when the apostle looked he saw that
they were raising themselves up in order to see him, and were
going up to high places; and the apostle said to them: 'You
men who have come to the assembly of Christ and intend to
believe in Jesus, take an illustration from this, and observe
that if you are not lifted up you cannot see me, the little one,
and you cannot look at me who am like you. If therefore you
cannot see me who am like you, unless you raise yourselves a
little from the ground, how can you see the one who dwells on
high and is now found in the depth, unless you first raise
yourselves up from your former conduct and unprofitable

practices and the lusts that do not last, from the wealth that is left behind here, from the earthly possession that grows old, from the clothes that rot, from the beauty that ages and vanishes, yes, and even from the entire body in which all those things are stored, and which grows old and becomes dust, returning to its proper nature! For all these things the body itself erects. But rather believe in our Lord Jesus Christ, whom we proclaim, so that your hope may be in him and you may have life in him for all eternity, so that he may himself become your travelling-companion in this land of wandering, and may become your haven in this stormy sea. And he will be for you a gushing fountain in this thirsty land, and a house full of food in the place of the hungry, and rest for your souls and a physician even for your bodies.'

38. When the crowd of those who had assembled heard this, they wept and said to the apostle: 'Man of God, the God you proclaim, we dare not say that we belong to him, because our actions which we have performed are alien to him and do not please him. But if he is sorry for us and pities us and delivers us by overlooking our former practices, and frees us from the bad things we have done when we were in error, and does not count it against us or bear in mind our former sins, we become his servants and we shall do his will to the end.' And the apostle answered them and said, 'He will not condemn you nor count against you the sins which you committed when you were in error, but will overlook the misdeeds which you have done in ignorance.'

THE SONG OF THE PEARL

108. All the prisoners saw him praying and asked him to pray for them. And when he had prayed, he sat down and began to utter this psalm:

'When I was a speechless infant in my father's palaces, resting in the ease and luxury of those who reared me, my parents provided me with means of support and sent me out from the East, our homeland. From the wealth of their treasuries they put together a pack, large and light, such that I could carry it alone. The pack from above consists of gold and unminted silver from the great treasures, of chalcedony stones from India and of pearls from the land of the Cushites. And they armed me with diamond ⟨which scratches iron⟩.[11] And they took off from me the suit encrusted with stones and shot with gold, which they had made in their love for me, and the robe of yellow colour to match my height. And they made an agreement with me, engraving it upon my mind that I should not forget it, and said: "If you go down to Egypt and fetch from there the single pearl which is there beside the devouring dragon, you shall (again) put on the suit encrusted with stones and the robe which goes over it; and with your brother, our second, become an heir in our kingdom."

109. 'I came from the East by a hard and terrible way with two guides, for I had no experience for travelling that way. And I came also along the border-lands of Mesene, where there is the hostel of the oriental merchants, and reached the land of the Babylonians ⟨and entered the walls of Sarbug⟩. But when I came to Egypt, the two guides who had travelled with me left me, and I made straight for the dragon and waited near his lair, watching for him to doze and fall asleep so that I might take away my pearl. And I was alone and foreign in appearance, and I looked strange even to my own (household companions). But there I saw one who was related to me, from the East, one who was free, a graceful and handsome boy, a son of noblemen. He came and associated with me, and I had him as my companion, making him both friend and partner in my journey. And I urged him to be on his guard against the Egyptians and the society of those impure men. But I put on their clothes, so that I might not appear foreign, as one from abroad, in order that I might get the pearl, and so that the Egyptians should not wake up the dragon against me.

'But I do not know[12] how they discovered that I was not from their land. But they cunningly devised a trap for me, and I tasted their food. I ceased to know that I was a king's son, and I served their king. I forgot the pearl for which my parents had sent me, and under the weight of their food I sank into deep sleep.

[11] In the Song of the Pearl, explanatory expansions from the Syriac version are placed in angled brackets ⟨ ⟩.

[12] This 'I do not know', namely, how the evil power obtains information about the world of light, recurs exactly in the Psalms of Thomas. The Psalms of Thomas stand in an intermediate position between Mandeism and Manicheism.

110. 'But as I suffered these things my parents also observed it and were sorry for me. And a proclamation was made in our kingdom that everyone should come to our gates. And the kings of Parthia and the potentates and the great ones of the East took a decision about me that I should not remain in Egypt. They wrote me (a letter) and the mighty ones each signed it: "From the father, the king of kings, and the mother who possesses the East, and the brother who is the second beside us, to our son in Egypt, greetings. Get up and sober up out of your sleep, and listen to the words of this letter. Remember that you are a king's son. You have come under a servile yoke. Think of your suit shot with gold; think of the pearl on account of which you were sent to Egypt, so that your name may be mentioned in the book of the valiant, and you may be an heir with your brother in our kingdom."

111. 'And the king sealed (the letter) because of the wicked, the children of Babylon, and the tyrannical demons of Sarbug. It flew in form of an eagle, the king of all birds. ⟨It flew and landed by me and became entirely speech.⟩ And at the sound and sight of it I started up from sleep, took (it), kissed (it) tenderly, and read. And it had written in it just what was written down in my heart. And immediately I remembered that I was a son of kings, and my freedom longed for its kind. And I remembered also the pearl for which I had been dispatched to Egypt. I began to charm the terrible dragon with spells and put him to sleep by uttering the name of my father ⟨the names of our second (son) and of my mother, the queen of the East⟩. I stole the pearl, took it away, and returned to my parents. And I took off the dirty garment and left it behind in their country. And at once I directed my course towards the light of the homeland in the East. And I found on the way (the letter) that had roused me. And this, just as it had by its sound raised me up when I slept, also showed me the way by the light (shining) from it; for the royal (letter) of silk stuff was before my eyes. And with love guiding and drawing me, I went past Sarbug. Leaving Babylon on the left I reached great Mesene, which lies on the coast.

112. ⟨My parents sent me by their treasurers my shining suit and my long robe.⟩ And I did not remember (any more) my brightness. For when I was still a child and quite young I

had left it behind in my father's palaces. And suddenly I saw
the suit which resembled (me) as it were in a mirror, and I spied
my whole self in it, and I knew and saw myself through it;
for we were partially separated from each other, though we
were from the same, and again we are one through one form.
Not only (so), but I saw also the treasurers themselves who
carried the suit as two, yet one form was present upon both,
one royal sign in both. They had wealth and riches in hand,
and they gave me precious things, the gorgeous suit which had
been skilfully worked in bright colours with gold and precious
stones and pearls of brilliant hues. They were fastened above.
And the image of the king of kings (was) fully present through
the whole (suit). Sapphire stones were set appropriately above.

113. 'I saw moreover that movements of knowedge were
emitted by the whole, and that it was ready to utter speech. I
heard it speak: "I am (the property) of him who is bravest of
all men, for whose sake I was engraved by the father himself."
And I myself noticed ⟨my stature, which increased in accordance with its impulse⟩. And all the royal movements extended
to me. It made haste, straining towards him who should take
it from his hand. And love roused me to rush to meet him and
receive it. And I reached out ⟨, adorned myself with the beauty
of its colours⟩, and drew my brilliant garment entirely over me.

'But when I had put (it) on I was lifted up to the gate of
acknowledgement and worship. And I bowed my head and
acknowledged the radiance of the father who had sent this to
me; for I had done what had been commanded, and he likewise, what he had promised. And in the gates of the palace I
mingled with those of his dominion. And he rejoiced over me
and received me with him in the palace. And all his subjects
sing with pleasant voices. And he promised me that I would also
be sent with him to the gates of the king, so that with my gifts and
my pearl I might together with him appear before the king.'

OTHER PASSAGES FROM THE ACTS OF THOMAS

From the second Act: 26. . . . They (King Gundafor and his
brother Gad) entreated him that they themselves also might
at last receive the seal of the Word (?), and they said to him:
'Since our souls are at ease and we are earnest about God, give

us the seal. For we have heard you say that the God whom you proclaim recognizes his own sheep by his seal.' The apostle said to them: 'I am glad and I entreat you to receive this seal and partake with me in this eucharist and praising of the Lord and be perfected by it. For this one is the Lord and God of all, Jesus Christ whom I proclaim; he is himself the Father of truth in whom I have taught you to believe.' And he ordered them to bring to (him) oil, so that through the oil they might receive the seal. So they brought the oil and lit many lamps; for it was night.

27. And the apostle stood up and sealed them. And the Lord was revealed to them through a voice, and said, 'Peace be with you (John 20: 19, etc.), brothers.' But they heard only a voice, and did not see his form. For they had not yet received the sealing with the seal. And the apostle took the oil, poured (it) on their head, anointed and smeared them, and began to say: 'Come, holy name of Christ which is above every name (Phil. 2: 9). Come, power of the Most High and perfect compassion. Come, highest gift of grace. Come, compassionate mother. Come, intercourse with the male. Come, thou who revealest the hidden mysteries. Come, mother of the seven houses, so that thy rest may enter the eighth house. Come, ambassador of the five members, of understanding, of thought, of prudence, of meditation, of intelligence, communicate with these young people. Come, Holy Spirit and cleanse their inward parts and their heart, and seal them in the name of the Father and of the Son and of the Holy Spirit.'

And when they had been sealed, there appeared to them a youth holding a burning torch, so that even their lamps were dimmed at the approach of its light. And he went out and became invisible to them. And the apostle said to the Lord: 'Your light is beyond our capacity, Lord, and we are unable to bear it. For it is too bright for our eyes.' But when daylight came, he broke bread and made them participants in the eucharist of Christ. And they were glad and rejoiced. And many others also believed and were added and reached the Saviour's refuge.

From the fourth Act: 39. . . . The apostle answered and said: 'O Jesus Christ, apprehended only by mind, of perfect compassion; O quiet and solitude, who now speakest even in the dumb beasts; O secret rest and our saviour and nurse, who art revealed through thy operations, who guardest us and makest us rest in alien bodies, thou saviour of our souls, thou sweet and unfailing well-spring, well-provided, pure, and never muddied fountain, succour and aid in combat of his servants, who turns and drives the enemy away from us, who in many combats fights for us and makes us conquer in all; our true and invincible champion, holy and victorious leader, highly honoured and providing for his own a joy that never passes and a relief that has no affliction at all, the good shepherd who sold himself for the sheep and defeated the wolf (John 10: 14 f.), set free his sheep and led them to good pasture, we glorify and praise thee and thy invisible Father and the Holy Spirit the mother of all created things.'

From the fifth Act: 44. And the apostle said: 'O uncontrollable wickedness; O insolence of the enemy; O slanderer that never rests; O mis-shapen one that subdues the shapely ones; O multiform—he appears however he likes, but his essence cannot be altered; O beyond the crafty and faithless; O bitter tree whose fruits are like him; O beyond the slanderer who fights for the foreigners; O beyond the deceit that uses insolence; O beyond the wickedness that creeps like a snake and is akin to that one himself!'

When the apostle had said this, the enemy came and stood before him, with no one seeing him but the woman and the apostle, and he spoke in a very loud voice for all to hear: 45. 'What have we to do with you, apostle of the Most High? What have we to do with you, servant of Jesus Christ? What have we to do with you, counsellor of the holy Son of God? Why do you want to destroy us when our time has not yet arrived? Why do you want to take our power? For until this present moment we had hope and time remaining. What have we to do with you? You have power over yours, and we over ours. Why do you want to behave like a tyrant towards us, especially when you yourself teach others not to behave tyrannically? Why do you need the aliens, as if you are not satisfied with your own? Why do you make yourself like the Son of God who did us wrong? For you are like him just as if you were born from him. For we thought to subjugate him also just like the rest. But he turned and got us under (his) control. For we did not know him. But he deceived us by his exceedingly ugly form and by his poverty and want. For when we saw him like that we thought he was a flesh-clad man, not perceiving that it was he who gives life to mankind. And he gave us power over our own, and (power) in the time in which we live not to release what is ours but to remain in it. But you want to possess more than is due and given to you and to overpower us. . . . 46. . . . I shall go and look for one who is like you,[13] and if I do not find her, I shall return to you again. For I know that in this man's proximity you have a refuge in him, but when he goes away from you you will be what you were before he appeared, and you will forget him, while for me it will be the time and free opportunity. . . .' With these words the demon became invisible, only as he departed fire and smoke appeared there. And all those who stood there were astonished.

47. When the apostle saw this he said to them: 'That demon has shown us nothing strange or alien, but his nature, inasmuch as he will be burnt up. For the fire will consume him and his smoke will be dispersed.' And he began to say: 'Jesus, hidden secret which has been revealed to us, it is thou that hast shown us very many secrets, that hast selected me alone of all my companions and told me three words by which I am set on fire and cannot tell them to others,[14] Jesus, man, slain, dead, buried, Jesus, God out of God, saviour, who makes the dead live and heals the sick, Jesus, the poor one, just as thou also canst rescue like the rich, who catchest the fish for breakfast and for dinner (John 21: 6, 11 f.), who makest all full with a little bread (Matt. 14: 19 f. par.), who restest from thy laborious wandering as man (John 4: 6), and walkest upon the waves as God (Matt. 14: 25), 48. Jesus, most high, voice rising up from the perfect compassion, saviour of all, right hand of the light, who overthrows the wicked in his own nature, and collects his whole nature together into one place, multiform, only-begotten, first-born of many brothers (Rom. 8: 29), God from the highest God, man despised until now, Jesus Christ, who dost not disregard us when we invoke thee, who became the cause of

---

[13] The woman whom the Apostle had healed.
[14] Cf. Gospel of Thomas, Logion 13.

human life for all, who for our sake was judged and guarded in prison and releases all those who are imprisoned, who is called deceiver and redeems his own from deceit; I pray to thee for these who stand here and trust thee. They ask to obtain thy gifts, hopefully confident in thy help, holding fast their refuge with thee in thy majesty, they attend with their ears to hear the words from us which are spoken to them. Let thy peace come and make its abode with them, and let it renew them, separate from their former deeds, and let them take off the old man together with his deeds, and put on the new, who is now proclaimed to them by me' (Col. 3: 9 f.).

49. And he laid his hands on them, blessed them, and said, 'The grace of our Lord Jesus be upon you for ever' (Rom. 16: 20). And they said, 'Amen'. And the woman also entreated him and said, 'Apostle of the Highest, give me the seal, so that yon enemy may not again return to me.' Then he made her step near him, laid his hands upon her and sealed her in the name of the Father and of the Son and of the Holy Spirit. Many others also were sealed with her. And the apostle ordered his servant to place a table nearby. And they set alongside a bench which they found there; and he spread a linen cloth over it and laid the bread of the blessing on it. And the apostle stood by it and said: 'Jesus, who hast deemed us worthy to participate in the eucharist of thy holy body and blood, see, we dare to approach thy eucharist and to call upon thy holy name. Come and be with us.' 50. And he began to say: 'Come, perfect compassion; come, intercourse with the male; come thou who knowest the mysteries of the elect one; come, thou who sharest in the contests of the noble contestant;[15] come, quiet who revealest the majesty of the whole greatness; come, thou who bringest the hidden things to light and causest what is secret to be revealed; holy dove that hatchest the twin chicks; come, hidden mother; come, thou who art manifest by thy deeds and suppliest joy and rest to those bound up with her. Come and take part with us in this eucharist which we perform in thy name, and in the love-feast for which we are assembled at thy invitation.' And when he had said this, he cut the cross in the bread, broke (it), and began to distribute (it). And first he gave it to the woman and said, 'This shall be to you for remission of sins and

---

[15] Cf. Cl. Al., *Exc.* § 58, 1 and p. 360.

eternal transgressions.' And after her he gave it to all the others who had received the seal.

From the sixth Act: 52. When the apostle heard this, he said: 'O senseless copulation, how do you extend into shamelessness? O uncontrollable desire, how did you stir this person to do these things? O work of the snake, how are you angry among your own?' And the apostle commanded water to be brought to him in a bowl. And when the water had been brought he said: 'Come, water from the living water, that which is from that which is, which also has been sent to us; rest which has been sent to us from the rest; power of salvation which comes from that power which conquers all things and is subject to its own will; come and dwell in these waters, so that the gracious gift of the Holy Spirit may perfectly be perfected in them.' And he said to the youth, 'Go, wash your hands in these waters.' And when he had washed them they were restored, and the apostle said to him, 'Do you believe in our Lord Jesus Christ, that he can do all things?' And he said: 'Though I am very unimportant, I believe. But I did this thing thinking to do something good. For I did ask her, as I also told you, but she would not listen to me, to keep herself chaste.'

From the tenth Act: 121. Mygdonia was standing before the apostle with her head bare. And he lifted the oil and poured it over her head saying: 'Holy oil, given us for sanctification, hidden mystery in which the cross was shown to us, thou art the unfolder of the hidden parts. Thou art the humiliator of stubborn deeds. Thou art the one who showest the hidden treasures. Thou art the plant of kindness. Let thy power come. Let it abide on thy maid Mygdonia, and heal her by this liberation.' When the oil had been poured out he ordered her nurse to strip her and dress her in a cloth. And there was just there a water-spring, to which the apostle went and baptized Mygdonia in the name of the Father and of the Son and of the Holy Spirit. And when she had been baptized and had dressed again, he broke bread and took a cup of water and made her a partaker of the body of Christ and of the cup of the Son of God, and said, 'You have received your seal; create for yourself eternal life.' And at once a voice was heard from above, saying, 'Yes, Amen.'

133. When they had been baptized and had dressed again, he laid bread on the table, blessed it and said: 'Bread of life, which those who eat remain imperishable; bread which satisfies hungry souls with its blessedness; it is thou that hast made us worthy to receive the gift, so that we get remission of sins and those who eat thee become immortal. We invoke thee, name of the mother, of the secret mystery hidden from powers and authorities; we invoke thee, name of Jesus.' And he said, 'Let the power of the blessing come and settle on the bread, so that all souls which consume it may be cleansed from their sins.' And he broke (the bread) and gave it to Siphor and his wife and daughter.

The last prayer of Judas before his death: 167. The prayer was this: 'My Lord and my God (John 20: 28), hope, redeemer, leader, guide in all lands, be thou with all who serve thee, and guide me as I come to thee today. May no one take my soul, which I have surrendered to thee. May the tax-collectors not see me, and the creditors not (falsely) accuse me. May the snake not see me and the great dragon's children not hiss at me. See, Lord, I have finished thy work and fulfilled thy command. I have become a slave; therefore today I obtain liberty. Thou who hast given it to me, finish it. I say this, not because I doubt, but so that they may hear it who ought to hear it.'

SELECT BIBLIOGRAPHY

The abbreviations correspond to those of the *Lexikon der Alten Welt*, Zurich and Stuttgart, 1965.

Translations of Sources and General Surveys

A. HILGENFELD, *Die Ketzergeschichte des Urchristentums*, Leipzig, 1884.

W. BOUSSET, *Hauptprobleme der Gnosis*, Göttingen, 1907.

W. SCHULTZ, *Dokumente der Gnosis*, Jena, 1910.

É. de FAYE, *Gnostiques et Gnosticisme*, Paris, 1925.

H. JONAS, *Gnosis und spätantiker Geist*, Teil I: *Die mythologische Gnosis*, Göttingen, 1934, 1964[3]; Teil II, 1. Hälfte: *Von der Mythologie zur mystischen Philosophie*, Göttingen, 1954.

K. KERÉNYI, *Mythologie und Gnosis* (Albae Vigiliae XIV), 1942; cf. id., *Humanistische Seelenforschung* (Werke in Einzelausgaben I), Munich/Vienna, 1966, 150–202, 404.

G. QUISPEL, *Gnosis als Weltreligion*, Zürich, 1951.

H. LEISEGANG, *Die Gnosis*, Stuttgart, 1955[4].

R. McL. WILSON, *The Gnostic Problem*, London, 1958.

G. R. S. MEAD, *Fragments of a Faith Forgotten*, New York, 1960.

R. M. GRANT, *Gnosticism, a Sourcebook of Heretical Writings from the Early Christian Period*, London and New York, 1961.

H. JONAS, *The Gnostic Religion*, Boston, Mass., 1963.

R. M. GRANT, *Gnosticism and Early Christianity*, London and New York, 1966[2].

R. HAARDT, *Die Gnosis, Wesen und Zeugnisse*, Salzburg, 1967 (with detailed bibliography on sources and literature) (ET Leiden, 1971).

Le origini dello gnosticismo, Colloquio di Messina 13–18 aprile 1966, Studies in the History of Religions (Supplements to *Numen*) 12, Leiden, 1967.

Works on Problems of Gnosis as a Whole

R. LIECHTENHAN, *Die Offenbarung im Gnostizismus*, Göttingen, 1901.

R. BULTMANN, *Das Urchristentum im Rahmen der antiken Religionen*, Zürich, 1954. ET, *Primitive Christianity in its Contemporary Setting*, London, 1956.

W. FOERSTER, 'Das Wesen der Gnosis', *WG* 15 (1955), 100–14.

C. COLPE, *Die religionsgeschichtliche Schule*, Göttingen, 1961.

W. SCHMITHALS, *Die Gnosis in Korinth*, Göttingen, 1965[2] (Introduction A: 'Die Gnosis', 21–80: on the redeemed Redeemer).

H.-M. SCHENKE, *Der Gott 'Mensch' in der Gnosis*, Göttingen, 1962.

K. Rudolph, 'Stand und Aufgabe in der Erforschung des Gnostizismus', *WZ Jena*, Sonderheft (Tagung für allgemeine Religionsgeschichte, 1963), 89–102.

C. Andresen, 'Erlösung', *RAC* VI (1966), 119–30.

J. Zandee, 'Gnostic Ideas on the Fall and Salvation', *Numen* 11 (1964), 13–74.

Works on Individual Teachers, Documents, and Systems

SIMON MAGUS

E. Haenchen, 'Gab es eine vorchristliche Gnosis?', *ZThK* 49 (1952), 316–49; reprinted in *Gott und Mensch, Gesammelte Aufsätze*, Tübingen, 1965, 265–98.

H. Schlier, 'Das Denken der frühchristlichen Gnosis', *Neutestamentliche Studien für Rudolf Bultmann*, Berlin, 1954, 67–82.

CARPOCRATES

H. Liboron, *Die karpokratianische Gnosis*, Leipzig, 1938.

BARUCH

E. Haenchen, 'Das Buch Baruch', *ZThK* 50 (1953), 123–58; reprinted in *Gott und Mensch, Gesammelte Aufsätze*, Tübingen, 1965, 298–334.

BASILIDES

P. Hendrix, *De alexandrijnsche haeresiarch Basilides*, Amsterdam, 1926.

W. Foerster, 'Das System des Basilides', *NTSt* 9 (1962/3), 233–55.

OPHITES

Th. Hopfner, 'Das Diagramm der Ophianer', *Charisteria für R. Rzach*, Reichenberg, 1930, 86–98.

G. Bornkamm, 'Ophiten', *RE* XVIII, 654–8.

BARBELOGNOSTICS

L. Cerfaux, 'Barbelognostiker', *RAC* I (1950), 1176–80.

APOCRYPHON OF JOHN

W. Foerster, 'Das Apokryphon des Johannes', *Gott und die Götter, Festgabe für Erich Fascher*, Berlin, 1958, 134–41.

H.-Ch. Puech, The Apocryphon of John, E. Hennecke–W. Schneemelcher (eds.), *New Testament Apocrypha*, ET I, London, 1963, 314–31.

VALENTINIANS

F.-M.-M. Sagnard, *La Gnose Valentinienne et le témoignage de Saint Irénée*, Paris, 1947.

W. Foerster, 'Die Grundzüge der ptolemaeischen Gnosis', *NTSt* 6 (1959/60), 16–31.

J. Mousson, 'Jean-Baptiste dans les Fragments d'Héracléon', *EThL* 30 (1954), 301–22.

Y. Janssens, 'Héracléon, Commentaire sur l'Évangile selon Jean', *Le Muséon* 72 (1959), 101–52, 277–99.

A. J. Visser, 'Der Lehrbrief der Valentinianer', *VChr* 12 (1958), 27–36.

MEGALE APOPHASIS

E. Haenchen, op. cit. (on Simon Magus).

NAASSENES

H. Schlier, 'Der Mensch im Gnostizismus', *Anthropologie religieuse*, Studies in the History of Religions (Supplements to *Numen*) 2, Leiden, 1955, 60–76.

W. Foerster, 'Die Naassener', *Studi di storia religiosa della tarda antichità*, Messina, 1968, 21–33.

ARCHONTICS

H.-Ch. Puech, 'Archontiker', *RAC* I, 633–43.

NICOLAITANS

L. Fendt, 'Borborianer', *RAC* II (1954), 510–13.

N. Brox, 'Nikolaos und Nikolaiten', *VChr* 19 (1965), 23–30.

POIMANDRES

R. Reitzenstein, *Poimandres*, Leipzig, 1904.

R. Reitzenstein, 'Vom Dāmdād-Nask zu Plato' in R. Reitzenstein–H. H. Schaeder, *Studien zum antiken Synkretismus*, Leipzig and Berlin, 1926, 3–37.

E. Haenchen, 'Aufbau und Theologie des "Poimandres"', *ZThK* 53 (1956), 149–91; reprinted in *Gott und Mensch, Gesammelte Aufsätze*, Tübingen, 1965, 335–77.

ACTS OF THOMAS

E. Preuschen, *Zwei gnostische Hymnen*, Giessen, 1904.

G. Bornkamm, *Mythos und Legende in den apokryphen Thomas-Akten*, Göttingen, 1933.

A. Adam, *Die Psalmen des Thomas und das Perlenlied als Zeugnisse vorchristlicher Gnosis*, Berlin, 1959.

A. F. J. Klijn, *The Acts of Thomas, Introduction, Text, Commentary*, Leiden, 1962.

G. Bornkamm, 'The Acts of Thomas', E. Hennecke–W. Schneemelcher (eds.), *New Testament Apocrypha*, ET II, London, 1965, 425–531.

G. Quispel, *Makarius, das Thomasevangelium und das Lied von der Perle*, Leiden, 1967.